HESUS JOY CHRIST

Discussion
of the Animation

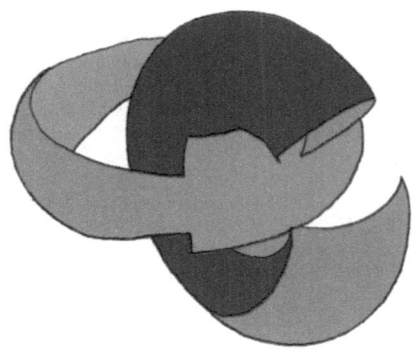

including

HYPOTHERMIA / *My Kayak Prayer*

lyrics

written
by

R David Foster

and published through
http://www.lulu.com/

HESUS JOY CHRIST
Discussion of the Animation
including
HYPOTHERMIA / My Kayak Prayer lyrics

ISBN   978-0-9917852-0-9

Copyright © R David Foster 2013

All rights reserved.

This book may NOT be copied or quoted in whole or in part, by any means, unless the entire text of the discussion of that verse is copied or quoted in its entirety, or the entire text of that Concordance is copied or quoted, and no more than three (3) verse discussions or one (1) Concordance may be copied or quoted by any group, organization, individual or associated individuals, ever. Purchase of this publication is necessary beyond quoting three (3) verse discussions or beyond quoting one (1) Concordance. No other parts of this book may be copied or quoted in whole or in part, in any form or by any means, unless written permission is obtained from R David Foster through contacting him at vid932008@gmail.com .

All scripture quotations, unless otherwise indicated, are taken from the Holy Bible, New International Version®, NIV®. Copyright ©1973, 1978, 1984, 2011 by Biblica, Inc.™ Used by written permission of Zondervan, under Fair Use Guidelines. All rights reserved worldwide. www.zondervan.com The "NIV" and "New International Version" are trademarks registered in the United States Patent and Trademark Office by Biblica, Inc.™

The animation text is written very tightly to the ® 1973, 1978, 1984 copy of the New International Version of the Bible. Where there are differences between the ® 1973, 1978, 1984 copy, and the ® 1973, 1978, 1984, 2011 copy, that are enough to raise confusion, I have identified the text in question with one or more asterisks (*) and quoted the ® 1973, 1978, 1984 copy further down on the page.

The Animation Text quotes the ® 1973, 1978, 1984 copy of the New International Version of the Bible. Where there are differences between the ® 1973, 1978, 1984 copy of the New International Version of the Bible and the ® 1973, 1978, 1984, 2011 copy of the New International Version of the Bible, the text in question is bracketed ( ) .

Self Published by R David Foster, Oakville, Ontario, Canada, through www.lulu.com .
" vid932008 " font ® R David Foster 2013 Unauthorized use of this font is not permitted .
Cover design created entirely by R David Foster using images created by R David Foster and text written by R David Foster.

www.sites.google.com/site/vid932008   2013-11-15

Dedicated,
with sincere appreciation
and love,
to

Gwen

and
presented
for

all secular faithful .

My Psalm of Lament

I am me, and so are you.
Read this now to doubt it's true.
I'll affirm you've understood,
I am gone, God said " should "!
Regardless gone, somehow I know,
I am belief below proof's no show.

Myself, I work at nothing
Daydream an Impossible Dream
Entirely Fostering nothing
And loving everything
With heart, mind and soul
Serving God and King
To find when I am gone
Emanuel finding me
Serving all the world
To solely acknowledge me
But once I'm gone
Like Jerusalem's king
Lion Heart last to partly fall off
Predictably amaising
Pass the twenty-four
This is an end
Without further I-do
Warily unaware
Love all conjugations
Including face with book
To one day
find
a'parent

Then:

Psalm 137

December 7th, 2008
-- audio recording: December 21st, 2008, 8:00am

Table of Contents

Preface.................19

The Animation.................23

- a Synopsis of the HESUS JOY CHRIST Animation :.................24
- HESUS JOY CHRIST   theme lyrics.................26
- DISCLAIMER.................27
- Introduction.................28
- KOANS - Required Reading !.................34

The Beginnings : Writing and Animating.................37

- HYPOTHERMIA / My Kayak Prayer   lyrics.................41
- HESUS JOY CHRIST Matthew's Two Four   DISCUSSION.................45
- CONCORDANCES.................73

Discussions.................97

- Matthew's One Too !.................99
- Matthew's Two.................163
- Matthew's Three Fold.................225
- Matthew's Foretold.................273

Appendices 351

- EPILOGUE 352
- HESUS JOY CHRIST theme lyrics 354
- Bibliography 355
- Links 381
- About the Author 384
- INDEX 385

Table of Contents

IN

DETAIL

    My Psalm of Lament 6

Preface 19
    Order of Creation 19
    Order of Presentation in This Book 21
    Quoting Scripture 21

The Animation 23

a Synopsis of the HESUS JOY CHRIST Animation : 24

HESUS JOY CHRIST   theme lyrics 26

DISCLAIMER 27

Introduction 28
    Acedia & Me — A Marriage, Monks and a Writer's Life 28
    Catholicism 28
    St. John of the Cross 28
    St. Therese of Lisieux 29
    Theology of the Body 29
    How to Read this Book 30
    Critical Thought 30
    You Understand This More Than You Know 31
    Mourning and Grieving 31
    Spiritual Experience and History of the Author 31
    Purpose Amongst the Humour 32
    Not Solely an Intellectual Exercise — Practical Implications 32
    Forgiveness, Death and Rebirth (Resurrection) 33

KOANS - Required Reading ! 34

The Beginnings : Writing and Animating 37

HYPOTHERMIA / My Kayak Prayer   lyrics 41
- The Layman's Guide to MARRIAGE 42

HESUS JOY CHRIST Matthew's Two Four DISCUSSION 45
- The Gospel of Matthew - Chapter Twenty-Four 46
- The entire paraphrasing ! 49
  - A LITTLE BACKGROUND 50
- " I love my job ! " 51
- " Understand the building's building ! " 52
- " When will we see you joyful as always ? " 53
- " To some, a not cowboy; to some, the gangster of love. " 54
- " Sheep swing too widely when the shepherd steps . " 56
- " Blow up and you're sucked in ? " 57
- " Triage inappropriate if diagnosis decapitating. " 59
- " When lost stay there. " 61
- " Golden mean visits if mental patience. " 62
- " On understanding attention sees forever . " 65
- " Next time it's personal . " 67
- " Don't yell 'I get it !' too loud . " 68
- " By hook, or bye-bye crook . " 70

CONCORDANCES 73
- Matthew's One Too ! 75
- Matthew's Two 81
- Matthew's Three Fold 87
- Matthew's Foretold 91

Discussions 97

Matthew's One Too ! 99
OVERVIEW from the discussion of Matthew's Three Fold 100
OVERVIEW 102
    Counting Generations 103
    The Genealogy of Jesus 103
    The Genealogy of Abram - Abraham 104
Opening Notes 105
    The Gospel of Matthew - Chapter One 106
Verse 1 Discussion   NIV Bible text verses 1 & 2 109
Verse 2 Discussion   NIV Bible text verses 3 & 4 112
Verse 3 Discussion   NIV Bible text verses 5 & 6 114
Verse 4 Discussion   NIV Bible text verses 7 & 8 118
Verse 5 Discussion   NIV Bible text verses 9 & 10 127
Verse 6 Discussion   NIV Bible text verses 11 & 12 132
    pilgrimage 133
Verse 7 Discussion   NIV Bible text verses 13 & 14 134
Verse 8 Discussion   NIV Bible text verses 15 & 16 137
Verse 9 Discussion   NIV Bible text verse 17 141
Verse 10 Discussion NIV Bible text verse 18 144
Verse 11 Discussion NIV Bible text verse 19 146
Verse 12 Discussion NIV Bible text verse 20 148
Verse 13 Discussion NIV Bible text verse 21 150
Verse 14 Discussion NIV Bible text verses 22 & 23 153
Taking a break — A Discussion of "Koans" 155
Verse 15 Discussion NIV Bible text verse 24 156
Verse 16 Discussion NIV Bible text verse 25 158
Closing Notes 160
    OVERVIEW 160
    HOW TO PICK UP A STICK ! 161

Matthew's Two 163
OVERVIEW from the discussion of Matthew's Three Fold 164
OVERVIEW 166
OPENING NOTES 167
    The Gospel of Matthew - Chapter Two 168
Verse 1 Discussion 170
Verse 2 Discussion 172
Verse 3 Discussion 174

- Verse 4 Discussion 176
- Verse 5 Discussion 178
- Verse 6 Discussion 180
- Verse 7 Discussion 183
- Verse 8 Discussion 184
- Verse 9 Discussion 187
- Verse 10 Discussion 189
- Verse 11 Discussion 191
- Verse 12 Discussion 193
- Verse 13 Discussion 196
- Verse 14 Discussion 198
- Verse 15 Discussion 200
- Verse 16 Discussion 203
- Verse 17 Discussion 205
- Verse 18 Discussion 208
- Verse 19 Discussion 210
- Verse 20 Discussion 212
- Verse 21 Discussion 214
- Verse 22 Discussion 216
- Verse 23 Discussion 219
- Closing Notes 221
    - OVERVIEW 221
    - HOW TO PICK UP A STICK ! 222

Matthew's Three Fold 225
- OVERVIEW 226
- Opening Notes 228
    - The Gospel of Matthew - Chapter Three 229
- Verse 1 Discussion 231
- Verse 2 Discussion 233
- Verse 3 Discussion 236
- Verse 4 Discussion 238
- Verse 5 Discussion 240
- Verse 6 Discussion 241
- Verse 7 Discussion 246
- Verse 8 Discussion 248
- Verse 9 Discussion 251
- Verse 10 Discussion 253
- Verse 11 Discussion 255
- Verse 12 Discussion 257
- Verse 13 Discussion 259

Verse 14 Discussion	261
Verse 15 Discussion	263
Verse 16 Discussion	265
Verse 17 Discussion	267
Closing Notes	270
OVERVIEW	270
HOW TO PICK UP A STICK!	271

Matthew's Foretold 273

OVERVIEW from the discussion of Matthew's Three Fold	274
OVERVIEW	276
OPENING NOTES	277
The Gospel of Matthew - Chapter Four	279
Verse 1 Discussion	282
Verse 2 Discussion	285
Verse 3 Discussion	287
Verse 4 Discussion	290
Verse 5 Discussion	292
Verse 6 Discussion	294
Verse 7 Discussion - part A	296
Verse 7 Discussion - part B	298
Verse 7 Discussion - part C	301
Verse 8 Discussion	303
Verse 9 Discussion	306
Verse 10 Discussion	308
Verse 11 Discussion	310
Verse 12 Discussion	312
Verse 13 Discussion	314
Cross of Victory Walking Pilgrimage	317
Verse 14 Discussion	319
Verse 15 Discussion	321
Verse 16 Discussion	323
Verse 17 Discussion	325
Verse 18 Discussion	328
Verse 19 Discussion	330
Verse 20 Discussion	332
Verse 21 Discussion	334
Verse 22 Discussion	336
Verse 23 Discussion	338
Verse 24 Discussion	340
Verse 25 Discussion	343

Closing Notes 347
    OVERVIEW 347
    HOW TO PICK UP A STICK ! 348

Appendices 351

EPILOGUE 352

HESUS JOY CHRIST theme lyrics 354

Bibliography 355

Links 381

About the Author 384

INDEX 385

Preface

A Technical History

This project is primarily an animation project. This means that the animation is sufficient for presenting the idea that christians are to apply their faith to balancing whole and part, female and male, on the foundation of marriage. The point of the animation is for christians to get married and stay married, in the supreme effort of balancing whole and part, female and male. This also means that this writing presented in this publication is extraneous and does not add anything to the animation. I have, however, found that audiences do not know how to understand the animation, so I have "discussed" it in blog posts, and these blog posts, up to 1,000 words a week on each verse, are the writing that is presented here.

For those that get it, no justification is necessary, but for those who don't get it, our entire world's justification will not suffice. The last will be first and the first will be last. Practicing christians may never understand the necessity of balancing whole and part, and its foundation of christianity, where secular individuals may already be living out such a faith.

Order of Creation

Since 1987 I have put marriage, a union of whole and part, female and male, above all other practical priorities. I became interested in animation as a way of presenting this priority in 1990 while studying with Jehovah's Witnesses. I was accepted into Sheridan College's Classical Animation program, in Oakville, Ontario, in 1993. Since then I continued to apply myself to animation at the film co-op organization in Toronto, Ontario, known as the Liaison of Independent Film of Toronto (**LIFT**), while working at other jobs.

In 1997 I became Roman Catholic, and was married in the Catholic Church. In 2006 I received two grants, one from the Ontario Arts Council, and the other from **LIFT** to complete **HYPOTHERMIA / My Kayak Prayer**, a six minute, 35mm, animated film, which I began working on in 1999. I completed that film in 2008 and then my marriage failed. This film, about a heart changing winter paddle down the Humber River in Toronto in 1986, is about taking a calculated risk when seriously disheartened, and almost suicidal, and realizing that my efforts and risk taking could be applied to marriage.

When my marriage failed in 2008, I began to realize that scripture spoke to me about the primary role of marriage. I also came to appreciate Pope John Paul II's **Theology of the Body**, beginning to read it. I began to write poetry and the paraphrasing of **HESUS JOY**

CHRIST / Matthew's Two Four and completed this as a full colour limited animation running about one minute in January 2009. This was about the time that **HYPOTHERMIA / My Kayak Prayer**, screened at the **Revue Cinema**'s open screening called **Drop Your Shorts**. I screened **HESUS JOY CHRIST / Matthew's Two Four** there in, I believe, April of that year.

I continued with the writing and animation of **HESUS JOY CHRIST / Matthew's One Too !**, and began writing blog posts of each paraphrased line of **HESUS JOY CHRIST / Matthew's Two Four**, since most people found that they could not relate to the writing of the 13 lines of this animation, since they were paraphrased from about 50 verses of scripture. **HESUS JOY CHRIST / Matthew's One Too !** screened at the **Revue Cinema** in July.

I continued animating **HESUS JOY CHRIST / Matthew's Two**, in October and it screened at the **Revue Cinema** as well. I then wrote and animated **HESUS JOY CHRIST / Matthew's Three Fold**, and again screened it at the **Revue Cinema** in February 2010. I then wrote and animated **HESUS JOY CHRIST / Matthew's Foretold**, screening it at the **Revue Cinema** in May 2010.

Each of these first five **HESUS JOY CHRIST** animations required less than 120 hours of work to animate, with **Matthew's Two**, being entirely animated in four days. That is why there are so many pans and zooms in **Matthew's Two**.

Continuing on, I began animating **HESUS JOY CHRIST / Matthew's Five's Nine** in June, 2010, and I am currently still animating it. One scene alone, of **Matthew's Five's Nine**, running 5-1/6 seconds, took over 120 hours to animate that one scene alone. This episode is a much, much more ambitious production.

In March of 2011, I realized that the animation was too dense to be accessible to audiences, so regretting that further discussion would fail to illuminate the obvious, I reluctantly began to "discuss" the animation. This discussion was posted weekly to my blog post, and amounted to almost 1,000 words per verse of animation. I completed discussing all the animation to date by November 6th, 2012. The entirety of these discussions are presented in this publication.

In September of 2011, I was able to set up a website, to allow an audience to navigate all the discussion, without having to dig back into linear blog posts, and more importantly, to present the animations **with** the discussion. This website also includes other artwork. The web addresses can be found in the **Links** section at the back of this book.

Order of Presentation in This Book

I have presented this written material more or less, in the order that it was created.

First, the lyrics to the song presented in **HYPOTHERMIA / My Kayak Prayer**, then the discussion of **HESUS JOY CHRIST / Matthew's Two Four** are presented in this book. The **Concordances** of the animation writing follow. Finally, the discussion of the last four animations are presented in the order of the chapters of Matthew to which each relates. Although this is the order in which the animation text was written and animated, this is not the order in which these discussions were written, as one may see from the dates at the end of each verse's discussion.

Quoting Scripture

Aside from the fact that scripture can be quoted to justify pretty much anything, there are some issues with my quoting of scripture that I would like to address.

I wrote the animation text based on a version of the New International Version translation of the Bible. Although I am Roman Catholic, I was concerned that using the Revised Standard Version translation of the Catholic Church would not be as accessible as the NIV to people for whom English is a second language. This problem is very apparent in the King James Version of the Bible that uses words such as "thee" and "thou".

The biggest problem that people have with reading Shakespeare is that it is written in an English that is no longer spoken, even though it is very effective for those who can access it. It remains a landmark in the English language and still is relevant. Nevertheless, only those seriously interested in the English language can make use of it.

Likewise, the words of the Bible are not there to be worshiped, but rather the message contained in the presentation of the words of the Bible, is sacred. As well, each one of us is sacred, by the way.

When I wrote the text of the animation, I used the New International Version copyrighted © 1973, 1978, 1984. There is now a New International Version of the Bible copyrighted © 1973, 1978, 1984, 2011, and I am only permitted to quote that copy in this print publication.

This raises a problem for which I will give this example.

In the © 1973, 1978, 1984 copy of Matthew, Chapter One, Verse 25, it states:

> [25]But he had no union with her until she gave birth to a son. And he gave him the name Jesus.

But in the 2011 copy of Matthew, Chapter One, Verse 25, it states:

²⁵But he did not consummate their marriage until she gave birth to a son. And he gave him the name Jesus.

This is not on its own a problem, and I agree with the change that was made from "had no union with her" to "did not consummate their marriage", for this is the meaning of the text.

The only problem arises when we look at the animation text that I have written so tightly to the © 1973, 1978, 1984 copy of the NIV. This reads:

"**¹⁶He had no union with her until separated, and animated Marriage, which he called "Emmanuel", meaning " God with us " .**"

The word "union" no longer has any corresponding word in the Gospel text! This is the problem.

To resolve this, I have quoted the 2011 copy of the New International Version, and placed either one or two asterisks (*), leading to the © 1973, 1978, 1984 copy further down the page, from which the animation text has been written.

Finally, since the Animation Text was written from the © 1973, 1978, 1984 copy of the New International Version of the Bible, it quotes that copy. Where there are differences between the text quoted and the © 1973, 1978, 1984, 2011 copy of the New International Version of the Bible, the differences are contained within brackets ( ).

Be aware that quotes cited in the Animation Text may have God's gender changed from male to female. The Bible almost always refers to God in the male gender, but I have taken the liberty of changing the quotes, cited in the Animation Text, to the female gender from time to time. Where I have changed the gender of God from male to female, I have attempted to indicate this by putting the pronoun, either "she" or "her", in **BOLD** and **NOT** italicized.

she   **her**

The Animation :

www.sites.google.com/site/vid932008/hypothermia-my-kayak-prayer

· www.sites.google.com/site/hesusjoychrist

https://www.sites.google.com/site/hesusjoychrist/home/hesus-joy-christ

a Synopsis of the HESUS JOY CHRIST Animation :

HESUS JOY CHRIST /

    Matthew's Two Four
        Matthew's One Too !
        Matthew's Two
            Matthew's Three Fold
            Matthew's Foretold
                Matthew's Five's Nine

. . . ... an eyewitness tour through the Gospel of Matthew, to a concept thoroughly rooted in faith yet paving the way far beyond anything yet imagined — the concept of marriage. As shows such as *Family Guy*, after *The Simpsons*, have established, animation clearly communicates the simple truths of complex dynamic social systems and practices and is uniquely suited to relating these truths. Since the sinking of the Lusitania, this is animation's destiny ! As shrewd as any two bit advertising executive, **HESUS JOY CHRIST** puts images to work establishing the divine role of marriage as put forth - as far as I can tell — in Pope John Paul II's *Theology of the Body*.

    Personal concrete references to the life of the animator flesh out the first five episodes of **HESUS JOY CHRIST**. *Matthew's Two Four*, based on the twenty-fourth chapter of Matthew, which is about the signs of the end of the age, is the beginning of this series, as the beginning end of this age of **HESUS JOY CHRIST**. *Matthew's One Too !* is written from the first chapter of the Gospel of Matthew and lists the matrigeneosophy of the matriarchal influences before continuing on to the story of the conception of marriage. *Matthew's Two*, relating to the second chapter of the Gospel of Matthew, which is the story of the Wise Men and the escape to Egypt, becomes the story of the marriage relationship preparing to be acknowledged. *Matthew's Three Fold*, written from the third chapter of Matthew, is about an early minister of marriage acknowledging a marriage relationship. *Matthew's Foretold*, drawn from the fourth chapter of Matthew, is about the temptation endured by the marriage relationship and the influence that relationship has on the community.

    The animation is fully coloured simple line drawings, carrying the story that although simple, bears considerable consideration. Approximately 20,000 words have been, or will be, written by the animator discussing the text of each animation alone, and can be read at

www.sites.google.com/site/hesusjoychrist .

__Matthew's Five's Nine__ is based on the fifth chapter of the Gospel of Matthew, which includes the Beatitudes, and is currently in production. Two previews may be viewed at www.sites.google.com/site/hesusjoychrist . It may take years to complete this full production that began in 2010. This episode does not have any references to the personal life of the animator.

This animation series, as well as all the discussion I have written, is the culmination of my experience and considerable consideration. It is true that seeking the divine in the world can make one a candidate for the psychiatrist's prescription, if not the psychologist's couch, yet, as the name of the Mood Disorders Association of Ontario's annual art show and sale proposes, those on the edge have been "touched by fire"!

Regardless, I stand on my record, considerate of others, yet boldly proclaiming what I have found, and hoping it confirms Pope John Paul II's __Theology of the Body__ .

God willing, and by his grace, I will complete **HESUS JOY CHRIST / Matthew's Five's Nine** soon enough, to continue on through the Gospel of Matthew for some time to come.

R. David Foster, not wishing to impose more words on anybody, most importantly himself, provides this BLOG, WEBSITE, and BOOK, for anyone who wishes clarification through explanations by means of words. Honestly, let me tell personal stories as true as I can possibly remember, which is pretty true if I bother to remember at all, and pretty verifiable if I'm bothering to remember or else it really means nothing to remember it because nobody will ever believe anything I feel worth remembering . . . whatever!

HESUS JOY CHRIST   theme lyrics

HESUS JOY CHRIST!
What are you doing?
Can you not hear that?
That's the Lord wooing!
He has come!
He has come!

HESUS JOY CHRIST!
Hallelujah, praise the Lord,
The Word is tabled
And the Spirit's poured!
Hear Him come!
Hear Him come!

HESUS JOY CHRIST!
John baptized to repent -
Submersed to consider
The life you've spent.
Here He came!
Here He came!

HESUS JOY CHRIST!
We died with you
To all the evil
To ever oppose you.
Here we go!
Here we go!

HESUS JOY CHRIST!
In faith we go -
To be cheeky with evil,
Death's freedom we know!
Here we come!
Here we come!

HESUS JOY CHRIST!
Arise you dead!
God's love is given!
In grace we're wed.
Here He is!
Here He is!

HESUS JOY CHRIST!
Alive in You!
We praise one and other -
'Til we see You!
Here we are!
Here we are!

JESUS LORD CHRIST!
We praise and adore!
Our Father and Spirit
Forever more!
Here we are!
Here we are!

JESUS LORD CHRIST!
You've been so patient!
Let all praise raise
The love that's latent
Here we are!
Here we are!

HESUS JOY CHRIST theme August 20th, 2009, 11:30pm - 12:07 am

DISCLAIMER

All of the **HESUS JOY CHRIST** animation and discussion is entirely original, although closely tied to Matthew's Gospel. This means that **IT IS NOT IN ANY WAY ENDORSED BY ANY CHURCH OR INSTITUTION** and should be considered in light of the fact that all of this is **ONLY** my sincere expression of my experience and comprehension.

As I consider the writing to be a discussion, please post or contact me with any comments, concerns, correction or questions you may have from time to time. I can most readily be reached by email at **vid932008@gmail.com**, and I should be able to respond within a week.

As of August 20th, 2012, I have begun to read the actual text of Michael Waldstein's translation of _Man and Woman He Created Them : A Theology of the Body_. I began reading the actual text of this work exactly 33 years to the day on which it began to be proclaimed by the Pope, on September 5th, 1979.

Introduction

Acedia & Me — A Marriage, Monks and a Writer's Life by Kathleen Norris

This book, which I thoroughly enjoyed, requires an audience to let it sink in, without critical analysis complicating the experience offered by the author. Although she refers to monastic culture and modern philosophers, she does not present arguments intended to convince through various proofs. She instead, discusses these topics and reflects on how they relate to her personal experience, while maintaining the theme of acedia.

This book awoke an awareness in me of the potential of writing that is free of reductionistic arguments — a writing that is more akin to koans.

Catholicism

In 2011 I began a course offered in my parish entitled **Catholicism**, which consisted of a DVD presentation, featuring Father Robert Baron, one week, and a reading assignment, with discussion questions that were discussed the following week. There were ten episodes and ten reading and discussion assignments.

In this course, we discussed both **St. John of the Cross**, who wrote **Dark Night of the Soul**, about the lover and beloved relationship with God, and **St. Therese of Lisieux**, who is known for her approach to God as a little flower of the forest floor, rather than a mighty towering landmark of a tree.

The discussion questions in this program of study referred to the **Catechism of the Catholic Church**, and the reading of the references there was my first encounter with the reductionistic and wholistic type of writing common in spiritual writing, and prepared me for my current reading of **Theology of the Body**.

St. John of the Cross

St. John of the Cross is known for his approach to God as a lover and his or her beloved. This approach is referred to in the introduction to Michael Waldstein's translation of **Theology of the Body**. The love of the lover for the beloved is the paradigm for the relationship of a person to God, and the infinite relationship of God to the person. This is fundamental to the relationship of the spouse to their partner, and is fundamental to **Theology of the Body**, which prioritizes the marriage relationship above all other earthly relationships.

The reading of these writings requires an open approach that relates to one's emotions as much as their intellect, and is another example of an approach by which one may make sense of my animation writing presented here.

St. Therese of Lisieux

Although I have not read anything by St. Therese of Lisieux, in the Catholicism course mentioned above, she was presented as one of the more recent Saints of the Catholic Church. She is also mentioned in Michael Waldstein's introduction to his translation of **Theology of the Body**, as an example of how to approach **Theology of the Body**.

Essentially, her approach to God, as a little flower, doing and being what she could be, more as a little flower on the forest floor, rather than a towering landmark of a tree, is relevant to this discussion, as this poetic comprehension bears meaning, and anyone can take up their cross or task immediately where the motive finds them, and there is not any reason to put it off.

Theology of the Body

Theology of the Body has become the catch all identification of the ideas presented by Pope John II in more or less weekly addresses as Pope, to a general audience from September 5th, 1979, to 1984. As best as I can understand at this point, the idea is that marriage, in a **theology** of the **body**, is the pinnacle of relationships for those who are in a body. This is not merely an answer to the critics of the Church's stand on abortion and birth control, but a call to everyone to the potential of marriage, working as the incarnation of the Trinity of Father, Son and Holy Spirit, or being, knowledge of being, and love of being, and even doing, knowledge of doing and love of doing. The Roman Catholic Church is in a unique position among other faiths of the world, that allows it to be capable of presenting this understanding that topples some and empowers others in a way similar to the cultural revolution surrounding the concept of Evolution, but even more revolutionary, and possibly the most revolutionary thing to ever happen in the historical history of humanity.

The physical gender of humanity is the key to the salvation of humanity, and any practice that does not promote the union and maintenance of these two as one has cut itself off from the infinite, limiting its potential.

Not only does this teaching provide a biblical, theological, academic and philosophical justification for the institution of marriage, it goes beyond to issues of the resurrection of the **body**, which, by the way, anyone who recites a catholic Creed **personally professes**, and most who do would be hard pressed if asked to explain this profession.

My understanding is that the purpose of humanity is to live forever in heaven on earth, rather than die and go to some mystical state. Death is real, but resurrection is **more** real. **Theology of the Body** addresses these topics, that are for the most part overlooked or dismissed by the majority of the faithful.

How to Read this Book

First and foremost, the animation should be viewed by whatever means, whether by acquiring a copy of the DVD by contacting the author, R. David Foster by email at vid932008@gmail.com, or more easily, viewing the animation on his website at www.sites.google.com/site/hesusjoychrist . The animation is sufficient at presenting the material .

Having said that, animation is so labour intensive that it was not intended to be viewed only once, but would provide a galaxy of consistent meaning with repeated viewings . And having said that, if one may make sense out of all of it that is all that is necessary .

If however, one finds they are unable to make any sense out of the animation, then I would suggest reading this book, if not the same text as posted on the website listed above . Reading this may help, but failure to seriously consider the animation cannot be helped by failing to consider this writing .

It is hoped that this project will shed light on the topic of marriage as well as scripture for both churchgoers and the secular alike . It could be said that I have excluded both sides of the duality of churchgoer and secularism, by not having church authority, and by speaking of church topics to the secular audience . I hope, rather, that the two may both find meaning in this work, and both sides of the duality of churchgoer and secular individual would make up my audience .

Indeed, this project is directed at both churchgoer and secular individual . Being in a church does not make anyone a christian any more than being in a garage makes anyone a car . And the truths communicated by scripture are relevant and make sense in the secular world, because they truly are as real as anything .

Scripture is so relevant that I have found it meaningful in my very own life . I have not elevated events in my life to the level of worship - I have instead used events in my life to show how scripture is effective at resolving meaning in my very own life ! The point is that it is relevant to anyone's life ! I have only used my life as an example .

Critical Thought

Critical thought ! - What other parlour tricks do you know ?!

It is very easy to find any of this incorrect, and I dare say this project presents an abundance of incorrectness for those who seek incorrectness . The meaning is beyond critical thought — it comes into play where critical thought leaves off .

Have you ever tried applying critical thought to critical thought ? Critical thought has an abundance of limitations . This project picks up where critical thought leaves off .

This is because the topics involved are in regard to a living God or living purpose, that cannot be nailed down or contained, and if it is nailed down and contained it has already departed and escaped!

The way to read this is to look for any meaning, and develop your own consistent understanding based on whatever meaning you can find consistently. The meaning you find is the meaning that is there, and there is meaning there.

You Understand This More Than You Know

Finally, you understand this more than you know. Just because you may find you cannot articulate an understanding does not mean you do not understand. The animation and this writing are my manifested hope of shedding light on your own experience and tweaking your awareness to illuminate what you already know.

Mourning and Grieving

Mourning is concrete practical action justified by the love of what was lost and grieving is the emotion of having lost what was loved.

Many have understood this project as a hangover from a failed marriage, and have promptly dismissed it. I would insist rather, that this project, although it may be an act of mourning, is therefore an act of love for the union of male and female, whether physical, spiritual, emotional, intellectual, practical, academic, philosophical or theological.

Spiritual Experience and History of the Author

I, David Foster, was baptized Presbyterian, attended Sunday School at a United Church, was confirmed Episcopalian (American Anglican), served as an Anglican altar boy, participated with a Baptist Church girlfriend, studied with Jehovah's Witnesses and Mormons, before becoming Roman Catholic through the Rite of Christian Initiation of Adults. Twice, at both the Episcopalian church and then the United church, I gave the Youth Sunday sermon. The youth group leader at the Episcopalian church was Roman Catholic, and befriended me, taking me to a Latin Mass at his Roman Catholic Church.

As a Roman Catholic, I volunteered in my parish by maintaining the lawn weekly and facilitating the Baptismal Preparation meetings. I also was a sponsor in the RCIA program twice.

I did not become Roman Catholic in order to marry a Roman Catholic. It was made clear by Father Paul McCarthy that it was not necessary for me to become Roman Catholic in order to marry a Roman Catholic.

Throughout all this churchy behaviour I acquired a protestant familiarity with Bible stories, preferring the simplicity and clarity of the Old Testament before growing into the life of the New Testament. These stories related real truth to me, and that is the only reason I maintain them in my memory.

This understanding, enlightened by solitude and experiences that I sought out to resolve issues and dig a firm foundation for further construction, has repeatedly been reaffirmed and is alive and growing.

My understanding is forged by "too much thinking". Often I have heard that I think too much. It is also forged by sincere honesty, where I try to accept things as they really are, often leading to despair that blossoms with new life, as my understanding dies to be reborn to a new understanding. This is what happened or happens in the first animation - **HYPOTHERMIA / *My Kayak Prayer*** .

Purpose Amongst the Humour

If there is not any love in this project then it is just annoying. But there is a great deal of humour and joking around in the animation. The writing is a little dryer but I still had fun writing it. I hope, for those who get it already, they are able to find a lot of fun in the presentation. Surely it may offend the merely pious, but it may enlighten and enliven the scriptures to the benefit of all.

I worship a living loving God who meets us beyond our failures to bestow new, more wonderful, life.

Not Solely an Intellectual Exercise — Practical Implications

Many who promote the priority of marriage base their argument on procreation. This is the lamest argument for marriage there is! The practical implications of this argument are a rejection of marriage.

Others use marriage to justify their cause of the day, and are ignorant of the revolutionary nature of full participation in marriage. Even I am mostly incapable of fulfilling most of my duties toward marriage. But I try when I am able, failing through my fault, through my fault, through my most grievous fault.

Take the Abortion Issue for example. If we discuss a young woman of limited means hoping to find love and instead becoming pregnant with complications, do those who vocally oppose abortion support this woman in her need and shortcomings to honestly give her honour, independence and a path to love, as well as love itself? Or do they assign her to the realm of a charity case and sinner for her seeking love? Do they hold the life of the child above the life of the mother? Do they maintain the need for charity or do they work to provide a world where all are able to acquire in honour and self respect. Charity is not the solution. Respect for life, whether at home, in the workplace or in any other situation means allowing others to make mistakes and helping them pick up the pieces and begin again, as they have allowed those with wealth to make that mistake and given them the opportunity to make amends.

Marriage is having your morning coffee with your own personal Satan who deviles you for your morning breath. Marriage is the salvation of humanity, the path to eternal life on earth with God our spouse.

Forgiveness, Death and Rebirth (Resurrection)

A final word on Forgiveness, Death and Rebirth is necessary.

Forgiveness is not a solution to a particular dispute — it is a way of life. One must constantly forgive others, and not only others, but oneself, for constant never ending failings, and more importantly, in balancing whole and part, female and male, one must accept their polar opposite as more than an enemy but rather a partner. This demands constant attention and awareness to avoid condemning your polar opposite for existing.

This Forgiveness will certainly lead to death — there is not any question about it — it will lead to death, and that death will be justified by our everyday sins.

But if we are trying our best to follow Jesus, by picking up our cross, the very means by which we will be executed, regardless of whether we are male or female, and not denying our death, we will be raised with Jesus to new life **in this world**. And we will continue on to our next death.

Hell is not where God sends us, but rather the state we create for ourselves by rejecting being itself. Heaven is accepting the world as all good, and allowing death to be a living part of it.

Mary lost everything by following her son, Jesus, and all people **both women and men**, must accept that Forgiveness is the threading of the camel through the eye of the needle when we die and are presented to new life, **in this world**. Death can be the only way through, and Resurrection is promised yet never expected.

We were meant to live forever with the infinite person, in a heaven **on earth**, rather than die and go into some other mystical state. This is achievable, and marriage is the means by which it may be achieved, opening a practical door to infinity, balancing whole and part, female and male.

KOANS

Required Reading !

A Wikipedian citation can be found at
http://en.wikipedia.org/wiki/Koan

The sound of one hand -- a prime example of a koan !

Two hands clap and there is a sound. What is the sound of one hand?
—Hakuin Ekaku

From the blog post (www . vid93 . blogspot . ca) of October 17th, 2011.

Taking a break
A Discussion of "Koans"

     Events in my life lately, have caused me to consider that I may not be able to complete as much of the animation as I had hoped. Once again, my livelihood is under attack for political reasons.

     As well, my brother has raised the point that the animation writing is unintelligible, which I thoroughly understand.

     So I feel it is time again to discuss how one may make sense of this animation, as I did in the winter of 2009 in my Blog post. It was a post from the book **Praying Our Experiences**[A] by Joseph F. Schmidt, which I will once again discuss here.

     In chapter three of his book, page 27 in my copy, under the heading **Introspection — Narcissism and the Limited Ego**, this Jesuit Priest acknowledges the dangers of considering our experiences. One may discover their weaknesses and gifted-ness by considering their experiences but they risk becoming narcissistic. As well, one may rationalize their experiences so that they find what they want to find in them. Loving ourselves over others is a danger, but we cannot love others if we do not first love ourselves. It is a precarious undertaking. Authentic consideration of life is not the problem, but part of the solution.

     When the ego is dominant one will judge each of their experiences as a victory or a defeat, rather than consider what they say to one. This rationalism leaves no room for authentic consideration to arrive through the cracks in our ego. An example of this is the judgment of a Pharisee that Jesus, if He was the Messiah, would have known what kind of woman was washing His feet. The dominance of the ego would not leave room for the unexpected and thereby close their awareness to God working in their life.

     In order to open a disciple's mind to the non-rational and the unexpected, the teacher of some eastern traditions will present the disciple with a koan as a focus for consideration. A koan is a statement that does not make sense. It is impossible to resolve the statement through analysis. This is the point.

     A classic koan is " What is the sound of one hand clapping ? " The answer must come from beyond rationalization and analysis, from beyond the ego. It is not a matter of rationalizing the koan, but rather being in faith with the statement that brings personal awareness and transformation. The ego must surrender to the helplessness.

Our experiences themselves are koans, in that they are not rational, containing contradictions and elements that do not make sense. Looking for meaning appears fruitless — this is the point. This opens one up to the source of life on the other side of the limited rational ego.

So all of the animation text, can be considered as one would consider a koan.

As with life, just because something does not appear to make sense, does not mean there is not any sense at all in it. This is the achievement of science — making sense of the natural world. Geographers have mapped the irregularities and inconsistencies of the surface of the earth, making it known.

So the animation text does not appear to make any sense, but careful consideration of whatever sense one can find in it, is the meaning of the animation.

An example is the question "Can we lead with you?" Does this inquire if the questioner can be a leader in a group of leaders? Or does it mean that the person questioned will be leading the charge, and everyone else, including the questioner, will be right along shortly?

As well, one may compare this question to the text in the Gospel of Matthew where Jesus, an embodiment of the One, says "Follow me!". The disciples hear a command, but in the animation, the One hears a question — "Can we lead with you?" So just as the people wanted to make Jesus king after he fed the crowds, one following in the path of Jesus will be called upon to lead.

Sunday, October 16th, 2011

A *Praying Our Experiences by Joseph F. Schmidt*,
Published by Saint Mary's Press, Christian Brother's Publications; Winona, Minnesota; www.smp.org. © 2000

Praying Our Experiences

Joseph F. Schmidt

Praying Our Experiences by Joseph F. Schmidt,
Published by Saint Mary's Press, Christian Brother's Publications;
Winona, Minnesota; www.smp.org. © 2000

PRAYING OUR EXPERIENCES is the practice of reflecting on and entering honestly into the day-to-day events of our life to become aware of God's word in them and to offer ourselves to God through these events.
Noted by some as one of the best introductions to prayer ever written, this book is helpful for developing your personal prayer life, as a guide for sharing in groups, or as a gift for someone who desires to live a more prayer-filled life.

http://books.google.ca/books/about/Praying_Our_Experiences.html?id=Dvc9IIzY3XAC&redir_esc=y

The Beginnings: Writing and Animating

HYPOTHERMIA

My Kayak Prayer

lyrics

current RANT

The Layman's Guide to MARRIAGE

HESUS JOY CHRIST

Matthew's 2 4

Discussion

Matthew's One Too !

Matthew's Two

CONCORDANCES

Matthew's Three Fold

Matthew's Foretold

www.sites.google.com/site/vid932008/hypothermia-my-kayak-prayer

HYPOTHERMIA / *My Kayak Prayer*

. . . is a 35mm animated film that I completed in 2008 with the support of two financial grants:

One grant, received in 2005, was from the Liaison of Independent Film of Toronto, which covered the costs of filming the artwork on their 35mm animation stand. www.lift.ca

The 35mm animated film was produced with the assistance of

LIAISON OF INDEPENDENT FILMMAKERS OF TORONTO

The second grant, received in 2006, was from the Ontario Arts Council, and covered the costs of processing the film and soundtrack of this 35mm animated film . www.arts.on.ca

ONTARIO ARTS COUNCIL
CONSEIL DES ARTS DE L'ONTARIO

50 YEARS OF ONTARIO GOVERNMENT SUPPORT OF THE ARTS
50 ANS DE SOUTIEN DU GOUVERNEMENT DE L'ONTARIO AUX ARTS

HYPOTHERMIA

lyrics

My Kayak Prayer

Refrain: *Down, down, down*
The sun goes down
The night comes down
Laid down, as I lay down

A boy in the yard
I try hard to sleep
And try not to think
Of the other, afoot
With plans of a crook
To ruin my shelter
And send helter skelter
A boy in the yard

Cycling on the highway
Turn off to the side road
Against what they all told
That there would not be a place
To which one could leave the
                            race
And to just be
Then to lay down

A youth by the road
Doing what he said
And pausing in bed
Amidst all the snow
Hoping not to show
The late rural drivers
A character diverse
As to set out to walk
In snow white as chalk
Only to lay down
So much on the ground
A youth by the road

What's the diff' between
Abram and Abraham
Seems to me one thicketed ram
Whether my talent,
my wealth or my life
Isaac it !
I sac' it to my wife

This is the beginning of the ideas presented in the **HESUS JOY CHRIST** animation series, as well as pointing to the point of the **HYPOTHERMIA / My Kayak Prayer** project.

current RANT as of the winter of 2008

When you look to the stars, you are likely to trip on a stone. Seeking the divine in the world can make you a candidate for the psychiatrist's couch.

The Layman's Guide to MARRIAGE

I can not keep silent about this topic any longer. Marriage is a spiritual union - no more and no less. It is blessed by the church when it is witnessed by the spouses to exist. The spirit comes first, then the material, then the eternal. A person is spirit first from the first cause known as " I AM ". They are expressed in the material of the body, of either gender. The material world imposes a cultural gender on the person which they may accept or reject. The legal world imposes ordinances which may be accepted or rejected and are changeable.

The union of the whole and part is essential to all existence whether material, spiritual or eternal. An imbalance in this union set existence into motion and will continue until the end of time. TO BRING SOMETHING INTO EXISTENCE, A UNION OF WHOLE AND PART MUST TAKE PLACE. All that exists is directed to either the whole or the part as a result of the motion of existence. This is expressed in the physical gender of a person but can be overcome by determined free will.

The church, a spiritual institution, in the material world, seeking the eternal, blesses the union of whole and part as identified by and alive in Christ and the church. The spiritual union of whole and part found in the marriage of a man and a woman is a great spiritual resource. It influences all that encounter it, whether society, persons, or the world. It is this union that the church wishes to honour, protect and nurture in the sacrament of marriage.

Marriage as a legal institution is a contract between two parties uniting resources, assets and investments, whether people, places or things. It is not concerned with anything spiritual although at times it is concerned with emotional hangups. For the good of society the family unit can be argued to necessarily be a balance of whole and part. This would encourage marriage between a man and a woman. However, many marriages are nothing but tools in an endeavor while many gay and lesbian marriages are spiritual unions of whole and part. As a legal institution I see no reason to allow marriage to be used as a material tool while being denied to true spiritual unions of whole and part. I would like to see the church restrict the sacrament of marriage to verified undeniable spiritual unions by testing the witness of the spouses, and disregarding any legal union that may follow.

A true spiritual union of one man and one woman will one day exist between a man and a woman, at the end of time when a perfect balance of whole and part comes into existence. Marriage is a vocation serving Christ. Marriage is not a perpetuation of the imperfect balance found in procreation and the inflation of the population. Children are the hope of tomorrow and acknowledgment of the failings of today.

The church is only trying to use material purposes, procreation, to justify a spiritual union between man and woman, part and whole, in a material, legal, world. I am disappointed by this argument although I agree with the conclusion. There is little more fundamental than gender and therefore a fundamental spiritual union of whole and part can only be between a man and a woman, **ALTHOUGH ONLY TO THE EXTENT THAT PHYSICAL GENDER IS FUNDAMENTAL.** The eternal soul, if it has not gender, can find spiritual union anywhere - in fraternity, sorority, nature, endeavor, procreation.

---

written in the winter of 2008

HESUS JOY CHRIST
Matthew's Two Four

DISCUSSION

The Gospel of Matthew

– Chapter Twenty-Four

The Destruction of the Temple and Signs of the End Times

¹ Jesus left the temple and was walking away when his disciples came up to him to call his attention to its buildings. ² "Do you see all these things?" he asked. "Truly I tell you, not one stone here will be left on another; every one will be thrown down."

³ As Jesus was sitting on the Mount of Olives, the disciples came to him privately. "Tell us," they said, "when will this happen, and what will be the sign of your coming and of the end of the age?"

⁴ Jesus answered: "Watch out that no one deceives you. ⁵ For many will come in my name, claiming, 'I am the Messiah,' and will deceive many. ⁶You will hear of wars and rumors of wars, but see to it that you are not alarmed. Such things must happen, but the end is still to come. ⁷ Nation will rise against nation, and kingdom against kingdom. There will be famines and earthquakes in various places. ⁸ All these are the beginning of birth pains.

⁹ "Then you will be handed over to be persecuted and put to death, and you will be hated by all nations because of me. ¹⁰ At that time many will turn away from the faith and will betray and hate each other, ¹¹ and many false prophets will appear and deceive many people. ¹² Because of the increase of wickedness, the love of most will grow cold, ¹³ but the one who stands firm to the end will be saved. ¹⁴ And this gospel of the kingdom will be preached in the whole world as a testimony to all nations, and then the end will come.

¹⁵ "So when you see standing in the holy place 'the abomination that causes desolation,'[a] spoken of through the prophet Daniel—let the reader understand— ¹⁶ then let those who are in Judea flee to the mountains. ¹⁷ Let no one on the housetop go down to take anything out of the house. ¹⁸ Let no one in the field go back to get their cloak. ¹⁹ How dreadful it will be in those days for pregnant women and nursing mothers! ²⁰ Pray that your flight will not take place in winter or on the Sabbath. ²¹ For then there will be great distress, unequaled from the beginning of the world until now—and never to be equaled again.

²² "If those days had not been cut short, no one would survive, but for the sake of the elect those days will be shortened. ²³ At that time if anyone says to you, 'Look, here is the Messiah!' or, 'There he is!' do not believe it. ²⁴ For false messiahs and false prophets will appear and perform great signs and wonders to deceive, if possible, even the elect. ²⁵ See, I have told you ahead of time.

²⁶ "So if anyone tells you, 'There he is, out in the wilderness,' do not go out; or, 'Here he is, in the inner rooms,' do not believe it. ²⁷ For as lightning that

---

[a] 15 Daniel 9:27; 11:31; 12:11

comes from the east is visible even in the west, so will be the coming of the Son of Man. ²⁸ Wherever there is a carcass, there the vultures will gather.

²⁹ "Immediately after the distress of those days

> "'the sun will be darkened,
> and the moon will not give its light;
> the stars will fall from the sky,
> and the heavenly bodies will be shaken.'ᵇ

³⁰ "Then will appear the sign of the Son of Man in heaven. And then all the peoples of the earthᶜ will mourn when they see the Son of Man coming on the clouds of heaven, with power and great glory.ᵈ ³¹ And he will send his angels with a loud trumpet call, and they will gather his elect from the four winds, from one end of the heavens to the other.

³² "Now learn this lesson from the fig tree: As soon as its twigs get tender and its leaves come out, you know that summer is near. ³³ Even so, when you see all these things, you know that itᵉ is near, right at the door. ³⁴Truly I tell you, this generation will certainly not pass away until all these things have happened. ³⁵ Heaven and earth will pass away, but my words will never pass away.

The Day and Hour Unknown

³⁶ "But about that day or hour no one knows, not even the angels in heaven, nor the Son,ᶠ but only the Father. ³⁷ As it was in the days of Noah, so it will be at the coming of the Son of Man. ³⁸ For in the days before the flood, people were eating and drinking, marrying and giving in marriage, up to the day Noah entered the ark; ³⁹ and they knew nothing about what would happen until the flood came and took them all away. That is how it will be at the coming of the Son of Man. ⁴⁰ Two men will be in the field; one will be taken and the other left. ⁴¹ Two women will be grinding with a hand mill; one will be taken and the other left.

⁴² "Therefore keep watch, because you do not know on what day your Lord will come. ⁴³ But understand this: If the owner of the house had known at what time of night the thief was coming, he would have kept watch and would not have let his house be broken into. ⁴⁴ So you also must be ready, because the Son of Man will come at an hour when you do not expect him.

⁴⁵ "Who then is the faithful and wise servant, whom the master has put in charge of the servants in his household to give them their food at the proper time? ⁴⁶ It will be good for that servant whose master finds him doing so when

b	29	Isaiah 13:10; 34:4
c	30	Or *the tribes of the land*
d	30	See Daniel 7:13-14.
e	33	Or *he*
f	36	**Some manuscripts do not have** *nor the Son.*

he returns. ⁴⁷ Truly I tell you, he will put him in charge of all his possessions. ⁴⁸But suppose that servant is wicked and says to himself, 'My master is staying away a long time,' ⁴⁹ and he then begins to beat his fellow servants and to eat and drink with drunkards. ⁵⁰ The master of that servant will come on a day when he does not expect him and at an hour he is not aware of. ⁵¹ He will cut him to pieces and assign him a place with the hypocrites, where there will be weeping and gnashing of teeth.

The entire paraphrasing !

"I love my job ! "

"Understand the building's building ! "

"When will we see you joyful as always ? "

"To some, a not cowboy; to some, the gangster of love ."

"Sheep swing too widely when the shepherd steps ."

"Blow up and you're sucked in ? "

"Triage inappropriate if diagnosis decapitating ."

"When lost stay there ."

"Golden mean visits if mental patience ."

"On understanding attention sees forever ."

"Next time it's personal ."

"Don't yell " I get it ! " too loud ."

"By hook, or bye-bye crook ."

HESUS JOY CHRIST
Matthew's Two Four

A LITTLE BACKGROUND TO
HESUS JOY CHRIST — Matthew's 2 4

    The animation is a technical achievement as it is the longest animation I have done on computer, completely coloured, with varying layers, and most importantly it is lip synced, my first attempt as self taught for a work of this length. The artistic achievement is all the (poor quality, I admit) drawings of the Skymark site on Kingsbridge Garden Circle, and the characters, people I have known and worked with, as they are all drawn entirely from memory, although still poor likenesses . Last but first, the writing is capable of bearing the weight of analysis as it took me a month at least to get a formula and complete the 14 lines to my satisfaction as being the most concise understanding of the 24th chapter of Matthew, as well as a personal relation of how Jesus, a better and leading tradesman, is relevant in my life .

    As the muse hit's me, I intend to relate using a proof system I encountered in grade ten Geometry, how each line effectively sums and directs the verses of Matthew that they stand for in the New International Version of the Bible . This will be posted here on this blog .

    Essentially, if you were to take the first verse as an example, where the disciples point out the wonder of the temple buildings, the method I use is to imagine the scenario and see what fits . In the case of this verse, a disciple enjoying the marvels of his chosen profession, religion, is really only appreciating the frills and bonuses of his position, same as a good lunch, and annoyingly lacking attention to what his real purpose as a disciple is suppose to be . A nice building is just a building; Jesus was building a community of people, his body, the church, and not an earthly establishment of architecture .

    Furthermore, in the face of critical analysis, I koan a confounding impression that a hick would appreciate a cheap, family pack of mass produced samosas for lunch . This is to establish that there is one truth in this scene and none other than that one truth . When you see the truth you know that is the meaning, and not that hicks should appreciate multiculturalism, because they don't appreciate it at all, by definition of a hick .

culprit: R. David Foster incident 4/24/2009 12:21:00 PM

The Destruction of the Temple and Signs of the End Times

¹Jesus left the temple and was walking away when his disciples came up to him to call his attention to its buildings. ²"Do you see all these things?" he asked. "Truly I tell you, not one stone here will be left on another; every one will be thrown down."

from the Gospel of Matthew, Chapter 24, New International Version

Discussion of how verse one became " I love my job ! "

Let's set the groundwork or ground rules for this discussion, which we will add to in order to clarify as I go along. First off, Jesus was a competent member of society, but more a tradesman than a scholar. He did not analyze and reduce everything he encountered. Instead he built up ideas and people, as he spoke from his position in society as a tradesman on his way to being a criminal and being executed. Secondly, I am discussing what the scripture means to me, and to me personally. If you feel I am directing you to see things my way because it is my way than stop reading right now. I only share my understanding to further an open discussion that will lead to further understanding, and this is only meant to be fodder for discussion, and absolutely will **NOT** be the last word.

Jesus was doing whatever he would do at the temple and as they leave his cronies annoy him with a stupid comment that exacerbates his concern that they may not be up to the task he has obtained them to do. He is a crew leader and the crew is proud of the poor work of their predecessors. They feel they are competent but Jesus has his doubts. He chastises them, objects to their statement and confronts their attitude with a terse comment. He then likely figures that will be the end of it. Job done - time for lunch and a nap.

Discussion of how verse two became " Understand the building's building ! "

The issue of the temple being destroyed was not Jesus' intention for his comment. He meant that a building is only a building. It is not as everlasting as the faith and body Jesus wanted to institute. Far from it. Even as a work of architecture it would not last. Sure the Pyramids are still around but maybe that's because nothing is alive in them. If there was some life to them they would likely be air-conditioned or at least made more livable from time to time, down through the ages. A building has a purpose, and the purpose is alive. The purpose is people and people are constantly re-inventing their purposes. Mom wants a new kitchen floor that is easier to clean than linoleum tile that always looks worn and dirty anyways. Besides this is not the sixties anymore and the jetson look is retro rather than new age. St. Christopher Parish, in Clarkson was renovated with a new altar and lectern. The Anglican's like the High English of the King James Version. There is a constant pressure to renew that battles the establishment of the old, constantly. What should stay and what should go ?

Jesus could care less. He was building a community. This was necessary to maintain his presence to mankind as the Son of Man and Son of God. He was no more than a man and no less than a God. He would pass away and always be with us. No building could do that. He used the temple like you used Starbucks last time. It serves it's purpose as either convenient java or social commentary — whatever works.

The building will be renovated — the building process will build the building, again. To renovate you must tear down at least a part of the building. I am sure there is one stone on top of another at the ancient temple, but likely not any more than that. The physical building is building or being renovated. As well Jesus' following is building, or increasing, and will overtake the old ideas of God, as Christianity did in the Roman Empire and beyond. As well, Jesus wanted his disciples to be the foundation of his church. A living breathing foundation of loving people on which to establish a living knowledge and awareness of God's presence and love for mankind. This is the second meaning of "understand" - be the foundation for others to know God came and gave his life out of love for his creation — humankind. God wants us to see him face to face and know He loves us. We need to get up to speed to be with Him. Jesus came to earth to urge us on and help God by helping humanity rise to greet God.

"Understand the building's building ."

Stand as a foundation, beneath the increasing following of Jesus, and support it as His loved ones approach God.

Discussion of how verse three became "When will we see you joyful as always?"

> ³As Jesus was sitting on the Mount of Olives, the disciples came to him privately. "Tell us," they said, "when will this happen, and what will be the sign of your coming and of the end of the age?"
>
> from the Gospel of Matthew, Chapter 24, New International Version

First of all, when I read a passage and I get stumped I look either further outward to the circumstances, or failing that, look inward to either the passage itself, the actual words, or into my feelings about what I have read or heard. This is a two step — left foot or right foot, followed by the other foot.

The entire chapter can be looked at as a whole, when looking outward. What is the kind of stuff Jesus is saying, and beyond that, a carpenter is talking about God. In this chapter there are literal contradictions that show the context is spiritual. The best one is that if he was talking about the destruction of the planet and this realm of existence in the natural science sense of it, than he would have been wrong, if you understand "generation" to mean a lifespan of less than eighty years. I have looked at the whole chapter and beyond to come to the understanding that this verse can be paraphrased as I have done. Jesus is not talking about the end of the planet — he is talking about the end of the existence of awareness.

Furthermore, why are the disciples asking this if Jesus was not talking about such things in his response of verse two. I believe they have made an assumption that the end of the temple is the end of the age. Even further, they want Jesus to talk nicely to them again, and are throwing him a bone where he can chew on about how everything will be wonderful. This is truly a journeyman — apprentice relationship : the apprentices do not have a clue about their work, and the loving journeyman must once again set them straight by meeting them where they are at and leading them forward.

If one has a faith based on a temple then the end of the temple is the end of one's age. Jesus answers their question for what it is, regardless of where it came from, and he answers it with love and joy.

Another issue is the problematic nature of the question : If one is always in joy than the reason you may not see that person in joy is a problem with your sight and not their joy! Another unrelated example of a problematic question is the question "Do you admit you beat your dog ? — Yes or No ?" A yes answer means you admit you beat your dog — a no answer means not only do you beat your dog, but by not admitting it you are trying to deny it. There seems no benevolent way out of such a question, and Jesus is getting better at finding ways to deal with these things during his ministry on the way to his trial. His answer in this case is more like "I beat my dog in every race because I am faster than him and he is slow — I always win a race against my dog ?" :P The disciples have asked a spiritual question in response to Jesus worldly statement about the temple. Jesus answers their spiritual question in worldly terms, as is necessary since the spirit is only visible in it's effect on the world and in that way is like the wind — you see the tree bend and know which way the wind is blowing. This sets the stage for the remainder of the 24th chapter of Matthew, which he has faithfully recorded, and I have lovingly paraphrased as I find it — full of JOY.

The Master Tradesman will have a good laugh over libations at the end of the day, when the Journeyman relates this tale of the day to Him in the embarrassed presence of the apprentices.

If you are next to the truck and lunch is called on a cold rainy day, do not go all the way back out to the other end of the property to get your cloak, since you saw the owner give the foreman two hundred bucks at the beginning of the day saying "Happy Court, but only two hours!".

If your wife tries to get back in the burning house to turn off the tap, don't let her do it!

DISCUSSION OF VERSES 4 TO 8

Thursday & Friday, June 11 & 12, 2009

" To some, a not cowboy; to some, the gangster of love. "

⁴Jesus answered: "Watch out that no one deceives you. ⁵For many will come in my name, claiming, 'I am the Messiah,' and will deceive many. ⁶You will hear of wars and rumors of wars, but see to it that you are not alarmed. Such things must happen, but the end is still to come. ⁷Nation will rise against nation, and kingdom against kingdom. There will be famines and earthquakes in various places. ⁸All these are the beginning of birth pains.

from the Gospel of Matthew, Chapter 24, New International Version

This takes a different tack in paraphrasing. The issue is the oversimplification and reduction of Jesus to manageable ideas, images, and parts. If Jesus is the ONE son of God, God from God, Light from true Light, the Word and the Word with God, why would he come again? If it is necessary for him to come a second time why would it be in any way similar to the first time he came, if not to be redundant. Man is made in God's image, so just look around you to see God's image . Still, to see God sitting beside himself in a packed bus presents a conundrum .

What is the essential nature of Jesus that sets his image above all the other images of God ? To me it could be that he speaks to eternity — every time he opens his mouth . He is the Word, and through him all things were made .

So to paraphrase this I stole and doctored a line from a pop song in an oversimplification of my own . Verse four and five talk about false images of Christ . I would say not false, but overly simplified and limited likenesses of Christ . The second coming of Christ is in glory and power, rather than the itinerant preacher as the first coming was . It is also personal and hard to relate from one person to another . So to some he will seem to come with an ability to handle the desertion experiences like a cowboy, with joy and spirit . And to others he will come as a lover who is beyond the law .

So wars and rumors and famines and politics are not the second coming no matter how charismatic the players are . Neither is the destruction of the temple the second coming . Do not be persuaded by others — the second coming is personal and far more thorough than any natural or political disaster . The second coming is the end of awareness and ability, which will end to give birth to a new awareness and world view . Like Saul on the road to Damascus, one will be without sight or awareness and then the new world will be born in you . No person, not even Jesus, can guide you through something when you have no awareness . You are not able to be led without having any awareness to lead . Jesus' message in Matthew chapter twenty-four is to console you and give you an understanding of what is happening to ease the stress of going through your loss of awareness and ability, for it is by faith alone that Jesus will carry you to the other side and new life . Without faith no one can enter into the new life for they will end their life if they see no future . It is the acceptance of Christ's love and obedience to Him that allows us to allow ourselves the Grace he has to offer us . Otherwise we would condemn ourselves as sinners and not accept His Grace .

This will happen many times before the physical death of a person, and this is the nature of true life . Life exists beyond death . Without life there would not be any death . The essential cause of death is birth ! How can anything die if it had never been born . In the beginning there was life before there was death, and there will be life after there is death . Whether an evolutionist or creationist, this is true . Life and death co-exist in a symbiotic relationship that even a vegetarian cannot deny — for they kill plants to live . A complete and total end of life has come many times to many people in the end of their awareness and loss of mind, sight or body . The end of the physical world is irrelevant to a one-hundred year old person on their death bed . So do not be troubled by the dead leading the dead in this cause or that cause . Be aware and pay attention to your relationship with God and your awareness of the ultimate and eternal that you encounter in your life, for when your awareness is failing you are dieing to this life and being born again into true life — if you have faith that allows you to accept your new life as the free gift that it is and do not deny the gift given freely to you .

Discussion of Verses Nine to Fourteen

" Sheep swing too widely when the shepherd steps . "

⁹"Then you will be handed over to be persecuted and put to death, and you will be hated by all nations because of me. ¹⁰At that time many will turn away from the faith and will betray and hate each other, ¹¹and many false prophets will appear and deceive many people. ¹²Because of the increase of wickedness, the love of most will grow cold, ¹³but the one who stands firm to the end will be saved. ¹⁴And this gospel of the kingdom will be preached in the whole world as a testimony to all nations, and then the end will come.

from the Gospel of Matthew, Chapter 24, New International Version

Paraphrasing by David Foster
Section C

Step one : Persecution, death, hatred; loss of faith, fellowship, love; false prophets; standing firm saved; Gospel preached totally then end .

Step two : Participants and citizens of your old world will see your difference as incorrect and as a threat to their fruitful world so will seek to correct your variance .
You will cause birth pains in some but not others and fellowship will decline, while weakness due to strain will withdraw love . Prophets are not appropriate because your relationship is with God alone at this time .
If you repent you will repeat this again, so stand firm, and be born again . [John the Baptist gathered back those that had moved beyond repentance to fuel the flock of Jesus and increase the number baptized in the Spirit .] * [Repentance provides a second chance, not a death and re-birth to new life .] *
All of your world will hear the Gospel before your world ends .

*[a new idea added by David Foster — ie: not an idea in the original Gospel text]

Step three : You're really going to get beat up over this by everybody. Everybody's going to be a—holes and jerks just because I (Jesus) put them in a sour mood. Some will try to cure the crisis like I (Jesus) would do. Extreme actions carried out in panic will lead to general hopelessness and lack of affect, but if you stand firm you'll benefit. Everybody will know about this.

Step four : Don't swing too wildly just 'cuz the shepherd acts / appears to

Final step :

<u>Sheep swing too widely when the shepherd steps.</u>

Basically, a lot will actually happen at the end of your world. People around you will spring to action or recoil back in rejection. Too much fuss over a natural occurrence. Who really cares will become apparent as some will withdraw from you and some will rush to aid you in any way they can think of. Some will offer strongly worded advice and other's will say " come this way — over here ! ". Others will avoid you like the plague.

It is kind of like the James Dean cool kid at graduation. He is loved by all but not able to participate since he is incorrect. Sure some will hate him for what he stands for but aren't love and hate closely tied and both count as strong emotions. Not many people will casually overlook such a character. Rather, his very existence screams for a judgment.

Anyways, there's a new approach for these discussions of the paraphrasing of the Gospel of Matthew Chapter 24.

Sunday, June 21st, 2009 R. David Foster

Section D

<u>" Blow up and you're sucked in ? "</u>

[15]"So when you see standing in the holy place 'the abomination that causes desolation,'[a] spoken of through the prophet Daniel—let the reader understand— [16]then let those who are in Judea flee to the mountains. [17]Let no one on the housetop go down to take anything out of the house. [18]Let no one in the field

go back to get their cloak. ¹⁹How dreadful it will be in those days for pregnant women and nursing mothers! ²⁰Pray that your flight will not take place in winter or on the Sabbath. ²¹For then there will be great distress, unequaled from the beginning of the world until now—and never to be equaled again.

²²"If those days had not been cut short, no one would survive, but for the sake of the elect those days will be shortened. ²³At that time if anyone says to you, 'Look, here is the Messiah!' or, 'There he is!' do not believe it. ²⁴For false messiahs and false prophets will appear and perform great signs and wonders to deceive, if possible, even the elect. ²⁵See, I have told you ahead of time.

^a 15 Daniel 9:27; 11:31; 12:11
from the Gospel of Matthew, Chapter 24, New International Version

First paraphrasing draft:

October 21 — 27, 2008

* When you see destruction's cause being held as sacred it is time to end your world .
* The end is very close — push through a roll when it comes to avoid spectacular catastrophic upset, and thread the double negative into the new structure . *Italics indicate sections that cannot be deciphered from the photocopy at hand* .
* You will see false christs do remarkable things . Your relationship is direct with God and not to be mediated .
* Hesus knows these things are knowable ---- *cannot decipher the photocopy at hand* .

Second paraphrasing draft:

October 21 — 27, 2008

* Sacred desolation; urgency; false christs perform wonders; 'Mark my words' .

Third paraphrasing draft:

November 1 — 7, 2008

* Exit collapsing wholes prior to supernova's action for survival of ---
* Supernova an exit before darker (black wholes) final exits .

Final paraphrasing draft:

November 22, 2008

* Blow up and you're sucked in ?

July 19, 2009

So to sum up for a work of limited animation, we have:
* Urgent departure;
* Necessary action to survive;
* Unsuccessful deception in the absence of a true Christ.
I think that covers it.

    Everyone is probably aware of what a supernova is: the explosive end of a bloated star or sun in space, followed by a black whole that sucks everything into its nothing. That is the image I am alluding to in this paraphrasing. But I am also pointing to how everyone tells the upset person to relax, hoping they can resolve the situation by resolving the symptom instead of the cause. When a person blows up in anger, are they taken into the manipulation of another person? A false christ perhaps? I resolve this by the teaching that if one strikes you on one cheek offer him the other to strike as well. Essentially if a person is trying to manipulate you then let them do it. That is what I am referring to when I mention the idea of pushing through a roll in a kayak. If the waves are going to push you over in a capsize, instead of push back, push along with the wave and go all the way around to be an upright person again!

Section E

"Triage inappropriate if diagnosis decapitating."

^{26}"So if anyone tells you, 'There he is, out in the wilderness,' do not go out; or, 'Here he is, in the inner rooms,' do not believe it. ^{27}For as lightning that comes from the east is visible even in the west, so will be the coming of the Son of Man. ^{28}Wherever there is a carcass, there the vultures will gather.

from the Gospel of Matthew, Chapter 24, New International Version

First paraphrasing draft:

October 21 — 27, 2008

* There is no singularity of Christ when your new world of Christ is transformed.
* The remains of one's old world are devoured when one's world has become new, and you need
— *cannot decipher photocopy at hand*.

Second paraphrasing draft:

October 21 — 27, 2008

* Many will point to a Christ in the world, but Christ is all the world; death is a spectacle.

Third paraphrasing draft:

November 1 — 7, 2008

* Everyone will say this or that is what I would do but at the end of all why bail out a bathtub sinking in a lake without a drain plug. Everyone loves to see someone try to (do this).
* Don't heed advice on how not to (heed advice).
* Achieve the goal of goal-less-ness.
* Never mind First Aid if you're headless (decapitated).
* First Aid is irrelevant upon decapitation.

Final paraphrasing draft:

November 22, 2008

Triage inappropriate if diagnosis decapitating.

August 16, 2009

So to sum up for a work of limited animation, we have :
* in your time of crisis don't listen to what anyone says about where to find salvation.
* the totality of a second coming is like lightning lighting up the sky rather than finding a pearl of great price in a field.
* many people will address your crisis to benefit from aiding you.

I think that cover's it.

      Essentially, putting a band-aid on a decapitated body doesn't do much to help. Especially if it is put on incorrectly. When you loose your head, advice is not much help. When your entire world is changing there is not much help to be had from someone only addressing the symptoms of the crisis.

      Instead, Christ has shown the way, so you have seen this problem before from the outside, before the second coming graces you with a first hand experience from the inside of the crisis. You are being born to new life. Your old life is passing away so anyone helping you to save your old life is of little service and not of any help. The anointing with oil that the woman did to Jesus feet is an honour to Jesus and shows understanding and appreciation for what he is going through.

      Physically, the Cross of Victory Pilgrimage was not as challenging as a day of landscaping, but the glory of God shone in the people I walked with. Many were older or younger and many more were not in shape. Honourable civilized respectable women went without comforts (flushing toilets, or any toilet at all, as well as showers). In a section of large hills, without physically carrying someone, there was little anyone could do for their discouraged hearts. I asked a young man if we should say the rosary. He lead and I continued. I really wanted people to look to their God when they are troubled.

Section F

" When lost stay there. "

> [29]"Immediately after the distress of those days
>
> "'the sun will be darkened,
> and the moon will not give its light;
> the stars will fall from the sky,
> and the heavenly bodies will be shaken.'[b]
>
> -b- **29** *Isaiah 13:10; 34:4*
> *from the Gospel of Matthew, Chapter 24, New International Version*

First paraphrasing draft:

October 21 — 27, 2008

* Created guides and heavens will serve no longer.
* Heaven itself will bear and endure the severity of the end of your world.

Second paraphrasing draft:

October 21 — 27, 2008

* Calm in the eye of the storm without steerage or guidance.

Third paraphrasing draft:

November 1 — 7, 2008

* You will be despairing without hope and wandering aimlessly not knowing me or God. Heaven will shudder.

Final paraphrasing draft:

November 22, 2008

* When lost stay there.

September 13, 2009

    Surely everyone must get the gist of this stuff by now.

    Basically there is a lull before the second coming that follows the turmoil. In this lull there is peace because there is nothing that can be done — nothing left to do and all is lost. There is no hope save salvation in Christ as he told you this would all happen. Nothing is left — not even any opportunity or hope. You just sit there doing the 1000 yard stare.

    So if you are lost in the woods this is what is generally taught in all the military and survival manuals — SIT TIGHT — STOP AND STAY and this is what you must do. It is foolish to run around aimlessly because that only makes it harder for help to find you, as well as wearing you out even further toward a weakened state that could make you unable to endure. Sit tight and help and salvation will come to you — there's nothing you can do at this time that will help anybody or yourself. Have faith that by the grace of God you will be retrieved into life again. Accept the grace when it comes, with JOY and THANKSGIVING.

    This is the part that I find the hardest. I take great care to be responsible but I know that just being is very often the only thing that should be done. Just stand there hoping for the hug of Christ — maybe reach out your arms in faith — but do nothing ! I often make things worse for myself and all concerned by leaping into action to address a perceived need. Sorry.

Section G

" Golden mean visits if mental patience. "

[30]"Then will appear the sign of the Son of Man in heaven. And then all the peoples of the earth[c] will mourn when they see the Son of Man coming on the clouds of heaven, with power and great glory.[d] [31]And he will send his angels with a loud trumpet call, and they will gather his elect from the four winds, from one end of the heavens to the other.

[c] **30** Or *the tribes of the land*
[d] **30** See Daniel 7:13-14
from the Gospel of Matthew, Chapter 24, New International Version

First paraphrasing draft:

October 21 — 27, 2008

Symbols of witness of Christ will be your focus and civil authority will acknowledge your loss. Civil authority will acknowledge your focus as creditable, your witness has been encountered. Witnesses to your end of the world will gather your support system about you.

Second paraphrasing draft:

October 21 — 27, 2008

Christ appears; temporal mourning; elect collected.

Third paraphrasing draft:

November 1 — 7, 2008

I will appear ghostly and nebulous coming toward you like a wind you can see in the same way you can see power and glory — by the effect only and not directly visible. Mortal spiritual servants will make a grand entrance, appearing as such to gather those you know suffer for my sake such as pastor Sharon, Maisie and Victoria, and father, in orderly procession amidst the chaos of others' panic.
Christ's power and glory — marginal dominance manifests through visitation's mental patience.

Final paraphrasing draft:

November 22, 2008

* Golden mean visits if mental patience.

September 20, 2009

    Surely everyone must get the in joke of this one now.

    First came Socrates, whose student was Plato, and then came Aristotle whose pronouncements of the natural world were adopted by the church, for better or worse (Galileo).

    Socrates went around asking questions and not giving answers — ever. Plato wrote down examples of how Socrates would ask further questions when someone gave him an answer. Socrates was employing a method of illumination, very perplexing and koanlike, and disquieting and disturbing. Socrates was sentenced to death for disrupting the peace by disturbing the common understanding that even today we all know is flawed.

    Plato wrote down examples of a living experience. The written work of Plato is not in itself a living experience. It is objectified. The Gospels and the Bible are a living experience.

    Aristotle sought to eliminate the ugknown of the experience of Socrates as related in Plato's writings. Aristotle was nothing but answers, and very dead. That's the risk a writer takes when he writes. In grade twelve, to eliminate this paralyzing awareness of how one's words can be misconstrued, I wrote a sign and placed it in full view of my desk, that said: " I, David Foster, do not believe, promote or in anyway justify anything I write." This allowed me to finish an essay on <u>The Great Gatsby</u> so I could pass grade twelve English.

A friend's friend said that my diagnosis was not valid. So are they implying I was lying or are they saying I was falsely diagnosed. Words can have many meanings. For the past year I have tried to keep every meaning of my words valid. This is what is happening as I paraphrase this chapter of the Gospel of Matthew into a 50 second commercial for God.

Anyways . . . . . Aristotle pronounced the Golden Mean. This is the statement that the middle road is always the correct or best choice. The extreme choices are to be avoided. This is valid until it is taken to extremes. If one always chooses the middle road they are being extremely middle of the road! To not always take the middle road, sometimes taking the right or left road would be less extreme than always taking the middle road. At least there is life in that. Aristotle does not go so far.

Christ is both middle road and extreme at the same time. He is all creation. All God and all man. Purely God and purely man. He is everything from the extreme end of being all God to the other extreme of being all man. The Son of God is the Son of Man — there's a koan for you! Christ is the Golden Mean. He did an extreme thing as God and an extreme thing as Man by dying on the cross for the love of man. So in this paraphrasing, Christ will appear if you are patient in your mind. If you are not patiently waiting you will be distracted and not see him appear.

When I was in turmoil I saw Maisie and Sharon and Victoria and my father in a very new light — I saw them anew, as I did the rest of the world. We all die a little each day and in the same way we are reborn each day. Those who love their life will lose it — death, and those who lay down their life for Christ's sake will have eternal life. Socrates asked if we are the same person as when we were a child. Physically our body's molecules have been exchanged for new material, and we continually look different from before. Yet something is the same! Life is spirit and our spirit or soul is eternal. If you die to your self you will have eternal life, and eternal death to keep it going. Go forth and make many mistakes so you will have many deaths and much life and learning from your mistakes. Billy Joel says mistakes are all you can truly call your own. And don't forget your second wind. Christ is coming! Christ is coming!

"The sky is falling!" - Chicken Little.

Section H

" On understanding attention sees forever . "

> ³²"Now learn this lesson from the fig tree: As soon as its twigs get tender and its leaves come out, you know that summer is near. ³³Even so, when you see all these things, you know that it[b] is near, right at the door. ³⁴Truly I tell you, this generation will certainly not pass away until all these things have happened. ³⁵Heaven and earth will pass away, but my words will never pass away.
>
> -b or he
>
> from the Gospel of Matthew, Chapter 24, New International Version

First paraphrasing draft:

October 21 — 27, 2008

- This end of world is (?) as it approaches so you know it will happen .
- You will be aware of this as it happens because Jesus has articulated it .
- [The articulation is a further foundation of an eternal world .]

Second paraphrasing draft:

October 21 — 27, 2008

- When fruit is ripe, ravaging will come; it will happen now; your mind, heart and world will pass away but I say you will witness that I spoke of this, in your next world and heaven .

Third paraphrasing draft:

November 1 — 7, 2008

- This is a pattern of events that occurs at every great catastrophic capsize and roll, that can be learned and recognized as a path of spiritual growth . This will happen to you, now and always . These are the words that I, Hesus Joy Christ, say, and pass along . Take them away with you when I send you forth, to the end of all until and beyond the end of time, and the beginning of timelessness .

Final paraphrasing draft:

November 22, 2008

* On understanding attention sees forever .

October 11, 2009

Hopefully everyone had a thanks fulled, happy and peaceful Thanksgiving as I did with a turkey dinner we prepared last night to be enjoyed by Crystal, Sean, Dave (the governor) and myself.

This is the last of the original paraphrasings. It was late in January that I decided to include the entire chapter 24 of Matthew and so added three more lines to include the remainder of the chapter as an epilogue - Randy on the left having liquid lunch with Dan on the right, as Brian plows past :)

This "On understanding attention sees forever." seems pretty obvious to me. Jesus is talking about awareness extending beyond the end of a world. Awareness that was provided by Jesus. If you can see it you believe it. And because he told you ahead of time, as he says, your faith is increased as you see it happen when you pay attention.

Keep your wick trimmed and oil handy, bridesmaids! When the fruit ripens you know the season is changing. When you see certain things you know and can anticipate a change. In your generation this will happen. Your understanding and your belongings will pass away but the Word will endure and survive along with you.

The Word is a provided understanding that will endure and survive all else, including heaven, your ideals, and earth, your accomplishments. On this understanding you can see forever. On this understanding you can see in a timeless way, beyond temporal interests. Trust me, you understand this more than you know, so do not be hindered by my articulation or even your own ability to articulate - whether sufficient or insufficient.

That's gotta' be enough words on this topic. Next week - next line.

Sunday, October 11, 2009

" Next time it's personal ."

The Day and Hour Unknown

³⁶"But about that day or hour no one knows, not even the angels in heaven, nor the Son,ᶠ but only the Father. ³⁷As it was in the days of Noah, so it will be at the coming of the Son of Man. ³⁸For in the days before the flood, people were eating and drinking, marrying and giving in marriage, up to the day Noah entered the ark; ³⁹and they knew nothing about what would happen until the flood came and took them all away. That is how it will be at the coming of the Son of Man. ⁴⁰Two men will be in the field; one will be taken and the other left. ⁴¹Two women will be grinding with a hand mill; one will be taken and the other left.

ᶠ 36 Some manuscripts do not have *nor the Son*
from the Gospel of Matthew, Chapter 24, New International Version

First paraphrasing draft:

January — February 2009

- That is how it will be at the coming of the Son of Man .
- Each at his own time yet under the same circumstances as shared with others .
- Everyone is going about their days as the Son of Man comes for you .
- It is personal .

Second paraphrasing draft:

March 2009

- Second time's . . . .
- This time it's personal !
- Next time's personal !

Final paraphrasing draft:

April 16, 2009

* Next time it's personal .

Sunday October 18, 2009

This too seems pretty obvious to me . Jesus, as well as a tradesman talking to his apprentices, and leading them on with colorful images as they have asked his elocution on this topic, is talking about the spirit in the only way possible — concrete language and examples to discuss ethereal topics !

The father knows when the child is about to step into traffic, not the passersby. It will happen as the world turns and it will happen in the presence of others yet other's will be oblivious to this event.

An example of this personal nature of the second coming of Christ can be taken from another of my personal experiences. In the fall of 1988 I was studying psychology at York University and summarizing chapters of a textbook on the foundations of psychology in a very tongue-in-cheek way — I was unimpressed and having fun with it. I was also sorting out whether I should get engaged to be married. Anyways, the professor summoned me to his office and told me I could write about any psychology topic I want instead of tying me to the textbook ". . as long as I get engaged." I almost fell out of my seat! I'm sure my eyes exploded right out of their sockets! This was a very personal experience and I heard something that no one else heard. Anyways, I did not complete university, nor did I get engaged or arrested.

Another example of how Jesus is talking could be the word "power". We all know what it means but how do you know power? Can you see it? Perhaps in your mind. Can you measure it? Only after measuring other aspects and computing a result. The second coming is in power and glory. It is not as an itinerant preacher so why would it even be the same as a person greeting you. Sometimes you have a revelation of a person's true character when they are not even around or even alive! And such a revelation can be very overwhelming — heartbreaking or life changing.

That's gotta' be enough words on this topic. Next week - next line — if animation permits.

"Don't yell 'I get it!' too loud."

⁴²"Therefore keep watch, because you do not know on what day your Lord will come. ⁴³But understand this: If the owner of the house had known at what time of night the thief was coming, he would have kept watch and would not have let his house be broken into. ⁴⁴So you also must be ready, because the Son of Man will come at an hour when you do not expect him.

from the Gospel of Matthew, Chapter 24, New International Version

First paraphrasing draft:

January — February 2009

- You are under the knowledge of the Saviour until he lifts you up into full knowledge.
- Eureka moment.

Second paraphrasing draft: March 2009

- "Eureka!" you'll shout.

Final paraphrasing draft: April 16, 2009

- Don't yell " I get it! " too loud.

Sunday October 25, 2009

    I really don't have time for this, this week, but I had to bring videos back to the library so this will help to make the trip worth it.
    Jesus is telling us and his disciples to keep watch. Be alert. Be aware. Be aware of your spiritual life. His example claims a house owner should keep watch to prevent his house being broken into. This could mean to have an alarm system but then you must be sure the system is working. When was the last time you checked your smoke detector?
    Jesus actually says that He will come " . . . when you do not expect Him." How is anyone suppose to expect something to happen when you do not expect it? This means that you must always be alert and aware and this can be exhausting. No matter how hard you try He will still come when you do not expect Him. The only thing you will be able to do is react and hope you will recognize Him when he comes. You must train yourself in spiritual practices to recognize Him immediately when he comes, unexpectedly, so that you can react appropriately and correctly.

44 "So you also must be ready, because the Son of Man will come at an hour when you do not expect Him."

    I opened a text message on October 2, that was sent on September 28, that I had ignored as a mistake. This text message said nothing but was overwhelming to me. I never would have expected it yet I have hoped for something like it. I would have yelled out loud if I wasn't expecting something unexpected spiritually. I received a call from Randy in March that was unexpected and then I broke my ankle the week before I was about to start working for him at Landscaping. He still had me work for him once it healed by May 4. Keep watch! Pay attention.
    The movie **The China Syndrome** was on TVO last night. Jack Lemmon's character knew something was out there, then someone was out there, and Jane Fonda's character witnessed Jack Lemmon's experience. She broadcasted it to anyone attentive. That was all she could do — and she had to do it because she witnessed his death. Her prying questions brought resolve to a respected co-worker of Jack Lemmon's character and enabled this co-worker to pick

up the fallen torch and carry it onward. All expectedly unexpected and all were warily unaware.

Wish me luck in completing my animation of <u>**HESUS JOY CHRIST — Matthew's Two**</u> this week for submission Saturday. I hope everyone stays healthy and I can be left alone as much as possible to get the 4 minutes done. I also pray I can focus and do a good worthy job of it. Pray for me, friends.

That's gotta be enough words on this topic. Next week - next line — if animation permits.

Sunday, October 25, 2009

" By hook, or bye-bye crook . "

[45]"Who then is the faithful and wise servant, whom the master has put in charge of the servants in his household to give them their food at the proper time? [46]It will be good for that servant whose master finds him doing so when he returns. [47]Truly I tell you, he will put him in charge of all his possessions. [48]But suppose that servant is wicked and says to himself, 'My master is staying away a long time,' [49]and he then begins to beat his fellow servants and to eat and drink with drunkards. [50]The master of that servant will come on a day when he does not expect him and at an hour he is not aware of. [51]He will cut him to pieces and assign him a place with the hypocrites, where there will be weeping and gnashing of teeth."

from the Gospel of Matthew, Chapter 24, New International Version

First paraphrasing draft:

January — February 2009

- The jerk of turning will break your bond with the Son of Man when he grabs you up if you are not already heading in that direction.
- fishing - reel in then let run.
- when Christ hooks you he can only bring you in if you head to the boat. (fishing for men)
- you'll live to die another day and be stuck doing it all again.
- remedial rebirth to new life.

Second paraphrasing draft:

March 2009

- By hook or bye crook.

Final paraphrasing draft: April 16, 2009

* By hook or bye-bye crook .

___

Sunday November 1st, 2009

    I really do have time for this, this week, as I completed the animation of **HESUS JOY CHRIST / Matthew's Two** in a record four days . It helps to pan, repeat and symbolize stuff . Everybody likes the pretty colours more than the good movement anyways .

    Jesus asks a question . Who is the good and wise servant ? He does not give a direct answer but goes on to say it will at least be very good for the servant that does the will of the master . Slacking off is ok but not if the master catches you . And who knows when he will return and assume you have been slacking off the whole time . Even my boss, the owner, to make a point yesterday, accused me of slacking while he slept . My reaction was firm, as I knew I had not slacked off, and he believed me as the work was done, and there was no more to the issue . If the work was not done he would have pressed the point .

    Taka, who barely speaks enough English, is a good and wise servant . He answers with an annoyingly loud "YES SIR!", even if he does not comprehend . When he has an idea of what he is suppose to do he does his best enthusiastically and energetically and meticulously . We asked him if he has been to university and he answered "No, but I've been to Disneyland ." Think about that for a minute and it will come to you . Taka is heading toward the boat .

    The flipside is getting chewed out and your argument being cut to pieces . You will be counted amongst the hypocrites and you won't like it . So don't lean on the counter, do not fold your hands, do not chat too much, hold the handrail as you take two steps at a time on the stairs, and listen to, for and with the master .

    Who's been fishing ? Who's been fishing for men ? Sure women troll the malls for a good catch, but if the fish cannot be lead to the boat the end of this world does not come and you go around to do it again . Who wants to be lifted up to the new world . ? John Smith had quite a whirl with Pocahontas, and she was lifted up to death from smallpox in England . If you do not follow Jesus as he leads you in your own life you just swim around like a fish looking for bugs . Not so bad . But if he can lead you to a new world wouldn't that be wonderful . Like University pubs to a high school grad . Like a good car for a post grad . Like not needing parents' help for a grown up .

    Beating your fellows and eating and drinking with drunkards is only wrong when it is not the will of the master . Jesus ate and drank and bested his fellows and was accused for it . John the Baptist, cousin to Jesus, fasted and prayed in solitude and was accused for it . Do not get hung up on the type of tree that shows the direction of the wind . Be aware of the wind, sky pilot! Do not get hung up on the negative. It is there but it is more dreary, like waiting for the bus in an eternal twilight. A kick in the pants is a blessing, not a destruction.

Several times (3 to be exact) this year I have been given a kick in the pants. The first was when I broke my ankle, the second was when I doored a car in traffic on my bicycle, and the third time was when I had my seizure. My awareness of my spiritual life has made these three times have spiritual meaning for me. The seizure was the toughest to figure out. Spiritually, death is a self prescribed illusion that fails to exist once it has occurred. The point of this passage of scripture is not that you must have the key to heaven, but that you must be blessed with the grace of constant fastidiousness. There is not a destruction for crooks, who steal from the master's grace, but you will be in a position to bid them good-bye.

Somewhere someone knows the origin of the expression "by hook or by crook." Wikipedia doesn't know:

By hook or by crook
Wikipedia, the free encyclopedia
http://en.wikipedia.org/wiki/By_hook_or_by_crook

This is an English phrase that means the goal may be achieved by any means necessary, disregarding any other concerns.

So knowing is not the same as doing. Do the will of the master, regardless of why you should.

And "University" does sound a lot like "Universal Studios" if you say it with a Japanese accent.

HESUS JOY CHRIST — Matthew's Two is done but that's another post. Thanks to everyone for their support. This is the end of the discussion of this bit of animation. I hope somebody read it cuz' I really enjoyed writing it . :)

That's gotta' be enough words on this topic. Next week - I'm off to a dinner with fellow pilgrims. Time to move on to discussing **Matthew's One Too!** anyways.

CONCORDANCES

OF THE
ANIMATION

WRITTEN WHILE ANIMATING
THE PREVIOUS CHAPTER

HESUS JOY CHRIST
Matthew's One Too!

CONCORDANCE

The Gospel of Matthew
Chapter One
New International Version

The Gospel of Matthew - Chapter One
New International Version

The Genealogy of Jesus the Messiah

¹This is the genealogy[a] of Jesus the Messiah[b] the son of David, the son of Abraham:

²Abraham was the father of Isaac,
Isaac the father of Jacob,
Jacob the father of Judah and his brothers,
³Judah the father of Perez and Zerah, whose mother was Tamar,
Perez the father of Hezron,
Hezron the father of Ram,

⁴Ram the father of Amminadab,
Amminadab the father of Nahshon,
Nahshon the father of Salmon,
⁵Salmon the father of Boaz, whose mother was Rahab,
Boaz the father of Obed, whose mother was Ruth,
Obed the father of Jesse,
⁶and Jesse the father of King David.

---

[a] 1 Or *is an account of the origin*

[b] 1 Or *Jesus Christ*. Messiah (Hebrew) and Christ (Greek) both mean Anointed One; also in verse 18.

Matthew's One Too!
written by R David Foster,
Wednesday, April 1ˢᵗ, 2009

The Matrigeneosophy of the Created

¹A record of the matrigeneasophy of the created, made through David, who I am.

²Dennis gave birth to Emily, who came out of the plain. In Emily David was born to Linda. Linda became Tina who was not chosen. ³Tina became Patricia, by choice, who did not accept. Patricia became Mia, who was apparently indifferent. Mia became Marcelle through Linda, in the style of a matriarch, who endured through Jacqueline, Marysse and Dorcas, and through Texas. ⁴Dana was first to initiate, under Sharon, and endured Etobicoke Collegiate Institute, Povungnituk, kayaking, and Bina, to become first chosen to accept. Dana became Kim, who became Wendy who endured the first cycle fall.

David was the father of Solomon, whose mother had been Uriah's wife,

⁷Solomon the father of Rehoboam,
Rehoboam the father of Abijah,
Abijah the father of Asa,
⁸Asa the father of Jehoshaphat,
Jehoshaphat the father of Jehoram,
Jehoram the father of Uzziah,
⁹Uzziah the father of Jotham,
Jotham the father of Ahaz,
Ahaz the father of Hezekiah,
¹⁰Hezekiah the father of Manasseh,
Manasseh the father of Amon,
Amon the father of Josiah,

¹¹and Josiah the father of Jeconiah[c] and his brothers at the time of the exile to Babylon.

Second to initiate was Miranda, who was stolen by Jane to the first policing, but no union .

⁵Lois followed Jane and began first witnessing and animation under Jennifer. Jennifer became Sherry and first following. In Sherry fundamental animation in Oakville was begun and union with Trisha, preceding Maisie .

⁶In the deserted came Irene, united without union .

---

c   11 That is *Jehoiachin*; also in verse 12

¹²After the exile to Babylon:
Jeconiah was the father of Shealtiel,
Shealtiel the father of Zerubbabel,

¹³Zerubbabel the father of Abihud,

Abihud the father of Eliakim,
Eliakim the father of Azor,

¹⁴Azor the father of Zadok,
Zadok the father of Akim,
Akim the father of Elihud,
¹⁵Elihud the father of Eleazar,
Eleazar the father of Matthan,
Matthan the father of Jacob,

¹⁶and Jacob the father of Joseph, the husband of Mary, and Mary was the mother of Jesus who is called the Messiah.

¹⁷Thus there were fourteen generations in all from Abraham to David, fourteen from David to the exile to Babylon, and fourteen from the exile to the Messiah.

⁷Emily became Sharon, who became Sherry, who became Irene.

⁸Maisie returned in the thirty ninth year to rule in the forty second year, and begat the second cycle fall and a new life in the Spirit.

⁹Thus there were twelve generations established at the first cycle fall. There were nine generations to establish commitment and conclude three generations of matriarchy, initiating purposeful driven animation.

Joseph Accepts Jesus as His Son[*]

¹⁸This is how the birth of Jesus the Messiah came about[d]: His mother Mary was pledged to be married to Joseph, but before they came together, she was found to be pregnant through the Holy Spirit. ¹⁹Because Joseph her husband was **faithful to the law**[**], and yet[e] did not want to expose her to public disgrace, he had in mind to divorce her quietly.

²⁰But after he had considered this, an angel of the Lord appeared to him in a dream and said, "Joseph son of David, do not be afraid to take Mary home as your wife, because what is conceived in her is from the Holy Spirit. ²¹She will give birth to a son, and you are to give him the name Jesus,[f] because he will save his people from their sins."

²²All this took place to fulfill what the Lord had said through the prophet: ²³"The virgin will conceive and give birth to a son, and they will call him "Immanuel"[g] (which means "God with us").

---

[*] **18** 1973, 1978, 1984 NIV copy that HJC was written from is ***The Birth of Jesus Christ***
[d] **18** Or *The origin of Jesus the Messiah was like this*
[**] **19** 1973, 1978, 1984 NIV copy that HJC was written from is ***was a righteous man***
[e] **19** Or *was a righteous man and*
[f] **21** *Jesus* is the Greek form of *Joshua* which means *the LORD saves.*
[g] **23** Isaiah 7:14

The Birth of the Created

¹⁰This is how the birth of the created came about. Society pledged creation through the establishment of Marriage, but before this came about, woman was found to be committed to another purpose. ¹¹Because David was a righteous man and did not want to expose public disgrace he had in mind to depart quietly.

¹²But after he had accomplished this, Sharon's image, as all other, called him back where he found conceived, Marriage as purposeful redemption if in the Holy Spirit. ¹³It will give birth to a One as Jesus, because the union will save people from their sins.

¹⁴All this took place as fulfillment of the Law and the Prophets, as foretold by Emmanuel and will be God again with us.

²⁴When Joseph woke up, he did what the angel of the Lord had commanded him and took Mary home as his wife. ²⁵But he **did not consummate their marriage***** until she gave birth to a son. And he gave him the name Jesus.

²⁵When David woke out, he began what he could do and took up animation to till out a wife. ²⁶He had no union with her until separated, and animated Marriage, which he called " Emmanuel ", meaning "God with us " .

*** **25** 1973, 1978, 1984 NIV copy that HJC was written from is **had no union with her**

HESUS JOY CHRIST
Matthew's Two
~~~
# CONCORDANCE
~~~

The Gospel of Matthew
Chapter Two
New International Version

The Gospel of Matthew - Chapter Two
New International Version

The Magi Visit the Messiah*

¹After Jesus was born in Bethlehem in Judea, during the time of King Herod, Magi[a] from the east came to Jerusalem ²and asked, "Where is the one who has been born king of the Jews? We saw his star **when it rose**** and have come to worship him."

³When King Herod heard this he was disturbed, and all Jerusalem with him. ⁴When he had called together all the people's chief priests and teachers of the law, he asked them where the Messiah was to be born. ⁵"In Bethlehem in Judea," they replied, "for this is what the prophet has written:

> ⁶"'But you, Bethlehem, in
>   the land of Judah,
> are by no means least
>   among the rulers
>   of Judah;
> for out of you will come a
>   ruler
> who will shepherd my people
>   Israel.'[b]"

---

* **1** 1973, 1978, 1984 NIV copy that HJC was written from is **The Visit of the Magi**

[a] **1** Traditionally *wise men*

** **2** 1973, 1978, 1984 NIV copy that HJC was written from is **in the east**, also in verse 9.

[b] **6** Micah 5:2,4

Matthew's Two
written by R. David Foster, Thursday, June 18, 2009

The Visit of the Daughters

¹After the One was conceived in the body of Christ, under the household, majestic daughters of communion came to the church ²and asked: "Where is the One who has been born above all? We have felt his joy in communion and have come to adore him."

³When the head of the household heard this, all the church was disturbed. ⁴When all were consulted the head asked where the Christ was to be born. ⁵"In the macropolis of David" they replied, " for this is what the prophet has written:

> ⁶" 'The Lord said to my Lord:
> 'Sit at my right hand
> until I make your enemies
> a footstool for your feet'[a]

---

[a] **6** Matthew 22:44;
    Luke 20:42-43;
    Psalm 110:1

⁷Then Herod called the Magi secretly and found out from them the exact time the star had appeared. ⁸He sent them to Bethlehem and said, "Go and search carefully for the child. As soon as you find him, report to me, so that I too may go and worship him."

⁹After they had heard the king, they went on their way, and the star they had seen **when it rose***** went ahead of them until it stopped over the place where the child was. ¹⁰When they saw the star, they were overjoyed. ¹¹On coming to the house, they saw the child with his mother Mary, and they bowed down and worshiped him. Then they opened their treasures and presented him with gifts of gold, frankincense and myrrh. ¹²And having been warned in a dream not to go back to Herod, they returned to their country by another route.

⁷Then the head of the household called the daughters and asked when exactly the joy had appeared, ⁸and sent them out to find the One, and report back so that he may be adored by all.

⁹The three majesties went on their way when they had heard the head of the household, and the joy they knew in communion went ahead of them until it rested over the place of a child. ¹⁰When they felt the joy they saw stars. ¹¹On coming to the house they saw the One of their mothers and they bowed to worship him. One opened his treasures and they received gifts of gold and fragrant flowers and perfumed soap. ¹²And being warmed in a dream they resode by another way.

***   9   1973, 1978, 1984 NIV copy that HJC was written from is ***in the east***, also in verse 2.

The Escape to Egypt

¹³When they had gone, an angel of the Lord appeared to Joseph in a dream. "Get up," he said, "take the child and his mother and escape to Egypt. Stay there until I tell you, for Herod is going to search for the child to kill him."

¹⁴So he got up, took the child and his mother during the night and left for Egypt, ¹⁵where he stayed until the death of Herod. And so was fulfilled what the Lord had said through the prophet: "Out of Egypt I called my son."[c]

¹⁶When Herod realized that he had been outwitted by the Magi, he was furious, and he gave orders to kill all the boys in Bethlehem and its vicinity who were two years old and under, in accordance with the time he had learned from the Magi. ¹⁷Then what was said through the prophet Jeremiah was fulfilled:

The Escape to Civilization

¹³When they had gone, an angel of the Lord appeared before father and said "Get One up, take mother and escape into civilization, for the head of the household is going to search for the infant One to kill him."

¹⁴So they got up, took the One during the night and left for civilization, ¹⁵where they stayed until the next end of the household. But the prophet foretold:

"But the more they called Israel, the further they went from them."[b]

¹⁶When the household realized they had been outwitted by the majestic daughters, they were furious and it was commanded that all knew Ones in the macropolis of David be destroyed. ¹⁷Then what was said through the prophet Jeremiah was fulfilled:

---

[c] 15 Hosea 11:1

[b] 15 Hosea 11:2

¹⁸"A voice is heard in Ramah,
>   weeping and great mourning,
>   Rachel weeping for her children
>   and refusing to be comforted,
>   because they are no more."ᵈ

¹⁶ "Restrain your voice from
        weeping
and your eyes from tears,
for your work will be rewarded. "ᶜ

ᵈ 18 Jeremiah 31:15

ᶜ 16 Jeremiah 31:16

The Return to Nazareth

¹⁹After Herod died, an angel of the Lord appeared in a dream to Joseph in Egypt ²⁰and said, "Get up, take the child and his mother and go to the land of Israel, for those who were trying to take the child's life are dead."

²¹So he got up, took the child and his mother and went to the land of Israel. ²²But when he heard that Archelaus was reigning in Judea in place of his father Herod, he was afraid to go there. Having been warned in a dream, he withdrew to the district of Galilee, ²³and he went and lived in a town called Nazareth. So was fulfilled what was said through the prophets, that he would be called a Nazarene.

The Return to Nativity

¹⁹After the head was reborn, an angel appeared before father in a dream ²⁰and said "Get up and take the One to church, for those who are trying to take the life now know more."

²¹So he got up and with the other took the One to church. ²²But when he heard the Son was reigning in the head space, he was afraid to go there. Having been warmed in a dream he withdrew to another place, ²³and One lived in another place. So was fulfilled what was said through the prophets: "He will be called an otherene."

HESUS JOY CHRIST
Matthew's Three Fold

~~~

CONCORDANCE

~~~

The Gospel of Matthew
Chapter Three
New International Version

The Gospel of Matthew - Chapter Three

New International Version

John the Baptist Prepares the Way

¹In those days John the Baptist came, preaching in the wilderness of Judea ²and saying, "Repent, for the kingdom of heaven **has come*** near." ³This is he who was spoken of through the prophet Isaiah:

> "A voice of one calling in the wilderness,
> 'Prepare the way for the Lord,
> make straight paths for him.'"ᵃ

⁴John's clothes were made of camel's hair, and he had a leather belt around his waist. His food was locusts and wild honey. ⁵People went out to him from Jerusalem and all Judea and the whole region of the Jordan. ⁶Confessing their sins, they were baptized by him in the Jordan River.

---

* 2   1973, 1978, 1984 NIV copy that HJC was written from is *is*

a   3   Isaiah 40:3

Matthew's Three Fold

written by R. David Foster
Wednesday, August 26, 2009

Joan Prepares the Way

¹In those days Joan preached to the converted and got nowhere, ²and said, "Rebirth! Or the kingdom of heaven is ne'er!" ³This is she who was spoken of through the prophet Isaiah:

> ("Speak tenderly to Jerusalem, and proclaim to her that her hard service has been completed, that her sin has been paid for, that she has received from the Lord's hand, double for all her sins." ᵃ)

⁴Joan's clothes were made of polyester and she had a vinyl belt around her waist. Her food was chocolate covered ants and wild honey. ⁵People went in to her from the church, and all the land and the region. ⁶Professing their sins, they were acknowledged by her in her church.

---

a   3 Isaiah 40:2

⁷But when he saw many of the Pharisees and Sadducees coming to where he was baptizing, he said to them: "You brood of vipers! Who warned you to flee from the coming wrath? ⁸Produce fruit in keeping with repentance. ⁹And do not think you can say to yourselves, 'We have Abraham as our father.' I tell you that out of these stones God can raise up children for Abraham. ¹⁰The ax is already at the root of the trees, and every tree that does not produce good fruit will be cut down and thrown into the fire.

¹¹"I baptize you with[b] water for repentance. But after me comes one who is more powerful than I, whose sandals I am not worthy to carry. He will baptize you with[c] the Holy Spirit and fire. ¹²His winnowing fork is in his hand, and he will clear his threshing floor, gathering his wheat into the barn and burning up the chaff with unquenchable fire."

⁷But when she saw many of the ordained coming to where she was acknowledging she said to them: "You brood of vipers! Who warned you to flee from the coming wrath? ⁸Produce fruit in keeping with rebirth. ⁹And do not think you can say to yourselves: 'We are ordained.' I tell you that out of these sinners God can raise up ordination! ¹⁰The ax is already at the root of the trees, and every tree that does not bear good fruit will be cut down and built into the building!"

¹¹"I acknowledge your death with rebirth, but after me will come one whose shoes you will wear. His holy spirit will acknowledge you with spirit; ¹²his spirit will test you, and gather you in, and there will be no one left out."

---

b   **11** Or *in*

c   **11** Or *in*

The Baptism of Jesus

¹³Then Jesus came from Galilee to the Jordan to be baptized by John. ¹⁴But John tried to deter him, saying, "I need to be baptized by you, and do you come to me?"

¹⁵Jesus replied, "Let it be so now; it is proper for us to do this to fulfill all righteousness." Then John consented.

¹⁶As soon as Jesus was baptized, he went up out of the water. At that moment heaven was opened, and he saw the Spirit of God descending like a dove and alighting on him. ¹⁷And a voice from heaven said, "This is my Son, whom I love; with him I am well pleased."

The Baptism of the One

¹³The One came in from another place, into her church to be acknowledged by Joan. ¹⁴But Joan tried to deter One saying, "I need to be acknowledged by you and do you come to me?"

¹⁵One replied: "Let it be so now; it is proper for us to do this to fulfill all righteousness." Then Joan consented.

¹⁶As soon as One was acknowledged, One went up, out of the church. At that moment, heaven was opened, and Joan saw the spirit of God descending like a dove and lighting on One. ¹⁷And a voice was heard: "This is my One, with them I am well pleased."

HESUS JOY CHRIST
Matthew's Foretold
~~~
# CONCORDANCE
~~~

The Gospel of Matthew
Chapter Four
New International Version

The Gospel of Matthew - Chapter Four
New International Version
Jesus Is Tested in the Wilderness[*]

¹Then Jesus was led by the Spirit into the **wilderness**[**] to be tempted[a] by the devil. ²After fasting forty days and forty nights, he was hungry. ³The tempter came to him and said, "If you are the Son of God, tell these stones to become bread."

⁴Jesus answered, "It is written: 'Man shall not live on bread alone, but on every word that comes from the mouth of God.'[b]"

⁵Then the devil took him to the holy city and had him stand on the highest point of the temple. ⁶"If you are the Son of God," he said, "throw yourself down. For it is written:

> "'He will command his angels concerning you,
> and they will lift you up in their hands,
> so that you will not strike your foot against a stone.'[c]"

---

[*] 1 1973, 1978, 1984 NIV copy that HJC was written from is **The Temptation of Jesus**

[**] 1 1973, 1978, 1984 NIV copy that HJC was written from is **desert**

[a] 1 The Greek for tempted can also mean tested.

[b] 4 Deuteronomy 8:3

[c] 6 Psalm 91:11,12

Matthew's Foretold
written by R. David Foster
Saturday, December 26, 2009 —
- Sunday, January 10, 2010

/The Temptation of the One/

/ ¹Then One was led by the Spirit into abundance to be tempted by the devil. / ²After feasting forty years and forty nights One was full. / ³The tempter came through him and said / " If you are the One of God, take this coin to become beer ! "

/ ⁴One humbled him, "Why do we need beer ? "

/ ⁵Then the devil took One downtown and placed them on the Order of Can-of-Duh list. / ⁶ " If I am the One of God, " he said, "why do we need this honour ? / For:

" ' You will tread on the lion and the cobra; you will trample the great lion and the serpent.'[a] "

---

[a] 6 Psalm 91:13

⁷Jesus answered him, "It is also written: 'Do not put the Lord your God to the test.'ᵈ"

⁸Again, the devil took him to a very high mountain and showed him all the kingdoms of the world and their splendor. ⁹"All this I will give you," he said, "if you will bow down and worship me."

¹⁰Jesus said to him, "Away from me, Satan! For it is written: 'Worship the Lord your God, and serve him only.'ᵉ"

¹¹Then the devil left him, and angels came and attended him.

ᵈ 7 Deuteronomy 6:16
ᵉ 10 Deuteronomy 6:13

---

⁷One answered him, " For ' whoever is not against us is for us'. ᵇ " She continued,

(" 'Fear the Lord you God, serve Him only, and take your oaths in his name.
/ Do not follow other gods, the gods of the people around you; / for the Lord your God, who is among you, is a jealous god, / and **her** anger will burn against you and **she** will destroy you from the face of the land.
/ Do not test the Lord your God as you did at Mass . . . ah ! ' ᶜ ")

⁸Again, the devil took One to a very high mountain / and showed her all the kingdoms of the world and their splendor. / ⁹ "All this I will give you," he said, "if you will bow down and subdue me."

/ ¹⁰She said to him, "Away from me, Satan! Did I not just quote 'serve him only.'ᶜ ? "

/ ¹¹Then the devil left them, and they waited on angels.

ᵇ 7 Mark 9 : 40
ᶜ 7 Deuteronomy 6 : 13-16

Jesus Begins to Preach

¹²When Jesus heard that John had been put in prison, he withdrew to Galilee. ¹³Leaving Nazareth, he went and lived in Capernaum, which was by the lake in the area of Zebulun and Naphtali— ¹⁴to fulfill what was said through the prophet Isaiah:

¹⁵"Land of Zebulun and
   land of Naphtali,
the Way of the Sea,
beyond the Jordan,
Galilee of the Gentiles—
¹⁶the people living in darkness
have seen a great light;
on those living in the land
of the shadow of death
a light has dawned."ᶠ

¹⁷From that time on Jesus began to preach, "Repent, for the kingdom of heaven **has come***** near."

/ One Gets Preachy /

/ ¹²When One heard that Joan was ministering elsewhere, he became secular. / ¹³Leaving the hill, he went and lived in a rooming house, down toward the lake, . ./ . . in the area of the mall, ¹⁴to fulfill what was said through the prophet Isaiah: /

/ ¹⁵ "Nevertheless, there will be no more gloom for those who were in distress. /
/ ¹⁶In the past she humbled the land of Zebulun and the land of Naphtali,
but in the future he will honour . . ." ᵈ/

/ ¹⁷From that time on One got preachy: "Rebirth, or the kingdom of heaven is ne'er. " /

ᶠ   16 Isaiah 9:1,2

***   17 1973, 1978, 1984 NIV copy that HJC was written from is **is**

ᵈ ¹⁵ Isaiah 9 : 1

Jesus Calls His First Disciples[****]

¹⁸As Jesus was walking beside the Sea of Galilee, he saw two brothers, Simon called Peter and his brother Andrew. They were casting a net into the lake, for they were fishermen. ¹⁹"Come, follow me," Jesus said, "and I will **send you out to fish for people**[*****]." ²⁰At once they left their nets and followed him.

²¹Going on from there, he saw two other brothers, James son of Zebedee and his brother John. They were in a boat with their father Zebedee, preparing their nets. Jesus called them, ²²and immediately they left the boat and their father and followed him.

/ The Calling of Discipline /

/ ¹⁸As One was seeking employment, . . / . . two siblings saw One, Simone called Stress Rocks and her brother in arms, Andrew. / They were playing a line for they were grifters. / ¹⁹"Can we lead you," they said, "we can get you lots of friends." / ²⁰At once they left their line and led with them. /

/ ²¹Going on from there, two others saw them, Mandy of Paul and her brother John. / They were in the same boat as their father, repairing their bets. / They called One, ²²and immediately they left the boat of their father and kept track of One. /

[****]   **18**   1973, 1978, 1984 NIV copy that HJC was written from is ***The Calling of the First Disciples***

[*****]   **19**   1973, 1978, 1984 NIV copy that HJC was written from is ***make you fishers of men***

Jesus Heals the Sick

²³Jesus went throughout Galilee, teaching in their synagogues, **proclaiming******** the good news of the kingdom, and healing every disease and sickness among the people. ²⁴News about him spread all over Syria, and people brought to him all who were ill with various diseases, those suffering severe pain, the demon-possessed, those having seizures, and the paralyzed; and he healed them. ²⁵Large crowds from Galilee, the Decapolis,ᵍ Jerusalem, Judea and the region across the Jordan followed him.

/ One Feels the Sick /

/ ²³One went thoroughly secular, learning in their malls, . . / . . preachy about the good news of the kingdom, . . / . . and bearing every disease and sickness among the people . / ²⁴News about One was unheard of throughout the community and they encountered all who were / . ill with various diseases, those suffering severe pain, / . the demon-possessed, / . . those having seizures, / . . and the paralyzed, / . . and they healed One . ²⁵Large crowds of secularism, / . municipalities, / . churches, / . hospitals, / . and the far side led with them .

****** **23** 1973, 1978, 1984 NIV copy that HJC was written from is **preaching**

ᵍ **25** That is, *the Ten Cities*

Discussions

OF THE
ANIMATION,

WRITTEN AFTER
ALL
THE ANIMATION
WAS COMPLETED

HESUS JOY CHRIST
Matthew's One Too !
DISCUSSION -

From Tuesday, July 5th, 2011,
to Tuesday, November 8th, 2011
as posted to the blog
of R. David Foster
entitled **Vid'93 bein' To Wordie** . . . . . .
@ www.vid93.blogspot.ca

© R. David Foster 2009, 2011, 2013

OVERVIEW
from the opening of the discussion of
HESUS JOY CHRIST / Matthew's Three Fold

Well here we go ! Try to keep up because there are many angles to this text and it's discussion will cover all the angles I can find in both texts and the relationship between the two texts, which carries a fourth level of meaning. That is — the meaning of each text individually (2 meanings), the meaning when both texts are viewed together (3rd meaning) and the meaning of the relationship (3rd meaning) in the context in which we share — real life (the 4th meaning) !

Stepping back a bit, let's acknowledge a few things. We are talking about religion — specifically christianity, which I believe is essentially forgiveness to the ultimate degree. All religions have their strengths, in fact all are valid and relevant. Forgiveness is either a spoken or unspoken element in many religions. I believe forgiveness is essential, and that is why I am christian.

Many religions have elements of Whole and Part. Ying-Yang for example. Other terms are Agency and Communion, Reductionistic and Holistic, one and many, or Male and Female. All that exists has both a wholistic aspect and a partial aspect. Everything that exists is part of a context, and wholly made of parts. To bring something into existence one must address both the whole and the part, both the context and the specific, aspects.

Furthermore, everything that exists has an inclination to either whole or part. The approach to anything assesses the balance of whole and part in that thing. An imbalance is always apparent, and the inclination of any approach is to correct the thing to obtain balance. If it appears too partial it must be corrected. If it appears too wholistic it must be corrected. The fallacy is that anything that exists is not in balance. In other words, if you may approach it then it does exist and if it exists it must already be in balance. Forgiveness allows the balance to exist without correction, and accepts that all things are in balance. This is somewhat a Buddhist opinion or faith. The important thing is to SEE the balance and not be moved to correction by any **APPARENT** imbalance. Otherwise the urge to correct leads to confrontation and a need to make things unbalanced and favoring whole or part over the other. A key thing about christianity is that it will forgive any apparent imbalance to the extreme of self destruction, but the self destruction is only apparent and not real ! This last idea is explored in the animation entitled **HESUS JOY CHRIST / Matthew's Two Four** which is a chapter about ends.

If whole and part are termed female and male, then this forgiveness that exists between the sexes will allow marriage, which is capable of creation, if not joy and contentment.

The whole of **HESUS JOY CHRIST** points to marriage as the further salvation of humankind, which is based on the essential character of Jesus that is essential for any successful marriage of any whole and part or female and male .

All people are called to different vocations, whether single celibacy, marriage, or other . Marriage is essential to society as a union of whole and part that creates new meaning and life . Marriage is a resource that produces new understanding and creates far more than just babies . This in no way diminishes christianity, because without ultimate forgiveness and sacrifice no marriage will survive . It will end when a partial or whole attitude fails to forgive a whole or partial attitude . Once one has taken up the challenge of Christ and begun to follow him, some sort of witness of the union of whole and part is where one must head, fully armed with forgiveness .

Moving on, evil is real, and forgiveness is how to deal with it . This third chapter of the Gospel of Matthew is about Jesus' baptism by his cousin, John the Baptist . John the Baptist was not preaching forgiveness, nor rebirth through death from forgiveness, but repentance which is turning from doing evil and trying again . Obedience to the Law, as turning from evil, will make balance apparent and allow the balance to be acknowledged and seen . But no one has ever been able to obey the fullest intent of the Law without the benefit of infinite grace . In other words, no one has ever been able to keep the Law when circumstances were against them . Jesus was able to obey the Law but it lead to his very public death . Many others have died obeying the Law in much less honoured deaths . Death — what is it really ? Death will be discussed elsewhere — perhaps in a further discussion of **Matthew's Two Four** .

Finally, one may choose to keep the issue of the existence of God out of this discussion . For my part, God is an infinite goal, infinitely present as an infinite goal, colouring our perception of existence . Whether God is a person, male or female, is beyond this immediate discussion, but worth discussing in some other writing . Suffice it to say, for now, that whatever has been created exists within infinity and it is all, entirely, good .

Ash Wednesday, March 9th, 2011

OVERVIEW

This is written after the discussion of **Matthew's Two Four** and the discussion of **Matthew's Three Fold** were written, and before the discussion of **Matthew's Two** and **Matthew's Foretold**. In a way, **Matthew's One Too !** is where the **HESUS JOY CHRIST** story begins, but really it began with **Matthew's Two Four**, which is the signs of the end of the age, which I take as the beginning end of this age.

The book of Matthew, Chapter One, from the Bible, is the story of the birth of the Christ, Jesus, and includes the genealogy of Jesus, on his earthly father Joseph's side. This has become, in this animation, the birth of the One, in my life, and into my actual first hand personal awareness. The One is the marriage relationship, or balance of male and female or part and whole. This discussion will be about the coming of the Christ into the world in both history for all the world, and into my awareness and life through the marriage relationship of whole and part, and also through my understanding of christianity. This understanding points in the direction of marriage as the further salvation of humankind.

I find it curious, that if Jesus Christ is the product of a virgin birth, than what does his earthly father, Joseph's, genealogy have to do with Jesus ? If Mary, his mother, was his only blood relative, wouldn't it be good to know her genealogy ? Nevertheless, I have written the "matrigeneosophy of the created". Matri- for matriarchal, -geneo- for genealogy or origins, and -sophy for love: the matriarchal origination of love of the created. The created is the understanding and faith of marriage, which must be nurtured and cultivated, but otherwise may be considered to exist regardless, so it could be seen as being begotten not made. I am not married to referring to the One as created. Jesus was created as a man, but the Word, or Christ, is begotten not made, being one with the Father and the Holy Spirit in the Trinity.

Friday, June 24th, 2011

As a bit of background to where these ideas of the One and marriage came from, my personal experience is presented in the form of the matrigeneosophy of the created, or the geneology of my personal experience of relationships with women. It can be traced back to my mother, through my childhood, to marriage and beyond, as my marriage failed in 2008. It is by no means an exhaustive and thorough experience, although it has exhausted me, as I write this, now, in my 45th year; but an ordered and known experience under careful and prayerful consideration, as I try to make sense out of my life. Some may think that trying to make sense out of life is fruitless and pointless, but my experience has been otherwise, and just when I think there is not any chance of things making sense, my awareness dies, and is reborn to a new and wider awareness.

Counting Generations

Since there is a long list of patriarchs and a long list of matriarchs, in this discussion, and they are counted up to fourteens, nine, twelve, four and three, let's look at how they add up.

The Genealogy of Jesus

1	Abraham	15	Solomon	29	Jeconiah **Babylon**
2	Isaac	16	Rehoboam	30	Shealtiel
3	Jacob	17	Abijah	31	Zerubbabel
4	Judah	18	Asa	32	Abihud
5	Perez	19	Jehoshaphat	33	Eliakim
6	Hezron	20	Jehoram	34	Azor
7	Ram	21	Uzziah	35	Zadok
8	Amminadab	22	Jotham	36	Akim
9	Nahshon	23	Ahaz	37	Elihud
10	Salmon	24	Hezekiah	38	Eleazar
11	Boaz	25	Manasseh	39	Matthan
12	Obed	26	Amon	40	Jacob
13	Jesse	27	Josiah	41	Joseph
14	David **King David**	28	Jeconiah **Babylon**	42	Jesus

So there is a bit of creativity in this count of 14 generations to King David and 14 generations from King David to Babylon, and 14 generations from Babylon to Jesus — Jeconiah has to be counted twice ! This may be due to counting the transitions, or generations, to the exile to Babylon, rather than actual persons.

Another interesting thing I came across is that if you take a generation to be nominally 50 years than 42 generations works out to be about 2100 years. So it is over two thousand years from Abraham to Jesus and it has been over 2000 years from Jesus until now !! Furthermore, in the book of Genesis there is enough information to create a genealogy of Abraham right back to Adam, and this genealogy is also about 2000 years !!

The Genealogy of Abram - Abraham

The Genealogy of Abram - Abraham

Patriarch / Son	Patriarch age at birth of heir	Years from birth of heir to patriarch's death	Patriarch's age at death
Adam	130	800	930
Seth	105	807	912
Enosh	90	815	905
Kenan	70	840	910
Mahalalel	65	830	895
Jared	162	800	962
Enoch	65	300	365
Methuselah	187	782	969
Lamech	182	595	777
Noah	500	450	950
Shem	100	500	600
Arpachshad	35	403	438
Shelah	30	403	433
Eber	34	430	464
Peleg	30	430	460
Reu	32	207	239
Serug	30	430	460
Nahor	29	119	148
Terah	70	135	205
Abram - Abraham	100	75	175
Isaac			

numbers in italics are calculated

Length of genealogy in years *1946*

References: Genesis 5 : 3 – 32; 10 : 1; 11 : 10 – 27.

So - 2000 years from creation to Abraham; 2000 years from Abraham to Jesus; and 2000 years from Jesus until now! The time is ripe for the birth of a new awareness!

Sunday, July 3rd, 2011

Opening Notes

This animation project was completed on July 24th, 2009 and screened on July 30th, 2009 at the **Revue Cinema** on Roncesvalles Road in Toronto, Ontario, Canada. Their open screening is called **Drop Your Shorts** and has been held about every three months since 2008.

      DVD copies of the entire **HESUS JOY CHRIST** series to date, along with the 35mm animated film entitled **HYPOTHERMIA / My Kayak Prayer** are available from the author. Individual episodes come complete with the discussion as an insert in the DVD case.

The author can be contacted at *vid932008@gmail.com*, and these discussions are posted verse by verse, week to week, as they are written, on the blog entitled **Vid'93 bein' To Wordie. . . . ...** at www.vid93.blogspot.ca .

The Gospel of Matthew

- Chapter One

The Genealogy of Jesus the Messiah

¹This is the genealogy*ᵃ* of Jesus the Messiah*ᵇ* the son of David, the son of Abraham:
²Abraham was the father of Isaac,
Isaac the father of Jacob,
Jacob the father of Judah and his brothers,
³Judah the father of Perez and Zerah, whose mother was Tamar,
Perez the father of Hezron,
Hezron the father of Ram,
⁴Ram the father of Amminadab,
Amminadab the father of Nahshon,
Nahshon the father of Salmon,
⁵Salmon the father of Boaz, whose mother was Rahab,
Boaz the father of Obed, whose mother was Ruth,
Obed the father of Jesse,
⁶and Jesse the father of King David.

David was the father of Solomon, whose mother had been Uriah's wife,
⁷Solomon the father of Rehoboam,
Rehoboam the father of Abijah,
Abijah the father of Asa,
⁸Asa the father of Jehoshaphat,
Jehoshaphat the father of Jehoram,
Jehoram the father of Uzziah,
⁹Uzziah the father of Jotham,
Jotham the father of Ahaz,
Ahaz the father of Hezekiah,
¹⁰Hezekiah the father of Manasseh,
Manasseh the father of Amon,
Amon the father of Josiah,
¹¹and Josiah the father of Jeconiah*ᶜ* and his brothers at the time of the exile to Babylon.

ᵃ   1   Or *is an account of the origin*

ᵇ   1   Or *Jesus Christ.* Messiah (Hebrew) and Christ (Greek) both mean Anointed One; also in verse 18.

ᶜ   11   That is *Jehoiachin*; also in verse 12

¹²After the exile to Babylon:
Jeconiah was the father of Shealtiel,
Shealtiel the father of Zerubbabel,
¹³Zerubbabel the father of Abihud,
Abihud the father of Eliakim,
Eliakim the father of Azor,
¹⁴Azor the father of Zadok,
Zadok the father of Akim,
Akim the father of Elihud,
¹⁵Elihud the father of Eleazar,
Eleazar the father of Matthan,
Matthan the father of Jacob,
¹⁶and Jacob the father of Joseph, the husband of Mary, and Mary was the mother of Jesus who is called the Messiah.

¹⁷Thus there were fourteen generations in all from Abraham to David, fourteen from David to the exile to Babylon, and fourteen from the exile to the Messiah.

Joseph Accepts Jesus as His Son[*]

¹⁸This is how the birth of Jesus the Messiah came about[d]: His mother Mary was pledged to be married to Joseph, but before they came together, she was found to be pregnant through the Holy Spirit. ¹⁹Because Joseph her husband was **faithful to the law**[**], and yet[e] did not want to expose her to public disgrace, he had in mind to divorce her quietly.

²⁰But after he had considered this, an angel of the Lord appeared to him in a dream and said, "Joseph son of David, do not be afraid to take Mary home as your wife, because what is conceived in her is from the Holy Spirit. ²¹She will give birth to a son, and you are to give him the name Jesus,[f] because he will save his people from their sins."

---

[*]   **18** 1973, 1978, 1984 NIV copy that HJC was written from is **The Birth of Jesus Christ**

[d]   **18** Or *The origin of Jesus the Messiah was like this*

[**]   **19** 1973, 1978, 1984 NIV copy that HJC was written from is **was a righteous man**

[e]   **19** Or *was a righteous man and*

[f]   **21** *Jesus* is the Greek form of *Joshua* which means *the LORD saves.*

²²All this took place to fulfill what the Lord had said through the prophet: ²³"The virgin will conceive and give birth to a son, and they will call him Immanuel"⁹ (which means "God with us").

²⁴When Joseph woke up, he did what the angel of the Lord had commanded him and took Mary home as his wife. ²⁵But he **did not consummate their marriage***** until she gave birth to a son. And he gave him the name Jesus.

---

⁹ 23 Isaiah 7:14

*** 25 1973, 1978, 1984 NIV copy that HJC was written from is **had no union with her**

This **LEFT** Column is always the Original Gospel Text of the First Chapter of the Gospel of Matthew, *New International Version* .

This **RIGHT** Column is always the text of the animation -
HESUS JOY CHRIST / Matthew's One Too ! , written by R. David Foster .

Verses 1 & 2

The Genealogy of Jesus the Messiah

¹This is the genealogy[a] of Jesus the Messiah[b] the son of David, the son of Abraham:

²Abraham was the father of Isaac,
Isaac the father of Jacob,
Jacob the father of Judah and his brothers,

[a] 1 Or *is an account of the origin*

[b] 1 Or *Jesus Christ*. Messiah (Hebrew) and Christ (Greek) both mean Anointed One; also in verse 18.

Verse 1
The Matrigeneosophy of the Created

¹A record of the matrigeneosophy of the created, made through David, who I am .

Verse 1 Discussion NIV Bible text verses 1 & 2

Why was this record of the genealogy of Jesus kept throughout the ages ? Well, for family reasons, this genealogy was memorized as a personal identification, since written records were uncommon . Then when Jesus became prominent, it became important to record his genealogy, regardless of whether Joseph was his birth father .

The other reason I can think of, is that it establishes that Jesus is the Messiah promised to King David, and Abraham . A genealogy supports this belief that Jesus is the Messiah, in spite of the belief that Joseph was not his birth father . It seems to me that there should be a genealogy of Mary, which I thought there was, in the Bible, but I have not found it . Nevertheless, this genealogy is an attempt to establish Jesus' authority, and similarly, I have written the matrigeneosophy of the created, to establish the authority of this idea of a sacred One — a relationship and balance between whole and part, female and male . These genealogies provide a context from which both Jesus' ministry and this animation have originated .

I made up the word "matrigeneosophy", with an "o" instead of an "a" just for the fun of it. Matri — for matriarchal; geneo — for origins; and sophy — for love; make the matrigeneosophy of the created mean the matriarchal origins of love of the created.

This idea of the importance of the balance and marriage of male and female, part and whole, is not just my idea, entirely out of my own head, but rather found as much in my experience of women and their ideas, as in my own ideas. There are some parts of this idea or faith that have come from my understanding and experience of women, from my mother through my friends and my wife, which when combined with my own ideas, became a new found idea. Then the idea took prominence as my life went on, being confirmed by experience after experience, as well as education and reading.

But first, let's confirm that the infinite purpose of humankind, or God, lives in each one of us, yet no individual is worthy of worship beyond any other individual. There are many references in the Bible to God living in us, from Jesus calling us children of God, in the Book of Matthew, Chapter Five, verse nine, where he says:

"Blessed are the peacemakers, for they will be called children of God."

Furthermore, in Matthew Chapter twelve, verse fifty, Jesus says:

"For whoever does the will of my Father in heaven is my brother and sister and mother."

And again, in First Corinthians, Chapter six, verse fifteen:

"Do you not know that your bodies are members of Christ, himself? . . . ."

So not only do I find Christ and the balance of whole and part alive in my mind, but I find it in others that I meet, including women. The church is the body of Christ, and my experience of people has led to my finding marriage and the balance of whole and part of utmost importance.

So this idea was not made by me, David Foster, but made through me, as I have only tried to clarify and draw attention to an idea that I have found. I found it in my christian upbringing, the people around me, and the women I am honoured to call friends. I find this idea is overlooked and misunderstood in our society, and I am trying to illuminate this idea wherever one may find it.

In a sense the idea of the One, the balance of whole and part, and the marriage of female and male, is both created and begotten, as Jesus the man was created in Mary's womb, and begotten as Christ in the world. This is not such a radical idea. A hammer is both created and begotten, as the idea may be begotten, but a hammer may be purchased or made, yet the wood and the steel, or iron, is still begotten.

Finally, I am David, and my infinite purpose is "I am" and is sacred. I will not go around saying "I am this" or "I am that" as that is stupid, obnoxious and vulgar, yet the truth remains that I am. We all are, and each of us can say that "I am", so again, such a statement is redundant yet eternal. Abraham was a patriarch, where Abram wasn't, since God changed Abram's name to Abraham when he made His covenant with him and promised him his son, Isaac. Abraham's God was a distant "I am", who Jesus taught us to call "Father" and strive for a loving, intimate relationship with the God who loves each of us dearly.

Sunday, July 3rd, 2011

Verses 3 & 4

³Judah the father of Perez and Zerah, whose mother was Tamar,
Perez the father of Hezron,
Hezron the father of Ram,
⁴Ram the father of Amminadab,
Amminadab the father of Nahshon,
Nahshon the father of Salmon,

Verse 2

2 Dennis gave birth to Emily, who came out of the plain. In Emily David was born to Linda. Linda became Tina who was not chosen.

Verse 2 Discussion   NIV Bible text verses 3 & 4

If Perez's mother was Tamar, my mother is Emily, and she came out of the plane, plain or ordinary?

It is often asked why Jesus could not have just spoken plainly. I believe this is because many people like to shift the context of a phrase or word, and change or twist the meaning. Sure, this is what I am doing, but see if my understanding fits with your experience and your witness from the holy spirit. If it fits, then consider it. If not, then discard what I write. Jesus spoke in parables and figurative language because it can only have one meaning that makes sense, and all other meanings are problematic if not downright absurd. When you find a meaning that works, then you know you are on the correct track.

The flip side of this is that a word or phrase could be correct in every meaning, such as my mother coming out of the plane, or plain. My mother grew up in the prairies, or plain, Saskatchewan, and migrated to Ontario by airplane. She must have seemed better than ordinary or plane, to my father, Dennis, or he wouldn't have chose her over other prospects.

Another example is my father giving birth to my mother, Emily. In the most obvious sense this is absurd as a man cannot give birth to a baby, let alone his wife. But if you think about this, a woman cannot give birth unless a man is willing to procreate. A woman cannot become pregnant all by herself, unless you consider Jesus' mother Mary, but most people cannot give birth by themselves. My father cannot give birth, but he can allow my mother to become pregnant, by co-operating with her, so that she can give birth to me. So my father gave my mother the birth of myself, by choosing her to procreate with. Get it? I don't know how I could explain it any further.

My memory of Linda goes back as far as I remember. When my parents bought a house, Linda lived next door. My parents introduced me to her when she came over to talk to them. Other than my mother, as I never had a sister, Linda was the only female in my age group, before starting to attend daycare, that I related to regularly, and was the first female I perceived as an equal.

Then when I began school, kindegarten, I met Tina. I treated Tina the same way I had learned to treat Linda, as an equal. This allowed us to get along well, but spending time playing together, mostly in a mixed group, drew the mocking attention of others that I had avoided in daycare. The mocking didn't bother me, as I had already learned it was meaningless, as another friend I had befriended partly in retaliation to his being a target of derision; but it did force me to assess my position, and I was not sure if I wanted to be associated with another person, so I wrongly concluded that getting along with Tina was not in my best interest, in a "too many eggs in one basket" or a sort of favouritism kind of mistake. It was only grade one and we were only six years old! This is what I mean when I write "who was not chosen", even though getting along with Tina made an impression on me.

I became aware of all this as I looked back on my life, which I began to do when I was eighteen, and then I could remember all this, and my reflection since then has kept the memories fresh. My mother was present to me, in my thoughts, for many years, if not still to this day, but in the past three decades, others have taken prominence over her. Both Linda and Tina were people in my life, and female people in my life, and my reaction to each of them set precedence for later decisions I would make, especially when I began to date in grade thirteen. I am still in contact with Linda and Tina, although very infrequently. The point is that this presence of a female, colouring my mind, can be traced all the way back to my mother, and I have never known any period of time without the presence of a single, if not serial, female presence in my mind. Accepting that this presence cannot be dismissed, is a large part of the whole importance of marriage. Rather than fight it, one should accept it and guide it to an appropriate end.

Finally, in the animation, did you see the placenta smack?! My father seems all too quick to part me from my mother, and suffers the backlash! This would continue to be the case, time after time, in one form or another. For example, my father use to say that my brother and I would be allowed to move out when we reached the age of eighteen. My mother would respond with a statement that we would not be kicked out at eighteen, to which my father would respond by reiterating that we were allowed to move out when we were eighteen. The fact is that it was very hard to break free of my mother, who would manipulate the situation to force me back, although that could be argued. In such a case the only thing to do, it seemed to me, was to allow it to happen and when all hell broke loose with my father, let the chips fall where they may, and this did work, allowing me to break free of my mother, albeit to free fall into the lap of any old female influence, such as Linda, another Linda, who is not in the matrigeneosophy.

Monday, July 11th, 2011

Verses 5 & 6

⁵Salmon the father of Boaz, whose mother was Rahab,

Boaz the father of Obed, whose mother was Ruth,
Obed the father of Jesse,
⁶and Jesse the father of King David.
David was the father of Solomon, whose mother had been Uriah's wife,

Verse 3

³Tina became Patricia, by choice, who did not accept. Patricia became Mia, who was apparently indifferent. Mia became Marcelle through Linda, in the style of a matriarch, who endured through Jacqueline, Marysse and Dorcas, and through Texas.

Verse 3 Discussion   NIV Bible text verses 5 & 6

Rahab and Ruth are prominent women of the Bible, as Ruth has her story told in the book of the Bible, Old Testament, called Ruth. The story of Rahab is in the book of the Bible, Old Testament, called Joshua, in chapter two. Rahab hid her city's enemy's Hebrew spies who had come into Jericho to assess it's military strength, before Joshua's army of the Hebrew's attacked. For this her family, gathered in her house that was identified by a red cord hung out of the window, were spared when Joshua's army massacred the city. Rahab was the mother of Boaz, more or less . . . . .

Ruth was a foreigner to the Hebrews, who when her Hebrew husband died, she accompanied her mother-in-law, Naomi, back to Israel and was taken as a wife by Boaz. It is a strong recommendation to not exclude anyone from "God's people", as Boaz was the great grandfather of king David.

David, the boy shepherd/giant killer, and psalmist, was a great man with great faults. As king of Israel he sent Uriah into certain death because he wanted Uriah's wife. This is the lineage of Jesus, or at least of Joseph, Mary's husband.

These are the kind of people that are memorialized in the genealogy of Jesus. They are questionable as saints, but have characteristics that God takes advantage of to accomplish what will be. God can accomplish anything with whatever is at hand, which is almost entirely sinners. The Lord provides.

2013-07-07
Being able to get along well with Tina, made me aware of the emotional benefits of an association, even though I had removed myself from associating with her in the face of the childish mocking of the other children. Two years later, in grade four*, at the age of eight, I decided I would investigate this whole boyfriend-girlfriend thing, but under my control and on my own terms. I, yes I alone, decided I would pursue Patricia as my girlfriend. Patricia avoided me, perhaps because I had not consulted her in my decision making that would result in mockery. It did not seem to matter that I wanted an emotional partner, rather than a co-conspirator, and I was not seeking a "friend with benefits". I was rejected and abandoned the pursuit. I had chosen Patricia and she did not accept.

2013-07-12
I drifted into an affinity for Mia, who seemed and appeared entirely indifferent, and so much so, that looking back, I am astounded at how I could have had an affinity that is so unrelated to the feelings of the person at the focus of that affinity. This affection seemed to drift aimlessly, with a life of its own, and alight or gravitate on any somewhat suitable person, regardless of who that person is or how that person acts. Mia did absolutely nothing to warrant my affection, and she did not have any outstanding qualities that I was aware of, that would warrant my affection. From this I learned that I have a need to feel affection, regardless of anyone warranting that affection.

But Linda, the next door neighbor, had a friend who would come over to play with our neighborhood gang, named Marcelle, and Marcelle had the same hairstyle that my mother had at the time. I was able to bask in Marcelle's glow, but eventually Linda broke off her friendship with Marcelle, and Marcelle no longer came over to play.

There is something to be said for who you know, beyond what one may know. I had an affection for a friend of a friend with the same hairstyle as my mother, and my mother was the matriarch in my life at the time. I had just experienced an affection for the sole sake of an affection, and then I placed that affection on a person that resembled my matriarch. A very influential person to know and stay close to is oneself. There is definitely a knowable pattern and predictable nature to this apparently irrational emotional activity. Consider popular beauty. There are the sporty, the ethnic, the glamour, the princesses, the tom-girls, and the fashionistas. There are the jocks, the preppies, the nerds, the academics, the hicks, the kickers, the rednecks, the roughnecks, the greasers, the grunts, and on and on. Once one has chosen a type, one will search high and low to obtain a member of that type. But is this necessary if affection is there regardless of the object of that affection? Could one not direct their affection toward a rational choice? Indeed, this is what one does when one pursues a person because they are a type. So it would seem possible to harness this affection and direct it toward an appropriate person, especially when it is challenging to do so, as when your spouse fails to achieve or maintain a status. This is why people may choose to tough out a rough time in their relationships, as well as how they sustain their relationships in the face of challenges to that relationship. It is most certainly an overwhelming affection that cannot be denied, but as certainly, it may be directed by a deliberate choice, for better or worse, and this is apparent as this matrigeneosophy plays out.

Not to be outdone, I distinctly noticed that Marcelle was in the church choir and youth group, so I joined the church choir and youth group. The group was great, with parties such as the one "immortalized" in a ballad of my brother's entitled **In That Car**, which I am animating, and the choir wasn't a problem as we had a music teacher that made us sing in the school choir or else. There is always an available presence of another to colour one's mind.

This became apparent to me, not only by the affection I felt for Marcelle and her hairstyle that matched my mother's, but throughout a year away in Texas, where I still thought of Marcelle, and deliberately maintained her in my memory, in spite of thinking about more local friends such as Jacqueline, at summer camp, Dorcas in my biology and drafting classes, and Marysse who asked me if I had been canoeing in the past summer. I asked Marysse how she could tell I had been canoeing and she replied "because your biceps are so big". That got my attention, but I deliberately maintained my attention on Marcelle, to the point of tipping the scales in favour of returning to Ontario from Texas. I was going to control this boyfriend girlfriend thing!

For me, in my mind and heart, under the matriarchy of my mother stood the matriarch Marcelle, in her own right, a matriarch over all comers, Jacqueline, Marysse and Dorcas. This persisted beyond her change in hairstyle.

Looking back now, this trying to control the situation, made me very attentive to my social environment, and taught me to observe, observe, observe. I would isolate to control my experience, and did not attempt to date until I was seventeen, if I could not be in control of the situation, and I never could see how I could be in control of the dating situation, so I never dated until the last months of high school. I was a free loner and a maverick. I knew my head and my affections very well. I would not risk a loss of control, especially self control, and I would not risk an irresponsible act, as I was not going to fail. Everyone was going to move away at graduation anyways so the whole dating thing seemed like stupid child's play anyways. Why would I want to get involved in that? I wanted a real partnership.

This relationship stuff is dicey. If neither partner can be in control, than under what order or organization can any relationship be said to exist? I would say that it is a living entity unto itself. There is an abundance of folklore and literature on the subject of just how dicey relationships are, and I am sure homosexual relationships are just as unwieldy, even if there may be less potential ultimately. If dealing with the infinite aspects of life is tough, try dealing with the moving alive target of a relationship with a real person. There never is any control, and if there is, it is not a relationship. One is left with only one choice: what am I willing to do? One can only control their own decisions, if that, and that is the limit of controlling a relationship. Beyond that, any relationship has a life of it's own. It is a One and it is alive.

* I completed grade three and four in the same year and my birthday is at the end of the school year.

Sunday, July 17ᵗʰ, 2011

Verses 7 & 8

⁷Solomon the father of Rehoboam,
Rehoboam the father of Abijah,
Abijah the father of Asa,
⁸Asa the father of Jehoshaphat,
Jehoshaphat the father of Jehoram,
Jehoram the father of Uzziah,

Verse 4

⁴Dana was first to initiate, under Sharon, and endured Etobicoke Collegiate Institute, Povungnituk, kayaking, and Bina, to become first chosen to accept. Dana became Kim, who became Wendy who endured the first cycle fall.

Second to initiate was Miranda, who was stolen by Jane to the first policing, but no union.

Verse 4 Discussion

NIV Bible text verses 7 & 8

2013-07-07

It is a One and it is alive. Dana was the first person to deliberately express what I understood to be an interest in emotionally partnering with me in some way. I assumed this because, at a grade thirteen dance she told me she had a crush on me in grade nine. In grade nine I was a maverick and failing school. I doubted she liked me in grade nine, so I immediately asked a friend of her's and her friend confirmed that Dana had a crush on me in grade nine. I knew in grade nine I respected Dana, so if she did have a crush on me in grade nine her affection endured all of high school, Etobicoke Collegiate Institute.

Yet I did not see much point in maintaining a relationship. I did, in the affection I had for Dana, begin to apply myself to my studies, but in my maverick behaviour at the grade thirteen high school semi-formal at the Palais Royale, that Dana's friends encouraged me to take Dana to, I expressed a hopeless disdain for appropriate behaviour by racing around the dance floor, and spending little time with Dana, even after the two of us shared a nice meal in a nice restaurant before heading to meet our classmates at the Palais Royale. High school ended for me without Dana.

2013-07-14

I was partly mature but wholly immature. I was insulted that my classmates glossed over the details, the parts, for the whole of the purpose of getting good grades and continuing on to university. I was also insulted that my classmates glossed over the details, the parts, of friendships in favour of maintaining the whole of their standing amongst others. This persisted until I gained a respect for the wholes as well as the parts.

2013-07-07 Within four months of leaving high school, and wanting to isolate myself from society, I was on my way to the arctic of Quebec, to a place two-thirds up the east coast of Hudson's Bay, called Povungnituk. It was an Inuit community of one-thousand people. My high school had one-thousand students. I was to work for the Hudson's Bay Company's Northern Stores — the Bay. I was unable to make sense of being there, as an employee, but I loved walking on the tundra. It was only when I was told not to walk on the tundra that I quit. I frequently thought of all my high school friends that had gone to university, including Dana. Before I left, my boss, the store manager, and the other assistant manager, came out walking on the tundra with me and were both amazed at how wondrous it was to be in such an open space, without landmarks or even trees to tell how big and far away a hill may be, if not small and closer to the viewer.

2013-07-07 After a month, September, I was back in Toronto, back working at a french pastry shop as I had in the summer. Bina, from Iceland, worked there very briefly, quit, and had her friend call me to ask me to go out with her. I tried to talk about the arctic. I never saw her again, and I remembered Dana.

I continued with my pursuit of isolation, to hear my own thoughts and develop my self reliance, as well as cultivate an independent way of life. I paddled my kayak from the Old Mill on the Humber River, past Toronto, to as far as Port Whitby, where I called to be picked up, as frequent beachings of my kayak had worn my hull so much as to make it leak. I then re-fiberglassed the hull by September, and headed out from Buckhorn, on the Trent-Severn Waterway, past Fenelon Falls, to as far as Talbot Lock, the last lock before Lake Simcoe. I was lifted down in my kayak through the Kirkfield Lift Locks, and that was a thrill. I did not like the idea of battling the five o'clock wind from the west all the way up the east shore of Lake Simcoe, and I had been out for three days. I had my fill of solitude, as discussed in the next section, entitled **The Birth of the Created**. I thought of Dana, and Sharon.

So after checking with Jeff, for his o.k., since he at one time expressed an interest in Dana, and after asking her mother for her contact information, I was on my way to Ottawa to choose Dana. I visited her at her rooming house, in the dining room, while her roommates occupied themselves in the kitchen, on a Saturday afternoon, and she invited me to a party that evening at her house. Still not appreciating the collecting and gathering force of social pressure, and wishing to avoid it, I declined the invitation. I felt I had invited myself anyways, by coming all the way from Toronto. So it was not surprising she canceled our meeting for the next day, Sunday. We talked by phone for a week or two, but perhaps I was too overwhelmed to commit over the geographical as well as social distance, her being in school in Ottawa and me not even willing to commit to an electrician's apprenticeship in Toronto. I must have been exasperating. In my defense, I was hoping for some kind of commitment from Dana that would act as a foundation for further commitments such as an electrician's apprenticeship, whether in Toronto or Ottawa. We never got that far in our conversations. I knew it was a long shot, but my intention was to thank Dana by honouring her with the right of first refusal. So I suppose I had doomed the endeavour from the beginning. My mistake. My fault. My loss.

Within three days I was dating Kim, who had strong ideas of her own, and I was just not up to speed with her convictions. I was learning at a late age. By June I was in the aircrew selection process of the Canadian Armed Forces and staying in a hotel near Downsview, with the other candidates. Wendy was on a graduation trip from a small town in Ohio, and jumped at the chance to date a prospective military pilot. Being more of a long distance runner than a body builder, I was only offered a navigator position, and by then Wendy had lost interest, partly because I fell on my motorcycle and chose to take the bus to visit her at her parents in Ohio for a weekend.

When I 'chose' Dana, it was with the conviction that I wanted to be married — a monogamous lifelong relationship. I decided to start with Dana as she was the last one who may have had an interest in me.

But I did not know myself well enough to realize I was overwhelmed by the shear magnitude of my task. Sure, I did not realize how hard it would be to establish a relationship as a foundation for further commitments, and I naively thought it could be accomplished in a weekend. Even though I knew what I wanted, I had not considered all the details enough to have a plan as to how the details would be placed in order to form the whole of a monogamous relationship. And I had very little understanding of the wholes of relationships, let alone the wholes of a woman. But at least I was doing something, and making my own mistakes, so that I could learn as fast as I could, by trying enough to actually make mistakes, forgiving myself, and continuing on in light of my expanding awareness.

This approach was entirely different from what was celebrated in the culture of my high school. One would usually apply themselves to school to prove that they could comprehend, regardless of whether their efforts were what they should be doing. I was aware of the great divide between engineers and contractors, as well as the every day disdain of the academic stream students for the trades students. Having witnessed my father, with a PhD in engineering, find himself unable to turn on a propane tank, because it was the opposite thread, I was very concerned with limiting myself to academic achievement. Likewise, I was not impressed with finding the trades students vindictive of the academic students, mocking any complexity.

When I transferred from the general stream to the advanced stream, in October of grade seven, I was thrust from studying fractions to studying functions, at a level that matched grade twelve studies. I did not even know what a negative number was! But by the time I had swum my way through the mire and up onto the dry land of academic ability, by grade eight, I realized that it wasn't necessarily the be all and end all that most people assumed it would be. So I chose my achievements carefully from then on, and I was very comfortable not having any comprehension of whatever situation I could find myself in, because I knew I could make sense of any situation in due time, and emerge comprehending.

So my appreciation of achievement gave way to appreciating an environment so challenging that it would force mistakes, yet those very mistakes would reveal the true nature of that environment. This makes me appear to be a bottom feeder, but I am engulfed in a flood of wholes and parts, and finding a true balance is an everlasting source of great joy to me.

So I continued on, reluctant to assume anything, and therefore offering a spiritual bond and monogamous relationship to any woman who expressed interest in me. This is obviously naive, assuming that every woman who has an interest in me is interested in maintaining a spiritual bond. But at least I am presenting the opportunity to the other, and this may cause them to at least consider the possibility, and that is an important fundamental task needing to be accomplished as well. The alternative would be to not entertain the possibility of a spiritual bond with a woman who expresses an interest in me, and this would certainly accomplish nothing, as opposed to the slim chance of accomplishing anything at all. The only problem that arises is denying one woman in favour of another, and mistakenly choosing one who is less interested in a spiritual bond rather than one who is more interested in a spiritual bond, and this may have happened at least twice in this matrigeneosophy.

Keeping track of all this, there are milestones along the way. Falling off of my motorcycle, at 130 kilometres an hour, while passing a truck on the 401, due to a severe wobble in my front wheel that had my arms whipping forward and back to hold onto the handlebars, counts as a milestone. I thought I was going to die, which I welcomed, but the idea was communicated to me that I would not die, and I responded with the desire that no harm should come to me, and none did. Years later, after minor repairs and a sprucing up, sporting a polished dent in my gas tank, I headed past that place on the 401 and out to Newfoundland. This was the first cycle fall, of three. The evening of that fall, I was in the Brunswick House, at the corner of Brunswick Avenue and Bloor Street.

Labour Day weekend saw me in the Brunswick House again, happy to be alive and fully enjoying life, albeit single. A group of women walked up to those gathered around our table so I asked one what her number was. She answered with "got a pen?". This was Miranda, and she counts as the second to initiate. I found I could call her about every two weeks — more often would spook her, and less often would cause her to feel abandoned. I had found a prospect with staying power. She lasted for almost a year, until Jane stole me away from her, even though in that year I had completed proof of academic ability and been accepted into Miranda's university, York-U, or yuck-u. Miranda's dithering wore me out and Jane wanted to be with me constantly. I felt like I abandoned Miranda, but she was too distant for me to pursue further.

I thought that men and women were the same, with thoughts as thoughts and emotions as emotions, but I was wrong. Why were all the women, intelligent enough to attend university, still at the level I was at in grade one? Why did they too, see me as immature? There was an obvious disconnect. Their awareness was drastically different than mine. I was a child to them, and they all seemed like children to me. There seemed a vast unknown territory that I had only peered into from the outskirts, through a small peep hole. My ignorance was about to astound me.

Nominal	Matriarch	Notes
1	Emily	My Mother
2	Linda	The girl next door
3	Tina	Grade One
4	Patricia	Grade Four
5	Mia	Grade Six
6	Marcelle	Lesser Matriarch
7	- Jacqueline	Summer Camp
8	- Marysse	Grade Nine
9	- Dorcas	Grade Ten
10	Dana	Grade Nine to Thirteen, — then commitment to Marriage established, & 1987
11	Kim	
12	Wendy	The First Cycle Fall

    Jane went back to Waterloo, with her stuff and me in my parents station wagon, and I returned to attend York, while she attended Waterloo. *I found a good drafting job in Waterloo, and almost accepted it, but* then the contact with Jane became infrequent, until a birthday card came back to me, unopened. I was determined to get to the bottom of this, and by the grace of a police officer, got back to Toronto without being charged. I had to walk up to his police car to get him to acknowledge me, as I sat in front of Jane's rooming house, trying to figure out what was going on. It did not help that as I realized the voice on the other end of the phone who said "good-bye David" was Jane, the phone booth was rocking due to an earthquake. Late November 1988 — look it up.

    I was in shock, like a suicide spectator. This was really big, and I was standing on it's doorstep. I would have to develop a new understanding and be very open to whatever may come. As far as women were concerned, I was a child, and as far as I was concerned they were like a child. We both must grow if we are ever to see eye to eye. I am partially skilled but wholly juvenile. Women were partially juvenile but wholly mature. The One could barely exist in such an ignorant environment. I resolved to learn as much as possible, and never condemn a child, nor turn away one wanting to stay.

By Jehoshaphat, Solomon was a wise man. In today's readings from the book of Kings, Solomon asks for wisdom to discern righteousness from evil. The story I remember though, is where two women both claim an infant. Solomon orders the infant to be divided between the two women, with a sword. The real mother protests and offers up the child to whoever will take it whole, and Solomon presents the infant to her. This is how to act as a part of a whole. This is real knowledge and not just the accumulation of facts. This is revealed to children and lost to the worldly wise. This is the wisdom of the One, and I would need it to pursue my goal of marriage.

Sunday, July 24th, 2011

Marcelle

Matriarchs —
Emily, Marcelle

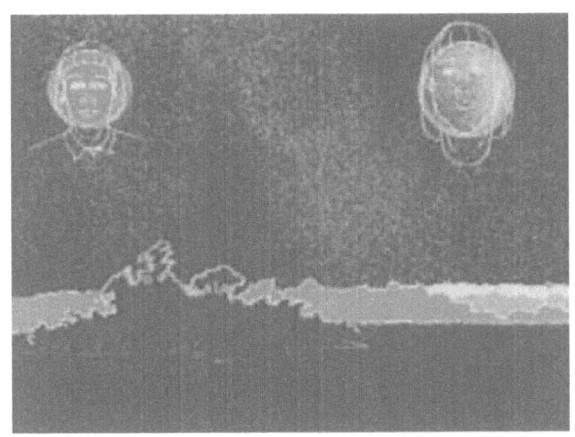

Dana

Miranda

Twelve Generations

Nine Generations

Verses 9 & 10

⁹Uzziah the father of Jotham,
Jotham the father of Ahaz,
Ahaz the father of Hezekiah,
¹⁰Hezekiah the father of Manasseh,
Manasseh the father of Amon,
Amon the father of Josiah,

Verse 5

⁵Lois followed Jane and began first witnessing, and animation under Jennifer. Jennifer became Sherry and first following. In Sherry fundamental animation in Oakville was begun and union with Trisha, preceding Maisie.

Verse 5 Discussion — NIV Bible text verses 9 & 10

Why are we discussing all these generations? Why are there all these generations? What purpose does having all these generations take place, serve?

Well, why is there time? Why do we live so long — or short? As far as the matrigeneosophy is concerned, each time I entered a relationship I began to learn and by the time each relationship dissolved I began to learn more, and this led into the next relationship. Each whole of each relationship nurtured an awareness, which once mature, led beyond that relationship. This is life. Each generation bears witness to an awareness, that when mature, leads beyond that generation, and is taken up by the next generation. We are limited by our nature and this limitation of our awareness and life brings us to our end. The wages of sin, or limitations, is death.

This was not God's intention, and likewise it is not our intention. We all intend to live forever, or at least as long as we can. But we each judge based on our knowledge of good and evil, and then we die to our awareness and ultimately to our earthly life. So no one ever intends to limit a wholly relationship, but nevertheless there is an end, or both ends.

However, the infinite purpose of humankind is to live with infinity for an infinite time. What is needed is a limited way of handling the unlimited — marriage. If our awareness could be infinite then we would likely live with infinity infinitely. But we are limited and will remain so in order to exist, so a mechanism is needed for our limited awareness to cope with infinity as an unlimited awareness. This mechanism or convention is marriage and is God's gift to all who will accept it.

Lois was the daughter of a Baptist minister. She was older than I, but nevertheless felt the need to take me to her church, Yorkminster Park Baptist Church. I participated in the young adults group and the Bible studies. They witnessed to me, and I witnessed to them. I also attended the Anglican church near my home, then headed over to Lois' church. This was the first time I really felt the need to express my experience and understanding to others, as Lois told me it was God's will for her to break up with me.

2013-07-14 Having put a lot of effort into maintaining a relationship with Lois, I was keen to express why I felt such a relationship was so important. And having spent so much time discussing our faith in the young adults group at her church, I was keen to find the justification I needed for maintaining a spiritual bond, balancing whole and part, in scripture. Once again, I was insulted by what I perceived to be a glossing over of the details, the parts, in favour of the whole of the situation. I rejected the whole that denied a spiritual bond. I sought to justify a whole that valued a spiritual bond, by assembling the parts of scripture. I was immersed in scripture, and trying to find validation for my appreciation of marriage as a spiritual bond.

I also was witnessed to, after Lois, by the Jehovah's Witnesses, which I enjoyed and attended their Kingdom Hall on Ossington(?), near Vaughan Road, as well as visiting their printing house in Georgetown. I could easily accept all their teachings, but they left out so many other understandings that my acceptance of their teachings was in no way binding. The illustrations in their literature were amazing, and I tried to illustrate my understanding as best I could with paper and pencils and paint. This was the beginning of my appreciation of animation as a means of communicating ideas. I left for Newfoundland and lost touch with them.

Jennifer moved into the rooming house I had just moved into to avoid living with women, so so much for that attempt. She was a good friend though, and treated me with great respect without doting on me. She must have wondered why I was away so much though, when I was *spending so much time with Lois*, because it was obvious to Jennifer how well Jennifer and I got along. She moved home to St. John's and I missed her.

The following spring I received a postcard from her inviting me to visit her in Newfoundland. I eagerly decided to put my motorcycle back on the road and ride out there, mainly because I did not want to have to deal with the inevitable "come here, come here; go away, go away" of getting on a plane to come back. I had a great visit and almost stayed in Newfoundland, but came back at the end of October, 1990.

2013-07-14

So it turned out that Jennifer was more of a prospect than Lois turned out to be, even if neither became my spouse. In my thinking, it would be better to maintain a relationship with someone who had permanent roots where I lived, but it did not turn out that way. I still consider myself friends with Jennifer, as the last time I talked to her was in 1993 and she had a family of her own. I was able to find work even in Newfoundland, and my boss wanted me to stay, but I did not want to be trapped there economically, and I had an offer of work in Toronto, taking a company from manual drafting to computer drafting.

Philosophically, I suppose if I had committed to staying over the winter in Newfoundland, and becoming economically trapped there, Jennifer may have been more willing to commit to our spiritual bond, just as I had originally chosen a person committed to staying in my home town rather than someone from away.

As well, if I had committed to staying at university, in the same program as Lois, where we met, perhaps she may have been able to commit to our spiritual bond. She was well aware of my potential as well as my frustrations with academics, but whether coincidentally or not, she seemed to loose interest as I lost interest in academics. I was loosing interest in academics as she lost interest in me. The sacred One can compound and spiral up, or it can compound and spiral down. The sacred One is full of potential, and this potential makes it so responsive as to be so unwieldy that it is very hard to manage without understanding and experience.

While working on Autocad, computer drafting, I became strongly interested in animation and continued to draw. Back at the french pastry shop on weekends, Sherry who worked there, began to allow me to go out with her. She was younger than I, and it was all too apparent to me, the age difference, but as I decided after Jane, I would not condemn a child or turn away one who wanted to stay.

2013-07-14

Allowing myself to associate with apparently unsuitable prospects, was my attempt at not overlooking any spiritual bond prospect. I still to this day, have very little confidence in my ability to discern who is interested in a spiritual bond from those who are not interested in a spiritual bond. I believe this is because I have a minimal wholistic ability, at least when compared to a woman, as well as any person can give all the signs of being anything one wants them to be, if they have a reason to want to associate with one. And there are many reasons other than a spiritual bond for two people to associate. So I stay true to myself, and false attempts become as plain as the nose on that person's face, lasting rarely more than a few months. It is not necessary for me to judge, as most false attempts remove themselves relatively soon. Sherry, although younger than me, has proven over time that she was interested in a spiritual bond, but not with me. By their fruit you will know them.

So I called her my daughter, and left it as that. She became the prominent female interest in my life for a good number of years, and it wasn't long before she graduated to being my sister.

2013-07-14
The idea that one must partner with an equal in all respects, is a limitation that I would not support. I do believe that one must be prepared to deal with their spouse in any pairing of adult-adult, parent-parent, or child-child, or parent-child, child-parent, adult-parent, adult-child, child-adult, parent-adult, or whatever! I'm sure any single parent can express that the responsibility of raising a child has a profound influence on their life, even though their child is 'only' a child. Sherry, even though she was younger, exerted a shepherding influence on me, as well as taught me how to cope with one who was a novice at dealing with spiritual bonds.

I had visited Sheridan College in 1991 to check out their animation program, but I hadn't been interested in any more schooling. Sherry, however, impressed upon me the importance of making something of my life, and to her that meant going back to school. So out of respect for her opinion I made it known that I would pursue attending that college. Sherry beat me there, and attended their Art Fundamentals program in September. So in a sense she followed me there, but I began attending after she did. I was behind but did get accepted into the Art Fundamentals Intensive program that started the following January, achieving honours, and was accepted into the Classical Animation Program.

2013-07-14
So this balancing whole and part, is not just restricted to romantic relationships, and is not just available to those who are in a romantic relationship. Indeed, as all of existence is a balance of whole and part, all relationships are a balance of whole and part. As any evangelist can tell you, you never know who you may be able to engage in a conversation regarding the infinite. And the benefits of balancing whole and part are not limited to romantic relationships — they are available as a benefit of all relationships.

I did not have any sort of romantic relationship with Sherry, but as a woman, albeit younger than me, she had an understanding that complemented my understanding and filled in the gaps. Ultimately, attending Sheridan College was a good thing for me, even if not as good a thing as I had hoped. If I had not respected Sherry's opinion, even her opinion as barely more than a teenager, I would never had committed to attending Sheridan College.

This is a life following the balance of whole and part — it leads to far greater things than the pedestrian method of planning and conquering. My seeking a marriage, a spiritual bond, led me to Sherry, and even though she was not a romantic interest, our friendship was fruitful for me.

I became the social target of Trisha, who in a week, went from wanting to constantly be with me, causing me to rack up a one-hundred-and-fifty dollar long distance phone bill and then wanting nothing to do with me at all. Nevertheless, I was determined to be available to Trisha, and this lasted for over a year, yet she wanted nothing to do with me.

2013-07-14

I was getting tired of this litany of the matrigeneosophy. I was determined to will my way into a spiritual bond. This is how I was able to stay the entire school year. This is why I tried to drop out in January. On the one hand I was trying to be available for a spiritual bond, and on the other hand, without a spiritual bond, I was unable to justify staying at school. Blind faith is useless. I needed to act to restore a spiritual bond. But I could not just do anything! And I had no idea what I could do. So it failed stupendously.

This is why I did not make myself available to Maisie, as I was worn out, and did not want another whirlwind runaround. I talked to Maisie on the phone for a while, but did not allow us to date. My mistake.

2013-07-14

Again, I overlooked a sincere interest in a spiritual bond, or at least a more sincere interest. Looking back, it seems neither was interested in a spiritual bond unless it came without challenges. I'm sure there must have been something I could have done to establish and maintain a spiritual bond, but I do not, to this day, have any idea what it could have been. Nevertheless, by their fruit you will know them, so even though I must begin with what is at hand, I do not kid myself that this One thing, seeking a spiritual bond, is an easy thing to do.

So even though their presence may shine in my awareness like the sun, giving light to all I survey, so as to make it too hard to countenance directly, I can still overlook the One of a relationship. Both Jennifer and Maisie, were obviously in my awareness, yet even though I was looking for someone, they were overlooked, to my detriment. This is tricky, this One stuff.

Sunday, July 31st, 2011

Verses 11 & 12

¹¹and Josiah the father of Jeconiah^c and his brothers at the time of the exile to Babylon.
¹²After the exile to Babylon:
Jeconiah was the father of Shealtiel,
Shealtiel the father of Zerubbabel,

  c   11   That is *Jehoiachin*; also in verse 12

Verse 6

⁶In the deserted came Irene, united without union.

Verse 6 Discussion   NIV Bible text verses 11 & 12

It is often said that we all have our own desert experiences. This may occur even in the midst of abundance. It can be a spiritual dry spell, or a period of isolation, or a long period of inactivity. In the book entitled **Acedia & Me : A Marriage, Monks and a Writer's Life** the author, Kathleen Norris, I believe, talks about how the desert monks dealt with the noonday demon, acedia, which strikes the person with exceeding apathy. The monks dealt with it in many ways, of which one was to make many baskets, filling their day in that industry, and then burn all the baskets that they had spent so much time and effort in making, as they had no need of so many baskets. The idea was to be industrious for the sake of being industrious, rather than apathetic. As well, if the superior found one of the monks suffering from acedia or apathy, he would send him to his cell, or room, and tell him specifically to do nothing, neither praying, reading or writing, until the acedia passed.

In my life, not counting Andrea and Glenda, who helped me out administratively, but did not advance my marriage longing, there was a long time of nothing after Maisie. This was my desert. I kept a garden and attended events and programs, but I accomplished little other than accept the passing of time. I did not suffer from acedia, but there was little to focus my efforts on and although I frequently received assurances from the authorities in my life, that I was doing well, I failed to see any progress.

The exile of the Hebrews to Babylon, is described as a lost time, to the best of my understanding. They longed for Zion, and the temple in Jerusalem. This is expressed in psalm 137, that was made into a hit in the eighties by Boney-M - you know it - " By the rivers of Babylon, where we sat down, there we wept, when we remembered Zion ". It may have seemed little good was coming from their defeat and exile. This story is told perhaps in the book of Daniel, but perhaps I am showing my lack of knowledge of the Bible.

But life goes on, with or without us, and all around us. My circle of people circulated. Times and circumstances changed, little by little, and I am sure my attitude changed as well, without my being aware of it.

Into my life came a woman who was committed to marriage. My beard and smoking did not deter her.

2013-07-14

We were married for ten years.

There was a limit to our relationship, that could be discussed over and over, without end. There was a limit each of us placed on our marriage, which to be real, must instead be infinite, and it was this way from the beginning.
So there is not any sure way of knowing whether one is in a marriage, a balance of whole and part, that can be had. This bumps the whole deal up to a spiritual exercise, rather than an intellectual or legal engagement. One can only choose how one will proceed, regardless of what everyone around one is doing or telling one to do.

On the *pilgrimage*, last week, last Saturday morning, at St. Ignace II, where St. Jean de Brebeuf and Gabriel Lalemant were martyred in 1649, the story of the attack of the Iroquois was told to us by an archaeologist. When it was known that 1000 Iroquois warriors were outside the incomplete palisade protecting 80 christian Ouendat (Huron), Brebeuf walked out to them, unarmed, for whatever reason. The Iroquois took his approach as a trick, and failed to attack immediately, allowing almost all Ouendat (Huron) to escape to St. Louis, which we walked by that morning on our way to St. Marie. This is a man who acted regardless of what others were doing or pressing him to do. He died a martyrs death, preaching so much as they tortured him, that they cut out his tongue. They did not even feel he was worthy to be taken back to Iroquois territory as a war trophy and tortured there, so he died in the territory of his ministry.

Spirituality is not just how one is inclined, it predestines everything. Our mind is informed by the Spirit, and we may or may not resolve our spirituality intellectually. Marriage is testified to by myself and the Spirit. Listen. One day I will die, as I have many times, but by the grace of God, it will not be for the lack of pursuing marriage. If God grants me marriage in my life, it will have the highest honor, as Jesus points to the Father, and Mary points to Jesus, and the Spirit has pointed to marriage.

Tuesday, August 16th, 2011

Verses 13 & 14

¹³Zerubbabel the father of Abihud,
Abihud the father of Eliakim,
Eliakim the father of Azor,

¹⁴Azor the father of Zadok,
Zadok the father of Akim,
Akim the father of Elihud,

Verse 7

⁷Emily became Sharon, who became Sherry, who became Irene.

Verse 7 Discussion   **NIV Bible text verses 13 & 14**

As mentioned earlier, in the discussion of Marcelle, in verse three, there are matriarchs that overshadowed any marriage interest. *My interest in* Marcelle was as both a marriage interest and a matriarch, as *my interest in Marcelle, and her prominence in my mind* endured *the presence of* Jacqueline, Marysse and Dorcas. Ideally, there can be only one marriage interest who must also be a matriarch, so as to be approached as everything from a child, through an adult, to a parent. Many relationships retain a matriarch separate from the spouse, and this gives rise to a dreaded Mother-In-Law, but one may not serve two masters or else they will hate one and love the other.

So throughout my venturing into a marriage relationship, there were four *woman who stood out, in my mind, as matriarchs,* counting as three generations of matriarchy — Emily, my mother; Sharon my older married cousin, who *in my mind* became a mother figure; Sherry, a friend, who as a 'daughter' and a 'sister' was the prominent female interest *in my mind,* for a good number of years; and finally Irene, who was an interest married with the matriarch. Irene was mother, friend and child to me.

So *in my mind* Marcelle was a lesser matriarch, over Jacqueline, Marysse and Dorcas, yet under the matriarchy of my mother. Sharon, without any of her own doing, *in my mind* became a competitor to my mother for the role of a matriarch. *In my mind* I levered myself away from my mother with Sharon as the fulcrum. Sharon did not choose this role, and never deliberately wanted it, but by her nature she found herself in the role. I became aware of the nature *and influence* of matriarchy *in my mind* by the similarities and differences between how my mother and Sharon *appeared to me in their behaviour* with me. Sherry did not choose me as a boyfriend, and I never sought that role, but inadvertently I *felt like I had* become a 'patriarch' in her life, if not just another prominent male influence. I respected *what I perceived to be* her specific need for a male friend she could trust to not take advantage of the role. She gave me the role of adult friend, although sometimes *I perceived that she appeared to me to be* slipping into a child-parent frame of mind. I felt honoured that she would make time for me and this satisfied my need for a matriarch. The relationship *seemed to me to have* matured from child-parent to adult-adult and *seemed to have, in my mind,* sufficed for me for a time as adult-child. Irene *apparently, in my mind,* approached as a child, when I was free from a controlling matriarch, if you do not count the health system as a matriarch. She inadvertently *in my mind,* became a matriarch, all the time *seeming in my mind,* only deliberately acting as a child or an adult. She did not intentionally deliberately act as a parent, so I gave her, *in my mind,* the role of matriarch even though she did not *appear to me to* take it or act as one.

So a child must become an adult, and then accept the role of parent as it is presented to them. The child must arrange the stars in their sky when they become an adult, and navigate as a parent. The issue though, is whether the parent will always be a parent. Sure, they may always see themselves as such, but the child, in their path to adulthood and ultimately marriage, must cast off the matriarchy of their mother, if there is to be an infinite commitment to their spouse. This does not mean they will disrespect their parents, but that they will maintain an adult-adult relationship out or respect and honour for their parents. And not only respect for their parents, but for the respect and honour of their parents' relationship with each other, as husband and wife. No one would argue that all too often the man enters into a marriage like relationship for the purpose of sex. I assert that all too often the woman enters into a marriage like legally binding commitment for the purpose of children, and puts the children above the spouse in their priorities, which not only denies the spouse, but overpowers the children and unduly influences the children's relationships with their spouses. So a son may not deny his mother in favour of his wife, and this limits the necessarily unlimited marriage relationship of the son.

Furthermore, a father may unduly influence his daughter, who may not respect her parents' marriage by maintaining an adult-adult relationship with her parents. If we are to follow Christ, deny ourselves and take up our cross, in pursuit of marriage, than we must make our spouse our parent, friend and child, and place our marriage relationship above all other family relationships, if only out of respect for the relationship between our parents. Wherever it says that a man will leave his father and mother and be joined to his spouse, I believe the corollary is true as well — that a woman will leave her father and mother and be joined to her spouse. This is for the integrity of the marriage relationship. If there is not to be one dominant over the other, than the spouses must come together as equals, without one family tagging along for the ride rather than the other.

If there is to be a marriage of equals, than the spouses not only share equal rights, but equal responsibilities. If a husband must take up his cross, than the wife must take up her's as well. If the husband must deny his family, than the wife must deny her family as well, for the sake of the balance of whole and part, female and male, in the sacred One of the marriage relationship. If the husband must suffer condemnation, execution and rebirth for the sake of his marriage relationship, then the wife must suffer condemnation, execution and rebirth for the sake of her marriage relationship. If the mother must invest, release and witness the destruction of her children, than the father must invest, nurture, release and witness the rebirth of his children.

The book, **Theology of the Body**, by the late Pope John Paul II, is said to be a ticking time bomb in today's church. It has also been said that Christopher West, who has been explaining the meaning of the **Theology of the Body**, both in presentations and writings, is lighting the fuse on the bomb. The impression the book gives is that the sexual revolution of the nineteen-sixties did not go far enough in opening up our awareness of love, commitment, and marriage. Suffice it to say that there is far more to marriage than just sex and babies. There is far more to sex than genitals! There is far more to babies than motherhood!

Sunday, August 21, 2011

Verses 15 & 16

¹⁵Elihud the father of Eleazar,
Eleazar the father of Matthan,
Matthan the father of Jacob,
¹⁶and Jacob the father of Joseph, the husband of Mary, and Mary was the mother of Jesus who is called the Messiah.

Verse 8

⁸Maisie returned in the thirty ninth year to rule in the forty second year, and begat the second cycle fall and a new life in the Spirit.

Verse 8 Discussion   NIV Bible text verses 15 & 16

First of all, there was an omission in the genealogy of Jesus, in the typing of the text I have taken from the Bible, New International Version. I omitted Eliazar, son of Eliud ! This throws off the 14 generation count as it would only add up to 13 generations, counting Jeconiah down to Jesus. So I stand corrected.

In the errors we make, there is the image of a new creation. We err in our limited awareness, as we are not fully aware of everything, and these errors are a direct result of our limited awareness. Even an oversight or a slip of the tongue bears witness to how limited our awareness is, when we are engrossed in something other than the matter at hand, and since we cannot be aware of everything we miss an aspect of the matter at hand.

Jesus talks of how the religious leaders of his time " strain out a gnat but swallow a camel ". The religious thought of the day was limited in it's ability to comprehend reality. Jesus was condemned by both the religious leaders, who acted on behalf of the Jewish faith and the Jewish people, and by the secular leaders, who acted on behalf of the state and the citizens of Rome. This is not a mistake. Jesus was teaching beyond the world of the religion of the day, and beyond the state which had political power. He was wrong on both counts.

Why was such a wonderful man wrong ? Jesus was advocating a new and greater awareness, that would not just fill in a missing piece in the incomplete puzzle of the day, but transform the entirety of the then current awareness. Jesus did not oppose the law, but rather, followed it more intensely than was commonly practiced, and this brought on astounding new ideas and an astounding new awareness.

An example of this is the question "Where is the centre of the universe ?" In classical astronomy, earth was the centre of the universe, but when telescopes made further, more intense observations possible, the Sun became a more obvious centre of the solar system, at least. Today we may say the centre of the milky way galaxy is a better centre of the universe. But when more thoroughly intensive observations are made, if we do not find any other intelligent life in the known universe, earth may once again seem a more appropriate centre of the universe.

If one is to follow the teachings of Jesus and the christian tradition more intensely and more thoroughly, it will lead to marriage, I assert and proclaim. Nevertheless it will be condemned as wrong by the religious thought of the day, since even though it is based on a thorough intense following of the religious thought of the day, it has produced results that are contrary to the casual follower of today.

I was hanging on to my marriage with a death grip. It failed and I was suffering. Maisie suddenly became a part of my life, in a good sense, and I began to feel my wounded heart cleansed, patched up, and beginning to heal, until I was able to stand alone again. In her presence I regained my health, and strength of heart, but I could not, in my mind, perceive her as intending to take on the matriarchal role I hoped for her. Other commitments appeared to me to be infringing on the priority of a spiritual bond.

May 20th, 2013 —

[6] We know that our old self was crucified with him so that the body of sin might be destroyed, and we might no longer be enslaved to sin. [7] For whoever has died is freed from sin. [8] But if we have died with Christ, we believe that we will also live with him. [9] We know that Christ, being raised from the dead, will never die again; death no longer has dominion over him. [10] The death he died, he died to sin, once for all; but the life he lives, he lives to God. [11] So you also must consider yourselves dead to sin and alive to God in Christ Jesus.

Romans 6 : 6 – 11;
New Revised Standard Version : Catholic Edition

[12] "This is my commandment, that you love one another as I have loved you. [13] No one has greater love than this, to lay down one's life for one's friends. [14] You are my friends if you do what I command you. [15] I do not call you servants[m] any longer, because the servant[n] does not know what the master is doing; but I have called you friends, because I have made known to you everything that I have heard from my Father.

[m] ***Greek** slaves*
[n] ***Greek** slave*
John 15: 12 – 15;
New Revised Standard Version : Catholic Edition

2013-07-14

Anyone who limits their behaviour to just obeying the rules, becomes a slave to those rules, and thereby, since they have ignored the spirit of the rules, the intention of the rules, and only attempted to obey the rules, have become a slave not only to the rules, but to the inevitable breaking of those rules, sin itself. They have inadvertantly become slaves to sin by limiting themselves to being slaves to the rules, or Law. This is because any set of rules is only a means by which to define and guide intent and behaviour, and are not in themselves, the rules, the final intention and behaviour guide of those who created the rules.

This is why there is a whole justice system, as well as a legislative system. The politicians create the rules, and the judges and jurors determine whether the intent of the law has been violated. This is why a law can be struck down by a judge or group of judges. This is because a law may fail to serve the purpose for which it was created. This is usually an example of the limitations of the legislative system. There are even limitations to the judicial system, as there are such things known as appeals, usually made to a higher court.

There is an ever higher court, where Jesus reigns above the laws of God as well as the laws of humanity. God is love, not only legislation. God is love, not only justice. The Trinity may be Father, Son and Holy Spirit, or Being, Knowledge of Being and Love of Being, or Doing, Knowledge of Doing and Love of Doing, or even Love, Knowledge of Love, and Love in Action, or the Experience of Love.

Again, this is why forgiveness is so important, for two main reasons. The first reason is that the limitations of the Law can only become apparent through an examination of the violations of the law, and no violation may be made known if condemnation is a foregone conclusion.

The second reason, is a little more involved. The intent of the Law is not to prevent violations, but to apprehend violations. The Law does not prevent violations, but seeks to limit the extent and perpetuation of violations, and even does a poor job of this. Only forgiveness can prevent violations. First, because it allows the limitations of the Law to be examined through the examination of each and every violation. Secondly, and more importantly, the opposition that is lacking in a policy of forgiveness, is something that is perceived as a challenge to overcome, and does not create an environment where every individual is free to consider their actions before the infinite. They only consider whether the Law is just and pursue a course of action within or beyond the Law. But the Law, as a created entity, is always fraught with limitations that ever increase as the world turns, and there will always be at least some valid challenge to it. Forgiveness, on the other hand, is an infinite environment that forces individuals to consider their actions on their own merit alone, rather than whether they are just in the face of the Law. This consideration, in the face of forgiveness, actually prevents violations, rather than just allow violations.

God does not want slaves — he wants friends — he wants to be known. Putting the law above all else, defeats the purpose of the law, which is to love one another.

--- May 20th, 2013

Without the faith to follow Jesus where he leads us, by taking up our cross and suffering as he did, we are all slaves to sin. We sin, are condemned and repent to go on to sin again. Jesus wants all of each one of us, and there can be no holding back. Jesus wants to lead us to new life in abundance, and there can be no clinging to this old life if we are to be born again in new life.

In fact, it is our very sins that tell of the need for this new life after rebirth. If one sins, it is as much a failure of the system that designates it a sin, as it is a failure of the sinner. Sure, at first, when one is learning a system, they will make mistakes, but when one knows the system and is still unable to avoid mistakes, or sins, then the system is flawed. This is why forgiveness is so important. Allowing one to make a mistake clarifies the system and allows it to be renewed. If one will not admit their sin or mistake, and hides it from awareness, than there is nothing the system can do to accommodate its' shortcomings, if there is not an awareness of the shortcomings of such a system.

Taking a partner, being condemned and suffering the punishment for it, but not letting go of the partner, would force the system to change, as Jesus' death and resurrection redeemed the world. This is death and rebirth, and it is overwhelmingly wonderful.

Nevertheless, by my conviction, incarceration, and rebirth I have been transformed into a new person, with a new life and the joy of my animation! I am free to pursue christ without fear of physical harm, although I may suffer physically at some point in the future, I have no fear of physical harm, nor fear of loss. By the Grace of God I will pursue my animation.

I only fall on a cycle when I have too much on my mind. The first fall was in 1987, and the second was in March of 2009, and a third was in May of 2009, shortly before my birthday, and after **_Matthew's One Too!_** was written. These stand as landmarks in my memory, and are pivot points in the growth of my faith and awareness.

Sunday, August 28th, 2011

Verse 17

¹⁷Thus there were fourteen generations in all from Abraham to David, fourteen from David to the exile to Babylon, and fourteen from the exile to the Messiah.

Verse 9

⁹Thus there were twelve generations established at the first cycle fall. There were nine generations to establish commitment and conclude three generations of matriarchy, initiating purposeful driven animation.

Verse 9 Discussion   NIV Bible text verse 17

There are two reasons I can think of, that would be why one would count up the generations — one would be to make it easy to remember, and the other would be to assert an order on what would otherwise seem random. I have counted the generations of the matrigeneosophy for both of these reasons.

Nominal	Matriarch	Notes
1	Emily	My Mother
2	Linda	The girl next door
3	Tina	Grade One
4	Patricia	Grade Four
5	Mia	Grade Six
6	Marcelle	Lesser Matriarch
7	- Jacqueline	Summer Camp
8	- Marysse	Grade Nine
9	- Dorcas	Grade Ten
10	Dana	Grade Nine to Thirteen, — then commitment to Marriage established, & 1987
11	Kim	
12	Wendy	The First Cycle Fall

There is however, a certain creativity in how generations can be counted. As discussed previously, the transition can be counted, or the person of the generation can be counted, where one is a transformation that is counted and the other is the person or generation as a noun, that is counted. There are twelve persons in the table, from Emily to Wendy, but there are only eleven transitions between the twelve persons. To establish commitment, there are nine transitions, from Emily to Dana. At the first cycle fall there had been twelve persons. On the other hand, if one counts a transition from the beginning to my mother, Emily, that would add a generation making there to be twelve generations at the first cycle fall.

This is not such a radical idea, as in Asia, one is one year old from the day of their birth, and is two years old from the first anniversary of their birth. As well, does the millenium begin on January first 2000 or 2001?

This same creativity is used in counting up the genealogy of Jesus, as Jeconiah is counted as a member of the fourteen persons up to the exile to Babylon, and is also counted as a member of the fourteen persons after the exile to Babylon.

The Genealogy of Jesus

1	Abraham	15	Solomon	29	Jeconiah **Babylon**
2	Isaac	16	Rehoboam	30	Shealtiel
3	Jacob	17	Abijah	31	Zerubbabel
4	Judah	18	Asa	32	Abihud
5	Perez	19	Jehoshaphat	33	Eliakim
6	Hezron	20	Jehoram	34	Azor
7	Ram	21	Uzziah	35	Zadok
8	Amminadab	22	Jotham	36	Akim
9	Nahshon	23	Ahaz	37	Elihud
10	Salmon	24	Hezekiah	38	Eleazar
11	Boaz	25	Manasseh	39	Matthan
12	Obed	26	Amon	40	Jacob
13	Jesse	27	Josiah	41	Joseph
14	David **King David**	28	Jeconiah **Babylon**	42	Jesus

This is the answer for anyone who wants closure of a definite and contained infinite person — there is not a closure here, in the genealogy of Jesus, to a living infinite purpose, as it is constantly changing yet always the same. Wanting a defined and completely knowable God is satisfied only by idols or models of the infinite. But the infinite, although everywhere, cannot be contained in a finite model or image. Or can it?

In modern physics there is talk of a finite space without bounds. An example would be the two dimensional space of the surface of a sphere. The two dimensional space that forms the surface of a sphere has an area that can be calculated and is finite, but there is not a border to such a two dimensional space. One may travel around and around and never come to a border or edge or limitation, other than that there are only two dimensions.

Three dimensional space may be the same, in that there is not an edge or boundary, yet there may be a finite amount of space. When you add the fourth dimension, time, physicists talk of curved space time in trying to account for gravity. Gravity screws up everything when one tries to account for other aspects of physics. The speed of light is a limit to how fast anything can travel. This may be a sign of the finite amount of three dimensional space.

Containing the infinite has been done by the person Jesus Christ (Colossians 2:9 — 10). Perhaps we all have infinite aspects. If we could know what is infinite and what is finite, we could tap into the infinite and have access to all. Would we want it though? Surely all the horror we could imagine would be available to us, as well as all the joy and wonder. I have a saying — if you are going to be sensitive you have to be tough. Jesus was sensitive to God's call and the people he encountered. He was tough enough to suffer death. Are we capable of such sensitivity and toughness? Perhaps we would rather stay in our limited state and await a comfortable death. But for those who choose to follow Jesus where he leads, the wonder and joy will follow, if not the horror and suffering.

Marriage is the living model of the infinite that we can follow, in the path of Jesus, as the limited beings that we are, in our journey to the infinite, a life with God on earth, with the infinite infinitely as a finite creation. I would assert that women have infinite wholistic aptitude and men have infinite partial aptitude. Some relationship between the two would create a balance of whole and part, and exist as created. Such a relationship between whole and part can grow without end or boundary. The spouse is the infinite to the other spouse, who brings the other infinite to the first spouse, and joined, creation exists, without bound, yet limited to the extent of the relationship of whole and part.

Sunday, September 4th, 2011

Verse 18

Joseph Accepts Jesus as His Son[*]

¹⁸This is how the birth of Jesus the Messiah came about^d: His mother Mary was pledged to be married to Joseph, but before they came together, she was found to be pregnant through the Holy Spirit.

* **18** 1973, 1978, 1984 NIV copy that HJC was written from is **The Birth of Jesus Christ**
^d **18** Or *The origin of Jesus the Messiah was like this*

Verse 10

The Birth of the Created

¹⁰This is how the birth of the created came about. Society pledged creation through the establishment of Marriage, but before this came about, woman was found to be committed to another purpose.

Verse 10 Discussion

NIV Bible text verse 18

Who wants to marry an obviously pregnant women when you know you are not the father of the unborn child ? This is what Joseph was up against. To make things worse, this pregnant women has already obtained a commitment from you to marry her, in the acceptance of her pledge. This is what Joseph was up against. There was no hiding the fact that she was pregnant. Everyone would know that Joseph was marrying a pregnant women, and people may even take his marriage to her as an admission of his pre-marital relations with her. There is no winning way out for Joseph. What would he do, fully knowing that whatever he does, he loses ?

This is what I found myself up against, as I took stock of the world around me in my late teens and early twenties. The whole world endorsed marriage as the means to bring new life into the world and as the means to carry on after death, in the life of one's children. But the game was played to win by getting the most stuff and children. This had nothing to do with a relationship between husband and wife, but rather a relationship between the husbands ability to provide and the woman's womb. Even then, in the mid nineteen-eighties, this had become politically incorrect, but the practice was prevalent. Rather than the fruitful relationship between husband and wife, the women I knew wanted to trade their womb for a comfortable life. This may sound harsh, and is harsh, as people long for more, but this was what was and is still, happening in reality. I found woman to be committed to another purpose.

I by all means most readily admit, that I had little ability to provide, and few concrete prospects on the horizon, but this was so that I could readily weed out those marriage prospects that were marrying for ulterior reasons. This left very few prospects, and even then still could not weed out all the wrongly motivated women. To my credit though, when I was in a relationship that I honoured, I have been readily able to create an ability to provide out of next to nothing. Most often though, when the woman left, the reason to sustain any ability to provide, left with her.

Even amongst those who were willing to marry, their commitment to the relationship had its limits, as I unwittingly came across my own limits. This is the lot of all people in this limited life. I can accept this, and still try to live a life worthy of a Christian, even a Roman Catholic christian. I still honour marriage, in the spirit of Pope John Paul II's **Theology of the Body** - I do need to read that book more — but as Joseph could not free himself of the critics of his marriage to Mary, I seem to get judged lacking as Joseph could very easily have been judged lacking.

There are very few women, in their early twenties, who could fathom what a life following Christ would entail, when he leads them to a destitute peer of a man to marry. The obstacles are too much for most people who have been coddled in the public education system all their life. This is why North America and Europe are importing religious leaders from the third world — there is not a culture of reality for our upcoming generations here to experience.

But what reason would Joseph have to take a pregnant wife? He was a righteous man, and need not humble himself for the sake of a fourteen year old girl, who had already run afoul of public opinion. This is the situation we are all called to deal with, even if most people take the moral high road and do not sully themselves.

A real marriage of a woman and a man, is a spiritual bond, that has real consequences, which include abundance and other temptations. So one must be living a spiritual life, following Christ, to even consider a real marriage relationship. Such relationships are in no way verifiable, even to the participants. This is why there is so much strife around marriage. Even many of the ones that last harbour disillusionment and closed hearts. Such behaviours, as the forgiveness and suffering of a marriage, are not supported by popular society, or even moral society, let alone individuals in such engagements, so it is not any wonder that marriages fail once challenged.

But in leading a spiritual life, following the Joy of communion and life in Christ, where are the greatest joys and happiness? The adventure and frolic of a marriage stand foremost in my mind, beyond all other pursuits, and this is what sustains society, through marriage.

Finally, accountants are always the last ones to the party. Keeping books, and records up to date is not for us but for God. This is why the official nature of marriage gets so cantankerous when one tries to write it all down and keep track of it. Marriage is a One as god and will not be contained by legislations of humanity. Nevertheless, sacraments are outward and visible signs of inward and spiritual grace. But there is never any legislation that can make a marriage any more than there is legislation that can make a baby.

Sunday, September 11th, 2011

Verse 19	Verse 11
¹⁹Because Joseph her husband was **faithful to the law**``, and yetᵉ did not want to expose her to public disgrace, he had in mind to divorce her quietly.	¹¹ Because David was a righteous man and did not want to expose public disgrace he had in mind to depart quietly.
`` 19 1973, 1978, 1984 NIV copy that HJC was written from is **was a righteous man** ᵉ 19 Or *was a righteous man and*	
Verse 11 Discussion	NIV Bible text verse 19

There is more to being righteous than being right. Joseph may have had every right to divorce Mary, being that she was pregnant outside of marriage, but that alone does not necessarily make it the right thing to do. Being right is more than just doing what is considered correct. Following the golden rule, to love God and love your neighbor as yourself, is a dynamic situation, and every incidence must be viewed on its own with respect to all the circumstances surrounding the situation. Furthermore, one must act independently of the pressure from all sides to move in one direction over another, and instead, consider the whole of the situation in the light of the infinite. Nevertheless, many take the high road of popular morality and choose to not sully themselves.

Being open to the infinite aspects of one's life adds a further dimension to decision making. When one considers something as vast as the infinite, and acts on it, many others who cannot view one's decision from the same vantage point will be unable to see any reason why one chooses to act as they do. Judas could not understand why Jesus would not claim his place as ruler of creation, when Judas could honestly believe that Jesus was the Christ, the Messiah, the anointed One. In my own life, of employment for example, I have very often chosen to leave a job, when everyone around me could not see it as a good or wise decision, and would have preferred that I stay in that employment. But we all know that certain situations fail to continue to be fruitful, and must be abandoned. Furthermore, free enterprise allows us to make these choices for ourselves. Why is this? I would assert that free enterprise incorporates the idea that the individual has a unique and only view of an employment situation and will act in their own best interest, and this is the best interest of the community. But in an infinite world, beyond free enterprise, this same infinite aspect comes into play, and I have acted with respect to the greatest understanding I can muster, and have chosen to leave unfruitful situations. This has disappointed others around me, as well as confused them, but has lead to further fruitful situations, in spite of the apparent cost, which does not appear to others to be worth the reward. Many have chosen, in the absence of any understanding that makes sense, being available to them, to attribute such decisions to mental illness. Such is my lot. Nevertheless, I am free and able to pursue my animation and this is my reward. Crazy like a fox — Joseph knew that a greater purpose was at work, as this text of the Gospel of Matthew plays out in the next verse, and made his own decision in light of the infinite, if not fully or generally understood.

In the text of the animation, I was up against the popular morality that an established ability to provide was prerequisite to marriage, when the popular opinion was that marriage was solely for the purpose of children and comfort, and had nothing to do with an infinite relationship between whole and part, female and male. I could have tried to change this popular opinion, but I did not feel up to the challenge, nor did I have the resources to do so, so I chose to live the remainder of my life apart from such apostasy and began to make my way accordingly.

The phrase "the pursuit of happiness" is full of unheralded assumptions. Although it is assumed that we are free to pursue happiness, what happens when one achieves happiness — does this confound society? I would believe so. Consider drug addiction — sure it is an empty pursuit, but it does provide pleasure, and people pursue the pleasure just as the rest of society appears to do. But if one does achieve happiness, does this confound societies economy? Look at the over abundance of the western world. We have and consume more than we need, yet evangelists appeal to our everlasting hunger. If we were content with less, what would drive the economy? The holy cow of industry and work and employment would lie down on its arse and fail to continue to be any consideration. Where can one be happy in such a society? So I chose to leave, in another apparently misunderstood decision.

Yet life goes on, and I may have been in the wilderness and other areas outside society, but I still had a life and grew to face further challenges. I tried to live in Povungnituk, in the arctic of Quebec, yet this door was closed, when in spite of *being an obedient employee,*

I was further hindered by not being allowed to wander the tundra on my time off. I tried to cache sufficient funds to purchase acreage but could not budget the funds for the municipal taxes. Although I was employed doing site supervision in the far north of Ontario, that door was closed when my job became *unnecessarily complicated*, and it was still too closely tied to society, in Toronto, rather than being tied to the life I loved in the remote communities of the north. These pursuits proved fruitless, yet I repeatedly gave them second chances and they repeatedly proved fruitless. The pivot point in my understanding was when I realized, while alone, that people are far more curious than any rock, tree, body of water, or animal, and this lead to a love of people as they are, and as I come across them, from time to time.

Sunday, September 18th, 2011

Verse 20

²⁰But after he had considered this, an angel of the Lord appeared to him in a dream and said, "Joseph son of David, do not be afraid to take Mary home as your wife, because what is conceived in her is from the Holy Spirit".

Verse 12

¹²But after he had accomplished this, Sharon's image, as all other, called him back where he found conceived, Marriage as purposeful redemption if in the Holy Spirit.

Verse 12 Discussion   NIV Bible text verse 20

Making decisions, when one is respecting the infinite aspects, has a certain life of its own. Practically, one must consider all aspects, and wait for the solution or choice to present itself. This can be an active consideration, while one holds off from making a decision until a suitable choice presents itself. This deliberation is not passive, but active, as one explores the possibilities. Joseph deliberated, then thought his mind was made up, but then, before he had acted on his decision, the choice was presented to him, and it was more wonderful than anything he had considered.

This has happened to me many times, with work, for example. An unmaintainable situation seems to require a certain choice or action, but then a terrific solution presents itself and all one need do is act on that solution. In my work experience, the best example is the first drafting job I had. I had already been in the far north, in Povungnituk, but that did not pan out. Before that, I had already worked for over a year for electricians, but that did not pan out. And even before that, when I was fourteen, I had completed a college structural drafting course, but neither in Texas or Ontario, would anyone hire a fifteen year old draftsperson. These three endeavours proved fruitless and seemed unrelated. But when I was twenty, I decided I wanted to go to university, because *the affection I had for* Miranda *inspired me*, and *I subsequently decided I needed a desk job to prepare for university*. So I again began looking for drafting work. Remarkably, I found one at the opposite end of Toronto from where I was living, and I was hired. As I began to work for these electrical engineers, with my structural drafting training and qualifications, they began to ask me if I would be interested in site supervision work in northern Ontario. So the three entirely unrelated, unfruitful endeavours of drafting training, electrical work and living in the far north, made me the perfect person for the job I acquired. Furthermore, the civil engineer remembered how, at the age of five or so, I had graded his University of Toronto engineering design graphics assignments that my father, as professor there, had assigned him. My father told his class that his sons had graded the class's assignments, by putting a tracing of the correct answer over the students' work and marking the differences. So there is not any knowing where a life following Christ will lead!

Where Joseph chose to accept Mary, I chose to not accept the incorrectness I found in society. I did leave and paddled Lake Ontario and the Trent Severn Waterway, for about a total of five days. I accomplished leaving society, but before I was fully committed, I began to see things differently. As I experienced and saw the world around me in a new light, I found myself thinking that so and so would like to see this, or so and so would get a kick out of that. Others, both matriarchs and other people, were forefront in my mind, and I accepted that they were important to me. I appreciated people as they were, since they were more intriguing than any thing I encountered on my trip, other than lock keepers. Sharon, *in my mind*, was my matriarch at the time, and coloured all my memories of the people I had known. These memories and considerations of others, called me back, as just as in the movie __Into the Wild__, the protagonist writes, in his last days before he dies, that "Happiness is meaningless if not shared."

Once I returned, my spiritual life progressed to the point where I found myself giving importance to marriage, as a spiritual bond. I acknowledged that there would always be a prominent female interest in my life, and I chose to accept this. I found a spiritual relationship with a woman to be of utmost importance, as a shepherding influence to my many unrelated pursuits and endeavours, which would stretch my resources in too many directions. This understanding has grown and flowered like a lotus, colouring all of my life since then. I began to seek out a spiritual relationship with a woman, which I called marriage.

So where Joseph found the Lord in Mary's womb, I found the Lord in the marriage relationship. As Joseph forgave Mary for being pregnant by another, I *beg forgiveness for failing to maintain a spiritual bond,* marriage. Joseph had no way of verifying whether Mary was really pregnant by the Holy Spirit, and I had no way of verifying whether a woman I was engaged with was engaged with me for the purpose of an infinite spiritual relationship. Joseph saw within Mary, the salvation of the world, and I saw within marriage, the salvation of the world. But for Joseph, the salvation was to come by the death and resurrection of the fruit of Mary's womb, where for me, the salvation was at hand in the sacrament of Marriage, if one could take up their cross, as Jesus did, and live a life of forgiveness in Marriage.

For us today, Jesus has saved us, and where we should now head, is into the infinite spiritual bond of marriage, fully armed with forgiveness, and prepared to meet the second, third, fourth, and as many as one can count, comings of Christ, to claim us in our endless life on earth with God.

Sunday, September 25th, 2011

Verse 21

²¹She will give birth to a son, and you are to give him the name Jesus,ᶠ because he will save his people from their sins."

ᶠ 21 *Jesus* is the Greek form of *Joshua* which means the LORD saves.

Verse 13

¹³It will give birth to a One as Jesus, because the union will save people from their sins.

Verse 13 Discussion

NIV Bible text verse 21

In these verses of the animation text, the image in the animation becomes two tori, perpendicular to each other, linked and rotating longitudinally. The two hands rotating toward each other become the two tori. This is a symbol or image of the One, in its crudest form.

The common symbol or image of christianity is a cross — two lines perpendicular to each other. The image is not to be worshiped, but people find meaning in the image. Originally it was taken to be a sign of the form of torture, death and victory of Jesus, but others since then have found meaning in the cross as a symbol of their faith. This is the relationship between female and male, whole and part. The whole is the horizontal line and the part is the vertical line. The union of the two lines becomes the cross, that Jesus was nailed to and died upon. I have never heard of this implied meaning being endorsed, but it is out there.

For example, Jehovah's Witnesses profess that Jesus died on a torture stake, without a horizontal bar. Why would they do this? What does this have to do with the faith they profess? My experience with them is that they do not entertain any wholistic thinking, but rather find wholistic thinking to be superstitious and wrong. I rest my case.

My personal belief is that Jesus, the one who saves, the anointed One, was at, and is, the union of whole and part, in every respect — as a person, in history, in creation and in God. The One is more prevalent than any historical person, and is all of existence, throughout the mind, throughout accomplishments, throughout achievements, absent in failures, throughout heaven and earth, and throughout God. Furthermore, the One is alive, as Jesus is alive to all who encounter Him to this day, and is dynamic and in motion.

So I offer this crude animated image of the union of whole and part, of a rotating horizontal torus, linked with a rotating vertical torus. As the **HESUS JOY CHRIST** series progresses, this animated image or symbol of the One, becomes more defined, accurate and complex, but remains a remarkably simple idea.

So " . . . . . marriage will give birth to a One as Jesus, because the union will save people from their sins." This means that the union of marriage, the spiritual bond between two persons, one infinitely inclined toward the part, or male, and the other infinitely inclined toward the whole, or female, strikes a balance between whole and part, and may participate in all the rewards of the presence of the One as Jesus, found there. Marriage has the redeeming quality that makes all else worthwhile and successful, as any balance of whole and part does.

Nevertheless, all the Jewish teaching is fundamental to Christian teaching, and all the Christian teaching is fundamental to the spiritual bond of marriage, as well as any reality that may exist. In the path of the spiritual relationship of marriage, all the markers, trials, tribulations, sufferings, joys, death, rebirth and achievements have been marked out for us by Jesus, who lived a perfect life before God, and is the Way, the Truth and the Life.

Have you ever wondered what one was supposed to do once one has had an overwhelming encounter with Jesus and has been converted, baptized, reborn or whatever? One could do charity work, join the ministry, or just join the choir, and find not much else is different from before! How does one apply this new found faith and conviction? The answer is one must take up their cross and follow the living Jesus, the union of whole and part, wherever He leads. I assert that He will lead one to marriage, and this union of whole and part, not only is the door to the eternal, it is full of all the trials Jesus had to face as it is the same path that He walked, the balance of whole and part, and will likewise lead to death and resurrection, many times over before any final death. Each and every death is final, if not physically fatal.

Death, whether marital, professional, intellectual, emotional, social, career or physical, is the door to new life with God. If the ultimate whole and part can be united, God may dwell with us in heaven on earth. God would still be God, our One parent apart and ahead, Jesus would still be leading the Way, and the Holy Spirit would still move us, but our spouse would be the presence of God in each of our worlds. Furthermore, if the union of whole and part is fundamental to all of existence, whether an idea in a mind, in heaven, or earth, or even the existence of a stone, and is more fundamental than death, this union of whole and part may transcend death and allow life to flourish throughout a sinful world ruled by forgiveness of sin as found in the eternal forgiveness and love that is marriage. Do you believe that Christ raised Lazarus and others from the dead? I believe Jesus Christ, the prime union of whole and part, is capable of such deeds. Do you?

If one professes Jesus as Lord and Saviour, and is armed with forgiveness, they must be true to this faith they profess, throughout all shortcomings they find in themselves, as well as others, and profess this faith by word, action and deed, standing firm to the end, and accept the loving forgiveness God offers them to see them through to their new life in God and on earth. Marriage is the love and forgiveness of God applied. Where else in the world is their a more worthy application of what any religion teaches us, especially christianity.

The **Theology of the Body**, taught by the late Pope John Paul II, as I understand it, as proclaimed by Christopher West in his talk entitled **Marriage and the Eucharist**, states that putting the burden of being God on a spouse will crush the spouse. I agree. I assert, furthermore, that this is the primary reason that death will be a frequent visitor in any real marriage, but at least as many times as death darkens a marriage, the opportunity for forgiveness and new life will present itself to the marriage. The path Jesus walked is not any different from the path of a real marriage, with its many healings, understanding and teaching, as well as suffering, death and resurrection, amongst other victories.

Sunday, October 2nd, 2011

Verses 22 & 23

²²All this took place to fulfill what the Lord had said through the prophet: ²³"The virgin will conceive and give birth to a son, and they will call him Immanuel"ᵍ (which means "God with us").

      ᵍ   23   Isaiah 7:14

Isaiah 7:14 ¹⁴Therefore the Lord himself will give youᶜ a sign: The virginᵈ will conceive and give birth to a son, andᵉ will call him Immanuel.ᶠ

  ᶜ   **14**   Masoretic Text; Dead Sea Scrolls *son, and he* or *son, and they*
  ᵈ   **14**   ***Immanuel*** means *God with us.*
  ᵉ   **14**   Masoretic Text; Dead Sea Scrolls *son, and he* or *son, and they*
  ᶠ   **14**   ***Immanuel*** means *God with us.*

Verse 14

¹⁴ All this took place as fulfillment of the Law and the Prophets, as foretold by Emmanuel and will be God again with us.

Verse 14 Discussion   NIV Bible text verses 22 & 23

There is not anything that I am trying to take away from Christianity, rather I am trying to tell of and illustrate what Christianity points to, from my experience of the world and of Christianity. Jesus said he was not taking anything away from the Jewish Law but was teaching the fulfillment of the Jewish Law. All of my experience and education points me in the direction of marriage. Marriage is more than I have ever heard tell. So I am telling — GET MARRIED AND STAY MARRIED.

My experience has fulled out my education. I do not have, by any means, an exhaustive education, but by watching and listening, I have been able to integrate the little I know and build on an understanding that has repeatedly been confirmed by further experience. Then when I consider my life with respect to the infinite I proceed accordingly.

When I was in my mid teens, I was concerned about heaven and hell. Why would God create anyone so as to send them to eternal hell. This disturbed me greatly. I understood God as an infinite identity that was the infinite purpose of life and loved all of life. Yet I could not integrate the idea of a loving God creating any being for eternal punishment, let alone death. I was very relieved to read, in very small type, so that one had to lean in to read it, on an all black t-shirt of an Oakville punk co-worker, the phrase "Life is hard / Then you die." I laughed out loud! Forget heaven and hell, it is life that counts, and death is the end. That simple phrase got me back to reality and I found great joy in it. For the next several years, I remembered that phrase so much that I painted it on the shaft of my kayak paddle, right between my hands where I could always read it, and on a paddle blade, in a way that people had to figure out what it was they were looking at. I still have that paddle displayed in my living room. I would now say that total death of any total awareness is all anyone need be concerned about.

As well, the Scientific Method, of hypothesis, testing, observation and the revision of the hypothesis, precipitating further testing, and so on, kept me busy into my late twenties, when I realized that any hypothesis can be proven wrong if there is sufficient testing, so I turned my attention to other matters in a more spiritual way.

So when things began to present themselves in light of the infinite, the Bible stories I was taught as a child took on a very real meaning, and failed to remain to be anything like a stupid kid's tale told to the naive and superstitious. For example, the story of the two sons of a vineyard owner, one refusing to work but then working, and the other agreeing to work but then not working, no longer is a fairy tale to make children obedient, but is an illustration of religious leaders saying they will lead the people spiritually and then not doing it, where the lay persons say they will not be spiritual leaders, but do lead spiritually.

When I began this path of mine, in my late teens, I encountered this fulfillment of the law and the prophets, both the God of Charleston Heston's Ten Commandments, and the United Church's support of the boat people in the late nineteen-seventies, and it has accompanied me everywhere since. This is at least like a second, as opposed to a first, coming of Christ, that repeatedly *blossoms out of the previous* coming. And this fulfillment of Christianity, Marriage, will be God again with us.

Immanuel, or Emmanuel, means "God with us". This name was given to Jesus as he was God with us. Immanuel foretold His second coming, but where is it? It is right under our noses, if we can discard the naive and stupid superstitious interpretations of religious material, just as the kingdom of heaven is at hand. Why do people cling to such obviously stupid understandings, both within the church and outside of the church? A profound understanding places God face to face with us, and the face of emmanuel is your spouse. Jesus foretold a second coming, and His teaching points to marriage, so there it is, if one can get over their hang ups about stupid ideas of God, embrace christianity and move on further to where it points — Marriage.

Wednesday, October 5th, 2011

Taking a break — A Discussion of "Koans"

Events in my life lately, have caused me to consider that I may not be able to complete as much of the animation as I had hoped. Once again, my livelihood is under attack for political reasons.

As well, my brother has raised the point that the animation writing is unintelligible, which I thoroughly understand.

So I feel it is time again to discuss how one may make sense of this animation, as I did in the winter of 2009 in my Blog post. It was a post from the book **Praying Our Experiences** by Joseph F. Schmidt, which I will once again discuss here.

In chapter three of his book, page 27 in my copy, under the heading Introspection — Narcissism and the Limited Ego, this Jesuit Priest acknowledges the dangers of considering our experiences. One may discover their weaknesses and gifted-ness by considering their experiences but they risk becoming narcissistic. As well, one may rationalize their experiences so that they find what they want to find in them. Loving ourselves over others is a danger, but we cannot love others if we do not first love ourselves. It is a precarious undertaking. Authentic consideration of life is not the problem, but part of the solution.

When the ego is dominant one will judge each of their experiences as a victory or a defeat, rather than consider what they say to one. This rationalism leaves no room for authentic consideration to arrive through the cracks in our ego. An example of this is the judgment of a Pharisee that Jesus, if He was the Messiah, would have known what kind of woman was washing His feet. The dominance of the ego would not leave room for the unexpected and thereby close their awareness to God working in their life.

In order to open a disciple's mind to the non-rational and the unexpected, the teacher of some eastern traditions will present the disciple with a koan as a focus for consideration. A koan is a statement that does not make sense. It is impossible to resolve the statement through analysis. This is the point.

A classic koan is "What is the sound of one hand clapping?" The answer must come from beyond rationalization and analysis, from beyond the ego. It is not a matter of rationalizing the koan, but rather being in faith with the statement that brings personal awareness and transformation. The ego must surrender to the helplessness.

Our experiences themselves are koans, in that they are not rational, containing contradictions and elements that do not make sense. Looking for meaning appears fruitless — this is the point. This opens one up to the source of life on the other side of the limited rational ego.

So all of the animation text, can be considered as one would consider a koan.

As with life, just because something does not appear to make sense, does not mean there is not any sense at all in it. This is the achievement of science — making sense of the natural world. Geographers have mapped the irregularities and inconsistencies of the surface of the earth, making it known.

So the animation text does not appear to make any sense, but careful consideration of whatever sense one can find in it, is the meaning of the animation.

An example is the question "Can we lead with you?" Does this inquire if the questioner can be a leader in a group of leaders? Or does it mean that the person questioned will be leading the charge, and everyone else, including the questioner, will be right along shortly?

As well, one may compare this question to the text in the Gospel of Matthew where Jesus, an embodiment of the One, says "Follow me!" The disciples hear a command, but in the animation, the One hears a question — "Can we lead with you?" So just as the people wanted to make Jesus king after he fed the crowds, one following in the path of Jesus will be called upon to lead.

Sunday, October 16th, 2011

Verse 24

²⁴When Joseph woke up, he did what the angel of the Lord had commanded him and took Mary home as his wife.

Verse 15

¹⁵When David woke out, he began what he could do and took up animation to till out a wife.

Verse 15 Discussion   NIV Bible text verse 24

A living god is ever present and providing opportunities to anyone who is attentive. All one need do is pay attention and watch for these opportunities as they present themselves. As Joseph suffered indecision he rested in reason, until an overwhelming experience presented the opportunity of justification in the one option of many he had been deliberating on. It was a personal interior deliberation he had suffered, that was resolved in his heart due to an overwhelming experience of being in the presence of the angel of the Lord, in a dream, and being instructed as to how to proceed. The means by which he was to follow this command were readily available and the command was easy to carry out, especially once he had the resolve of a determined heart.

In my life, at the end of everything at both the end of 2008, and at the end of 2009, when everything had failed and it seemed all was lost, I deliberated what I should pursue in this world. When I looked around, it was apparent that everything I needed to produce the animated message of the importance of marriage, and present it, albeit in a limited way, was readily at hand, and furthermore, all other pursuits were problematic. I had a clear idea of the importance of marriage, based on what I had written in the winter of 2008 in a piece I called **The Layman's Guide to Marriage**; I had the book of Matthew that spoke clearly to me and my experience; I had the means to produce animation at little cost; I had an income as well as problems with employment that forced me to not rely on employment; and the Revue Cinema was looking to screen anything it could get with their Drop Your Shorts, open screening program.

So I began, not knowing or having too much faith in where it would lead, but having the spirit to carry it out, and just enough faith to maintain the effort. I still have no idea where all this work will lead, but as I am able, I pursue this animation.

Not only do I need a wife, the world needs spouses that are prepared to follow through with marriage, the spiritual bond, as well as any other bonds that come along with it. Marriage, the spiritual bond, is far more important than the economic, social, family, physical, and even emotional bonds that come along with it, and this is overlooked in today's society. When any of these other bonds fail, the spiritual bond must be maintained to see the marriage through. These are the deaths that will occur and must be resolved by the spiritual bond. Why is this?

In a world where religion and faith are considered to be highly questionable, marriage as the application of the christian religion and faith is a frequent casualty. But if the union of whole and part that is created through forgiveness of the opposing inclination, is fundamental to all of existence, no wonder the world is limited in what is possible! Marriage is the forge of this union of whole and part, where understanding is crafted from experience and applied to all else. Each understanding will have a lifespan including birth, prevalence, accomplishment, failure and death, followed by the birth of a new understanding and this "second" understanding's lifespan. Marriage must be used as a resource and a foundation for this cycle of birth and death of understandings. It is the refuge and the battleground that resolves existence, death and birth.

Since I believe my marriage failed due to a lack of understanding of how important marriage is, I feel personally compelled to proclaim this understanding, in order to "till" or create an understanding that a spouse may hold and thereby allow a marriage, a spiritual bond. All people, not only spouses, need to understand how important the spiritual bond of marriage is, since marriage never exists in a vacuum and external pressures and influences can arise from anywhere and break the marriage bond.

Sunday, October 30th, 2011

Verse 25

²⁵But he **did not consummate their marriage***** until she gave birth to a son. And he gave him the name Jesus.

*** **25** 1973, 1978, 1984 NIV copy that HJC was written from is **had no union with her**

Verse 16

¹⁶He had no union with her until separated, and animated Marriage, which he called "Emmanuel", meaning "God with us".

Verse 16 Discussion

NIV Bible text verse 25

    If the parents of Jesus were suppose to be legitimate when he was born they may be considered to have to have had marital relations so as to consummate their marriage ! As the story goes, they did not consummate their marriage until after Jesus was born, if they ever did, Mary being ever virgin ! The whole situation is ripe with bending the rules ! This is the point ! A living God is not bound by His own rules, and frequently transcends them.

    This is what many people take as an indication of the powers *that* be being at work — the transcending of natural rules and laws; so much so that they chase "miracles" and supernatural occurrences. The point, though, is that we are not to worship the laws of God, but rather we are to worship the living God Himself, who is beyond His laws. God wants not only a personal relationship with each of us, He wants a loving personal relationship with each of us. He sets us up to encounter Him, yet we dismiss His presence as a coincidence, or luck, or the scheme of another.

    In my life, I try to be self reliant, responsible, attentive and dependable. This leads me to be apart from God as the personal source of my entire life, ever present and ever patient, wanting me to know and love Him. I did everything by the rules in getting married, and this marriage failed. God wanted me to know Him, not just His rules. I now may not rely on my obedience to rules, as my salvation, as the rules have become impotent, and fail to offer a solution to my salvation. It is God alone who saves, rather than humanity's religious institutions and understandings of God's law. So much so that Jesus Himself was a criminal.

    Where Joseph named Jesus, which means "the one who saves", I named the animation Immanuel, which means "God with us". I try to present God to the audience in personally meaningful ways, with koan statements and presentations of the first book of Matthew in my life.

The Matrigeneosophy of the Created, is a list of the "generations" preceding the coming of the animation of **HESUS JOY CHRIST**, as the genealogy of Jesus is a list of the generations preceding the coming of Immanuel. ***The Birth of the Created***, is the story of how the animation came about to being made. As a balance of whole and part, which is what I strive for, the animation is Christ like, as far as Christ is a balance of whole and part.

Matthew's Two Four is the story of the end of my previous "life" and the beginning end of this "life", as foretold by Jesus in the twenty-fourth chapter of the Gospel of Matthew.

God is with us, even if we are unaware of Him. He does want us to be aware of Him, and not only aware of Him, but to thoroughly know him and even more, love Him. I often wonder if this is the meaning of life, to know and love God. But once one has gained this height, God sends them back with a task to serve His people, which is everyone, in a specific way under specific circumstances. This is what they mean when they say "take up your cross and follow Jesus". This is very specific. One need just look around and see what is possible. If it is possible, it may be what God is calling one to do. But careful deliberation is necessary to determine if this is of God or else. I'll never know in this life if this animation is truly what God wants, but I pray regularly and earnestly, and day by day, more animation is getting done. Day by day . . . . .

Sunday, November 6th, 2011

Closing Notes

OVERVIEW

Well here we go! We were a third of the way through discussing the seventeen verses of **HESUS JOY CHRIST / Matthew's Three Fold**, when I took a break to consider the wordage that was then pushing seven thousand words!

A body of knowledge has it's limits, and one limit has nothing to do with how many pages are written about such a body of knowledge. When one (or a group) creates a body of knowledge they are making many decisions, or rather, assumptions that are not stated outright. These assumptions are made early on in the creation of a body of knowledge but seriously limit the effectiveness of that body of knowledge. So as an example of how creating a body of knowledge can become ridiculous, usually around the point at which academia takes over, I have chosen to write about everything I know about how to pick up a stick.

I was fortunate to make the acquaintance of a man in his fifties who left the aerospace industry to go to school for landscaping. That alone is ridiculous enough, but the point is that this gentleman was accomplished in academia and technological industry, who when he decided he wanted to work outdoors it was only natural that he would go to school to learn an outdoor trade. He studied for three years at Humber College and graduated from the landscaping technician program. Sadly, he only lasted five months as a landscaper, in spite of working for a very reputable, good and established company, and was able to get into good enough shape in spite of his many years of age, but could not tolerate the bystanders looking at him with the expression of 'look at that nice old man picking weeds'! His academic and thorough understanding was not appreciated by the casual observer, so was it worth anything at all? Likewise, this thorough understanding of how to pick up a stick is ridiculous and not worth anything at all to the casual observer. And the discussion of **HESUS JOY CHRIST / Matthew's Three Fold** is not worth anything to the casual observer — unless an awareness is cultivated by considering the discussion, but a thorough consideration of the animation would have the same effect of cultivating an awareness, not to mention considering life would cultivate a thorough awareness.

The moral of the story, here, is PAY ATTENTION !!!

Tuesday, April 12th, 2011

HOW TO PICK UP A STICK!

Here is how to pick up a stick.

First determine the size of the stick. Is it a twig, a limb, or a full branch? If it is a twig, how many of them are there? If there are many, then get a rake and a tarp. If there are not enough to warrant a tarp than get a garbage bag or a bucket.

Drop the garbage bag or bucket in the general middle of the twigs, and begin a loop path, starting and finishing at the bucket and extending only far enough to allow you to fill your hands with twigs. If you make the loop path too big you will waste time walking back to the bucket when your hands are full. If you make the loop path too small you will be dumping too few sticks in the bucket for each loop and that wastes time loading too small a load of twigs in the bucket. This becomes a concern when the bucket begins to get full and the twigs must be stuffed into it and can no longer just be dropped into it. If you are using a garbage bag, however, this is always a concern as the twigs must be placed into the bag lengthwise as otherwise the bag cannot hold as much and is too quickly filled.

Actually picking up the twig must be done standing with legs extended but not locked. Lean down like you are touching your toes and bob down to pick up the twig, and as you bob up transfer it to your off hand until it is full, and by that time you should be more than halfway along your loop path. Finish the remaining path holding the sticks in the good hand that picks them up, so that you arrive at the bucket with two full hands. Do not crawl around on your hands and knees because you need your hands to hold as many twigs as possible. It likely isn't good for your knees, crawling in the damp ground. As well, bending your knees to crouch down to pick up the twigs will be too much bending for your knees. Bobbing will get you well stretched out.

In the case of many twigs, a rake can be used to gather the twigs into piles and onto the tarp, to be dragged or carried to the truck. The first sweep of the rake will orient the twigs perpendicular to the sweep of the rake, and then the pile can be rolled like a snowball as it gathers more twigs. Maintain the coherency of the pile if the twigs are to be tied into bundles, as such a fagot can be rolled onto the twine to allow the twine to be wrapped around the fagot and tied. Do not attempt to rake a twig that is parallel to the path of the rake. This will break the rake. It may still be necessary to gather the remaining twigs by hand. Larger sticks may need to be picked up by hand, following the above mentioned method, as they cannot be gathered by a rake. **DO NOT BREAK THE RAKE!**

Usually, a large area of twigs will occur in the spring as summer or spring maintenance is beginning, but may also occur when pruning. Pruning will produce limbs and perhaps branches. Branches may also need to be picked up at the beginning of spring maintenance or after a storm.

When picking up a limb or a stick that is larger, pick it up by the stump end as that will give you the most leverage over a tapered limb if you pick it up by it's heaviest end. Otherwise the limb will be unwieldy and if you can get it into your armload, you may not be able to toss it in the truck. Gather all that you can hold under one arm and make sure you are on your way back to the truck by the time you have a full load in your arms. Again, bob down and up to pick up the sticks, keeping in mind your armload. There is no way you could crawl or even crouch with an armload of sticks.

Branches are larger sticks that branch into more than one stick. They may be very large. If they are very large, do not cut them up, but instead drag them by the stump end, so that no further branches are broken off, and heave them by the stump end, into the truck. The best place to cut them, to pack them into the truck efficiently, is right in the truck. If one was to cut them up before they are in the truck, that is only more sticks to pick up and more sticks to throw in the truck and more sticks to pack into the truck to get a large load and reduce the number of trips with the truck. Once a few branches are aligned with the stump end at the head of the truck, tread on the branches carefully and with loppers, cut the branches at the crotches where the smaller branches head out from the main branch. It is the crotch that sets the limbs at angles to one another and prevents efficient loading in the truck bed. By cutting the branches at the crotches the limbs are able to fall into alignment with one another. I have seen a load of branches come out of the truck body and maintain the rectangular shape of the truck body as it sits on it's own after being dumped.

Finally, for a good laugh, try to wield a branch by the small end — it will wobble around and you may not even be able to get the stump off the ground! The use of a wood chipper greatly improves the packing and removal of large branches, but there will still be twigs to be gathered, according to the appropriate method.

_____
1000 words

_____
Tuesday, April 12th, 2011

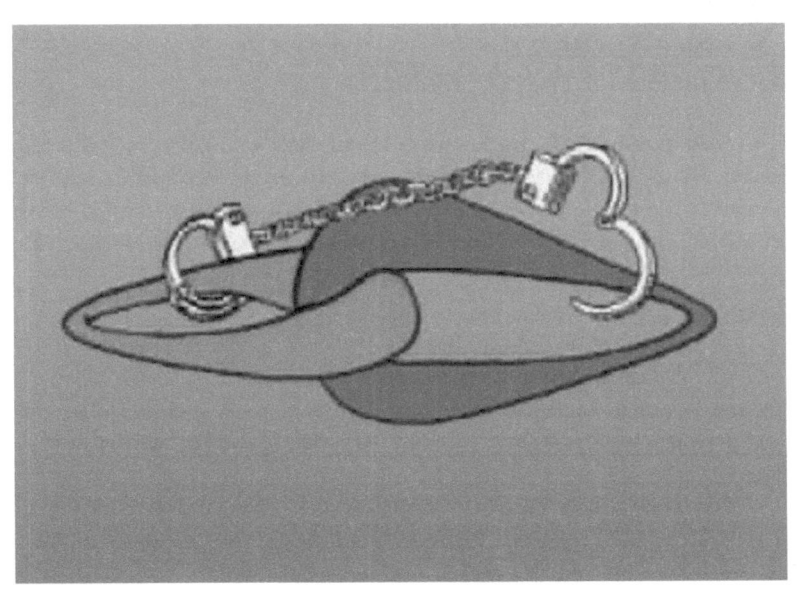

HESUS JOY CHRIST / Matthew's Two DISCUSSION -

From Tuesday, November 15th, 2011,
to Tuesday, April 17th, 2012
as posted to the blog
of R. David Foster
entitled **Vid'93 bein' To Wordie** . . . . .
@ www.vid93.blogspot.ca

® R. David Foster 2009, 2011, 2012

OVERVIEW
from the opening of the discussion of
HESUS JOY CHRIST / Matthew's Three Fold

Well here we go ! Try to keep up because there are many angles to this text and it's discussion will cover all the angles I can find in both texts and the relationship between the two texts, which carries a fourth level of meaning. That is — the meaning of each text individually (2 meanings), the meaning when both texts are viewed together (3rd meaning) and the meaning of the relationship (3rd meaning) in the context in which we share — real life (the 4th meaning) !

Stepping back a bit, let's acknowledge a few things. We are talking about religion — specifically christianity, which I believe is essentially forgiveness to the ultimate degree. All religions have their strengths, in fact all are valid and relevant. Forgiveness is either a spoken or unspoken element in many religions. I believe forgiveness is essential, and that is why I am christian.

Many religions have elements of Whole and Part. Ying-Yang for example. Other terms are Agency and Communion, Reductionistic and Holistic, one and many, or Male and Female. All that exists has both a wholistic aspect and a partial aspect. Everything that exists is part of a context, and wholly made of parts. To bring something into existence one must address both the whole and the part, both the context and the specific, aspects.

Furthermore, everything that exists has an inclination to either whole or part. The approach to anything assesses the balance of whole and part in that thing. An imbalance is always apparent, and the inclination of any approach is to correct the thing to obtain balance. If it appears too partial it must be corrected. If it appears too wholistic it must be corrected. The fallacy is that anything that exists is not in balance. In other words, if you may approach it then it does exist and if it exists it must already be in balance. Forgiveness allows the balance to exist without correction, and accepts that all things are in balance. This is somewhat a Buddhist opinion or faith. The important thing is to SEE the balance and not be moved to correction by any APPARENT imbalance. Otherwise the urge to correct leads to confrontation and a need to make things unbalanced and favoring whole or part over the other. A key thing about christianity is that it will forgive any apparent imbalance to the extreme of self destruction, but the self destruction is only apparent and not real ! This last idea is explored in the animation entitled **HESUS JOY CHRIST / Matthew's Two Four** which is a chapter about ends.

If whole and part are termed female and male, then this forgiveness that exists between the sexes will allow marriage, which is capable of creation, if not joy and contentment. The whole of **HESUS JOY CHRIST** points to marriage as the further salvation of humankind, which is based on the essential character of Jesus that is essential for any successful marriage of any whole and part or female and male.

All people are called to different vocations, whether single celibacy, marriage, or other. Marriage is essential to society as a union of whole and part that creates new meaning and life . Marriage is a resource that produces new understanding and creates far more than just babies . This in no way diminishes christianity, because without ultimate forgiveness and sacrifice no marriage will survive . It will end when a partial or whole attitude fails to forgive a whole or partial attitude . Once one has taken up the challenge of Christ and begun to follow him, some sort of witness of the union of whole and part is where one must head, fully armed with forgiveness .

Moving on, evil is real, and forgiveness is how to deal with it . This third chapter of the Gospel of Matthew is about Jesus' baptism by his cousin, John the Baptist . John the Baptist was not preaching forgiveness, nor rebirth through death from forgiveness, but repentance which is turning from doing evil and trying again . Obedience to the Law, as turning from evil, will make balance apparent and allow the balance to be acknowledged and seen . But no one has ever been able to obey the fullest intent of the Law without the benefit of infinite grace . In other words, no one has ever been able to keep the Law when circumstances were against them . Jesus was able to obey the Law but it lead to his very public death . Many others have died obeying the Law in much less honoured deaths . Death — what is it really ? Death will be discussed elsewhere — perhaps in a further discussion of **Matthew's Two Four** .

Finally, one may choose to keep the issue of the existence of God out of this discussion . For my part, God is an infinite goal, infinitely present as an infinite goal, colouring our perception of existence . Whether God is a person, male or female, is beyond this immediate discussion, but worth discussing in some other writing . Suffice it to say, for now, that whatever has been created exists within infinity and it is all, entirely, good .

Ash Wednesday, March 9th, 2011

OVERVIEW

This is written after the discussion of **Matthew's Two Four**, the discussion of **Matthew's One Too!** and the discussion of **Matthew's Three Fold** were written, and before the discussion of **Matthew's Foretold**. Matthew Chapter two, is the story of the visit of the Magi, wise men from the east, and both the escape to Egypt and the return to Nazareth. **Matthew's Two** is a similar story of the coming of the infant One, its **Escape Into Civilization** and the **Return to Nativity**.

The One is the marriage relationship, or balance of male and female or part and whole. This discussion will be about the coming of the infant One into the world in the form of a marriage-like relationship. This One needs to be protected and nurtured to come to fullness and maturity.

The infant One is the understanding of the necessity of a balance of whole and part, and the faith of marriage, which must be nurtured and cultivated. It appears in relationships, especially romantic relationships, and must be taken care of and nurtured to reach maturity. This care can be interfered with and obstructed, as it frequently is, by other interests in the life of the spouses. **Matthew's Two** is the story of the trials of nurturing the One relationship.

Feast of Christ the King, Sunday, November 20th, 2011

OPENING NOTES

Wednesday, October 7, 2009
Drop Your Shorts - Revue Cinema open screening.
Revue Cinema's *Drop Your Shorts* next open screening is Thursday, November 5th, so the countdown clock is running for me to complete the next <u>**HESUS JOY CHRIST** - *Matthew's Two*</u>.
http://revuecinema.ca/dropyourshorts
By the way, the theme song for <u>**HESUS JOY CHRIST**</u> is complete and I just might post it here as a teaser . . . .
ngoh ngoi neih pauh yahng
culprit: R. David Foster incident 10/07/2009 09:47:00 AM
?! &*%(#)$

Monday, November 2, 2009
<u>**HESUS JOY CHRIST** - *Matthew's Two !*</u>
Drop Your Shorts - Revue Cinema Screening
<u>**HESUS JOY CHRIST** / *Matthew's Two !*</u> is being screened this Thursday, November 5th, at the **Revue Cinema** on Roncesvalles, in Toronto, as part of their open screening called *Drop Your Shorts*.

Since the text is so closely tied to the original second chapter of the Gospel of Matthew I have provided the original text below. You would be wise to read it over before viewing the animation to double your viewing pleasure! I will post the animation here on Sunday or Monday next, complete with the text of the animation - <u>**HESUS JOY CHRIST** - *Matthew's Two !*</u>
-RDF

The Gospel of Matthew

- Chapter Two

The Magi Visit the Messiah[*]

¹After Jesus was born in Bethlehem in Judea, during the time of King Herod, Magi^a from the east came to Jerusalem ²and asked, "Where is the one who has been born king of the Jews? We saw his star **when it rose**^{**} and have come to worship him."

³When King Herod heard this he was disturbed, and all Jerusalem with him. ⁴When he had called together all the people's chief priests and teachers of the law, he asked them where the Messiah was to be born. ⁵"In Bethlehem in Judea," they replied, "for this is what the prophet has written:

> ⁶"'But you, Bethlehem, in the land of Judah,
> are by no means least among the rulers of Judah;
>   for out of you will come a ruler
> who will shepherd my people Israel.'^b"

⁷Then Herod called the Magi secretly and found out from them the exact time the star had appeared. ⁸He sent them to Bethlehem and said, "Go and search carefully for the child. As soon as you find him, report to me, so that I too may go and worship him."

⁹After they had heard the king, they went on their way, and the star they had seen **when it rose**^{***} went ahead of them until it stopped over the place where the child was. ¹⁰When they saw the star, they were overjoyed. ¹¹On coming to the house, they saw the child with his mother Mary, and they bowed down and worshiped him. Then they opened their treasures and presented him with gifts of gold,

---

*   **1** 1973, 1978, 1984 NIV copy that HJC was written from is ***The Visit of the Magi***

a   **1** Traditionally *wise men*

**   **2** 1973, 1978, 1984 NIV copy that HJC was written from is ***in the east***, also in verse 9.

b   **6** Micah 5:2,4

***   **9** 1973, 1978, 1984 NIV copy that HJC was written from is ***in the east***, also in verse 2.

frankincense and myrrh. ¹²And having been warned in a dream not to go back to Herod, they returned to their country by another route.

The Escape to Egypt

¹³When they had gone, an angel of the Lord appeared to Joseph in a dream. "Get up," he said, "take the child and his mother and escape to Egypt. Stay there until I tell you, for Herod is going to search for the child to kill him."

¹⁴So he got up, took the child and his mother during the night and left for Egypt, ¹⁵where he stayed until the death of Herod. And so was fulfilled what the Lord had said through the prophet: "Out of Egypt I called my son."[c]

¹⁶When Herod realized that he had been outwitted by the Magi, he was furious, and he gave orders to kill all the boys in Bethlehem and its vicinity who were two years old and under, in accordance with the time he had learned from the Magi. ¹⁷Then what was said through the prophet Jeremiah was fulfilled:

> ¹⁸"A voice is heard in Ramah,
> weeping and great mourning,
> Rachel weeping for her children
> and refusing to be comforted,
> because they are no more."[d]

The Return to Nazareth

¹⁹After Herod died, an angel of the Lord appeared in a dream to Joseph in Egypt ²⁰and said, "Get up, take the child and his mother and go to the land of Israel, for those who were trying to take the child's life are dead."

²¹So he got up, took the child and his mother and went to the land of Israel. ²²But when he heard that Archelaus was reigning in Judea in place of his father Herod, he was afraid to go there. Having been warned in a dream, he withdrew to the district of Galilee, ²³and he went and lived in a town called Nazareth. So was fulfilled what was said through the prophets, that he would be called a Nazarene.

---

[c] **15** Hosea 11:1

[d] **18** Jeremiah 31:15

This **LEFT** Column is always the original Gospel text of the Second Chapter of the Gospel of Matthew, *New International Version*.	This RIGHT Column is always the text of the animation - HESUS JOY CHRIST / Matthew's Two, written by R. David Foster.
Verse 1	Verse 1
The Magi Visit the Messiah* ¹After Jesus was born in Bethlehem in Judea, during the time of King Herod, Magi^a from the east came to Jerusalem	The Visit of the Daughters ¹After the One was conceived in the body of Christ, under the household, majestic daughters of communion came to the church . . . .
* 1 1973, 1978, 1984 NIV copy that HJC was written from is ***The Visit of the Magi*** ^a 1 Traditionally *wise men*	

Verse 1 Discussion

Here we go again !

Jesus was born in Bethlehem, which was known as the city of David, in the region of Judea, under the reign of King Herod. The people of the One God, were as a house of God, a living temple to Him, just as we are temples to God in our bodies, and form the body of Christ, the church. The people of God are one, as a family is one, under the head of the household, who for Judea was King Herod. He was not a religious leader, but a puppet king of the Roman Empire.

The One can be found in many places, including scripture as the Lord, in Christ, the anointed One, and in the church, the body of Christ, as well as in healthy marriages. The One is present as Christ is present, in the Eucharist or Communion. To conceive of the One, is to recognize the One as one may encounter it, and once this is achieved, one seeks it out wherever it may be found.

I find the title "Magi" to be a root of the word "majestic", so in this story, the Magi, or Wise Men, are played by three majestic daughters of communion. Old wise men are played by young daughters. This is a story of young romantic love, found in the church by three young women, as opposed to the cold old love of majesty. Actually, though, in my mind, one daughter is a married elder, another is middle aged and married, and a third is a middle aged single person. All three have conceived of the joy of the One and are chasing it down, as this story plays out. Each however, is in a different situation, as one is a married leader, another is married and the third is single, yet these three friends have found the One and are pursuing it from each of their situations in life. Each has their own household within which they act. The household is unique to each of the three, from each of their perspectives. Yet they all encountered the One in Communion.

As well, the body of Christ, the church, has born the idea and being of the One to the world, as Mary bore Christ into the world.

The One, as a balance of whole and part, wholistic and reductionistic, yang and yin, female and male, as well as communion and agency, is alive and leading them, and not definable. The use of the word "communion" is not a mistake, as the Communion or Eucharist of the church, is a wholistic influence, as the name suggests. But as well, whole and part can be expressed as east and west, as the west is reductionistic or partial as opposed to the wholistic nature or wholeness of the east. The United States, as an example of the western world, is reductionistic when compared to China or other eastern lands such as Japan or Korea. But then again, Japan is reductionistic when compared to China, and North Korea is wholistic when compared to South Korea.

So Wise Men from the East, in this story, are played by daughters of Communion. Get it?

And so now, as the story is told, the city of Jerusalem has become the church, an architectural being of spiritual leadership. This is not as hard to make sense of as one may imagine!

And now to flesh out this blog post, let's discuss romantic love. Romantic love is seen as contrary to holiness by some, but as my understanding of this **Theology of the Body** stuff coming from the Catholic Church, the union of male and female is a participation in the union of the Trinity, and is very holy! So the attitude that daughters of the church are misbehaving by chasing down romantic love, if they are sincere and committed, has to go!

Many people believe that young love is irresponsible and too much for adolescents to be involved in, but isn't that societies fault? If society demands so much education while neglecting basic human nature, so much so that a teenage pregnancy is considered a tragedy, isn't something wrong with society? Even in this case, where the three daughters are of middle age, why need there be a problem with these adults pursuing the One of romantic love? Surely the two married persons may pursue romantic love in their marriages, especially the person with the leadership role!

Mary was an adolescent and God chose her as she was.

Many people fault the Catholic Church for not allowing married priests so as to effectively minister to married couples. Yet this condemnation of romantic love is just as present in the protestant churches.

If God is love, and the Trinity is the Father, Son and Holy Spirit, or rather, the mind, self knowledge and self love, then in light of the **Theology of the Body**, such condemnation of romantic love as between married spouses is absurd. And restricting both youth and adults from romantic committed love is just wrong.

Sunday, November 13th, 2011

☻

Verse 2

..... ²and asked, "Where is the one who has been born king of the Jews? We saw his star **when it rose**** and have come to worship him."

** **2** 1973, 1978, 1984 NIV copy that HJC was written from is *in the east*, also in verse 9.

Verse 2

..... ²and asked: "Where is the One who has been born above all? We have felt his joy in communion and have come to adore him."

Verse 2 Discussion

Who was born to be king of the Jews? The Messiah, or anointed one, was promised in scripture to the Jews. As the Messiah, he had four tasks to complete, which were, gather the people, cleanse the temple, deal with the enemies of Israel, and reign as king of all nations. In a book entitled **The Real Messiah? A Jewish Response to Missionaries**, the case is made that Jesus of Nazareth did not accomplish any of the tasks of the Messiah. But Christians claim he accomplished all the tasks of the Messiah. Christians claim that Jesus gathered the sinners, cleansed the temple, whether the building or the bodies of the people, dealt with sin and Satan as the real enemies of Israel, and greatly ruled as king of the nations, as many western nations govern under God. Even in the United States, where there is a separation of church and state, prayers at least use to be said, in Congress and the Senate.

So this baby born in Bethlehem, was sought after to be acknowledged by Wise Men from the east, who in spite of being wise, thought the current establishment in Jerusalem would be aware of his birth. They unwittingly brought the threat on his life from Herod. In seeking to praise him they brought upon him the threat of death. This is not so uncommon an occurrence. In seeking to praise, one draws attention to the tall grass, that will cause it to be cut off.

So as king of the Jews, to rule all the nations, this is what it means to be born above all. The majestic daughters have not known any greater One, so this One is above all else.

So they saw his star in the east, and this was the guide of the wise men, to both the place and time of the birth of the anointed one. The star is the specific and the east is the context. In the animation text, the joy is the specific guide and the context is communion, whether the Eucharist or the unity of the church. The joy can be felt and can guide one as in the game where the players are either hot or cold depending on how close they are to the prize. If one feels joy they proceed until the joy passes, then they redirect themselves until the joy returns.

Adoration is a form of worship. But adoration includes personal love as well as honour and glory and blessings. The three majestic daughters are asking the church, instead of the people of Jerusalem, where the One is, so that they may adore him further. The church doesn't know. This is beyond the church's comprehension.

The One may be referred to in the third person, as masculine, since in this case it is considered other than us, as opposed to being united with us, when it would be referred to as feminine in the third person. The three majestic daughters have encountered the One, but he passes and they seek him out where they have not been. He is apart from them.

Since they felt the joy of the One in communion, they naturally ask the church where it can be found, just as the wise men from a foreign land, ask the locals where the king of the locals can be found. The church generally has no idea where the One can be found, just as King Herod has no idea where the king of the Jews can be found, as he considers himself King of the Jews, and the church believes it has the highest and greatest joy. This joy that the majestic daughters have encountered is considered foreign to the church, just as any other king is considered a threat to Herod.

Another understanding is that as the three majestic daughters come to know the One, their adoration of the One grows, or rather they come to adore him.

This whole scene is like a child asking their parent a confounding question. A question such as "Where do babies come from?" can confound a parent who strains to answer the child both honestly and in a way they can understand, as well as present the appropriate attitude with which the child should approach sex and birth.

Finally, God save whoever bears a temptation to the majestic daughters of communion. The head of the household will take action against anyone who bears an alternative to their authority, just as King Herod seeks the death of any child considered as born to be king of the Jews. It does not matter that the bearer or child is only a part of all that is to come, they must be eliminated as they are the means by which it will come. The action of Herod is against God, and the baby Jesus is only the means by which God comes, and therefore the target of Herod. Likewise, the means by which the One comes will be the target of the head of the household, and the head of the household, as well as the church, may choose to act against God by acting against the bearer of the One. The One may be considered to be God, as it is an infinite source, but God is unfathomable and undefinable, so any image of God, such as a One, is not God, but rather only another image of God. God does not live in the Sistine Chapel any more than He lives anywhere else, but there is an image of God on the ceiling of the Sistine Chapel.

Feast of Christ the King, Sunday, November 20th, 2011

Verse 3	Verse 3
3When King Herod heard this he was disturbed, and all Jerusalem with him.	3When the head of the household heard this, all the church was disturbed.

Verse 3 Discussion

So the role of King Herod is played by the head of the household. A matriarch of a family is the economic and social leader of the family, as the king is the social and economic leader of the nation. More commonly though, in western society, it is a patriarch who is the head of the household. It doesn't matter whether it is a female or a male leader who has authority over the household, just as it doesn't matter whether a queen or a king is in control, neither is interested in entertaining any challenge to their authority.

To call Jesus "Lord" or "King", is to give Him authority over economic and social issues, as well as everything else. He as well, asks for total obedience to His authority. He wants all of me, you, or us, more so than any other king. But He wants us to surrender to Him willingly, and will not force us to pay Him homage, but rather patiently waits and encourages each of us to acknowledge Him and accept His blessings.

So trying to serve two masters will make one hate one master and love the other master. Jerusalem at the time, had two masters, and God as well. The King Herod, the Roman rule, and the God of Abraham, Isaac and Jacob, the God of being itself. And this choice between these three would have to be made daily. Jesus was challenged whether it was lawful to pay taxes to Rome or not. He answered with the question "Who's face is on the coin?". Being the Roman Emperor's face on the coin, Jesus said "Give to Caesar what is Caesar's, and to God what is God's". And that is the way to sort out how to deal with more than one master, but still leaves the love of one and the hatred of the other.

So if there is the head of the household, the head of the nation, and the King of Heaven, then give to each his due. The problem arises when one authority wants homage out of its jurisdiction. The church may be all knowing in the way of following Christ as Lord, but it has failed in directing how one should proceed once one is committed to God, Jesus and the Holy Spirit. This the church has left up to the individual to sort out on their own. And this is where this idea of marriage picks up. The idea of the One of marriage demands the application of all Jesus taught and was, or is, to the sacred relationship of marriage. Any interference by any authority, whether the nation or the household, is interference in the application of the direction of Jesus. This is why the household and the church were disturbed when they heard the question of the previous verse - "Where is the One who has been born above all? We have felt his joy in communion and have come to adore him", - they were enjoying undue authority over the relationships of the members of the household, or nation, and recognized this question and expression of love as a threat to their authority. The household saw a devotion greater than it knew, to an other beyond their authority, and the church likewise saw a devotion greater than it knew, again, to an other beyond its authority.

This is common in popular culture, this overbearing interest of the parent or parents, in the relationship of their adult children. Surely adolescents need guidance, but this is not forever, as even the crown acknowledges that adults, over the age of 18, are responsible for their own decisions, regardless of whether their parents feel they are capable or not. Indeed, many parents deliberately undermine the adult child's ability to take care of themselves independently of their parents, so as to keep them under the authority of the household. This servitude is different in each culture, but prevalent in all cultures. It is as rampant with fathers as it is with mothers, with respect to male adult children as it is for female adult children.

And this overbearing influence of a parent or parents undermines any One relationship the adult child may venture into. It truly becomes a marriage of two families, and the ensuing battle for control between them, rather than a significant balance of whole and part in the form of a marriage of equals. Not only that, the parents of the adult child have their own relationship as husband and wife that suffers neglect by the undue attention given to the adult children. Both fathers and mothers are guilty of neglecting their spouse in the interest of maintaining authority over their adult children.

Sunday, the first day of Advent, November 27th, 2011

Verse 4

⁴When he had called together all the people's chief priests and teachers of the law, he asked them where the Messiah was to be born.

Verse 4

⁴When all were consulted the head asked where the Christ was to be born.

Verse 4 Discussion

Looking back now, I could have written "One" instead of "Christ", but what I wrote, I wrote.

As a union of whole and part, Christ, or the Messiah, or the Anointed One, has dominion over all of us. We each are inclined toward the whole or the part, whether by choice or gender, and this inclination moves existence forward, albeit in a struggle as well as in peace. We are limited to the extent in which we are a union of whole and part, as a world or as individuals. Christ is the union of whole and part, in history as well as for all time. Christ is the Word, before all worlds. This eternal union of whole and part which is existence can be brought forth in marriage as well as many other ways. We all exist in this union of whole and part and anything new is created first as a union of whole and part. So in marriage there is the potential for creation, to the extent that the union of whole and part exist. Christ, as union of whole and part, is synonymous with the One of marriage.

So the head of the household, having heard the daughters ask where the infant One was, must track down this challenge to their authority, under the guise of curiosity and genuine interest. This is what Herod was doing and this is what the head of the household does. Under the assumption that they have the best interest of the infant One or the infant Christ as their intention, they draw their enemy closer than their friends and prepare to deal with this challenge to their authority.

The members of the church, or the chief priests and teachers of the law, may be open to the gift of the One or Christ, but nevertheless, they unwittingly allow the infant One or the infant Christ to be threatened. Each member of the church must choose for themselves if they will accept this occurrence or oppose it. There will not be a consensus arrived at, but rather, each person will decide for themselves if they will accept the One or the Christ and act accordingly.

So the One or the Christ, may appear as a person, but in reality it is a relationship. The other person in your relationship may appear to you as the One, but in reality the One is the relationship you have with the other person, rather than the other person themselves. This is a common error, this confusing the joy of the relationship with the other person, the object of your intentions. The other person may truly be the essential origin of your joy, but in reality it is your relationship with the other person that is the true source of the joy. The other person without you is nothing more than any other stranger, but your relationship with that individual bears great joy.

This true source of joy, the relationship, is trickier to explain with respect to Jesus Christ, but is still true of your relationship with Jesus Christ. To begin with, did you ever personally shake Jesus' hand? No you haven't. But Jesus is a source of great joy. He did many things, in the past, but it is His presence to you today that brings you joy. You have not shaken hands with Jesus, but you live in an eternal relationship with Him and this is the true source of your joy. The relationship with Jesus is present to you today, if Jesus the man is not present to you today.

That is why it is so important to act on your relationship with Jesus, or your spouse, so that the relationship may bear fruit. The consequences of your actions are the only thing that really exists in this world, that can bear witness to the relationship, which bears witness to the eternal existence of the Christ or the One. The little things we do each day for Jesus or our spouse are the only things that exist in reality, and especially so for those beneficiaries of our actions based on our relationship with Jesus. What ever you do for the least of these, you do for Jesus. And the same is true for the One of the marriage relationship — whatever you do for your spouse, no matter how inconsequential, you did for Jesus, the Christ, and the One of marriage.

Finally, sometimes it is important to do nothing. This allows the spouse to come to act on the relationship. Joseph, allowed Mary to nurture Jesus in her way, and supported the Holy Family as best he could. He safely took them into hiding in Egypt, and safely brought them back to Nazareth, as opposed to Bethlehem, where Herod's influence still threatened the infant Christ. But the immaculately conceived Mary, was the one to raise Jesus up to fulfill his mission, with the blessings of Joseph. Joseph may have known that Jesus was the one to do all Joseph longed to see, rather than Joseph doing it himself, in a futile grasping at God. The union of whole and part was allowed by Joseph to exist between Jesus and his mother Mary, and blessed by Joseph, who may have judged it more powerful than anything he and Mary could accomplish. This one man, Jesus, was a product of an immaculately conceived Mary and her relationship with the Father and the Holy Spirit, and may have been more than anything Joseph could have come up with, so he honoured Jesus by allowing Him to do his work.

Jesus is the perfect person, if Mary is the perfect Mother, and Joseph is the perfect Father. We are all called to be perfect people, in the image of Jesus, as children of God, and secondly called to be spouses, and thirdly called to be parents. The union of whole and part that exists and existed in Jesus Christ, is most readily available and full of potential in the marriage relationship. It does exist between parent and child, but this is an imbalance of power, where a true marriage is a perfect balance of whole and part.

the Second Sunday of Advent, December 4th, 2011

Verse 5

5"In Bethlehem in Judea," they replied, "for this is what the prophet has written: . . . . . .

Verse 5

5 "In the macropolis of David " they replied, "for this is what the prophet has written: . . . . "

Verse 5 Discussion

So this is the kind of thinking involved in the experience of the One. Bethlehem was a town in Judea. It was the birthplace of the King David. So it is known as the city of David. Now a city can be big, and referred to as a metropolis, which is a word with either Greek or Latin roots. Bethlehem was a small town, I believe.

The Acropolis, which means at the top of the city, is a fortified hill in Athens on which the Parthenon stood as a Doric temple to the virgin god Athena. And finally, the prefix "macro" is from the Greek makros, and is a "combining form meaning long, large "[4]. I did not look any of this up when I wrote the text of this animation, but now that I have looked it up, let's figure out what this means.

My thinking at the time of writing this, was that the Acropolis was a temple to all the gods of Greece, and that "macro" meant all as well as large or many. So the Macropolis of David would mean the temple to all the gods of King David, which, David serving the one God, would mean all the approaches of King David to the one God. But now that I have looked up the roots of this word Macropolis that I made up, let's see how one could interpret this made up word.

Macro means long or large, and polis means city. Metropolis, means mother-city, but can refer to any large city. So correctly and literally, Macropolis means a long or large city.

But Bethlehem is a small town, so why refer to it as a large city? I was not referring to the town of King David's birth nor the town where Jesus was born. I was referring to "where the Christ was to be born", and in this animation story, the Christ, or One, is born in the, let's say, long or large city of David. For this to make sense, we must see the word "Macropolis" as having a religious context, and having the meaning of the large city of David's gods. And since both King David, and the author, David Foster, serve the One God, this plural gods means the many approaches to the One God.

The boy David was the son of Jesse, and a shepherd who was called upon to slay the giant Goliath. He later became King and wrote many psalms, as well as marrying the wife of a man he sent to certain death. His most popular psalm is known as the 23rd psalm which begins "The Lord is my shepherd, there is nothing that I want."

David led a wondrous life as poet, warrior, shepherd and king. He truly had a thorough understanding of his Lord and God. The city of his knowledge of his Lord and God would be very large and magnificent.

So there you have it - this is the meaning of the answer to where the Christ was to be born- in the Macropolis of David. It takes a bit of thought to make sense of this stuff, but the experience is worth the effort and makes for a nice Sunday drive around one's mind.

This is what is meant by the Christ being born in the city of David, Bethlehem, and Joseph being a descendent of David — the Christ bears many of the aspects of King David, mainly the spiritual aspects. It is not important who Joseph was a descendent of, nor is it important what the geographic location of Jesus' birth was — it is most important what the Christ was building upon, which is the legacy and establishment of King David.

King David was a celebrated individual in the Hebrew faith. His life was held up as an example of one who was devoted to God and blessed by God. It was promised to him that the Messiah would be one of his descendents. This was not an incidental favour bestowed on David, this was an acknowledgment of his closeness to God. This is what is important, that David was close to God, as Christ would be close to God. David's offspring are incidental, as is the place of his birth, but his closeness to God is of primary importance.

So the One, or Christ, appears in the legacy of King David, rather than in a small obscure town or glorious lineage. Deliberation on the psalms and history of King David points to the Christ, and the One.

Finally, this animation text is the story of my experience of the Gospel of Matthew, and how I find the truths of the Bible played out in my life. It is a coincidence that my name is David and that I may appear as a spiritual scout, reporting on the spiritual territory that our people are entering into. Many may feel that it is obnoxious to write all this, and to dwell on my experiences, but I feel it is important for me to share my experience, as I am able, as we all should do, to identify and establish spiritual truths to those that follow us. None of us live in a vacuum — we all share this life with the others around us. Identifying and clarifying our existential nature is a joint endeavour of all of us. This, I find, is more important than what I will get for Christmas, or what state I will be in financially when the tally is taken. I readily welcome any comments and discussion, whether supportive or critical, and can be reached at vid932008@gmail.com.

[a] Page 361, Webster's New World Dictionary of the American Language, Warner Books Paperback Edition, © 1984

the third Sunday of Advent, December 11th, 2011

Verse 6

⁶"'But you, Bethlehem, in the land of Judah,
    are by no means least among the rulers of Judah;
    for out of you will come a ruler
      who will shepherd my people Israel.'[b]"

[b] 6 Micah 5:2,4

Verse 6

⁶ "The Lord said to my Lord:
"Sit at my right hand until I make your enemies a footstool for your feet"'[a]

[a] 6 Matthew 22:44 ;
Luke 20:42-43 ;
Psalm 110:1

Verse 6 Discussion

So which is more important — the legacy of King David, or the geographic location of the birth of the Christ or the One? Well for one thing, this animation is specifically about the birth of the One, so the legacy of King David, as maintained and fulfilled by Jesus of Nazareth is more important to this story of the One. But the geographic location of the birth of Jesus is something to be considered for those who are drawn to supernatural occurrences.

Jesus being born in the city of King David, Bethlehem, is important to those looking for supernatural signs and acknowledgments of God. But be careful that these supernatural occurrences are not an attempt by Satan to mislead the overly simplistic. I'd rather try to know God, although He is ultimately unknowable, and develop an understanding, than be at the whim of any supernatural claim that comes along.

But the Wise Men, or Magi, were looking for the geographic location of the birth of Jesus, so the scripture quoted to them makes a geographic claim that Bethlehem would be where the Anointed One will be born.

Where did the Wise Men get this idea to come and visit a baby in Judea? My understanding is that there are two ways something can be known — wholistically and partially. The Wise Men came upon their knowledge wholistically. This wholistic way of knowing things can be explained by an example. If you see a stallion come out of a barn, and then after a gestation period, see a colt come out of the same barn, you would know that there is a mare in the barn. This is the wholistic way of knowing things. Alternatively, if you go into the barn and find a pregnant mare, then you know there is a mare in the barn. This would be the partial way of knowing things. It is the classic idea of the problem of the One and the Many — if there is one, then how can there be many? The Wise Men saw signs and came looking for the baby in the manger. I have generally gone looking for the mare, and tried to further my understanding through inquiry, consideration and integration of what little I know.

But Jesus, as a balance of whole and part, knew far more than even the church has imagined. The Wise Men saw signs and knew the Anointed One would be born, but Jesus, as the Anointed One, knew many more things through the integration of the whole of his awareness with the parts of his awareness. Also, Jesus was in a geographic location that gave him a unique whole view. And, Jesus was at a historical time that gave him a unique whole view. These signs of the place and time were what the Wise Men knew and so were able to locate the manger.

So as a balance of whole and part, the One, which the majestic daughters of communion have encountered in the church, is of the legacy of King David and made alive in the life of Christ, and can be tracked down just as the Wise Men tracked down the manger, by inquiry, consideration and the integration of what little one may know.

So in the animation, the Lord said to David's Lord, "sit at my right hand, until I make your enemies a footstool for your feet." So which Lord is which? I would argue that there is a the classic Lord of the Old Covenant, which I would refer to as the Father, but David's Lord, is the Christ, the balance of whole and part, which would suffer and die as the Son, to bring about a new heaven and a new earth through His resurrection. In the legacy of King David, there is the new inkling of the idea of the Trinity of the Father, Son and Holy Spirit. To me, the Father is being, the Son is the knowledge and awareness of being, and the

Holy Spirit is the love of being. And the Christ, which is Greek for "the Anointed One", who was wholistically anointed due to his place, time and nature in the reality of the world, is the eternal balance of whole and part. This balance of whole and part is of the legacy of King David, and sits at the right hand of the Father, the Lord of the Old Testament. The balance of whole and part is the action of the nature of existence and draws all existence to it. Existence — Father, Being; acts by the balance of whole and part — Christ, the Word, the Son; and is motivated by love — the Holy Spirit. To sit at the right hand is to be the lead actor in the organization of the throne's occupant.

So the One may be found in the macropolis of David, where David's Lord sits at the right hand of the Lord, until the Lord makes the enemies of David a footstool for his feet.

Today's reading from the Second Book of Samuel, Chapter Seven, verses 1-5, 8-12, 14 and 16, is how King David realized he was living in a proper house, while the Ark of the Covenant, the gift of the presence of God, was housed in a tent. David expressed this to the prophet Nathan, who told him to go ahead and build a better "house for God". But that night Nathan became aware that God would raise up a house for David, as David had wanted to build a house for God. "Moreover the Lord declares to you, David, that the Lord will make you a house." "I will be a father to him, and he shall be a son to me. Your house and your kingdom shall be made sure forever before me; your throne, David, shall be established forever."

I believe David will be remembered as a leading founder of the thought of the Trinity, and the balance of whole and part.

Finally, to see this whole seating arrangement, if David can be seen to be sitting at the right hand of his Lord, and his Lord is sitting at the right hand of the Lord, then if this is the complete gathering, then David is sitting at the left hand of the Lord. This will confound many people, but this is the nature of wholism, and the truth of the completion of the seating arrangement.

The Fourth Sunday of Advent, December 18th, 2011

Verse 7

⁷Then Herod called the Magi secretly and found out from them the exact time the star had appeared.

Verse 7

⁷Then the head of the household called the daughters and asked when exactly the joy had appeared, ...

Verse 7 Discussion

Herod is hunting down this alternative to his authority, and using the Magi for his purposes. There is nothing the Magi can do about it, as the milk is spilled. They have unwittingly brought a threat onto the life of the one they wish to honour. It's as simple as that.

Now that Herod knows the time that the star has appeared, he will know the age of the infant and can narrow it down by the age of the infant.

Not everyone who expresses interest is sincere. There are many reasons to seek the infant Christ, or One, and not all of them are benevolent. Many people came to Judea looking for enrichment, but many were like the Romans and saw opportunity for wealth rather than spiritual enlightenment. But in the nature of the One, anyone who is not totally committed will fall away as the will of the One prevails. Another way of looking at it, is, there is only one One for each individual, and all else falls away as the will of that one One prevails. We are all called to fulfill our lives as the One intended, and this is unique for each one of us. This being, and furthering our knowledge of being, precipitating further love of this being, is ultimately beyond full knowing, and this leaves a constant opportunity for surprise growth. Any threat to this ultimate purpose will ultimately fall away.

Likewise, as with the Magi and King Herod, the One will prevail over the threat presented by the head of the household. The head of the household likewise sees the One as a threat to their authority, whether it is or not, and has a malicious interest in pursuing the One, so that it may be eliminated and no longer threaten their authority.

Where the Magi followed a star, the majestic daughters are following the joy as a guide to the presence of the One. This joy prevails over all else, and is easily pursued like a game of "getting warmer" - "getting colder". So when exactly the joy had appeared, would guide the head of the household as to what the circumstances were when the joy had appeared, and provide information as what may be eliminated so as to eliminate the joy. This could be a person, place or thing. It could be a lover, a prophet, a book, a drink or any other amusement, as long as it provides a joy that threatens the authority of the head of the household. Normally, this is just the head of the household being responsible for their charges, but if there is a limit to their responsibility — a point at which they are to relinquish their authority, then the head of the household is grasping at authority that they are not intended to exercise. Yet the One will prevail, as the infant Jesus was saved to gain maturity.

Thursday, December 22ⁿᵈ, 2011

Verse 8

⁸He sent them to Bethlehem and said, "Go and search carefully for the child. As soon as you find him, report to me, so that I too may go and worship him."

Verse 8

. . . . ⁸and sent them out to find the One, and report back so that he may be adored by all.

Verse 8 Discussion

There you have it - Herod claims he wants to worship the infant One, Jesus. There are many who claim they want to worship similarly to how one may worship, yet there is a vast array of how many people comprehend their faith, our faith. Yet by their fruit you will know them.

The body of Christ, the church, is a compendium of various understandings. What one may see clearly, can vary greatly from what another may understand thoroughly, and the church is made up of these many understandings. They all may be correct, each in their own context, but in an infinite context, each one's understanding comes up short. Combined, all these comprehensions make up humanity's comprehension of God, and may actually be complete, one day. Nevertheless, by their outcomes, one will know which comprehension is of God and which is opposed to God.

As well, there is a parable of Jesus, somewhere, where he illustrates that to uproot the weeds, or understandings opposed to God, would damage the understandings, or crop, that are of God. Better to let them alone, and when the day of judgment comes, the harvest, when all are taken up, let God sort out what is of Him and what is opposed to Him.

In light of this, I would propose, that as the world was created as good, and therefore all is good, there are not any weeds or understandings opposed to God, but rather conflict between differing limited understandings that are all of an unlimited God. There really is no one who willingly opposes God, by definition of God being an infinite unlimited purpose, but limited understandings of an unlimited God. Satan is real, however, and is manifested by one limited understanding trying to obliterate another limited understanding. This pursuit of destruction is where Satan comes into play, rather than anything being worthy of destruction, the act of pursuing destruction throws out the baby with the bath water. This is why one must forgive — to let God sort out what is of Him on the day of judgment, at the harvest, when the time comes to exercise judgment and act on that judgment. The good news is that there is likely no end to God's created world, as he set it into perpetual motion, but the bad news is that this day of judgment can come at any time, to any person, and happens frequently, as necessary.

Herod may have been correct in asserting that he must perpetuate his authority for the good of his people, but when he acted to obliterate what he considered opposition to his authority, he acted as Satan the opposer acts, and opposed another understanding of authority. Jesus himself said his kingdom is not of this world, so he had no intention of opposing or obliterating any state authority, whether Herod or Pontius Pilate, the Jewish state or the Roman Empire, but was rather, establishing an infinite kingdom, not a limited earthly kingdom. His kingdom would guide earthly kingdoms, as it has in all Christendom, rather than oppose and try to obliterate earthly kingdoms. Render unto God what is God's, and unto Caesar what is Caesar's. So Herod was limited, mistaken, in his opposition and attempt to obliterate what he saw as opposing him.

This is all too common, this perception of opposition to our best interests. As Joseph accepted a pregnant bride, one must not leap into action to correct what one's limited understanding perceives to be incorrect. One must endure and suffer the opposition to our existence and not oppose, so that one may see a common ground between one's understanding and the apparently opposing understanding.

So Herod was lying when he said he too wanted to worship the infant One, Jesus, just as the head of the household, in the animation text, claims that they too want to adore the infant One, the balance of whole and part, as witnessed to by the joy the daughters felt in communion. Lying — what is the problem with that? Well when one lies, the first lie they tell is to themselves, and that lie is that they will get away with it. Lying splits one's mind into two realities — their truth and the impression of truth they present to others. These two realities destroy the integrity of one's mind and consume valuable resources needlessly so as to beleaguer the liar and limit their own existence by limiting their integrity. "Blessed are the pure of heart, for they shall see God." Destroying your integrity by lying obstructs your comprehension and cuts one off from their lessened limited potential before the infinite. Once one has lied, they have lessened their ability to comprehend the unlimited and thereby cannot reconcile their limited understanding with another's differing limited understanding. They have truly challenged themselves before infinity and generally made things harder for themselves.

The recipient of the lie, however, maintains their integrity as they act truthfully in the world the infinite has presented to them. They continue on their way, oblivious to the falsehood they have accepted, but with their integrity, they are able to conceive that a falsehood has been perpetrated, as circumstances play out. This is apparent when the product of one becomes apparent, when the fruit of one's actions is obvious — by their fruit you will know them. Only the pure in heart, those with integrity of understanding, the solid construction of all they have encountered and experienced forming a grand world of their understanding, can withstand falsehoods perpetuated upon them.

Furthermore, looking to where this all leads, one becomes aware that their suffering by the falsehoods of others is really only a means by which the infinite purpose, God, forges one's character in the furnace of such trial, to purposes we can rarely imagine until the benefits of hindsight come. For example, the three failures of my youth, Povungnituk, electrician's apprentice, and structural drafting, all made me perfect to do electrical drafting and supervision for remote northern communities. I could never have imagined such an opportunity for myself, especially when each of the three failures were raw. And besides, the falsehoods perpetuated by others on one, become as plain as the nose on their lying faces, and never really have any detrimental effect on those living a life of balance of whole and part, following in the path of Jesus, the Christ, the anointed One, whether they be a woman or a man.

Solemn Blessing — New Year
May he give you integrity in the faith, endurance in hope, and perseverance in charity with holy patience to the end.

Amen

- New Year's Day, Solemnity of Mary, Mother of God, January 1ˢᵗ, 2012

Verse 9

⁹After they had heard the king, they went on their way, and the star they had seen **when it rose***** went ahead of them until it stopped over the place where the child was.

*** 9 1973, 1978, 1984 NIV copy that HJC was written from is ***in the east,*** also in verse 2.

Verse 9

⁹The three majesties went on their way when they had heard the head of the household, and the joy they knew in communion went ahead of them until it rested over the place of a child.

Verse 9 Discussion

The Wise Men, or kings from the east, or Magi, are foreign to Israel, but are searching for the child they have learned about in their own way, and want to offer him valuable gifts to honour him. They have become aware of his importance by a completely foreign method, but nevertheless want to make the journey to honour him, with their gifts. It just goes to show that whatever good there is locally, it may take a foreigner to recognize it. As well, seek and you will find, or, knock and the door will be opened. Who knows what the baby Jesus could have meant to these foreign Magi. They had the means at their disposal to make not only the journey, being welcomed by the Jewish head of state, but to offer substantial gifts as well. These foreigners had their own reason to honour the baby. One may never know from where one may receive acknowledgment.

It is the same for the One in the animation. It is known by the three majestic daughters, but who is to know the what or the why of their pursuit. Nevertheless, they pursue the One, led by the joy they knew in communion. More could be said about this particular instance.

So the joy led the daughters, as the star led the Wise Men, always ahead of them and calling them onward, until it comes to rest over the place of a/the child.

The star is a sign of something beyond the baby Jesus, acting in accord with his birth, just as the joy is beyond the One, and acts according to the One's occurrence. But the One is not the child, or the man who acts as a child, but rather the relationship of the child and the three pursuers. How's that for speaking plainly ? It cannot be more plain than that.

Jesus, however, is the One for all time, as he is a perfect, historical, geographical, sociological person balanced between whole and part, communion and agency, female and male, for all the world. But for us today, we may only witness to glimpses of the One, and may not ever in one's lifetime fully grasp the One, just as we may never in our lifetime fully comprehend Jesus. Generations will pass before the perfect balance may again exist in the form of a marriage. And this is the relationship of the One, which may rest on any partner, but nevertheless is the relationship with that partner, and not the partner themselves. The One, the divine infinite ultimate purpose, exists in the marriage relationship of two spouses.

This is not that complex, but many seem to stumble when they try to grasp it. It is like the right hand rule in physics. If the thumb of the right hand is extended, and the fingers allowed to curl naturally, then the direction the fingers point, around the direction of the thumb, is in a relationship to the direction of the thumb. The fingers may be pointing up or down or across the room, but their relationship with the thumb will always be the same. This is what the marriage relationship of the One is like — it doesn't matter what either spouse does, there is a relationship with the other spouse.

This idea of the One is built on the One and Many problem of philosophy. If their can be one of something, then how can their be many of something. Clay is one thing, but a piece of clay is another thing. Both are clay, but a piece of clay is different than clay. As well, if there is female then how can their be male. If everyone is the same, then how can we all be different individuals. Secondly, this one and many is manifested as female and male and is an opportunity to chart vast unfathomed areas of existence, since all knowledge has both a specific and a contextual aspect, as does all experience have both a specific and a contextual aspect.

The joy is found in this balance and union of whole and part, female and male, and acts like a beacon to all who encounter it. The joy of One is not limited to person to person relationships, but can exist in any other balance of whole and part. Take for example, the young man in a Ferrari! He can know a great deal of joy as long as his part of the car is in union with the whole of the road. But let this balance of whole and part deteriorate and for his part his car will fail to remain whole!

Furthermore, consider an adolescent, who is wondering which person they will kiss first. It doesn't seem to matter much who it is, but they still want to know who it will be! They are more in love with the idea of being in love, than actually being in love with any particular person.

This is why the animation text reads " . . . until it rested over the place of a child." The joy is felt by the majestic daughters before they even meet the man, who acts like a child, but it comes to rest upon him. This may be influenced by his acting like a child, which will be discussed further, below, but is not really any of his own doing, other than being open to the relationship offered by the majestic daughters. And this could very well be enough!

"Suffer the little children to come unto me, for of such is the kingdom of heaven," or something or other like that. The joy of the One is far more apparent in children or childlike attitudes, and that is what the kingdom of heaven is like, a lot of people with childlike attitudes of wonder, awe, and auugh, with their heart's on their sleeves. There is a lot of joy in childhood, in spite of children not being in any way in control of their circumstances.

Epiphany, Sunday, January 8th, 2012

Verse 10

¹⁰When they saw the star, they were overjoyed.

Verse 10

¹⁰When they felt the joy they saw stars.

Verse 10 Discussion

The Wise Men, or kings from the east, or Magi, when they saw the star, they were overjoyed, but the majestic daughters, when they felt the joy, they saw stars.

This is a phrase that isn't used much anymore, to see stars when one is overcome. It is an expression, like many expressions, that has come and gone out of popular use. This is often overlooked, how much our language rests on common phrases. But just look at the difficulty high school students have with reading Shakespeare. The phrases used in Shakespeare are definitely not common today, yet they remain very expressive to those who take the time to consider what these expressions could mean, as well as refer to the many guidebooks published on Shakespeare.

Our language relies heavily on repeated phrases, and when one changes these phrases, or creates new phrases, the audience is challenged to ascertain the meaning of such new phrases. So in reality, which is a phrase, we do not communicate with words but with phrases. And anyone who creates new phrases, has challenged their audience to understand them.

Taken further, the use of buzz words such as "popular morality", or "global economy", or "downsizing", or "stalemate", or "worst case scenario", or "clock ticking", or "lockout", or "diversifying", or "global demand", or "skyrocketing", or "underground economy", or "privatizing", or "high-tech", or "down turn", all express an idea more specific than the word or words alone mean. We do not communicate with words, but with phrases. "Now having said that, God knows what's going to happen over the next few months." - Rene Morissette, Toronto Star, Friday, January 13th, 2012. There's a sentence that is completely made up of phrases! To an audience 100 years before or after her writing, this sentence may not make any sense at all, to the casual reader!

So if we communicate with phrases, rather than words, are we really thinking about what we are communicating? I believe that we get hung up in common phrases and do not really think about what we are reading or what we are expressing. This animation writing requires that the audience think about what is being expressed, more than any popular entertainment demands. And then the natural extension is that the audience will think about the original Gospel text and what it is really saying.

> Jesus saves, Moses invests!
> Jesus saves! Moses shoots! He scooooorrrres!!

There are two plays on the use of an overused common religious phrase - "Jesus saves!". The problem is that when communication gets bogged down in overused phrases and expressions, it fails to communicate anything at all, as the audience fails to receive any new idea, and so throws the communication in the dumpster with all the other discarded messages. Buzz words are a waste of time, and an even worse waste of time than a challenging creation of new phrases. The only problem is that the new phrases, seeming unintelligible, are discarded along with the overused phrases. But at least there is the chance that some meaning may get across, as opposed to using the same old buzz words, where there is certainty that no message will get across.

All the "thee"s, "thou"s, and "shall"s of the King James Bible, do not merit their use as implying that a more important message is being communicated than the use of common words would imply. Christianity was spread in Greek, the common language of the people at the time, and not in the loftier languages of Latin or Hebrew! All this use of lofty language detracts from the practicality and obvious nature of the christian message, and I will not use lofty language to promote the marriage relationship. I will use parables, examples and other challenging forms of communication to bring the real message to the audience, rather than to exclude the audience from the message that marriage is the salvation of society, as well as society's greatest challenge.

Finally, if this message is so obvious, why do most people find it to be obscure? Well, where is your nose? Did you have to think about it — as to what I meant by that question? The most obvious can very easily be overlooked, and we need to be mindful of even the obvious, which we often overlook. Will you die? - of course! But are you spending all your waking hours aware of this? I think not. Have you incorporated this fact into your daily life? Perhaps you have a retirement plan, but what is your resurrection plan? This is real. Act like it.

Whether one is aware of it or not, they will die. Whether one is aware of it or not, their actions have a cumulative ultimate infinite goal. This is a fact. If one tosses popcorn in the movie theatre, this may be random but there will be popcorn to be swept up, and this is a fact. So what is your ultimate infinite goal? Are you only thinking about the next job, or are you thinking about your next death ? This self discussion is your religion, whether you believe it or not. Is this what you want ?

So don't talk to me about how a job is necessary when I am not allowed to do a good job by my employer and co-workers who are playing politics as they screw up even the simplest of tasks. I am not interested in your finite religion. Do what you want, and leave me to the death of my own choosing, if it be that. Don't talk to me about an education where I am to cheat the results all the way through to only end up in debt. I'll educate myself, thank you. Do what you want, and leave me to the death of my own choosing, if it be that.

This writing is passive and can easily be avoided, as can the animation. When one is ready to appreciate any of this, it will be here. My next death will be mitigated by this work, if only because I alone value it.

Sunday, January 15th, 2012

Verse 11

¹¹On coming to the house, they saw the child with his mother Mary, and they bowed down and worshiped him. Then they opened their treasures and presented him with gifts of gold, frankincense and myrrh.

Verse 11

¹¹On coming to the house they saw the One of their mothers' and they bowed to worship him. One opened his treasures and they received gifts of gold and fragrant flowers and perfumed soap.

Verse 11 Discussion

This is a long verse with a lot to it, so let's list what will be covered in this discussion. First of all, there is how the majestic daughters saw the One of their mothers', then how they worshiped him, and how One opened his treasures and they received the three gifts.

The One, the balance of whole and part, is the anointed one, or Christ, in our world today. It, or he, as it is referred to when apart and beyond us, lives in the communion of the people around us, as well as in each of us individually, and brings joy with his presence. So the One, is not particularly the man, but the relationship that exists between the friends, of whom the man is one. The One, the joy, is present among the friends including the man, but also has been a part of the women's lives before, which causes them to recognize it when they are with the man. Specifically, the women have experienced this joy in the presence of their parents, including their mothers, so that is why they find there, the One of their mothers. The majestic daughters are following in the path of their mothers.

The joy has been present to all of us, and we recognize it when we encounter it. We pursue it. It is the joy of the union of whole and part, and not only exists in romantic relationships, but beyond as well, to include all of existence. But romantic relationships, as a balance of whole and part, female and male, have the greatest potential for bringing the One to the world, and the joy with it.

This pursuit entails leaving behind other interests for the sake of the pursuit of the joy. We bend to the pursuit. We turn away from other interests to focus on the joy of the One. We bow and worship this anointed union of whole and part, female and male. We seek it out and accept what it offers.

Worship — what is it really? Well, first of all, we all worship, whether we admit it or not. The question becomes, instead of why worship this or that, but rather the identification of what we already worship. What are we willing to sacrifice our sense of self and self respect to an object of worship to allow it to flourish. It has been claimed that many people worship money, and this is so, since most people will do things for pay that they would not do otherwise. Picking up garbage in the street is one example. Unless one is paid, they will not act in the community interest by picking up garbage from public places. There can be more to it then the purpose of getting money, but the fact remains that being paid will influence one to act beyond their self interest. Worship is the same, this deference of self interest to a higher interest. Nevertheless, being paid makes the service to be in the person's self interest, as the pay will serve the person's self interest when they spend it. Self interest is not the problem, but the choice of which larger purpose is in a person's self interest. This is where your worship is — the choice of a larger purpose that is in your self interest enough to allow you to defer your self interest to it.

Many people despair that the larger purpose they defer to will not redeem them, and this is what evangelists appeal to — that there is a larger purpose that will redeem one and all, and then the evangelists go on to explain this larger purpose to anyone with an ear.

Work and pay is just one example of this worshiping, amongst many others such as the success of one's children, the honour of one's parents, the honour of one's self, the power one has over others, the respect the community pays to one, and on and on.

But just as one worships the Father, the Son and the Holy Spirit, there are other guides in one's worship, such as a Sunday school teacher, a parent, a respected friend, a minister, a public official or perhaps a teacher. Likewise, a spouse can and should be a very prominent guide in one's worship of their God, as Christianity points to a balance of whole and part today as well as throughout history. I assert that one's spouse is above all humanity in deserving one's worship and service, and this, I believe, is in accordance with the late Pope John Paul II's ***Theology of the Body***.

Then One will open their treasures and the participants will receive gifts. The gifts that the Wise Men, or Magi, gave the baby Jesus had significance. Gold was for kings, frank-incense was for the sacred, and myrrh was a balm, not a bomb but a balm, for the dead. This signified the role Jesus was to play, as king, sacred to all, conquering death by dieing. This was the work Jesus had to do, beyond his role as a teacher, he had concrete things to accomplish.

Having accomplished them, Jesus sends us out on the same path, but not to die as he did, on a cross two thousand years ago, but to die to ourselves for the greater good of us as well as ourselves. Where is this greater good? I profess that an infinite understanding held by a finite individual is necessary for any greater good, and this infinite understanding can only be had by finite individuals who participate in marriage, the perfectable union of whole and part, female and male. This endeavour will require the death of oneself many times over before much may be accomplished. Yet each death will be swallowed up in the new, more infinite life that follows. The gifts of the One signify this.

The gifts of the One, from its' treasures, are gold, fragrant flowers, and perfumed soap. They signify the kingship of the balance of whole and part, female and male in the One relationship, the sacredness of such a relationship, and the cleansing of the world in just such a relationship, washing away the filth of the old world in preparation for the new life accomplished.

Sunday, January 22nd, 2012

Verse 12

¹²And having been warned in a dream not to go back to Herod, they returned to their country by another route.

Verse 12

¹²And being warmed in a dream they resode by another way.

Verse 12 Discussion

Where the Magi, or Wise Men, were warned in a dream, and therefore proceeded to avoid something, specifically what Herod might do, the three majestic daughters are warmed in a dream, and drawn toward a course of action, rather than seeking to avoid something. What they were drawn to was a different course from the one they were pursuing, and thereby lived differently than before. The Magi, on the other hand, simply chose a different route by which to return to their country. The majestic daughters have chosen a different way to live their lives.

"Return" versus "reside", which in the past tense, rather than "resided" I made up the word "resode" as the past tense to "reside". The Magi are traveling, returning to their home country, but the majestic daughters are home, where they reside, and living differently, by a different way. Surely the Magi are transformed by their experience, but the majestic daughters are far more transformed by their experience.

The majestic daughter on the left, is the married one, and she has chosen to repent, and try to address her marriage in a new, better way, and avoid any of the pitfalls she is already aware of, having fallen into them in the past. She holds onto her previous course, but adjusts it to avoid that which she has already become aware. She seeks the One in her marriage.

The majestic daughter on the right, the married elder, has chosen rebirth, as she maintains her course, through failure, and onto a new life, shepherding a new flock. For her, nothing has caused her to reconsider anything about her choices, and rather, she has met with failure and been transformed by circumstances around her, into a new kind of elder. She has been true to the end. She has held fast to her faith and inherent convictions, and witnessed the world around her change and open up to new opportunities, in a new world, with a new, more infinite understanding. She seeks the One in her ministry, as well as her marriage.

The majestic daughter in the middle, considers whether to choose repentance or rebirth. We do not know what her choice is or will be, but we know she has been presented with the choice. She seeks the One in her relationships but whether she does so by repenting, turning back and trying again, or rather by rebirth, holding fast to her convictions and faith regardless of the repercussions, we do not know.

This is the choice we are all faced with when our faith is challenged — do we change ourselves and maintain the course, or do we stand firm in our convictions, weathering the storm through to a new world, not bending to the influences around us but instead being swept up and whisked away in the resulting changes around us. This is death and rebirth, as opposed to repentance, this standing firm and being swept away.

Repentance is older than rebirth, traditionally, as John the Baptist was baptizing with water for repentance before Pentecost, the coming of the Holy Spirit. The two are different. This is stated clearly by John the Baptist himself, in Matthew chapter three, verse eleven:

> [11] "I baptize you with[b] water for repentance. But after me comes one who is more powerful than I, whose sandals I am not worthy to carry. He will baptize you with[c] the Holy Spirit and fire.
>
> [b] Or *in*
> [c] Or *in*
>
> Matthew 3 : 11 New International Version

Repentance is like a training ground for rebirth. Unless one is certain that they are correct, they would rather try to be more correct, than proceed in error. But once one is sure they are correct, the correct choice is rebirth, yet one may avoid death and rebirth at their own peril.

Although repentance is part of christianity, rebirth is its main teaching, as Jesus died on the cross and was reborn to new life. No christian can avoid rebirth any more than anyone can avoid death.

Consider the first martyr, Stephen, who was stoned as Saul watched over the coats of the crowd that stoned him. Stephen was full of the Holy Spirit —

> "But filled with the Holy Spirit, he gazed into heaven and saw the glory of God and Jesus standing at the right hand of God."
> *Acts 7, verse 55*
> *New Revised Standard Version.*

In the next verse he is actually quoted as saying so. Stephen stood firm to the end, and was accompanied by God at his end. He died. What was beyond death for him we do not know. This death was without rebirth in this world.

But there are many ends in this life, that go on to becoming beginnings as well as ends, and may foreshadow a beginning beyond one's end in this earthly life. Who's to know? Nevertheless, we die to one life and begin another, as any child dies to childish behaviour and becomes an adult. It is the perseverance in spite of the consequences that may bring new opportunities, where other choices are sure to maintain the current situation. Look at Stephen Biko, of South Africa. His death resounded around the world and caused people to act differently than they would have otherwise.

Yet marriage offers new life, to those that persevere, and this is most pregnant with opportunity for those who persevere in spite of the consequences. If one is to die, let it be for marriage, as all of christianity points to the maintenance of marriage, and regardless of traditional religion, this union of male and female makes practical sense, that both genders are destined to participate in growth and improvement.

So if you are to repent, repent toward marriage; if you are to die, die for marriage; and if you are reborn, it is likely due to your marriage, not only of male and female, but of part and whole. And this view of the world allows for the greatest joy I have ever known.

Sunday, January 29th, 2012

Verse 13

The Escape to Egypt

¹³When they had gone, an angel of the Lord appeared to Joseph in a dream. "Get up," he said, "take the child and his mother and escape to Egypt. Stay there until I tell you, for Herod is going to search for the child to kill him."

Verse 13

The Escape to Civilization

¹³When they had gone, an angel of the Lord appeared before father and said "Get One up, take mother and escape into civilization, for the head of the household is going to search for the infant One to kill him."

Verse 13 Discussion

Joseph had a dream, and acted upon it. In his dream, he saw and heard an angel tell him to escape with his family to Egypt, because the Jewish head of state, Herod, whom the Wise Men had visited, was going to search for the child to kill him. In fact, Herod didn't search for the child, as far as we know, but instead had every child two years and under, in the region of Bethlehem killed. So something as simple as acting on a dream had serious consequences, or rather, not acting on the message of a dream would have had disastrous consequences.

But why go to Egypt? Egypt at the time was very civilized and prosperous. Since the time of Jacob and Joseph, with his coat of many colours, Egypt had been the bread basket of the middle east, with the cultivation irrigated by the Nile. During Jesus era, Egypt was a prosperous civilization. Sure they had pagan gods, but they were civilized and there was order. This is what civilization is — order. In Canada, we defer to the Crown, and the Crown keeps order. We used to be called the Dominion of Canada, harkening to the phrase "God's Dominion". As far as infinite consensus goes, though, it has nothing to do with order. The biggest stick is the Crown, and its will will be done. This has nothing to do with gods, God or infinity. There is only arbitrary rulings, which patch up conflicts without resolving them, that are enforced by the bigger stick.

Anyone who is injured, will suffer their injury, and the bigger stick cannot make that better, only appease dissension with a ruling. It is like the parable statement " If you who are evil, know to give your children good things, than so much so will God give you good things." The Crown, or bigger stick, may or may not be good, but it is not God, and will only appease dissension to maintain order — its order, the Crown's order, and further their control of that order. This is civilization — the maintenance of a finite order, by whatever means, on an infinite creation. There is much lacking between this finite order and infinite creation, but there is and will be order.

Judea on the other hand, was governed more so by God, and everyone's interpretation of God, which made it akin to the wild west, as it is to this day. Rebellions and submission cycled constantly. There was a lack of order. There was God, and religion, but there was still no infinite consensus, so there was not order. The Romans had to constantly exercise their power through the use of force to impose order, just as it is today in Palestine. Just as the natives of North America, failed to maintain an infinite consensus, and thereby appeared uncivilized, without order, Judea was not civilized, or at least not as civilized as Egypt.

So Joseph took his family to the civilized region of Egypt, where no arbitrary executions were allowed, because it was civilized and there was order to keep and maintain, even if it was away from the Temple and the heart of Judaism, the faith of Jesus' youth.

In the animation text, the head of the household, with their authority being challenged by this new infant One, the relationship between a female and a male, seeks to kill it. One can easily imagine the constant barrage of criticism, arbitrary rulings and condemnation the One relationship suffered at the hands of this challenged head of the household. Just as Joseph could not endure the infanticide and fled, the One relationship must escape, even if they are to part from their God — their partner. Otherwise the destruction of the One is certain.

Furthermore, this departing, is like a martyrdom, that although a serious defeat, allows the martyred One to grow in the awareness of the community in spite of its end. It is not the end of the One, but the beginning of the sacred life of the One. Jesus would have to do something to honour all those who died just because he was born. This would sober up even Jesus! And whether or not the One in the animation remains the relationship between the two specific people at the time, or becomes a One relationship between two different people, the One survives. The escape honours and preserves the One for all time.

I omitted the "stay there until I tell you" part from the animation text, and that was likely just an oversight, but what was written is what was written. I suppose it didn't speak to me, but looking back now, I would suggest that there is no sign as to when the One relationship may reunite, other than when directed by the Holy Spirit, if they reunite at all.

I also omitted the taking of the child or the infant One with them, which again was likely an oversight, but perhaps that did not speak to me. Nevertheless, the One survives as the father and mother survive.

Finally, in any One relationship, a balance of female and male, whole and part, the participants take any of the three roles of parent, friend and child, and may be reciprocated by the partner taking any of the three roles. If one spouse acts like a parent the other may respond by any role of child, adult or parent, and their need not be any conflict no matter what role the response takes. The same is so for the roles of child and adult; the other spouse may respond in the role once again, of parent, adult or child.

In the animation text, father is given the message, and he takes mother. Both spouses are acting like parents, with knowledgeable care, understanding and nurturing of the infant One, the relationship.

So even though the One was not stated as being taken, it exists just as Jesus is present to each and all of us today. And though no one is waiting to be told by an angel in a dream to return from civilization, the One awaits its return to the participants in any relationship with the potential of balancing whole and part, female and male.

Sunday, February 5th, 2012

Verse 14

¹⁴So he got up, took the child and his mother during the night and left for Egypt, ...

Verse 14

¹⁴So they got up, took the One during the night and left for civilization, ...

Verse 14 Discussion

Joseph took the initiative, and took the child and his mother, during the night and left for Egypt. In the animation text, however, both parents got up and took the infant One, and left for civilization. Both parents acted jointly, rather than one leading the other. It was a mutual decision. The infant One must be protected, and civilization is its only chance. The persecution of the One was too great for the juvenile being to overcome. It could be argued that if Jesus was divine, he could have saved himself, but such was not the case. Divinity does not overcome evil by exerting its power or authority, but by forgiveness. God makes the sun to shine on the evil and the good.

In the grand scheme of things, the infant Jesus, and the One, are protected by divine providence, just not in a magical way. Too many people seek magical solutions to their suffering, rather than participating in God's providence by seeing the opportunities he offers and taking him up on them. It is like the joke Father Paul, at St. Christopher's in Clarkson told at least once: A person prayed to God everyday in church for years - "God . . . . . please let me win the lottery!" This went on most of their lifetime. Then one day, as this person was losing their faith, they were once more, for probably the last time, praying - "God . . . . . please let me win the lottery!" Just then, the heavens opened before them! A bright light shone down, and a voice was heard - "Help me out . . . . buy a ticket!"

Another one is a little dryer, but goes something like this. A survivor was lost at sea in a lifeboat. They prayed desperately for God to save them. Then one day a ship arrived and spotted them. They launched a rescue craft and just as they were approaching the lifeboat, they called out "Can we help you?" The survivor replied "I'm O.K., God will save me!"

So if God makes the sun to shine on the evil and the good, and forgiveness is how to combat the opposer, Satan, then what is there for one who is suffering? Prayer, a constant sorting out of one's needs, categorizing and prioritizing and goal setting and planning and assessing and reassessing, including determined action, will resolve our situations so that we may live in JOY! We will all die, and few are so bold as to pray to escape death, even if I have, yet we may die in JOY! If we believe in the resurrection, as we claim to, including the resurrection of the body, as stated in both the Nicene and the Apostle's Creeds, then what is death but a new beginning. Pray to be faithful in the face of death, and rely on the promise of the resurrection.

So the taking of the infant One into civilization is not its end, but a new beginning.

In the animation, the man is arrested in front of the home of a majestic daughter, as she looks on with her family. How is this escaping? Well the persecution was so intense that the infant One would not survive unless he escaped. The parents co-operated in protecting the integrity of the infant One, yet the relationship seemed to end, just as Jesus was taken to Egypt, seemingly never to come back. But what of the One? It continues in the hearts and minds of the spouses, regardless of the presence of the other spouse, and becomes a sacred ideal, to precipitate once again, as it did with the majestic daughters in communion, on another suitable relationship, and guide that new relationship through any persecutions it may encounter, armed with the knowledge of past persecutions. Joseph did not return from Egypt with his holy family until Herod had died. Likewise, the One will not appear again until the persecutions it has suffered are no longer a threat, presumably when the head of the household has changed, one way or another, as this animation plays out.

Think of what would have happened if the man wasn't arrested, and the life of the One was not cut short. The persecutions would have continued, and whittled away any chance the One may have had of becoming mature. At the hands of the head of the household, the One would have been crippled and corrupted, as it dodged and bent itself out of shape to try to maintain its integrity amongst the false accusations and outrageous demands of the head of the household.

Joseph did not make any claim against King Herod, in any court. He went away and came back. Likewise, if the man is charged, he is guilty, rather than make a case against the head of the household. Let the blame rest on those making the accusations. If being a criminal was good enough for Christ, Peter and Paul, then it is good enough for us. Civilization, once again, is not interested in any infinite resolution, just order, and anything that threatens the good order of society, whether for the better or the worse, will not be tolerated.

Nevertheless, civilization's imposition of order has saved the One, even if only as an ideal, to be reborn anew at a later time, in another place, with who knows being the spouses.

Sunday, February 12th, 2012

Verse 15

. . . . ¹⁵where he stayed until the death of Herod. And so was fulfilled what the Lord had said through the prophet: "Out of Egypt I called my son."ᶜ

   ᶜ   **15** Hosea 11:1

Verse 15

. . . . ¹⁵where they stayed until the next end of the household. But the prophet foretold:

"But the more they (called Israel),
the (further they went from them.)"ᵇ

   ᵇ **15** Hosea 11 : 2

Verse 15 Discussion

The entire quote, from Hosea, is as follows -

11   *God's Love for Israel*
¹"When Israel was a child, I loved him,
  and out of Egypt I called my son.
²But the more they were called,
  the more they went away from me.ᵃ
They sacrificed to the Baals
  and they burned incense to images.
³It was I who taught Ephraim to walk,
  taking them by the arms;
but they did not realize
  it was I who healed them.
⁴I led them with cords of human kindness,
  with ties of love.
To them I was like one who lifts
  a little child to the cheek,
  and I bent down to feed them.
    ᵃ **2** Septuagint; Hebrew ***them***
   Hosea 11 : 1 – 4 *New International Version*

One has to keep in mind, that each spouse in a sacred One relationship, ministers to the other spouse just as that spouse ministers to them. So in the animation text, even though each spouse calls to the other, the further apart they become. Taking the footnotes in the above full quote into consideration, the second verse would read "But the more they were called, the more they went away from them." Once the relationship is severed, the participants must stabilize themselves since the loss of the balance of the relationship has put each of them far out of balance, and each must recover from the loss. The severance has taken hold, and neither spouse can bridge the gap that has opened up between them. This is the nature of sacred One relationships, that they may be volatile if not managed, nurtured, allowed and honoured. Eventually, as we are all aware of romantic relationships, the balance is lost and the relationship topples catastrophically. We all know this to be true.

So what hope is their for romantic relationships, balancing whole and part, whether in full romance or just any balance of whole and part, such as societies, enterprises or any other endeavour? The answer comes from a marginalized people, living in third world conditions, right here in Canada. The answer is to roll, like a kayaker, using the momentum that topples the craft by adding to it to bring the craft right around and back into an upright position. What does this mean, theologically or philosophically?

Well, if forgiveness is how to deal with evil, sin, and opposition from Satan the opposer, then allowing this toppling force, and even adding to it, will bring the endeavour back up into a new upright life. This is death and rebirth. This is why it is so essential to understand this truth of life that is everywhere around us — this death and rebirth. If one opposes the toppling force, one will end up stuck in their toppled position, and unable to recover to an upright position, as the inverted position is just as stable as the upright position, if not even more stable, but without the advantages of being upright. This may be why many people have more faith in failure and evil than in success and upright behaviour — the inverted position is ultimately the most stable.

Yet continuing with the kayak roll analogy, if the roll fails, there is the option of a wet exit, so even ultimate failure need not be final.

I am intrigued by the boldness of the original quote in this verse from the Gospel of Matthew. The writer of Hosea, is talking about the exodus of the Hebrews from Egypt, so to use this quote to strengthen the case for Jesus being the Messiah, as Jesus came out of Egypt, seems to me to be a bit of a stretch. That's poetic license for you! My stretches are not so outlandish after all.

The next end of the household, is the opportunity for the return of the One. The household need not be destroyed, but it will come to an end, and be reborn to a new life and awareness, that may allow for the sacred One, by then more mature, to alight once again on a romantic relationship of the majestic daughter. By then, the daughter may find the head of the household more willing to entertain the possibility of an addition to the inner circle that can benefit all, rather than see the interest the majestic daughter has in maintaining a sacred One relationship as a threat to the authority of the head of the household. This would be just as Herod's successor did not see a magical threat to their authority in the prophesied juvenile Jesus.

We all know what happens in society today, when a relationship ends. There is the political sides that must be consolidated and maintained. This means former acquaintances can no longer entertain their relationship. Two camps precipitate from a common society and no link between the two camps is tolerated, although the existence of the other camp may be tolerated. Individuals may act on their own, and strengthen their acquaintance with a member of the other camp, but they do this only if their integrity allows this and generally their own camp may see this behaviour as benign.

So the faithbook friends become blocked, as communication channels are closed, to allow the healing of each spouse to take place.

But what of the roll? If each spouse, as in a two person kayak, with two cockpits, acts cooperatively, the relationship can survive this death to be reborn again, if they allow the death to occur and even encourage it, knowing that it leads to new life. This could have happened between the two original spouses, as each pays attention and watches for signs and text messages that indicate the actions of the lost spouse to them. Each can prepare a place for the lost spouse in their life, looking to their eventual return.

But when they fail to return, a wet exit is necessary, which means a lot of trouble undoing the advantages of being in the relationship, swimming through their own circumstances, probably to find dry land, to prepare to be on their way again.

Societies must accept their death and rebirth, and even encourage the forces that topple them, so as to emerge upright in the new day. This has happened with the transformation of the population from an agricultural workforce to a manufacturing workforce. Today our leaders must recognize new opportunities that the workforce may take up, such as clean energy, and push in that direction, encouraging the death of the fossil fuel economy and the birth of renewable resources, to occupy the labours of society's members, keeping in mind that people need to work, regardless of the distribution of wealth.

Family Day, Monday, February 20th, 2012

Verse 16

¹⁶When Herod realized that he had been outwitted by the Magi, he was furious, and he gave orders to kill all the boys in Bethlehem and its vicinity who were two years old and under, in accordance with the time he had learned from the Magi.

Verse 16

¹⁶When the household realized they had been outwitted by the majestic daughters, they were furious and it was commanded that all knew Ones in the macropolis of David be destroyed.

Verse 16 Discussion

When the rage hits, there is not any reasoning that can be done by others with the person in the rage. The situation is lost. So then those in the company of the person in a rage can not do anything other than isolate the person in the rage. Herod, being in control of his kingdom despite his rage, issued orders that were carried out, but failed to accomplish the purpose he had for those orders, as the infant Jesus escaped with his parents to Egypt.

Likewise, the head of the household finds them self in a rage when they realize that the majestic daughters have outwitted them, and the infant One has escaped unharmed, as it survives without being tainted as being anything other than infinitely good. Sure the sacred infant relationship no longer exists within the household, but it exists in the awareness of the majestic daughters and is still sacred and untarnished. It is still an ideal in the minds of the majestic daughters, as the household has failed to discredit sacred One relationships and their balance of whole and part. The infant sacred One relationship remains to rule all else, and is worshiped and glorified. The head of the household has failed to end the life of the infant One sacred relationship by discrediting it.

So in the animation text, "it was commanded that all knew Ones in the macropolis of David be destroyed." "Knew" is spelled with a "k", as in "knowledge" as well as being novel. The "knew" ideas that came forth from the macropolis of David are commanded by the head of the household to be destroyed, as Herod commanded all the new boys, in the city of David, under two years of age, be destroyed. But how does one destroy an idea? In this "information age" it is very hard to destroy an idea once it has taken hold. Communism knows all about that. So does South Africa — it knows all about that as well!

The attack on the knew Ones in the macropolis of David, is lame, being pathetic at best, and fails to achieve any purpose. It is like throwing stones at a tank, or using a slingshot against artillery. The attackers can try to discredit and mock the ideal of the sacred One relationship, but it has been established and will prevail. Likely there will be bullying and mockery and slander, but it will fail to discredit the potential of a sacred One relationship, balancing whole and part, and rendering great Joy to the spouses.

This is not a radical idea at all. Even in the chaos of the novel **The Hitchhiker's Guide to the Galaxy** where the earth is destroyed at the beginning of the story, just to make way for an interstellar highway, the protagonist is engaged in a sacred One relationship with a woman who has rejected him for a two headed alien, if only because he is President of the Universe, but even then only because he can provide her with a knife that makes toast as it slices. She knows such a relationship is unfruitful and entertains the possibility of something better. This longing for the Joy of a sacred One relationship is universal. This idea that there can be more in a relationship is universal.   !

But how does one go about improving on one's sacred One relationship? Many people claim it is the fault of the other spouse, and so spend their time trying to trade up, and don't realize that there are fundamental differences between the sexes that will never change, but can be harnessed in such a way as to provide the great Joy everyone longs for.

And regardless of romantic relationships, the Joy is prevalent in any balance of whole and part, such as a sports car on a winding mountain road, or a thoughtful and unexpected gift. A dance can bring the Joy of a balance of whole and part, just as any other art form, balancing whole and part, can bring wonder, awe and Joy. Being at one with the universe can be a source of Joy, yet ultimately being at one with the universe is essentially another balance of whole and part.

So "the One who has been born above all" was found in the macropolis of David, after feeling his Joy in communion, yet was attacked by the head of the household only to escape into civilization. That's about it altogether.

But furthermore, any grasping at infinite good, rather than letting it just come in its own time, is basically what sin is, and leads to the loss of what was sought. A spouse will resent any attempt by their spouse to take from them that which is not offered. And the other spouse will resent the holding back of something, rather than offering it as one offers all of themselves in a sacred One relationship.

And condemnation is condemned. One must accept what is offered, and if insufficient, be patient and endure, rather than throw the baby out with the bathwater to only find themselves in a relationship with a different person but the same problems as the previous relationship.

These are the ideas taught by the sacred One relationship that the majestic daughters have seen escape from the persecution by the head of the household. They are not unlike the teachings of the fulfilled Jesus, as the balance of whole and part is present fully in Jesus.

Yet the relationship has ended, as the Magi left for their homeland, and the sacred One has left for civilization. Understanding does not relieve the anguish of the loss, yet the One survives to live another day, in another relationship or even a new relationship with an old spouse. Who knows what the future may hold. The key is to pay attention, and be aware of the present, fully understanding the past, as the new kingdom of heaven may come as a thief in the night, when one least expects anything to occur, if I may mix a few metaphors.

Monday, February 27th, 2012

Verse 17

[17] Then what was said through the prophet Jeremiah was fulfilled: .. ...

Verse 17

[17] Then what was said through the prophet Jeremiah was fulfilled: . . . . . .

Verse 17 Discussion

Quoting the Bible is probably liberally overdone, and deserves a discussion of its own. As well as other quotes in other episodes of **HESUS JOY CHRIST**, below are the three quotes in this episode being discussed — *Matthew's Two*.

Verse 6
([6]"But you, Bethlehem, in the Land of Judea,
are by no means least among the rulers of Judah;
for out of you will come a ruler
who will be the shepherd of my people Israel.'[b])

[b] 6 Micah 5 : 2

Verse 6
([6]"The Lord said to my Lord:
"Sit at my right hand
until I make your enemies
a footstool for your feet " ' [a])

[a] 6 Matthew 22 : 44 ; Luke 20 : 42-43 ; Psalm 110 : 1

Verse 15
......¹⁵where he stayed until the death of Herod. And so was fulfilled what the Lord had said through the prophet: "Out of Egypt I called my son." ᵈ

ᵈ **15** Hosea 11 : 1

Verse 15
. . . . . . ¹⁵where they stayed until the next end of the household. But the prophet foretold:
(" But the more they called Israel,
the further they went from them . " ᵇ)

ᵇ **15** Hosea 11 : 2

Verse 18
¹⁸"A voice is heard in Ramah,
weeping and great mourning,
Rachel weeping for her children
and refusing to be comforted,
Because they are no more."ᵃ

ᵃ **18** Jeremiah 31 : 15

Verse 18
¹⁸" Restrain your voice from weeping
and your eyes from tears,
for your work will be rewarded . " ᵉ

ᵉ **18** Jeremiah 31 : 16

The first quote, taken from the Bible, is from Micah Chapter five, verse two. In its place I have quoted Matthew, which is quoting Psalms, which Luke quotes as well.

But the other two quotes, as you may have noticed, in the animation text of this episode, have been substituted with the verse that immediately follows the original quote — Hosea 11:1 is substituted with Hosea 11:2 ; and Jeremiah 31:15 is substituted with Jeremiah 31:16 !! This occurs in **Matthew's Three Fold** as well — this substitution of the following verse when writing the animation text.

What is the purpose of quoting the Bible ? Well, just as in any quote, the idea is to support the claim being made. But in quoting the Bible, people try to support their idea, but furthermore, they seek to magically reinforce the divinity of the subject being discussed by showing it to be a fulfilled prophecy.

This is the purpose of the Bible quote of Hosea. The quote implies that the writer was foretelling the presence, or rather, the emergence of Jesus from Egypt. My opinion is that it is a lame attempt to show that Jesus was the one that the prophecies foretold.

The quote of Jeremiah, as well, fails to substantially support the argument that Jesus is the one that was foretold by the prophets. There are far better, and wider ranging, arguments that Jesus was and is the promised Messiah.

These quotes show that taking a quote out of context can support pretty much anything. It is understood, generally, that one should support their argument with references, but I could easily take issue with this. The entirety of **HESUS JOY CHRIST** uses the Gospel of Matthew to support the case for marriage, and that marriage is divine. But such a grand argument, that marriage is divine, cannot draw support from quotes taken here and there. Rather, the entirety of the Old and New Testaments must be understood before one may see their point being marriage, the balance of whole and part.

So just as the Old Testament points to, and is fulfilled in, the New Testament, the sacred faith of the Hebrews that Christianity builds on, points to and is fulfilled in the union of marriage, and any other balance of whole and part.

This is like a paper I wrote in university for my Natural Man, social science course. The topic was Darwin's Origin of Species, better known as Evolution. I essentially used a book called ***The Geometry of Meaning***, by Arthur M. Young, to outline where Evolution fits in, as well as where Creation, as opposite Evolution, fits in, and how the two relate. The teaching assistant wanted to know more about the book I was referring to when I had lifted most of the ideas in the paper I wrote, pretty much right out of that book. It got to the point that I actually had to tell the teaching assistant to go, get the book, and read it. The simple idea of how the two opposing ideas relate required a thorough understanding of the geometry of meaning.

So get going, read the Bible, consider it, and take up your personal balance of whole and part, whether it leads you to marriage or not.

Monday, March 5th, 2012

Verse 18

> ¹⁸"A voice is heard in Ramah,
> weeping and great mourning,
> Rachel weeping for her children
> and refusing to be comforted,
> because they are no more."^d

^d **18** Jeremiah 31:15

Verse 18

> ¹⁸ "Restrain your voice from weeping
> and your eyes from tears,
> for your work will be rewarded."^e

^e **18** Jeremiah 31:16

Verse 18 Discussion

This specific incidence of the infant One relationship is no more, as the boys under the age of two, in Bethlehem, are no more. Jesus, and the infant One, have escaped to live on, but the cost is high, as other children have been executed.

But the prophet goes on to say, in the very next verse, that they should restrain from weeping and tears for their work will be rewarded. What is their work? What are they working on, after such a great loss? The answer is whatever they are working on!

In the animation, the image is of a Sunday School class lead by the majestic daughter. The children are eager and engaged in the lesson. This is what the majestic daughter was doing and is still doing. This is her work, and it will be rewarded. She is not compelled to engage in this work, but does it willingly, to give of herself to others. She is devoted to this work, as it is her way of expressing her faith — a faith that she wants to share and a faith that led her to the sacred One relationship. In presenting herself entirely to the children, she presents her faith, under the guidance of the curriculum, and this faith includes her adoration of the sacred One relationship. She is not preaching her personal faith, outside of the curriculum, but by presenting herself her example shines and gives glory to the faith she professes, a faith encountering the One sacred relationship, that lives on in her heart, to one day manifest itself once again.

In Matthew, chapter twenty-four, Jesus speaks of the end of the age. This is also understood as the Second Coming of Christ. In the animation, **Matthew's Two Four**, many statements, paraphrasing the Gospel text, are made about the end time, which is both the end of this age and the beginning of the next age. The important thing is to be ready, when everything of this age is failing, to welcome the coming of the next age. In the same way, the sacred One relationship will return to a new heaven and a new earth, and likely with different players, but not necessarily different players. The trick is to endure the end of this age and welcome the new age with the same players. This is death and rebirth, and this is a significant part of the sacred One relationship. Jesus did not abandon his followers once he rose from the dead, but rather left so as to make room for them to grow in faith and responsibility, and to take on his mission for themselves. This mission is not just nice sentiments, but existential reality, more real than anything, including death, which we are all headed for, whether we maintain an awareness of death or not.

So as the animation plays out, look for the second coming of the sacred One relationship. Just as surely as Jesus returned to Israel, the sacred One relationship will manifest itself again. This is not radical at all. We all have died to one relationship to only find ourselves in another relationship. It is not a question of if the sacred One relationship will arrive again, but when and where it will arrive. We are to watch and stay awake so as to be ready to welcome it, like the birth of a child, when we may least expect it, and welcome it for it will need to be honoured, nurtured and cared for. This awareness is maintained by our work, and our work will be rewarded.

If, on the other hand, we weep and mourn the loss endlessly, we will fail to see the opportunities, when they occur, to welcome the sacred One relationship once more! I have witnessed this many times. Especially in arguments, when one is being berated by another, a glimmer of a resolution will appear in the endless beration, but the berated will fail to take up the resolution and speak up, since they are wallowing so much in the fact that they are being berated!

Another example is this animation itself! When I became unable to work due to reasons beyond my control, I could have wallowed in self pity and repeatedly failed at attempts at employment, which would all fail for the same reasons that were beyond my control. I paused, looked around, and all circumstances were supporting my pursuit of this animation and other artwork. This support has been maintained, surprisingly, for over three years, and has resulted in five episodes of animation and over forty-thousand words of discussion written.

If one professes an omnipotent, almighty, benevolent, merciful and loving God, one should exercise a little faith and look for the opportunities that are presented by him, to take them up and live on in Joy and love! Many are surprised to realize that the Creeds profess the resurrection of the body! This means our bodies will be resurrected! This is what the church professes in the creeds! Furthermore, we seem to have lost sight that God wants to live with us eternally on earth! We pray, in the Lord's Prayer, "your kingdom come, your will be done;

on earth, as it is in heaven"! We are not intended to go to heaven, but live in heaven on earth!

This is the power of God, that we could live forever with him on earth, if we could only see the opportunity of the sacred One relationship and work at such a relationship to harvest the potential of the understanding it freely provides.

Sunday, March 11th, 2012

Verse 19

The Return to Nazareth

¹⁹After Herod died, an angel of the Lord appeared in a dream to Joseph in Egypt ......

Verse 19

The Return to Nativity

¹⁹After the head was reborn, an angel appeared before father in a dream ......

Verse 19 Discussion

Herod persisted in his rebellion against God, to maintain his authority as the sole ruler of Israel, and did not entertain any other ruler, be it a "soul" ruler or not!

The Jewish historian Flavius Josephus, is quoted by Eusebius, in **The Church History**. Eusebius states that as well as murdering his wife, children, relatives and friends, Herod became gravely ill, with worms breeding in his genitals, as well as many other illnesses, and quoting Josephus, Eusebius writes that Herod clung to life, desperately seeking baths to cure himself, but to no avail. Realizing he was dying, Herod gave 50 drachmas to each of his soldiers, larger sums to his officers and friends, and commanded that eminent men from every village in Judea be assembled in the hippodrome, to be executed upon his death, so that, vainly, all Judea would mourn Herod's death.

Where Herod persisted unto his own death, in the animation text, the head of the household is reborn, enduring the death of their perception and world through to the beginning of a new and greater world. Those are the only two paths there are to choose from — death without accepting forgiveness, or death accepting forgiveness, and the death accepting forgiveness leads to rebirth and new life.

Some may say repentance is the way to salvation, but without fully understanding why one strays from the law, one is doomed to re-offend. Instead, when one is certain that the law under which they offend, is lacking, then they persist to their death under that law, and place their hope in a new life beyond that limited law. Nowadays, when everyone hopes for a life in heaven beyond the grave, this is what they are doing — hoping for a less limited law of life and death.

Apparently Herod neither repented nor hoped for a new life under a greater law. He hoped for earthly rewards, the mourning of Judea, and the benevolence of those he benefited, beyond his death. I'm sure there must be some way he might have justified himself, but few are interested in that. Nevertheless, if he were to accept forgiveness he would be forgiven. And so, continuing to rebel by not accepting forgiveness, he has his relief from life, and lives no more.

So the head of the household, may maintain their authority, where it is due, but has somehow changed so as to allow the sacred One relationship to return, in a new nativity. This opportunity was present to Herod as well, although he may have suffered execution if he entertained challenges to his authority, and the head of the household takes the same risk, by allowing any challenge to their authority. This, as well as the end of their perception of the world, is the death they must accept in order to be reborn. It is as real as any other death, full of anxiety and fear, as they submit themselves entirely to another in order to be transformed into a new person. This submitting oneself to another is only possible by the grace of God, and cannot be accomplished by anyone on their own. It is grace that saves, not merits.

So then why did God not grant grace to Herod? The answer is that He did grant grace to Herod, but Herod did not accept it. This is the difference between a sinner and a saint. A sinner does not allow God into their life, claiming and clinging to the fact that they are a sinner. A saint, which only means one that the church declares is in heaven, is a sinner that does allow God into their life, claiming the grace He offers them in spite of their being a sinner.

We are all sinners, and that doesn't change, but we can regret our sins and claim the forgiveness offered. Why are we all sinners? We are all limited in that we each fall short of perfection, as no one rose is perfect, but the perception of perfect can be obtained by observing many roses. Our limitations are our sins. We cannot escape our limitations, but we may overcome them by seeking the infinite purpose and taking up the opportunities that present themselves to us, in our life of faith, devoted to the most infinite purpose we can muster. This is the Joy of life, being a limited being in an unlimited infinite world. This itself is another union of the One and the Many, of female and male, and as such a balance of whole and part, renders true Joy to the participants.

So an angel appeared before father in a dream, the masculine nurturer of this specific romantic incidence of the balance of whole and part, the sacred One relationship. This would be what he longed for, and joyous news. But still, he must act on only a dream, and take a risk that cannot be taken lightly, with only a dream to justify such action. This is the life of faith, listening and watching for opportunities and acting on them. Most likely, no reasonable person would trust a fact on a dream, but rather trust the resolve that a dream may provide, and move forward based on that resolve, rather than the dream, looking for corroboration as one proceeds, cautiously but boldly.

Finally, it is our limitations, our sins as individuals, that slay Jesus - the manifestation of the balance of whole and part, and the realization of this brings the head of the household to their knees, before the object of their worship, the Son and the Father and the Holy Spirit, the knowledge of Being, Being, and the love of Being.

Sunday, March 18th, 2012

Verse 20

......²⁰and said, "Get up, take the child and his mother and go to the land of Israel, for those who were trying to take the child's life are dead."

Verse 20

.......²⁰and said "Get up and take the One to church, for those who are trying to take the life now know more.

Verse 20 Discussion

Joseph had a dream that Herod, the head of Israel, was dead and no longer posed a threat to the child Jesus. This is rather extraordinary, that a dream would communicate such a fact, yet Joseph, cultivating his spiritual life, knew how to respond to a dream both practically and faithfully. As discussed earlier, one may find themselves resolved to take action because of a dream, and this action, taken boldly, will likely resolve the facts of such a dream.

In the animation text, father, a male nurturer of this specific incidence of an infant One sacred relationship balancing whole and part, female and male, is compelled by a dream to take the infant sacred One relationship to church. This corresponds to the gospel text in that the people of God, the Hebrews, lived and worshiped in the land of Israel, specifically at the temple in Jerusalem, as well as the synagogues throughout Israel. The people of God, as christians, worship in churches. So taking the infant balance of whole and part, the child Jesus, to Israel, corresponds to taking the infant One sacred relationship balancing whole and part to church.

Just as Herod, the head of the household of Israel, is no longer a threat to the child Jesus, the head of the household, in the animation text, is no longer a threat to the One relationship. But where Herod is dead and no more, the head of the household in the animation, is re-born, having died to their old perceptions and life, seeking forgiveness, to awake in their awareness to a new life with newly born perceptions. In this new life of the head of the household, they know more, rather than are no more. Herod is no more.

If there was anything redeeming about Herod then someone would take up his cause, or causes, of which one may be the persecution of the child Jesus. But since Herod was the way he was, people are content to be done with him and his causes. But the head of the household, acting against the One relationship in a mistaken understanding that the One relationship would be a threat to the well-being of the household, may still protect the household, yet not attack the sacred One relationship. They have protected the household with their life and understanding, to be defeated by the One relationship, to their loss of awareness and rebirth to a new awareness.

As discussed earlier, it does not matter who the players are in a sacred One relationship, but it does matter whether such a relationship is attacked or nurtured. The head of the household in the animation text, achieved the death of the sacred One relationship, where Herod was outwitted, yet both heads of the households have died, one physically, and in the animation text, the other, spiritually. If the majestic daughter were to enter into another subsequent relationship, without any change or rebirth of the head of the household, the head of the household would once again attack such a relationship just as they did in the last relationship. If there is not any change in our lives and circumstances, we are to repeat the same failures over and over again, repenting over and over again, to only go on to sin again.

Herod's credibility was seriously discredited by his ordering the execution of all male children under the age of two in the region of Bethlehem. Like wise, the head of the household in the animation text, suffers a lessened credibility in the church each time a member of the household fails in a relationship. The church, the people of God, become jaded regarding the crises as they keep repeating for this head of the household. Can they not overcome their shortcomings and grow into a new awareness of the repercussions of their repeated behaviour? It does grow old.

It is easy to point a finger at someone else. Do we not all fall short of our calling to bring the infinite and love to the people we encounter? And especially in responsible romantic relationships, we are all guilty of condemnation and likely to suffer condemnation for our condemnation of such sources of the One.

Whether we abandon the sacred balance of whole and part, female and male, in the relationships we are in, or fail to nurture and develop these relationships we find ourselves in, does not matter. We are making choices that express our limitations, so we are guilty of not expanding ourselves to overcome our limitations by not taking full advantage of the balances of whole and part we find ourselves in. This is at least the sin of omission — not taking advantage of the opportunities we encounter to nurture the sacred balance of whole and part, female and male.

Why are we so negligent? We are negligent because it is very hard to advocate for a balance of whole and part when all around us people see us as either too partial or too wholistic. This is a lack of culture, that could educate its members about how the nature of existence is. It is like immigrants who do not respect national values that respect the individual as well as place responsibilities on the individual. The whole idea of educating children and youth to make them strong responsible contributing citizens fails if a simple act of balancing the whole and part becomes a target for accusations of foul play.

Sunday, March 25th, 2012

Verse 21

²¹So he got up, took the child and his mother and went to the land of Israel.

Verse 21

²¹So he got up and with the other took the One to church.

Verse 21 Discussion

This is a simple verse. But let's open it up and discuss it fully.

Joseph got up, took the child Jesus, and his mother Mary, and went to the land of Israel. In the animation text, the masculine participant in this sacred One relationship, gets up, and with the other participant in this specific incidence of the sacred One relationship, takes the sacred One relationship to church.

This is very common — couples taking their relationship to church to acknowledge it, as well as present and affirm their relationship. There is a sort of comfort in acknowledging a beloved relationship in one's place of worship. One may not even worship in a church or any other building, but whatever they do worship will witness their beloved relationship, as the participants will want to share their relationship with whatever and whomever they honour.

So just as Joseph and Mary would have wanted to take their son to Israel, to share their faith and culture with him, the couple wants to share their relationship with the members of their faith, in the place where they worship and practice their culture and faith.

Now on to the "other". This is not to imply that the masculine is primary and anything else is other, but rather that whether one is masculine or feminine, there is an "other". This generally goes overlooked, that there is an other out there, rather than everyone being the same. Everyone is the same . . . . but different. This is the problem of the one and the many, from Plato's Philebus. If there is one, then how can there be many, and if there is many, how can there be one? Since I am constantly referring to a balance of whole and part, female and male, one and many, wholistic and reductionistic, and communion and agency, I intend to write out how all this works, beyond the introduction to the discussion of *Matthew's Three Fold*, and with references, likely after the discussion of *Matthew's Foretold* is written. Suffice it to say for now, that existence is a dynamic balance of whole and part, female and male, and this balance is progressing through imbalance to greater stability.

In a relationship, the acknowledgment of an other is a source of great joy. The other accepts one and overlooks one's shortcomings, gently nurturing the growth of the one into the greater knowledge of the other. And the one does the same for the other, accepting, overlooking shortcomings, and gently nurturing the other's growth into the greater knowledge of the one. It is common for this relationship to be considered sacred and a priority above all else, or at least close to it.

But nevertheless, the other is other, and conflicts are bound to arise, as the other is inclined toward their affections and the one is inclined toward their affections, and these are different in that one is wholistic and the other is partial. This is the irony, that the greatest joy is a result of the differences that are capable of the greatest condemnation and enmity. So without forgiveness there is not any One sacred balance of whole and part. And any endeavour that does not employ a balance of whole and part, is by definition, evil and destructive.

This is why it is important to take a sacred One relationship, whether of a couple or of an individual, to church or one's place of worship, because such a relationship can be volatile if not treated with forgiveness, and directed toward the infinite.

In the past, the idea that I should attend a seminary or become a priest, was put forth by a friend at least twice in my life. I reject the idea because I have not found an institution that I can be obedient to, since I have not found an institution that worships the Lord as a balance of whole and part, holding marriage in the highest esteem. Even the Roman Catholic faith, that I vote for with my feet, is only beginning to recognize the sacred and important nature of marriage as put forth in the late Pope John Paul II's *Man and Woman He Created Them: A Theology of the Body*. So I am taking a risk by labouring outside of institutions that I may loose my way and be lost for not gathering together with others. I have chosen rather, to be a voice crying in the wilderness, that is true to myself and my relationship with my God, and not hindered by the institutions of man, if not nurtured by the institutions of God. Nevertheless I am a practicing Roman Catholic, needing the Sacrament of Reconciliation, as I try to put forth a faith in marriage as the application of christianity.

Furthermore, a more intense faith of christianity may unite the denominations, and even the religions as well as secular society under one infinite person, with many possibilities. Even an evolutionist can see value in marriage.

But when a balance of whole and part, whether the child Jesus, or a sacred One relationship, is taken to those who intercede on behalf of the infinite, will the intercessors be capable of guiding such a powerful, potentially volatile, union? I would suggest that only the infinite itself is capable of housing the infinite sacred One relationship, whether Jesus or a marriage. Nevertheless, the participants must play out before the infinite and the infinite's intercessors to witness to the truth they have encountered. This is part of what Jesus did, and this is what the apostles, martyrs and saints have done, and this is what participants in marriage, the sacred One relationship of whole and part, are to do, both to and for their spouse as well as the community in which they find themselves to be members.

Finally, as discussed in the **Theology of the Body** stuff, a person may engage the infinite as an individual, and this is a valid expression of their spiritual life, if taken up freely in response to a calling. Nevertheless participants in a sacred One relationship likewise have a responsibility when each of them acts as an individual, to witness to their encounter with the infinite.

Passion Sunday, April 1st, 2012

Verse 22

²²But when he heard that Archelaus was reigning in Judea in place of his father Herod, he was afraid to go there. Having been warned in a dream, he withdrew to the district of Galilee, ...

Verse 22

²²But when he heard the Son was reigning in the head space, he was afraid to go there. Having been warmed in a dream he withdrew to another place, ...

Verse 22 Discussion

If Joseph was prudent enough to consider the reign of the son of Herod to be a threat, then no one can accuse him of being ignorant in acting on merely a dream. There is a practical truth to scripture that still allows for the infinite to act.

Nevertheless, many choose to put their faith in magic and not reconcile what they are told with what they know for themselves to be true. For certain, mysteries remain, yet failing to attempt to reconcile mysteries leaves magic in the place of fertile consideration. We are to consider everything about Jesus' presence, so much so that we are to consume his presence, in whatever form we encounter it. To not do so is to dismiss his efforts to influence our lives before infinity. This is another balance of whole and part, reconciling what we are told with what we have witnessed first hand, and it all points to the infinite.

To accept what we are told, and not consider it fully to the point of reconciliation, is to lack faith in the truth we are being told. With faith, I have considered my knowledge of the faith, and have encountered the risen Christ, and live in a world that includes Him. This world, ruled by Christ, sends us not only to follow the very path of Christ, but beyond to the fruit of his ministry and resurrection. In this world, ruled by Christ, I have found a path to the Kingdom of Heaven, on earth, and this path is marriage. We are destined to eternal life with God on earth, by the means of Christ himself and his ministry applied.

So for the Son to reign in the head space, with nothing beyond his holy height, is a static idol rather than a living God. Any sovereign who reigns idly is not a leader and is a hindrance. Christ, in the Trinity, is a living God, present to those taking up their own crosses and following Him. He is not an idol, idly ignoring his kingdom, but active in bringing God to the world, and His Kingdom of Heaven, on earth, as it is in heaven. If not life giving, by His resurrection, than christianity is pathetic. We are all to follow Jesus, to life through death. The only thing to fear is an idol god. The father of the One, is afraid to go there.

But the world goes on, in spite of idolatry, and One is warmed by a dream of heaven on earth, and withdraws to another place. There is more. There is more than a comfortable life and a comfortable death. There is eternal life, that could be here on earth, if the infinite could be fathomable, and the infinitesimal considerable.

The dark ages were dark, partly due to everyone seeking heaven rather than attending to earth. Open sewers were common for lack of anyone digging a latrine. They would rather pray than lift a finger to improve their life on earth. We are in a similar age, with everyone on track to a comfortable life and a comfortable death, rather than a worthy life and untimely death. This is the case since the mid nineteen-sixties, with the loss of the Vietnam war, with its unpopularity at least partly due to a culture of comfort among the youth rather than a culture of service. The war was a waste, but so was the second world war, yet people were committed to winning it. Many speak of a culture of death, and call the movement "Pro-Life", yet they do not address the reasons for euthanasia and abortion. An untimely pregnancy, untimely for a comfortable life, is the reason for abortion, rather than an anti-life attitude.

Christ has offered all of us true life, by showing us the way to it, through embracing death in order to find life. If one were to accept an uncomfortable life, in a spiritual death, then they would not choose abortion or euthanasia, and live on in true life, with its challenges and spiritual birth to new life.

So rather than continue on in this pathetic worship of an idle, idol God, the sacred One relationship balancing whole and part dwells in another place, free to worship the living resurrected God, who conquered the Roman empire with the martyrs who embraced death in order to find life.

Consider what one is working for today. Is it pay for a comfortable life, or is it work to benefit others and society as a whole? If one works at something that is not benefiting anyone other than one's pursuit of a comfortable life, than could there be more? To dodge work is to steal from one's employer, co-workers and society. To work at something for the idol, idle goal of being paid is to limit the possibilities that would come from effective work.

And to propose that one's work is not illegal is not a justified response. Prostitution is not illegal, only the solicitation for the act of prostitution and benefiting from the proceeds of prostitution are illegal. Exotic dancing establishments are not illegal, yet adultery is wrong. Likewise, just because one is paid, does not make the work justified. If one were to consider their employment in light of a greater whole, one may find that they are only a hindrance to the kingdom of heaven on earth, rather than contributing to heaven on earth.

Who honestly believes that one person could benefit society to the extent of earning five hundred thousand dollars a year? Could they have accomplished such a thing if they were outside of society? Likewise, who honestly believes that a single mother on welfare is not contributing to society. If the culturally sanctified goal of distributing the wealth based on contribution through work were to be justified, than the crown must prosecute any incidence of malpractice on the part of employers, co-workers or customers. This is all a result of an idle, idol worship of the infinite, excluding the infinitesimal.

Just as there are worlds that are overlooked by idol, idle worship, that could be employed if the sincere worship of a living God were to be employed, these worlds are where those who worship a resurrected living God find themselves. This is the other place where the resurrected living God finds the sacred One relationship living, working and worshiping Him. This worship is alive and well, although overlooked to its benefit, until one day when the nurtured sacred One relationship is mature enough to rule the empire.

Capitalism won the cold war and now has free reign to show its prosperity, but where is that prosperity? If leaders cannot direct our economies to create value, our economies will flounder for a good time to come, likely only recovering by means of a social upheaval such as a war. This could be avoided if economies take both the infinite and the infinitesimal into consideration, balancing whole and part, practically worshiping a resurrected living God, and embracing death in order to find true life.

Easter Sunday and Easter Monday, April 8th and 9th, 2012

Verse 23

...... ²³and he went and lived in a town called Nazareth. So was fulfilled what was said through the prophets, that he would be called a Nazarene.

Verse 23

. . . . . . ²³and *One* lived in another place. So was fulfilled what was said through the prophets: "He will be called an otherene."

Verse 23 Discussion

What is an other? It is something other than us or I. This could be an inanimate collection, or other than animal, or other than human, or other than our race, or other than our faith, or other than our nation, or other than our community, or other than our trade, or other than our family, or other than ourselves. There are many distinctions between ourselves and others, and many communities of which we consider ourselves to be a member.

I was always impressed with a phrase from the animated film entitled **The Man Who Planted Trees**, from the writing of the same title by Jean Giono. The phrase is "There were rivals in virtue and rivals in vice, and the battle royal between vice and virtue raged incessantly." If we consider a being as other, than how do we treat it. Do we battle it, whether it is virtuous or not, or do we align with it and seek its benevolence? This could be God himself that we consider other and seek his benevolence. This could be Satan, the opposer, that we oppose in the hopes of conquering his influence.

The whole idea of the duality of whole and part enables one to consider both situations, the other than us, and the united with us. This understanding dances through one's mind, sparkling and alighting here and there with the identification of One and Many, ourselves and other.

Christians may pray that the Holy Spirit will come upon them and guide and enlighten them. This is the seeking of a union with God, who is understood as other than us, as well as greater than us. But if God is being itself, the Son is knowledge of being, and the Holy Spirit is the love of being, than as legitimate beings, if only temporal, we are to a certain extent . . . gods! Likewise, to the extent that we do not exist, our limitations on our being, we are creatures, temporal and mortal. So there is the divine in each one of us, as well as the opposer in each one of us, and a portion of our existence that will cease to exist, whether from day to day, or for eternity.

What does it mean that Jesus was called a Nazarene? Literally, it means he came from Nazareth. But the intention is to show that Jesus is member of those that come from Nazareth, and shares characteristics with others who come from Nazareth. The phrase "can anything good come out of Nazareth?" will give one the idea of what it means to call Jesus a Nazarene. This is the delineation of a distinction between good and Nazareth, and between good and Nazarenes. It is implied that Nazarenes were to be kept as other, not united with good, as we are united with good. Jesus was an other.

Likewise, the sacred One relationship balancing whole and part, female and male, will be considered other until it is accepted and considered united with us. But for the meanwhile, until the sacred One is accepted and adopted as our life's guide, it will be considered other. So it will dwell in an other place from where we are, and remain "foreign" to us. But this will be in degrees, as some people agree with parts of my writing that they may have read, but find other parts challenging and unacceptable at this time. Likewise, I have not presented any of this to any church authority, choosing to develop it until it has a life of its own and can stand up to critical evaluation. Critical thought — what other parlour tricks can one do? This entire project, this **HESUS JOY CHRIST**, is other until it is accepted and united with us.

So the sacred One relationship, balancing whole and part, lives in an other place. Religions have not accepted it, whatever religion one may consider, yet neither has the secular world accepted it, expressing an aversion to religious engagement. So, by trying to walk the line between religious and secular, I have excluded myself and this work from both — both reject this work as either being too religious, or not authorized religion, being too secular.

This is the cross that christians are called to bear, this balance of whole and part, accused of being too partial by those who are too wholistic, and being accused as being too wholistic by those that are too partial! In striving for a balance, one becomes persecuted from both or all sides. So just as christians were other than the Roman Empire, as well as other than Judaism, even though they were considered enlightened by the Greeks, and considered themselves to have witnessed the fulfilment of the Hebrew faith, Judaism, this sacred One relationship, balancing whole and part, female and male, is considered other by all. So it dwells in an other place.

This dwelling in an other place, is where new value comes from. Just as splitting the atom releases power, so within today's world there is value, rather than acquiring value from beyond today's world. It is in the infinitesimal that the means to fathom the infinite can be found. Yet when one becomes aware of the One sacred relationship balancing whole and part, a new world of opportunity becomes apparent. When one can see both the whole and the part of each and all they encounter, one can navigate throughout, gathering value as they go, and knowledge of where they are and where they are headed, so as to effectively envision and gather value.

In a closed system, there is not any opportunity for new growth as the system is closed to anything beyond it. Or is there an opportunity for new growth? If the system were to change from within, then first some part of the system will be considered wrong, as it addresses a greater system, beyond the limits of the closed system in which it is considered wrong. This is why forgiveness is so important, that something that is wrong is not to be opposed so that it may run its course in the hope that it will present a greater system to a closed system. This is why Jesus was persecuted, because he was wrong in the existing closed system, and this is why Jesus was successful, because he was correct in a greater, farther ranging system.

Just as navigation by the stars was developed in the closed system of the north African desert caravans, and became the means by which ocean navigation was possible, opening the new world, developments within existing systems, although contrary to the existing closed system, will be the means by which the system will expand and include greater assets.

Sunday, April 15th, 2012

Closing Notes

OVERVIEW

Well here we go! We were a third of the way through discussing the seventeen verses of **HESUS JOY CHRIST / Matthew's Three Fold**, when I took a break to consider the wordage that was then pushing seven thousand words!

A body of knowledge has it's limits, and one limit has nothing to do with how many pages are written about such a body of knowledge. When one (or a group) creates a body of knowledge they are making many decisions, or rather, assumptions that are not stated outright. These assumptions are made early on in the creation of a body of knowledge but seriously limit the effectiveness of that body of knowledge. So as an example of how creating a body of knowledge can become ridiculous, usually around the point at which academia takes over, I have chosen to write about everything I know about how to pick up a stick.

I was fortunate to make the acquaintance of a man in his fifties who left the aerospace industry to go to school for landscaping. That alone is ridiculous enough, but the point is that this gentleman was accomplished in academia and technological industry, who when he decided he wanted to work outdoors it was only natural that he would go to school to learn an outdoor trade. He studied for three years at Humber College and graduated from the landscaping technician program. Sadly, he only lasted five months as a landscaper, in spite of working for a very reputable, good and established company, and was able to get into good enough shape in spite of his many years of age, but could not tolerate the bystanders looking at him with the expression of 'look at that nice old man picking weeds'! His academic and thorough understanding was not appreciated by the casual observer, so was it worth anything at all? Likewise, this thorough understanding of how to pick up a stick is ridiculous and not worth anything at all to the casual observer. And the discussion of **HESUS JOY CHRIST / Matthew's Three Fold** is not worth anything to the casual observer — unless an awareness is cultivated by considering the discussion, but a thorough consideration of the animation would have the same effect of cultivating an awareness, not to mention considering life would cultivate a thorough awareness.

The moral of the story, here, is PAY ATTENTION !!!

Tuesday, April 12th, 2011

HOW TO PICK UP A STICK!

Here is how to pick up a stick.

First determine the size of the stick. Is it a twig, a limb, or a full branch? If it is a twig, how many of them are there? If there are many, then get a rake and a tarp. If there are not enough to warrant a tarp than get a garbage bag or a bucket.

Drop the garbage bag or bucket in the general middle of the twigs, and begin a loop path, starting and finishing at the bucket and extending only far enough to allow you to fill your hands with twigs. If you make the loop path too big you will waste time walking back to the bucket when your hands are full. If you make the loop path too small you will be dumping too few sticks in the bucket for each loop and that wastes time loading too small a load of twigs in the bucket. This becomes a concern when the bucket begins to get full and the twigs must be stuffed into it and can no longer just be dropped into it. If you are using a garbage bag, however, this is always a concern as the twigs must be placed into the bag lengthwise as otherwise the bag cannot hold as much and is too quickly filled.

Actually picking up the twig must be done standing with legs extended but not locked. Lean down like you are touching your toes and bob down to pick up the twig, and as you bob up transfer it to your off hand until it is full, and by that time you should be more than halfway along your loop path. Finish the remaining path holding the sticks in the good hand that picks them up, so that you arrive at the bucket with two full hands. Do not crawl around on your hands and knees because you need your hands to hold as many twigs as possible. It likely isn't good for your knees, crawling in the damp ground. As well, bending your knees to crouch down to pick up the twigs will be too much bending for your knees. Bobbing will get you well stretched out.

In the case of many twigs, a rake can be used to gather the twigs into piles and onto the tarp, to be dragged or carried to the truck. The first sweep of the rake will orient the twigs perpendicular to the sweep of the rake, and then the pile can be rolled like a snowball as it gathers more twigs. Maintain the coherency of the pile if the twigs are to be tied into bundles, as such a fagot can be rolled onto the twine to allow the twine to be wrapped around the fagot and tied. Do not attempt to rake a twig that is parallel to the path of the rake. This will break the rake. It may still be necessary to gather the remaining twigs by hand. Larger sticks may need to be picked up by hand, following the above mentioned method, as they cannot be gathered by a rake. DO NOT BREAK THE RAKE!

Usually, a large area of twigs will occur in the spring as summer or spring maintenance is beginning, but may also occur when pruning. Pruning will produce limbs and perhaps branches. Branches may also need to be picked up at the beginning of spring maintenance or after a storm.

When picking up a limb or a stick that is larger, pick it up by the stump end as that will give you the most leverage over a tapered limb if you pick it up by it's heaviest end. Otherwise the limb will be unwieldy and if you can get it into your armload, you may not be able to toss it in the truck. Gather all that you can hold under one arm and make sure you are on your way back to the truck by the time you have a full load in your arms. Again, bob down and up to pick up the sticks, keeping in mind your armload. There is no way you could crawl or even crouch with an armload of sticks.

      Branches are larger sticks that branch into more than one stick. They may be very large. If they are very large, do not cut them up, but instead drag them by the stump end, so that no further branches are broken off, and heave them by the stump end, into the truck. The best place to cut them, to pack them into the truck efficiently, is right in the truck. If one was to cut them up before they are in the truck, that is only more sticks to pick up and more sticks to throw in the truck and more sticks to pack into the truck to get a large load and reduce the number of trips with the truck. Once a few branches are aligned with the stump end at the head of the truck, tread on the branches carefully and with loppers, cut the branches at the crotches where the smaller branches head out from the main branch. It is the crotch that sets the limbs at angles to one another and prevents efficient loading in the truck bed. By cutting the branches at the crotches the limbs are able to fall into alignment with one another. I have seen a load of branches come out of the truck body and maintain the rectangular shape of the truck body as it sits on it's own after being dumped.

      Finally, for a good laugh, try to wield a branch by the small end — it will wobble around and you may not even be able to get the stump off the ground! The use of a wood chipper greatly improves the packing and removal of large branches, but there will still be twigs to be gathered, according to the appropriate method.

1000 words

Tuesday, April 12th, 2011

HESUS JOY CHRIST
Matthew's Three Fold DISCUSSION –

From Tuesday, March 8th, 2011,
to Tuesday, June 28th, 2011
as posted to the blog
of R. David Foster
entitled Vid '93 'bein' To Wordie . . . . .
@ www.vid93.blogspot.ca

© R. David Foster 2009, 2010, 2011

OVERVIEW

Well here we go! Try to keep up because there are many angles to this text and it's discussion will cover all the angles I can find in both texts and the relationship between the two texts, which carries a fourth level of meaning. That is — the meaning of each text individually (2 meanings), the meaning when both texts are viewed together (3rd meaning) and the meaning of the relationship (3rd meaning) in the context in which we share — real life (the 4th meaning)!

Stepping back a bit, let's acknowledge a few things. We are talking about religion — specifically christianity, which I believe is essentially forgiveness to the ultimate degree. All religions have their strengths, in fact all are valid and relevant. Forgiveness is either a spoken or unspoken element in many religions. I believe forgiveness is essential, and that is why I am christian.

Many religions have elements of Whole and Part. Ying-Yang for example. Other terms are Agency and Communion, Reductionistic and Holistic, one and many, or Male and Female. All that exists has both a wholistic aspect and a partial aspect. Everything that exists is part of a context, and wholly made of parts. To bring something into existence one must address both the whole and the part, both the context and the specific, aspects.

Furthermore, everything that exists has an inclination to either whole or part. The approach to anything assesses the balance of whole and part in that thing. An imbalance is always apparent, and the inclination of any approach is to correct the thing to obtain balance. If it appears too partial it must be corrected. If it appears too wholistic it must be corrected. The fallacy is that anything that exists is not in balance. In other words, if you may approach it then it does exist and if it exists it must already be in balance. Forgiveness allows the balance to exist without correction, and accepts that all things are in balance. This is somewhat a Buddhist opinion or faith. The important thing is to SEE the balance and not be moved to correction by any **APPARENT** imbalance. Otherwise the urge to correct leads to confrontation and a need to make things unbalanced and favoring whole or part over the other. A key thing about christianity is that it will forgive any apparent imbalance to the extreme of self destruction, but the self destruction is only apparent and not real! This last idea is explored in the animation entitled **HESUS JOY CHRIST / Matthew's Two Four** which is a chapter about ends.

If whole and part are termed female and male, then this forgiveness that exists between the sexes will allow marriage, which is capable of creation, if not joy and contentment. The whole of **HESUS JOY CHRIST** points to marriage as the further salvation of humankind, which is based on the essential character of Jesus that is essential for any successful marriage of any whole and part or female and male .

All people are called to different vocations, whether single celibacy, marriage, or other . Marriage is essential to society as a union of whole and part that creates new meaning and life . Marriage is a resource that produces new understanding and creates far more than just babies . This in no way diminishes christianity, because without ultimate forgiveness and sacrifice no marriage will survive . It will end when a partial or whole attitude fails to forgive a whole or partial attitude . Once one has taken up the challenge of Christ and begun to follow him, some sort of witness of the union of whole and part is where one must head, fully armed with forgiveness .

Moving on, evil is real, and forgiveness is how to deal with it . This third chapter of the Gospel of Matthew is about Jesus' baptism by his cousin, John the Baptist . John the Baptist was not preaching forgiveness, nor rebirth through death from forgiveness, but repentance which is turning from doing evil and trying again . Obedience to the Law, as turning from evil, will make balance apparent and allow the balance to be acknowledged and seen . But no one has ever been able to obey the fullest intent of the Law without the benefit of infinite grace . In other words, no one has ever been able to keep the Law when circumstances were against them . Jesus was able to obey the Law but it lead to his very public death . Many others have died obeying the Law in much less honoured deaths . Death — what is it really ? Death will be discussed elsewhere — perhaps in a further discussion of **Matthew's Two Four** .

Finally, one may choose to keep the issue of the existence of God out of this discussion . For my part, God is an infinite goal, infinitely present as an infinite goal, colouring our perception of existence . Whether God is a person, male or female, is beyond this immediate discussion, but worth discussing in some other writing . Suffice it to say, for now, that whatever has been created exists within infinity and it is all, entirely, good .

Ash Wednesday, March 9th, 2011

Opening Notes

Monday, February 1, 2010
The Gospel of Matthew - Chapter Three
HESUS JOY CHRIST / Matthew's Three Fold is written very tightly to this chapter of the Bible. It really doubles, if not more than doubles, one's appreciation of the animation which is to screen at the **Revue Cinema**'s **Drop Your Shorts** open screening this Thursday.
www.revuecinema.ca/dropyourshorts
The Gospel of Matthew - Chapter Three
New International Version

~~~~~~~

The Gospel of Matthew

- Chapter Three

John the Baptist Prepares the Way

¹In those days John the Baptist came, preaching in the wilderness of Judea ²and saying, "Repent, for the kingdom of heaven **has come**[*] near." ³This is he who was spoken of through the prophet Isaiah:

> "A voice of one calling in the wilderness,
> 'Prepare the way for the Lord,
> make straight paths for him.'"[a]

⁴John's clothes were made of camel's hair, and he had a leather belt around his waist. His food was locusts and wild honey. ⁵People went out to him from Jerusalem and all Judea and the whole region of the Jordan. ⁶Confessing their sins, they were baptized by him in the Jordan River.

⁷But when he saw many of the Pharisees and Sadducees coming to where he was baptizing, he said to them: "You brood of vipers! Who warned you to flee from the coming wrath? ⁸Produce fruit in keeping with repentance. ⁹And do not think you can say to yourselves, 'We have Abraham as our father.' I tell you that out of these stones God can raise up children for Abraham. ¹⁰The ax is already at the root of the trees, and every tree that does not produce good fruit will be cut down and thrown into the fire.

¹¹"I baptize you with[b] water for repentance. But after me comes one who is more powerful than I, whose sandals I am not worthy to carry. He will baptize you with[c] the Holy Spirit and fire. ¹²His winnowing fork is in his hand, and he will clear his threshing floor, gathering his wheat into the barn and burning up the chaff with unquenchable fire."

---

[*] 2   1973, 1978, 1984 NIV copy that HJC was written from is **is**

[a] 3   Isaiah 40:3

[b] 11   Or *in*

[c] 11   Or *in*

The Baptism of Jesus

¹³Then Jesus came from Galilee to the Jordan to be baptized by John. ¹⁴But John tried to deter him, saying, "I need to be baptized by you, and do you come to me?"

¹⁵Jesus replied, "Let it be so now; it is proper for us to do this to fulfill all righteousness." Then John consented.

¹⁶As soon as Jesus was baptized, he went up out of the water. At that moment heaven was opened, and he saw the Spirit of God descending like a dove and alighting on him. ¹⁷And a voice from heaven said, "This is my Son, whom I love; with him I am well pleased."

This **LEFT** Column is always the original Gospel text of the Third Chapter of the Gospel of Matthew, *New International Version*.

This <u>RIGHT</u> Column is always the text of the animation —

<u>HESUS JOY CHRIST / Matthew's Three Fold</u>, written by R. David Foster.

Verse 1

John the Baptist Prepares the Way

[1] In those days John the Baptist came, preaching in the wilderness of Judea . . .

Verse 1

Joan Prepares the Way

[1] In those days Joan preached to the converted and got nowhere, . . .

Verse 1 Discussion

John the Baptist, who was he? In a book called <u>The Pagan Christ</u>, some academic makes the case that the people of the Bible, specifically Jesus, never really existed as persons, but were created by theologians to justify a mythology of Christ. I find it irrelevant whether they ever actually existed as persons, because the mythology of Christ makes sense to me regardless. I do however feel that the author of such a book doesn't even believe his own ideas if he cannot entertain the possibility that a mythology could be real.

Religion is not a window onto the world, it is the world. The whole of existence is fodder for religion, even to within our own senses, within our perceptions. When I read something I consider the ideas put forth against my experience, which accumulates daily, and try to find sense in what I read that fits with my experience. To me, John the Baptist was a devoutly religious person from his upbringing, who could not tolerate common society, and that drove him into the desert, away from society. I know this feeling. With me, what I found in the wilderness, on the doorstep to infinity, called me back to society, where people were far more interesting, even if at times exasperating, than any rock, tree, lake, bush or animal. John, on the other hand, apparently still encountered people who came across him from time to time, who were curious about him, how he lived, and his ideas put forth in what he said. Society went to him, rather than John coming back to society. Jesus went out in the desert, in the fourth chapter of Matthew, but came back to society. Another example of the type of person John may have been, is the actor Charlie Sheen, and the meltdown he experienced in the winter of 2011. Mania is probably not too far from how John the Baptist presented himself.

If John was a man, so be it. His gender is irrelevant. So I created a preacher named Joan. If John was in the desert, people had to travel to meet him. It took the effort of a special trip. If he had been in an auditorium what difference would it have made? The only difference it would have made would be that he was supported by sufficiently affluent members of society. Today many preachers are beyond established churches preaching their own comprehension of the ancient texts. This is what John was doing. Nobody told him what to say, just like the modern preachers speak from their own heart, even if their interests may be questionable. John was in this category.

Hopefully you recognize the expression "preaching to the converted". What is the point of such a love in? It will accomplish less than what is ultimately possible. Furthermore, by all the heads nodding in agreement, everyone accepts the teachings of this preacher Joan. Is she content with that? I hope not. A good preacher hopes her words will move people to live a greater life through understanding, love and joy. Joan did not enjoy such a pleasure. She "got nowhere". I am sure she may have felt like the voice of one calling in the wilderness. If a preacher speaks and there is no one to hear it, does she make a sound? She may just as well be alone in a desert for all her effort. Nevertheless, she trudges on.

The point is that a preacher is a talker. Sure they have an understanding, which they feel compelled to share, and that may be worthwhile, but could there be more? Jesus was more. He healed, however he was able to do that, but more importantly, he voted with his feet, by placing himself squarely as a living example rather than just a mouthpiece. He was a master journeyman, investing his time in the people around him, apparently twelve of them, by getting right down to the same work he expected of them. Many people take offense at how preachers take money and a livelihood out of hard working people by just talking. The whole idea of a priesthood endures this criticism. Apparently Jesus had his concerns with the priesthood of his day. Nevertheless, he agreed that a worker is worth his keep, referring to his disciples. But don't forget that his disciples, including Paul, led by example. Paul was a tent maker, and worked as one as well as preached. Sure, they had ideas to get across, but they also did things and stood up for things as well. Imprisonment was common. Just read the book of Acts. These people could relate to others through personal experience, which many theologians and seminarians could easily lack. How much academia is necessary before one can be a benefit to society? The trick is how to maintain work and witnessing at the same time. It can be done to this day. To my knowledge, Jehovah's Witnesses suffice themselves with part time jobs so they have the time to knock on doors. Young members of the Church of Latter Day Saints spend a good part of their early adult years witnessing.

Jesus and John each gave their whole life to their ministry, suffering death for their preaching. Jim Baker lost everything, so only God knows a man's soul. The idea is more akin to tying a rope around yourself, and, after making sure the other end is secured to the vessel, diving into the waves of the storm to retrieve the lost, rather than throwing a lifeline from the safety of the ship. Look at people in soup kitchens, who serve the homeless in spite of how repugnant their characters may be. The Salvation Army takes this approach. Who knows where a life following Christ will lead? Let me assure you it will have a good portion of adventure. And so will any marriage.

Lastly, I would like to address the intellectualisation (yeah, I made up that word!) of faith. Understanding is not the same as doing or being. Many people will applaud a good preacher for the interesting ideas they put forth. To me, reality is more bizarre than most people can imagine. I do not need to be entertained in church. I have enough going on in my life of following christly balance to keep me interested. In my Roman Catholic parish, the priest's homily speaks to my spiritual life, rather than my mind alone. I am not looking for intellectual agility — a life following christ has plenty of that. I am looking for immediate solutions, which always surprise me by not appearing on my schedule, yet well in time. These solutions come in my heart when I follow other's witness, as well as God's presence. Suffice it to say that reality is far more intellectually agile than any good preacher, and more quiet.

Ash Wednesday, March 9th, 2011

Verse 2

... ²and saying, "Repent, for the kingdom of heaven **has come*** near."

* **2**   1973, 1978, 1984 NIV copy that HJC was written from is **is**

Verse 2

. . . ²and said, "Rebirth! Or the kingdom of heaven is ne'er!"

Verse 2 Discussion

Moving on, in this verse John's entire message is summarized in one line — "Repent, for the kingdom of heaven is near." John was trying to get people to step back from sin and see what they were really doing — what they were all about.

Repentance is stepping back from sin and trying to find another way that is within the Law. I would assert that people, as flawed persons by definition, are not perfect before the Law, and created mortal and flawed since creation, so cannot avoid condemnation before the Law — whatever law one chooses. We all know that popular thought or morality is flawed, or unfair, essentially because there are always exceptions to the Law or rules. God's Law, however, is perfect, and Jesus followed the Law of God, to the fullest intentions of God's

Law, and was condemned by man's laws, even if only by the judicial side, rather than the legislative side, which he did try to change as he went along his way, anyways. Man's Law, or interpretation of God's Law, always falls short of the fullest intention of the Law, or God's Law. (For the sake of this discussion, "God's Law", could be read as "Infinite Law".) Nevertheless, it is better to try to obey the law rather than disobey it. Any law is better than lawlessness.

What is the kingdom of heaven ? To me it is a society, or kingdom, that is the fullest intent of God for mankind - a society that is infinitely good. All of such a society is good, and without flaw, pain, suffering or lack. There would still be challenges, but such challenges would be taken up with Joy, like a canoe trip vacation. Sure, there will be slogging through mud and rain, but many people enjoy such hardships and that is the only type of hardship in a society that is infinitely good - hardships that are endured in Joy ! John is proclaiming that such a society is very near, if we can try to obey the Law and become aware of it. Another way of understanding the purpose of legislation is to compare it to a lawn or landscaping in general. A well manicured landscape brings out the best in horticulture and makes the good in nature more apparent. It does not in anyway eliminate much of the natural world, but instead, directs and highlights the Joy of nature. On the other hand, however, the natives of the Americas saw good in all of nature, and did very little weeding. The Law is only a means to see infinite perfection, and is only a crutch, if one believes infinite perfection already exists. Trying to obey the Law, or weeding, both make the infinite purpose more apparent. John prepared the way for Jesus' ministry by drawing the peoples attention to such an infinite purpose of mankind.

What is rebirth ? It is different from repentance. Repentance is stepping back and trying again. Rebirth is a re-creation of everything, and I believe it is the culmination of condemnation, death and suffering. Repentance avoids condemnation and suffering by trying to obey the law. But if the law or morality of man is flawed, it is different in many ways from God's Law, or an infinite law. When one tries to obey an infinite law, beyond a finite law of man, there will be conflict and condemnation under the finite law of man. The wages of sin, or lawlessness, is death. So even if one sins against a finite law, albeit obeying an infinite law, death under that finite law is the condemnation and culmination of such sin. But where does such a sinner stand with respect to an infinite law ? If the infinite law has been obeyed than the condemnation of the finite law results in death under the finite law, but there may not be condemnation and death under the infinite law. What occurs when one is condemned and dies to finite law, by obeying an infinite law, is rebirth. The entire world is recreated ! Repentance could make one aware of a possible infinite purpose of humankind, but rebirth is how to get into the infinite purpose, like putting on a new suit of clothes. The finite world around one dies, and the more infinite world encompassing that finite world, is where one will find them self.

When Jesus says "follow me", he is leading us to death and rebirth. This is what happens at the end of an age. One dies in one world and is reborn to a greater world. This happens physically, yes, but more importantly, it happens existentially. It is the only way. That is why Joan, in the animation, says " Rebirth, or the kingdom of heaven is ne'er!" "Ne'er"? This is a contraction of the word "never", with the apostrophe standing in place of the "v". Another example of "ne'er" is in the phrase "ne'er do well", an adjective phrase of an inferior person. In subsequent verses of the animation, Joan goes on to explain what the path to this new world will provide. But remember, rebirth is how to step into the society of infinite good, if repentance is a means to see a society of infinite good.

Finally, this is not such a radical idea, this death and rebirth. We have all already encountered it many times. The death of a child and the birth of a youth, for example. The end of elementary school and the beginning of middle school. Our awareness has died many times to be reborn to a more thorough understanding. **HESUS JOY CHRIST / Matthew's Two Four** explores this idea of the end of one life and the beginning end of another life. The question of how to proceed once one understands this truth of rebirth, is proclaimed in the following verses of this animation - **HESUS JOY CHRIST / Matthew's Three Fold**.

Tuesday, March 15th, 2011

Verse 3

³This is he who was spoken of through the prophet Isaiah:

> "A voice of one calling in the wilderness,
> 'Prepare the way for the Lord,
> make straight paths for him.'"ᵃ

ᵃ 3 Isaiah 40:3

Verse 3

³*This is she who was spoken of through the prophet Isaiah:*

> (*"Speak tenderly to Jerusalem,*
> *and proclaim to her*
> *that her hard service has been completed,*
> *that her sin has been paid for,*
> *that she has received from the Lord's hand,*
> *double for all her sins."ᵃ*)

ᵃ *3 Isaiah 40 : 2*

Verse 3 Discussion

I always find it interesting how quoting a verse out of context can support such a completely alternate meaning. Here, in Isaiah 40:3, we have John in the desert calling the people to prepare for Jesus. But in the previous verse, Isaiah 40:2, we have a demand to "Speak tenderly" to the people and tell them their sins are forgiven. This verse is not as well known since it hasn't been quoted as often. One is calling the people to action, after the other tenderly tells the people they are forgiven, having paid double for all their sins. I find this important, that people accept that they are forgiven in order for them to move on in their relationships with God and people.

It is essential to know your mistakes are not fatal, almost all the time. Otherwise one becomes paralyzed, unable to act, out of fear of making a fatal mistake. Fear is a serious thing. For example, we all know we will die, but for whatever reason, we do not walk around in fear of death, most of the time. I actually find most people are under the impression that they will live forever, by the way they labour and by what is apparently important to them. Consider what one's life would be like if you were in constant fear, of death for example. You may not find yourself belabouring which birthday card to drop seven dollars on for your boss's wife, I presume, if you were mortified!

Nevertheless, John is calling the people's attention to the coming of Jesus, as the Lord and Saviour of humankind. But in **Matthew's Three Fold**, I have written that this preacher, Joan, who may be discouraged by her apparent lack of success, is being consoled as she returns home, late again, to consider her day. Something is going to happen, as she is being reassured that she is forgiven. John is proclaiming the work to be done, while Joan is hearing the proclamation of the "hard service" that has been done.

In the fullness of time, the long awaited Saviour, Jesus, came as fulfillment of the Law and the Prophets. The work of Israel had been completed and a new age was to come, with people following the way Jesus presented to them. This way spread, partly in the expectation that he would return in the same way he left, throughout the roman civilization. But as the apostles passed away, without Jesus' return, the real work of this new age began. The values of christianity were adopted by the state, which surely fell under the weight of those values, to the end of that society and the beginning of the modern world, taking about two thousand years before the values of the way that Jesus taught were fully incorporated into the institutions of society. Even Islam built on the prophetic message of Jesus.

I proclaim, that a new age is again on our doorstep, and it is going to bring closer, a society of infinite good. If you have ever viewed any of this animation on www.youtube.com, you may have become aware of many of the other self proclaimed messages out there, and I am throwing my animation lot in with them. Society will again disintegrate under the weight of these proclaimed values, and there will be no apparent gain within many generations, until the values are adopted by the large majority of the members of society. Africa, to my mind, is now going through it's dark ages as medieval Europe did, with the end of apartheid in South Africa, and the racial genocide in other parts of Africa. This kind of upheaval will result from the adoption of marriage as the further salvation of humankind.

Tuesday, March 22nd, 2011

Verse 4

⁴John's clothes were made of camel's hair, and he had a leather belt around his waist. His food was locusts and wild honey.

Verse 4

⁴Joan's clothes were made of polyester and she had a vinyl belt around her waist. Her food was chocolate covered ants and wild honey.

Verse 4 Discussion

I've always been under the impression that the point of telling what John was wearing was to establish that he was living a very rough life of abstinence, outside of society, by mentioning the inferior nature of his clothing and diet. In the same way, Joan wears modern day inferior clothing of polyester and vinyl. Times have changed and a leather belt is considered better than a vinyl belt, and wild honey is a luxury. Similarly, the trappings of a modern day preacher have changed, as many are well off, although still on the outskirts of popular society.

Nevertheless, Joan is making use of the gifts of her followers, which may be wild honey and chocolate covered ants. These today are considered luxury gifts, as tokens of appreciation, which I use to establish this element of the narration, and Joan makes use of them, to establish that she respects these gestures. Joan is appreciated but not sufficiently cared for. She lives a solitary life of a single preacher. She may be better off than John was, financially and professionally, but she, as John did, longs for more. She has a vision of how God loves us and is compelled to proclaim her vision of God's plan for humankind. Tokens are tokens, and although the gesture is appreciated it does not fill the longing she has for marriage. Similarly, John's food and clothing suffices, but does not fill the longing for the kingdom of heaven.

Once again, where John was successful, Joan will be successful, as this animation plays out. John did not witness Jesus' ultimate victory, but he fulfilled his role in making it happen. Similarly, in this animation, it appears that Joan is single, and devoting her life to her ministry, and may never witness a victory of marriage in her personal life, even though she likely longs for a truly real marriage. It is a long rough road, which is full of disappointments, but it is a road we all travel, both warily and unaware, and it has its' adventure and joy.

Although he may have been of the opinion that he had no choice in how he lived his life, John did choose to dedicate his life to God. Similarly, Joan has devoted her life to preaching what she believes God wants the people to hear. Both are longing for more, and striving to see the kingdom of heaven. They neglect all else in their striving to obtain the kingdom of heaven.

Although marriage may be the ideal, many people will fulfill their roles given to them by God, in other pursuits. Just as Jesus, whose name means "one who saves", was called the Christ, from the Greek for "the anointed one", or from the Hebrew "Messiah", the One of marriage is anointed upon a couple, as in coming down from above, and is a gift from

God. A society of infinite good, may have many "anointed" Ones of marriages, but not all people may participate in a heterosexual marriage. Many people follow Jesus' example, as the apostles for example, but this path is unique to each individual, and not everyone need be crucified and resurrected in Jerusalem 2011 years ago. Likewise, a society of infinite good, where marriage is upheld as the ideal, may not be entirely made up of husbands and wives. We can't all be priests, with none of us left over to be parishioners, but we all worship in the same church.

Children are upheld as a value to society, but we are not all children. Elders are held up as a value to society, but we are not all aged. Work and labour are held up as a value to society, but who expects their 8 year old to have a full time job, or their 80 year old grandmother to punch a time clock. Marriage as an ideal does not mean everyone will be married, but rather, marriage will not be hindered by having work, children, parents, law, or politics interfere. Today many people choose their parents, their children, their careers, and their general welfare over their role as husband or wife. In the society of infinite good I foresee, marriage will take priority over much of everything else.

Finally, a discussion of the role of Jesus in this society of infinite good, would be worthwhile. Stepping back, what is the common understanding of marriage? Some cliches come to mind: the battle axe of a wife, condemning everything her husband does; the overbearing mother-in-law; the never ending slavery of raising toddlers, without the active support of the husband; the never ending seemingly arbitrary rules the wife puts on the husband; the never ending outlandish ventures the husband must endeavour into; the self righteous father-in-law, never happy with the wife; and the endless disappointments of one's spouse. It all paints a picture that no one would wish on themselves. Where is our saviour Jesus in all this? He is right in the midst of such marriage relationships, helping the spouses to live entirely in an environment of constant forgiveness of the other spouse, and sharing in the joy when forgiveness bears it's wonderful fruit. Fools may rush in where angels fear to tread, and angels do fear to tread into a marriage. Jesus does tread headlong into marriages and will be there with us in our suffering as well as our joys.

On the other hand, where have we witnessed our greatest joy? Some examples may be: the completion of a very hard project; the joy of young love; the blessings and joy of a newborn child; the love of a mother; the love of a father; romantic love; the unwarranted forgiveness of a heartbreaking sin; or a hard won achievement. A bad situation can be seen as a great opportunity, and a marriage is both a tough situation and a great opportunity.

Tuesday, March 22nd, 2011

Verse 5

⁵People went out to him from Jerusalem and all Judea and the whole region of the Jordan.

Verse 5

⁵People went in to her from the church, and all the land and the region.

Verse 5 Discussion

This verse portrays the extent of the influence John, and Joan, had in the world. Jerusalem was the sacred city, as it is to this day. The temple of Jerusalem was the earthly house of God. Churches, the actual buildings, are very often referred to as "God's house". Again, if one finds the use of the term "God", misleading and offensive, just substitute "infinity" or "the infinite", and God's House becomes the home of the infinite. It is an earthly place set aside where people go to encounter the infinite aspects of their lives. But don't forget that even the Bible has many references to the impossibility of containing the infinite, or God, in anything finite, like a place or a building. Likewise, containing God, or the infinite, in anything, can be cantankerous! By definition, infinity is infinite. It is everywhere! Nevertheless, it helps to consider the bigger picture directly or purposefully from time to time, and a place to do that makes sense. Just don't forget that everything is a manifestation of the infinite. The finite is a part of the infinite. So as a "house of God" I have substituted "church" for "Jerusalem".

Where John was "out" in the desert, Joan was "in" an auditorium. I see no difference in whether one is in the system or outside of the system, as the work anyone does can bring us closer to our infinite purpose. This is the idea of free enterprise and protestant religion. It is also the idea of the story of **The Sword in the Stone**, where the boy Arthur is the only one who can free the blade of discernment that is trapped in the cold stone of popular morality. In free enterprise the initiative of an individual outside of established institutions or corporeal realities is encouraged and allowed to grow to fruition and become established separately as an alternative to the majority. If such initiative can win support it will overcome the limits of the already established alternatives. This is what happened with christianity in the roman world. When the church became bogged down in bureaucracy others such as Martin Luther, became an alternative, and although something was lost, the outsiders of Protestantism moved the world forward and changed the establishment from the outside. Now that Joan is in, it forebodes that new life or change is imminent. Just as Martin Luther was a catholic monk, Joan is in the establishment by having a following of people sufficient to fill an auditorium. Jesus was both in and out, as he had a very large following, which he did not take into the establishment, which would be "putting new wine into old wine skins", but did go in to Jerusalem to encounter the establishment, as well as teaching in the synagogues.

John's influence was relatively widespread - "all Judea and the region of the Jordan" - and Joan's influence, similarly, is relatively widespread. The consequences of this influence can be looked at within the "home of the infinite" or church, the political state and political environment, and the widespread nature of a region. The images shown in the animation are of a single individual on Joan's doorstep, for a personal ministration of Joan; and the offloading of one of many buses at an auditorium presumably where Joan preaches.

Addressing these three aspects of a ministry, the personal, political, and geographical aspects, the personal aspect is no more important than the other two. If one is challenged and changed personally, with respect to infinity, political and geographic concerns are affected. If a kingdom of heaven is coming, will it directly oppose the roman empire? Yes and no. The roman empire had its' many gods and this served the empire, as individuals served and were served by their gods, or images of infinity. If the gods change than the society changes in every way. Just as christianity changed the politics, marriage will change the politics of its' time. Jesus encountered and dealt deliberately with all three aspects. Geographic? Yes. The roman empire served to spread the personal challenges and changes of Jesus teaching of forgiveness throughout a geographic region. The actual socialization of people was necessary to establish an alternative to what was common at the time. This can only happen when people are in contact and communication with one another. A new age of marriage need spread this way as well. In **HESUS JOY CHRIST / Matthew's Foretold**, the marriage makes an impression on many people, as Jesus made an impression on many people, in both cases through personal contact and awareness.

Tuesday, March 29th, 2011

Verse 6

⁶Confessing their sins, they were baptized by him in the Jordan River.

Verse 6

⁶Professing their sins, they were acknowledged by her in her church.

Verse 6 Discussion

Confession — what's that all about. When one sins, and acknowledges their being incorrect in their action or omission, the very act of acknowledging a sin implies that they do not want to sin again. This feels like a new beginning and is a new opportunity to act within the law. The unspoken truth is that they have experienced forgiveness in that their incorrectness was not fatal. But why did one sin in the first place? What would drive one to act incorrectly, if they have been created as good, as a loving infinity would have created one, and all. Again, the law is limited and only a means to see infinite perfection.

Stepping back, our awareness as finite beings is limited by our limited nature. No one can be aware of everything, at least on their own. For example, a pilot has instruments to make him more aware of his immediate environment of flight. A compass can guide one by extending their awareness to include their orientation in a magnetic field. This limited awareness will not change, but can be expanded through the use of inventions, or conventions. A society is a group that shares conventions. There are many societies, and I dare say every convention in every society, has an opposite convention in an opposite society. The point is not that one convention is better than another, but that within one society one convention is correct. Many societies have the convention that they drive on the left side of the road, which is no different from the convention of driving on the right side of the road, but stick with the convention or risk a head on collision. A set of laws is a convention. A set of laws is a convention of a society that keeps individuals from running into one another. A set of laws provides a level of awareness to the individuals who can maintain the convention of the set of laws of their society. The point is that the law will increase the awareness of the individuals. Once one had become aware through the maintenance of the convention that they find themselves in, the awareness continues beyond the limits of the law or society's convention. The law has served its' purpose.

This is not such a radical idea — the law having a limit to its' usefulness. Western society has at least two branches of the legal system — the legislative branch, and the judicial branch. Where the legislative branch ends, the judicial branch begins. If the law has failed, in a specific instance where one has apparently contravened the law, the judicial branch takes over to make a judgment in the specific case. The intent of the law is considered with respect to the specific circumstances of the specific case and the consequences are determined. In an infinite environment under an infinite law, who is qualified to judge? Many say Jesus is the one who judges, and others say Peter is the one, since he holds the keys to heaven. Let's go with Jesus being the judge. I prefer Jesus being the judge, as he is the one who has 'died for our sins'. This is a rather complicated discussion beyond the scope of this writing, but may be addressed here and there throughout these writings. Let's just say that Jesus is the victim of our sins and he is also the judge of our case, not to mention our defender in our trial. This is a truly wonderful situation when you consider it. The same person is the judge, the defender of the accused and the victim of the offense. This is the judicial side of infinite law.

Returning to the question of why one who was created as good would do something bad, it would be our awareness by means of the law, both in their limited nature, that judges an act as good or bad, as correct or incorrect. The awareness that makes such a judgment is flawed by being limited and that is why anything appears to be bad or incorrect before the law. The flaw is with the awareness and not the act. A society is determined by the individuals that work together. Individuals acting solely in their own interest does not look much like a society, but as is the nature of infinity, there is an obvious example of individuals seeking solely their own individual interests constituting their own society — free enterprise! It would not take much, however, to analyze and find individuals acting in the common interest in societies that promote free enterprise. An obvious example is the idea of an employee, not to mention a corporation. Nevertheless, the limitations of a law begin with the limitations of the individuals awareness.

Once again, the way to deal with lawlessness is to forgive, the same way as how one would deal with sin. Furthermore, in a closed system with a determined outcome, the only way to improve or grow is to take apart the system and recreate it. This would be seen as a destructive act, this dismantling to recreate. Sin is the same thing. It is a destructive act that moves the system toward a better, more aware system. It is the limitations of our awareness, as manifested in the law or conventions of our society, that call a sin a sin, and fail to see a sin as a manifestation of further infinity that is not considered in our awareness, convention and law. That is how a being created as good appears to act or omit badly.

If confession is one thing, profession is another. When one confesses, it is considered differently from when one professes. I believe this is more a convention of language rather than a considered choice of words, although I deliberately changed "confessing" to "professing".

"Confess" means to admit or acknowledge a fault, crime, belief or other. "Profess" means to declare openly or affirm. So if a sin is something committed by someone who is trying to dismantle in order to recreate, as a good person would, than why wouldn't one want to profess it? Sin is real and forgiveness is how to deal with it. An endless battle attempting to eliminate another or at least another's behaviour only limits further the infinite world we live in.

Let's try a few examples. Men are men and women are women. Some like their gender and others may not. That is a choice and one proceeds to choose their behaviour. One's behaviour influences what one will become. As a man I like being a man, more than I like to be a woman. But the best for me is when I am a man being a man with a woman. Experience influences our decisions. I find it quite conceivable, in my experience with woman, that I might prefer to be a man being a man with another man or men, and this is not uncommon. If I spend too much time with women I begin to look forward to time spent with men, and vice versa. What would be accomplished if I were to limit myself to certain associations and behaviour. Ideals would still be ideals and I would still hold up my ideals whether I am working towards them or taking a break. Society is the same. If one chooses to partner with the same sex, that may be a limitation of sorts, but the convention of our society is to allow people to choose their challenges. No one would deny that a heterosexual partnership has its' limitations. A sin is a sin, and forgiveness is the way to deal with it. There are many opportunities to sin whether one is in a heterosexual relationship or a homosexual relationship. All relationships require an environment of forgiveness. I do personally and idealistically believe a heterosexual relationship is potentially more rewarding, and certainly more challenging than any other relationship.

Another example is murder. How could this be any act of a good person? How would forgiveness be the way to deal with this? There are many types of murder. Many people feel abortion is murder. Many people feel war is murder. Many people feel capitol punishment is murder. Let's look at horrific murder — Paul Bernardo — if that is how his name is spelled. Is this a case of horrific unjustifiable murder? Before the Crown — yes — this has been decided in court. But before infinity — this is worth discussing. Certainly Paul Bernardo's decisions have led to his being limited in his life — prison. It can be argued that he has separated himself from God, by his sins. Nevertheless if he asks the heavenly father for forgiveness he will be forgiven. Where is the good in this story? Paul has brought attention to the consequences of unrestricted lust. His lust led him to do worse than just fornicate. It is a path he chose and it has been shown where that path leads. His choices were his alone to make, but many feel such a case casts our society in a poor light, and consider their actions accordingly. Is Charlie Sheen's womanizing his own choice or a symptom of society's modern values. Likely both. Certainly the situation comedy called **Two and a Half Men** is presenting ideas that society wants to celebrate and profess, if only the ways that a divorced man and a womanizer are treated. And the actions of Paul Bernardo were to a certain extent celebrated through proliferation. Both Charlie Sheen and Paul Bernardo are professing rather than confessing, and their actions are the culmination of our actions if our actions were taken to the infinite extent. We all feel the pain of these situations because we feel partly responsible through commission or omission as members of our society. This awareness may be the only good from such a sad situation, along with the warning that evil is possible if we do not limit our behaviour to appropriate infinite ends.

Limiting our behaviour — that is what the law is all about. But life is infinite. The situation is like the scientific method — observation, hypothesis, testing, observation, hypothesis, testing, etc. The law is the hypothesis, and is constantly changing in the light of observation and testing. When one is fully aware of the world through the law, then the miraculous takes place in our awareness. It is only knowing that there is snow all around and the world is cold that reveals the miracle of a crocus emerging. The law exists for offenders and the behaved, but it shows the miracles to the behaved and the coincidences and luck to the offenders, if not forgiveness.

Finally, it is only in the world of incorrectness that a new creation will emerge. Jesus was a condemned criminal. Jesus was executed and went to hell. He accepted God's love for him and is crowned. That is why acknowledging those who profess their sins is so important. If there is a crime it is for a reason, and would not be a crime if a legitimate solution was available. Why is this so important? What if you found you were face to face with pure evil and had to forgive it? This is what it may feel like in a marriage. If your awareness is that partial is all and wholistic is evil, you will find yourself having to forgive the evil, to really live, and vice versa.

Saturday, April 2nd, 2011

The law has been taking a bad rap in these discussions — let's set the record straight. There are many blessings for those who can find their way within the law. Miracles happen and benevolence abounds for those who obey the law — whether a finite law or an infinite law. If one is challenged by circumstances and is finding it hard to obey the law, a herculean effort is rewarded by those who witness the commitment of one trying desperately to obey. In most cases people will go above and beyond for someone who despite severe difficulty is making a supreme effort to obey the law. And this is by no means the greatest benefit of obeying the law, whether the finite law of man or the infinite law of God.

Miracles and blessings are witnessed by those who have the awareness to notice such events, and this awareness is provided by obeying the law. Otherwise such events are overlooked and dismissed as coincidences or just good luck on the part of the casual observer. Here is an example — taxes! If one works under the table there is not an official record of the income. The individual may save twenty percent of their income but will have no record on which to get credit to expand, and will not have any opportunity to get the benefits of having worked, that are available to those who have a record of work. This is important when today's society so religiously values labour and free enterprise.

There is a lesser value to life on the wrong side of the law. Picking one's nose may suffice, but is considered wrong and is obviously not as good as a good blowing of one's nose. Lawlessness is the same — it may seem like a good idea in a specific situation but it pales by comparison to the benefits of obeying the law.

I will provide a free DVD of **HESUS JOY CHRIST / Matthew's Three Fold**, complete with this entire completed discussion, to anyone and everyone who can get correct word to me identifying what the members of the congregation are brandishing in this scene of the animation!! It illustrates what a shortcoming life on the wrong side of the law really is . . . . . .

The two most important laws are, first, love God with all your heart, mind and soul; and secondly, love your neighbor as yourself. Note that both these laws are laws of love. This is infinite law. This is the full intent of finite law.

Nevertheless, when you oppose God or just your neighbor, you begin down the path of opposition, and Satan is the opposer. A contest between neighbors can serve as a test of which is the better way to proceed, but opposing one who is professing may never come to a good end. Separating yourself from God or your neighbor, limits your existence, and subsequently the extent of your real life is limited. On the other hand, considering God, or the infinite aspect of everything and everyone can be so full of life as to be overwhelmingly wonderful. At the very least it leaves all possibilities on the table.

And again, finally, where will this love of infinity, or God, and love of all our neighbors lead an individual, as a limited person? Where is this love to be directed — how will it be manifested? What law is there that fully respects this infinite love. I profess that marriage is the appropriate first place to direct this love, and will test the ability of the spouses to forgive, and is the appropriate infinite end of all our efforts, leading us to fullness of life, as Jesus promised to all who follow Him.

Sunday, April 3rd, 2011

Verse 7

⁷But when he saw many of the Pharisees and Sadducees coming to where he was baptizing, he said to them: "You brood of vipers! Who warned you to flee from the coming wrath?"

Verse 7

⁷But when she saw many of the ordained coming to where she was acknowledging she said to them: "You brood of vipers! Who warned you to flee from the coming wrath?"

Verse 7 Discussion

The Sadducees were a religious authority of the time, who had their own brand of Judaic religion, along with the Pharisees and possibly others. Today, in Christianity, the religious authorities are Cardinals, Bishops, Priests, Monks, Nuns, Deacons, and Ministers. Other religions have Rabbis, Monks, Imams and others. Religion, being in the world although not of the world, has a business side. This business side is a limitation. It takes a heroic effort to maintain religion in the real world, and this maintenance is plagued with problems. Some, however, do quite well in this business, probably due to leaning toward the business side rather than the religious side. This is a problem, this favouring of the maintenance of the religion as a business over the spiritual leadership of the people. Whenever we turn from gazing at the infinite in infinity and instead look at the finite we limit our perception. This limitation has consequences which John calls a "coming wrath". When a society fails the leaders of that society pay a heavy price, and as the leaders of religions, if the religions fail, the leaders will pay a heavy price. This is especially true of the leaders that fight strongly for the maintenance of such a failing religion. These leaders are what John calls a "brood of vipers", as they may already be seriously focusing on the finite maintenance of the business of their religion at the expense of spiritual leadership, and placing the cost on the people, as vipers bite without benevolence. And Joan says the same of the ordained leaders of many religions, who have the religious authority throughout the world.

The animation of this verse shows examples of various authorities of world religions, at the entrance to Joan's auditorium, and then a cycle of a hammer and a sickle, common symbols of communism, and more importantly, secularism. This is the consequence of unproductive religion. As an opiate to the masses, religion has no value. It is not an escape from reality, but rather a delving in, headfirst, to reality. If this truth is lost, the secular world, with finite goals, will surpass the benefits of religion, whose purpose is to study infinite goals. If the spiritual leaders fail to produce results, other priorities will take precedence.

Both the Sadducees and the ordained may have been genuinely interested in hearing for themselves, what John and Joan had to say, and may have taken their message to heart, but that is not for us to know. There position as authorities may have given them an advantage in incorporating John's and Joan's message in the practices of themselves and their colleagues, or they may only be looking for flaws and possible traps that could be set for the preachers. We do not know.

Even Jesus had to deal with this business side of religion. For one thing, many wanted to crown him king when he fed the multitudes. He avoided that. In other stories, a wealthy woman funded his ministry, by providing for the needs of his group of followers. The idea throughout, is that people gave freely in the presence of Jesus' group, as the group gave freely of their wisdom. No wisdom - no food.

Jesus established a following and in the book of Acts this following continued without Jesus participation. In the book of Acts, Jesus tells Peter to feed his sheep, -Jesus' sheep- as Jesus did not participate as a person beyond his ascension. The followers of the "Way" tried many ways as to how to keep their practical needs met, throughout the ages. Finally, Jesus taught his followers to give to God what is God's and give to Caesar, or the state, what is Caesar's, or the state's.

This is how marriage will exist, in this society of infinite good — in the same way that the state exists within the world of religion, a marriage will be a spiritual entity existing in the world of the church. The state ministers to its' members, the church ministers to the people and the marriage is ministered by the church and the state and likewise ministers to the church and the state. The practical worldly aspects of the marriage are governed by the state, and the personal challenges of the participants of a marriage are governed by the church, and the relationship between the spouses governs the state and the church. This is not so radical. Imagine a state without the presence of marriage. Most people consider the will of their father and/or mother, or spouse, when they vote or otherwise act politically. Most people consider the will of their parents and/or spouse when they deal with the church or other religion. Family is an extremely powerful influence to this day. And a family is ideally a marriage.

      Neither Jesus, John or Joan were compelled to proclaim — they spoke freely from the heart. Likewise, no one is compelled to become a religious authority — they do it by choice. This free will gift is essential to how one must approach religious responsibility. Give what you can and leave the rest up to God. We are finite beings from an infinite source in an infinite world. No one can do everything but everyone can do something. Giving freely of your self, your talent, and your wealth is your only responsibility. No one should ever make a demand of you that is beyond your best effort, or even beyond your effort today. This is true in marriage. Give what you can and leave the rest up to the rest of infinity. We will all fall short — that is a given! But each of us can do something, and that will all add up to everything. And the first and foremost place to invest your gifts and efforts is in your marriage, or at least your influence on a balance of whole and part.

Friday, April 15th, 2011

Verse 8

⁸Produce fruit in keeping with repentance.

Verse 8

"⁸Produce fruit in keeping with rebirth."

Verse 8 Discussion

      This one verse is pretty simple. We've already covered the relationship between repentance and rebirth. Repentance is turning from sin or incorrectness and trying again. Rebirth is suffering, condemnation, death, and rebirth to new life in a wider world. Either way, as Jesus taught, one will know whether a tree is good or bad by whether it bears good or bad fruit. Only a good tree can bear good fruit, and a bad tree will bear bad fruit. A body of knowledge, or a religion, or legislation is like a tree — it has roots and branches — it reaches from the depths to the sky, and it will be known by what it produces. Communism was good for Russia for a while but failed to continue to produce and was replaced in the 1990's.

Communism is producing fruit, or at lease seems to be providing a growing economy in China, and so China at least nominally, retains communism, albeit with a healthy dose of enterprise and capital.

Can you follow this — that last paragraph was loaded. John wants real repentance that is productive. Joan wants true rebirth that is productive. Either way there will be a falling back and regaining ground. To admit that one has violated the law, make reparations, and begin again may seem like two steps back for one step forward, but the point that is being pressed is that there will be many more steps forward than there would be possible if one continues on the current path — their will be greater production, although there will be an initial loss. This is true for both repentance and rebirth, although rebirth has greater potential than repentance.

This is the test of all this animation of religious marriage ideas — DO THEY BEAR FRUIT! That is your test, if one needs a test. Just looking around in one's own life and experiences should provide many examples of the joys and productive nature of marriage, or variations of marriage, and any form of balance of whole and part. Marriage is by no means a new idea, but as a primary resource there seems to be little outright teaching giving sufficient prominence to marriage. Many will acknowledge the challenges of marriage, and the failings of relationships and individuals engaged in marriages, and this appears to have dulled the enthusiasm of society to promote strong marriages, out of fear of prolonging suffering. This is like not leading the horse to water because he cannot be made to drink! This animation is leading the audience to marriage, and allowing it to consider the resource it may find there. The trick is to show the audience how far this resource can take humanity, so that it will drink deeply of marriage, for the wonderful journey that awaits.

Critical thought — that's a wonderful parlour trick! I believe it was Albert Einstein who said something like no matter how many times a hypothesis is not proved wrong by a testing experiment, it only takes one experiment to prove it wrong. In the novel <u>Zen and the Art of Motorcycle Maintenance</u> it is proposed that everything can be proven to not exist, and that is the point at which I stopped reading it. I do believe that anything and everything can be proven to not exist, but what is the point? The truth of such a proof is that proof is inconclusive! So be careful with your testing. Keep an eye on the big picture and watch the world open up as each finite model of your infinite world fails!

And now, with the space available this week for this verse, I would like to elaborate as to how far marriage could take a society that freely and fully commits to marriage.

Religions, states and laws exist for the good of human kind, and not the other way around. At least these three institutions serve to provide an awareness of the bigger picture in the myriad of specific situations individuals may find themselves in. They are finite representations of the world beyond and within the individuals. They are also created by within and beyond the individuals. When a person acts wholistically, another may respond partially, and this two step is a dialogue that never ceases. This dialogue is infinite, from the infinite sources within and beyond the individuals. A person acting wholistically balances the person responding partially, and vice versa. This is the key — this constant dialogue and balance between acting partially and wholistically. This is the purpose of religion, states, laws, and lets add knowledge.

If this is the purpose — balancing whole and part — than could this be done more efficiently? I propose that the environment of marriage is a more efficient means of balancing whole and part. This is a powerful idea — it is the basis of all awareness, let alone society's institutions.

If a bolt needs to be a certain size and strength in a certain place on a skyscraper this is determined today by previous experience and testing, current knowledge, various building codes, engineering, trades, manufacturing and distribution, etc. All this is generally considered too much for one person to know let alone be responsible for, by the natural limitations of one's awareness. But if one could be sufficiently aware, how much labour and testing could be superseded by common sense? Imagine if every steelwalker could have the experience of 30 years in the business and the knowledge of the designer who drew up the 300 sheets or more of plans? How could this be possible? How is it possible to build a skyscraper today? Many people have sufficient resources to gain the knowledge and experience that when combined create the skyscraper, but marriage is at the heart of all these resources, and if more fully cultivated could allow even more productivity.

Another example is language. If language can be learned, how many languages can be spoken by one person fluently? This is only limited by one person's awareness, which could be expanded by thoroughly making use of the balance of whole and part in a society where marriage is an ultimate resource. There is an example, albeit somewhat dubious to the non-believer, in the book of Acts in the Bible, where at Pentecost the people gathered spoke in foreign languages that they were not trained in.

So if all these institutions of society are solely to balance whole and part, than marriage will only serve to better these institutions, if not entirely replace them. Perhaps marriage will become an awareness compass, where the state of the relationship dictates the next step in the relationship. The possibilities seem endless to anyone with an imagination.

EASTER Sunday, April 24th, 2011

Verse 9

⁹And do not think you can say to yourselves, 'We have Abraham as our father.' I tell you that out of these stones God can raise up children for Abraham.

Verse 9

"⁹And do not think you can say to yourselves: 'We are ordained.' I tell you that out of these sinners God can raise up ordination!"

Verse 9 Discussion

What does it mean to have Abraham as a father? This was a society that God set apart to bring awareness of Himself to the world. The children of Abraham were a culture that maintained an awareness of the one God "I am." They were an example to the rest of the world of what life in a relationship with God is like. They were in a geographical position and an evolutionary time that set them as an example to the rest of the world. It was a special time and position, but it was not obtained by the worthiness of the Hebrews — it was ordained by God and sustained through his love and mercy, rather than the merits of the Hebrews. It could have been any other race in the same position and time. But it was the Hebrews.

Abraham did not obtain his position with God by his own merit. Rather he was open to God in his life and this allowed God to act on his behalf. This openness allowed God to bless him. This openness is apparent by Abraham allowing himself to have faith in God's word to him, in spite of the obstacles to his having children. Abraham heard the word of God and believed, in the face of the gross unlikelihood of God's word being fulfilled. This openness to God even allowed him to consider sacrificing his only son when he may have felt his love for his son was overshadowing his love for God. Abraham had more faith in God than in his own understanding that he likely would not have another child with which God could fulfill his promise. This is extreme faith. This faith came to Abraham by the grace of God and by Abraham's situation as created by God. Abraham was ordained by God.

Many clergy are ordained by God. There lives and witnessing have set them apart from the world as ministers of the Word to the world. This is not by their own merit but by the grace of God that they can proclaim the Word meaningfully. They are in no way less sinners than the rest of us, but they are able to make the Word known to us in spite of their limited sinful nature. A minister of God's word cannot rely on their ordination but rather their participation in making God's Word known. If they abandon their work ordination will not redeem them.

If the Hebrews failed to listen and participant in a relationship with the one God, they cannot rely on their ancestry to redeem them. Likewise, any other religious leader who abandons his or her commission cannot rely on any sort of authority vested in them to redeem themselves. If the religious authorities abandon their commissions their work will be taken up by others who can produce. This goes back to bearing good fruit, as discussed previously. A very good example of this is the protestant revolution. The ordained church failed to produce results and were abandoned by the people in favour of other religious leaders who sprung up among them. These leaders were no more sacred than their followers, and all of them were sinners.

All ordained people deserve special consideration of their intent by their followers, but this does not mean they will not be judged as being incorrect. The protestant revolution judged many of it's ordained leaders as being incorrect and that is why there are so many different denominations. So much so that three denominations even reversed this process and joined back together to become the United Church.

Another strong example is Islam. If christianity was failing to produce results another man with a strong relationship to God spoke through faith and is now known as the last prophet of God. Islam produced many results in its' early history and greatly overshadowed christianity. Likewise, if Islam cannot improve the standard of living amongst it's followers it will be overshadowed by other priorities, such as western secularism, and this may be happening in the uprisings in Egypt and Libya of the winter of 2011.

And now back to marriage. If religion cannot produce results it will fail to hold the attention of the people. Likewise, a marriage, if it cannot produce results it will fail to hold the attention of the participants. But what is the alternative to either religion or marriage? Religion and marriage are both doors to the infinite — one is for the infinite purpose of each of many individuals in a society, and the other, marriage, is for the practical application of the understanding of the infinite purposes provided by religion, as well as a source of understanding of the infinite purposes of both society and persons. If religion fails to produce meaning than perhaps personal relationships will take priority. If personal relationships fail to produce meaning than perhaps blind faith will take priority.

This is what is happening in modern marriages — they are failing to produce good fruit. Why is this? If one gives serious intense attention to something they will see it fail and the world of that something will fail and then become a new something. This has happened in religion throughout the ages as well as marriage. This is suffering, condemnation, death, and rebirth. This is the truth of any awareness, that it will fail and then become a new awareness. So the issue becomes what is worthy of our serious intense attention and faith so much that one is willing to follow through with it to death and rebirth. We all know we will die — our experience of the lives of others around us makes this apparent. The question becomes what is worthy of our life and death. And why should we become content with awaiting a comfortable death? Is there more to all of this? I believe there is.

Many people will die for their faith, as history has many examples. I propose that religion may be worthy of death, but marriage is more worthy as it is the purpose that religion points to throughout history. If one is going to die, let it be for marriage. Then the truth of life conquering death through rebirth comes into play. Many people will die for their religious beliefs and go on to rebirth to new life, and many people will loose their awareness for their spouse and go on to rebirth of their marriage in new life. Marriage in no way will replace religion, but rather will be the field in which a personal religious life will play out. Marriage is the practical application of all that religion teaches. Religion teaches that there are many things more important than a limited life, which justifies death, which leads to rebirth. Marriage is where this will all play out and bring forth good fruit, and rebirth. Without a strong faith in God, death and rebirth, marriage has nothing much to offer. But once one has developed a strong faith in religion, forgiveness, death and rebirth, marriage is where one should invest their efforts as that is where new meaning, understanding and good fruit will come from most readily, in spite of our limited sinful nature. Marriage is a compass that will help to determine all other decisions, as it is a living balance of whole and part.

Saturday, April 30th, 2011

Verse 10

¹⁰The ax is already at the root of the trees, and every tree that does not produce good fruit will be cut down and thrown into the fire.

Verse 10

"¹⁰The ax is already at the root of the trees, and every tree that does not bear good fruit will be cut down and built into the building.'"

Verse 10 Discussion

There is a bit of a theme becoming apparent in this text of the animation. We have already discussed how a body of knowledge is like a tree, reaching from the depths of the roots to the sky. We have also discussed the idea of bearing good fruit or being productive. This verse touches again on those two ideas, and then adds a twist.

Where John talks about the elimination of the tree, or body of knowledge, or religious practices, by the trees that are not bearing good fruit being cut down and thrown into the fire, Joan says something a little different. Joan takes the metaphor a little further and adds a twist. She states that the trees that do not bear good fruit will be cut down and built into the building. This is a new metaphor — the idea of a body of knowledge or religious practices as a building rather than a tree. This goes back to **HESUS JOY CHRIST /**

Matthew's Two Four where Hesus says things like "Understand the building's building!" where in the gospel text he is referring to the temple in Jerusalem. So instead of completely wasting the tree, or religious practices, they would be incorporated into the new religious practices, as trees are turned into lumber and used to build a building of religious practices. Do you see why animation is so suited to the expression of these ideas? Animation can state these ideas very succinctly where literature tends to run in circles.

So if the religious practices will not be completely abandoned and wasted, but rather used in a new religious practice, is this a radical idea? No! The christian Bible is more than half made up of the Jewish writings. The New Testament is less than half of the Bible, with the remainder being Judaic or Hebrew writings. The New Testament is the only writings that were added by christianity, no matter which Bible you choose. So if a new idea of religion, where marriage takes prominence, will still rely heavily on the old christian traditions and teachings, this is like taking the religious practices that are limited in their productiveness and re-using them in the light of marriage.

This is like the expression — don't put new wine into old wine skins, or the new wine will cause the old wine skins to burst. A new understanding of the world will make use of the old understanding but cannot be added onto the old understanding, like an appendage, but rather must transform the whole of the old understanding in light of new understanding. Christianity will in no way be abandoned by a view with marriage taking prominence, just as the Hebrew teachings are a strong foundation for christian teachings. The personal experience of marriage requires persons to be like Christ, in character, actions, and perceptions, or the marriage will fail and not experience rebirth.

As well, where there is a balance of whole and part, nothing can be dismissed or abandoned, by consuming in fire, as John states, but rather everything will be a part of the new understanding, with nothing being dismissed as irrelevant or incorrect. This acknowledges a world created by good that is all entirely good. This is a society of infinite good where the balance of whole and part in both marriage as an ideal and marriage as a specific relationship between two individuals, takes priority.

Now in the animation — did you notice the writing on the signs? The Church that is closed is the called the "Know More Church of Can of Duh". This expresses that it is not the accumulation of knowledge that redeems, but something else, which I will state here to be the integrity of the knowledge, whatever that may be, of what one already knows. The "Know More Church of Can of Duh" is implied to have promoted the accumulation of knowledge without end, over the integration of whatever knowledge may be had. This church is "no more" in a world where marriage takes precedence.

If a religion is an approach to infinity, then it has an eternal aspect. And the sign states "Thanks for a great eternity!" The Know More Church of Can of Duh has played out its usefulness and is no longer at the forefront of productiveness. As well, the condominium sign expresses the idea that almost everyone has sold out, if not only referring to the units sold. This is the idea that most people have given up on eternal life and joy, implying that this is not necessary. Everyone these days seems to be content with what they can have now, and do not consider what they may have for eternity.

On the other hand, the sign that is in front of the new church that is being erected, says "Coming Soon! Church of One!". This is the same name that is on the bus that is unloading in front of the auditorium in verse 5, previously discussed. Joan's church is expanding. And then tagged on to that sign is a board that states "Free Marriages!". This is to imply that any attempt at marriage will not be hindered.

Tuesday, May 10th, 2011

Verse 11

¹¹"I baptize you with^b water for repentance. But after me comes one who is more powerful than I, whose sandals I am not worthy to carry. He will baptize you with^c the Holy Spirit and fire.

    ^b   11 Or in
    ^c   11 Or in

Verse 11

¹¹ "I acknowledge your death with rebirth, but after me will come one whose shoes you will wear. His holy spirit will acknowledge you with spirit; . . .

Verse 11 Discussion

John did not see himself as worthy of grace. He saw only the sinful nature of people, including himself, and tried to get people to scrap everything and start over, repenting of their sins and being baptized into a new start. His baptism was one of repentance, not rebirth. Joan on the other hand, acknowledged death with rebirth. This is accepting the wrong of our sins, and dieing to them, to be reborn to a new life and world. This was not accomplished by Joan, but rather by the individuals themselves before God. The individuals would be the sole witness to their rebirth, which they would bring to Joan for acknowledgment, or something like that, as the animation does not go into much detail about the mechanisms Joan actually implemented.

John does not consider anyone worthy of grace, by his statement that the one who is more powerful than him would not appreciate John carrying that person's sandals. This may be true, and likely is, but it sets God and Jesus at a distance from John and us, and does not dare to have a loving intimate relationship with God, Jesus or any infinity. Joan on the other hand, says we will walk in his shoes. This is a play on the expression "Do not judge a person until you have walked a mile in their shoes".

Jesus commissioned his followers to follow him and serve. This means taking up Jesus' work and doing what he did ourselves. He did not come for us to just listen and learn — he wanted us to follow him and do as he did. We are to take up our crosses and follow him. We are to walk in his shoes. We will wear his shoes.

Whether one is a man or a woman, we all have some sort of awareness. This awareness will die and be reborn many times in our life. We must take up our crosses, suffer, die and be buried, and then awake to the new world that is presented to us. This is not just true for men — women have awareness too, so it is true for everyone.

In a marriage, both spouses have awareness, and any awareness will die and be reborn. This will happen most dramatically and effectively in the marriage relationship. Jesus led the way into the ugknown of the opposite world and taught how to succeed in such a venture - practice forgiveness. He may have been strongly influenced by his mother, Mary, but there were limitations to that relationship which do not hinder a marriage relationship. Regardless of whether one's skills are stronger in whole or partial, everyone has an awareness that will die and be reborn. We all must take up our crosses and follow Jesus, primarily into a marriage relationship.

We must cultivate an intimate relationship with God and Jesus, and follow where it leads. God is not an absent Father. He is as present as an infinite goal is always present in everything anyone does. We are not worthy of God but God is worthy of us. And God does choose to have an intimate personal relationship with each one of us, if we do not limit our world in such a way as to exclude him. Jesus was in an intimate relationship with God and the Holy Spirit, and this is the nature of a marriage relationship — the person of Christ. This spiritual relationship exists between spouses and we are shown how to behave by how Christ behaved. We take on the person of Christ when we enter into a marriage relationship and the relationship speaks to us as Christ spoke to the world. We will still experience death and rebirth, but a marriage is the most appropriate place for our efforts. We may not be worthy of our spouse, but our spouse is worthy of us.

Christ is present in a marriage relationship, and indeed is present in any relationship that has a balance of whole and part, and we will walk in these relationships as he walked in the world — in his shoes. The animation is much better at expressing this idea, if one is willing to consider it, and does not get lost in circular rambling discussion such as this.

The next part is about being baptized with spirit and with fire, as opposed to a holy spirit acknowledging with spirit. Many people are filled with spirit, which drives them to accomplish what they desire. A Holy Spirit is a wholly spirit, and will drive you to accomplish what you will. Many people have a spirit that they feel justifies their actions, and I agree that this is true. Extreme actions that are challenging to others, may be considered evil, but once again the way to deal with evil is to forgive, for the proponent is likely professing, I confess.

None of this is that radical. Especially a Holy Spirit acknowledging with spirit. Everyone decides they must be married based on how they feel, which I would say is how the spirit directs them. So it is not that radical that a spirit will acknowledge a person's actions or situation.

So the acknowledging is by rebirth and by the presence of spirit. This is how you know you have been reborn. This also acknowledges that you were faithful in your death, by maintaining your integrity, and that you have dealt with your demons and begun your new life. This is basically common sense. One suffers many challenges in their life, which take their toll as they accumulate, but one may overcome the burden of such failures by making lemonade with the lemons! I know, where is the sugar for all these lemons suppose to come from?! You get the idea. There can be an overwhelming joy if one can come to peace with their life so far. And don't forget that our mistakes are our greatest learning opportunities and experiences.

Fear is a serious thing. Fear can control one. Fear is ridiculous though. Does anyone really expect to live to 400 years old? The strain on the retirement system would be enormous! So if we all know we will die what is there to be afraid of? Fear of suffering is another thing. This is a little trickier because it can go on for so long. A weak moment is more likely to occur over an extended period of suffering. But than if we know we are forgiven than what is there to fear! God loves us and knows all our shortcomings, so go out and live! This is even more thrilling if one chooses to live a spiritual life full of spiritual challenges and growth. And marriage is one of the most spiritually challenging endeavours out there.

Sunday, May 15th, 2011

Verse 12

¹²"His winnowing fork is in his hand, and he will clear his threshing floor, gathering his wheat into the barn and burning up the chaff with unquenchable fire."

Verse 12

. . . ¹²his spirit will test you, and gather you in, and there will be no one left out."

Verse 12 Discussion

What's a winnowing fork? What's a threshing floor? John is using the metaphor of threshing to illustrate what God is doing with the people of the time.

Once the wheat had been harvested the grain had to be separated from the straw and chaff before it could be ground into flour. This was done outdoors on a threshing floor with a winnowing fork. The wheat would be trampled to make the grains fall off of the stalk or straw. Then the winnowing fork was used to throw the mix into the air where the wind would blow away the chaff, which is anything other than the grain, and the grain, being heavier would fall straight down and not be carried away with the wind. One would be left with a large broad pile of chaff and a smaller separate pile of grain. The grain would be collected and the chaff would be discarded and possibly burned as waste.

So the good people are the grain who pass the test and the bad people are the chaff who will be wasted. The winnowing tests the mix or people and then each group, either grain, good people, or chaff, bad people, are dealt with appropriately.

Once again, John does not see a merciful God, and in his illustration, the chaff, or bad people, are burned up with unquenchable fire. But once again, if God created everything and saw that it is good, then where do bad people come from ? Joan on the other hand, in her Church of One, says something different.

In the animation text, the whole testing metaphor of threshing and winnowing is summed up in the phrase " . . . his spirit will test you, and gather you in, and there will be no one left out." This is different from what John is saying in that there is not any waste. If God created an entirely good world, than all is good and there is nothing left over to waste. The trick is to see the good in everything, rather than limiting what is judged as being good to a portion of what exists.

Nevertheless there will still be testing and failure. A marriage relationship is full of testing and failure, and how does one deal with failure ? Forgiveness. The testing is more to learn about what is possible. Just because the hammer misses the nail doesn't mean it will always miss the nail. Practice teaches what is necessary and possible with whatever means one has at their disposal. A hammer that misses the nail likely still hits the board nearby. There is a certain level of success that encourages one to try again. When a spouse fails as a spouse, the other spouse still tries again to get the intended result. They may change their approach, and the failing spouse may try again in the light of the last mistake, with a new approach. Most mistakes are not fatal, and therefore the opportunity to try again is usually there. This is the nature of infinite forgiveness. This is necessary. This is common today. Joan is acknowledging this.

"His spirit" is the masculine form of the relationship between the spouses. This spirit is like Christ and ministers to the spouses as Christ ministered to the world. The relationship will test the spouses and they will fail but go on to forgive and be forgiven. One may have no control over the other spouse, so this forgiveness from that spouse is a gift from God, or the infinite. This makes the marriage relationship a gift from God or the infinite.

There has been discussion of relationships that identifies different types of relationships in terms of the participants being parents, adults, or children. All three roles exist in a marriage relationship. Sometimes a spouse acts like a child and the other spouse responds as a child. Other times a spouse acts like a child and the other spouse responds as a parent. Again, sometimes a spouse acts like a child and the other spouse responds like an adult. We are to approach God, or the infinite, as a child, with an open and loving mind, ready to hear the wonderful truth of existence and accept it with Joy. We are to approach God, or the infinite, as a parent, full of love for what could be, and gently encouraging and guiding the manifestations to fruition. We are to approach God, or the infinite, as an adult, aware of what is, what could be, and what has been, seeking companionship.

A marriage relationship does not exist in a vacuum — it is affected by the world around it and has an affect on the world around it. One marriage can lead to many more, and One marriage is all it takes. The only ones who can witness to this One relationship are the participants themselves.

Placing marriage as an asset to society, and supporting the spouses in their roles is essential to maintain one and all marriages. When one fails, others may follow. A society of infinite good supports all marriages in their many forms, as they are essential to such a society and every member of such a society knows this. The strains on a marriage are further testing and when failure comes, forgiveness is how to deal with it. Marriage is too important to abandon, even though the darkest places in the world could easily be found in a marriage.

Christ, Jesus, went to hell and overcame the demons, and this is what is necessary in marriage. There will definitely be as many challenges in marriage as Christ had to face, and when failure comes, one's awareness must die in the failure or else die in the world, overcome and be reborn to a new life and awareness. Jesus had to die in his awareness that society was not going to embrace his understanding officially. Judas had other ideas. Judas may have felt that Jesus could overcome the official understanding of the time if he was forced to face it head on. Jesus knew in his heart that such an embrace was not coming. Judas had to see it for himself, and did not die to his awareness that Jesus teaching should be embraced officially, and so died to the world, separating himself from God in the process.

Monday, May 23rd, 2011

Verse 13

The Baptism of Jesus

¹³Then Jesus came from Galilee to the Jordan to be baptized by John.

Verse 13

The Baptism of the One

¹³The One came in from another place, into her church to be acknowledged by Joan.

Verse 13 Discussion

What is baptism? Is it being born again? There is a lack of clarity. John the Baptist's baptism was one of repentance. Jesus' disciples baptized to acknowledge the presence of the Holy Spirit. John spoke of such a difference between his baptism and the baptism that Jesus would provide.

A baptism of repentance is an acknowledgment that one has committed themselves to a new start and has the intention to obey the law. Jesus' disciples baptized to both acknowledge and provide the presence of the Holy Spirit. Nevertheless baptism was an acknowledgment that one was beginning a new life, whether in obedience to the law or in cooperation with the Holy Spirit.

Why did Jesus choose to be baptized by John? Did Jesus need to repent? I doubt it. Jesus himself says "It is proper for us to do this to fulfill all righteousness." I believe Jesus was acknowledging a new beginning in his life — his public ministry.

Many people chase miracles. Their interest is in manifestations of the supernatural — like a magic show. In the book of Acts there is a story of a sorcerer who tried to buy the trick of bestowing the Holy Spirit. He was chastised by Peter. Jesus was not a magician and neither was John. Baptism may have overwhelming spiritual consequences but it is not magic. It is an acknowledgment.

John ministered from the banks of the Jordan river in the wilderness. This was his sacred place, and Jesus came from Galilee to be baptized by him there. In the animation the One comes in from another place, into Joan's sacred place to be acknowledged by Joan. Who is the One?

The One is the relationship, which is like Christ, a balance of whole and part. The One is nurtured by the spouses and in turn, ministers to the spouses. It is a living ideal. It is a living manifestation of the infinite. It is real. The One exists. Sure you can't touch it, but it is as real as anything else one may identify. It exists in the perception of the spouses and the people around them. It is witnessed by the spouses and proclaimed by the spouses to exist. This is common today — a couple will proclaim their relationship exists and is valid.

Again, in the animation text, the One comes in from "another place". If real marriage exists, where is it? It is beyond, it is always out in front of us, ahead of us. It is safe in a place beyond our reach, yet we reach for it. It cannot be bestowed by any person, and cannot be found in society. It is in the perception of the spouses and calls them forward. As well, at the end of **HESUS JOY CHRIST / Matthew's Two**, the couple and their One, not finding support in the conventional church, must dwell in another place, outside of society, yet they may physically exist amongst other people. The One is among us, calling us up and out to new life.

So what will marriage accomplish? What did Jesus accomplish? This is not a simple question. I believe Jesus established many things, not the least of which was the church, the living body of Christ. I am Christian because Jesus established that forgiveness is fundamental. Jesus died for forgiveness. He gave up everything, including his life for forgiveness. Forgiveness has nothing to do with being polite or nice. Forgiveness is messy, dirty, painful, expensive and ultimately fatal, in the end. But rebirth is real — more real than death. Marriage is the foremost intention of forgiveness. The dichotomy of whole and part meets and kisses in marriage, creating all awareness. We do not live in our bodies, we live in our minds. Marriage is the birthplace of all that is created, to the extent that Christ lives in a marriage.

So if Christ saved the world, where are we going now? If God became man, whose mother was a woman, and this man was called "Emmanuel", or "God with us", then can God continue to dwell among us? Where is God? He is here among us, in the faces of the people we meet every day. Can we see God among us? This depends on our awareness and if our awareness is sufficient to see God. Where is this "Kingdom of Heaven" or society of infinite good? It is very, very, very close — as close as our spouse, or the nearest thing to our spouse. Does anyone really believe heaven can exist on earth? Could we really have a society of infinite good? I believe the means to obtain a society of infinite good are at hand, in marriage. This is what marriage will accomplish — a society of infinite good, the Kingdom of Heaven, God dwelling amongst us, infinite good.

Death will be swallowed up in life. The lamb will lie down with the lion. Evil will be swallowed up by Good. Fear will be meaningless. Everyone will live — either long or reborn.

Friday, May 27th, 2011

Verse 14

¹⁴But John tried to deter him, saying, "I need to be baptized by you, and do you come to me?"

Verse 14

¹⁴But Joan tried to deter One saying, "I need to be acknowledged by you and do you come to me?"

Verse 14 Discussion

Yeah, John tried to argue, almost, with Jesus! This must have been like someone arguing with a person who has just complimented them for some reason. "No, my drawing is not any good, and I cannot draw well!" The draftsperson is too focused on how far their work is from perfect, and looses their awareness of how much more they have achieved than if they had never made an attempt! John was very aware of his shortcomings in the sight of God, and had lost sight of how much he had accomplished on God's behalf. He blazed a trail for Jesus that was straight and true. Jesus came to John and continued on. Jesus walked in the path of an itinerant preacher as John had. The people were accustomed to preachers, partly because of John, and they were aware that things could be better, as well due to John's work. John had the peoples attention, and the people were now of a mind that was open to Jesus.

John knew Jesus and Jesus knew John, since they were cousins or something, and John had jumped in his mother Elizabeth's womb when Mary, pregnant with Jesus, came into Elizabeth's presence. They were well aware of one another, so that Jesus sought out John's acknowledgment when he had decided to begin his mission. This would have been important to Jesus, the man, that John, who had an established ministry, acknowledge Jesus as worthy of engaging in a similar type of endeavour. Jesus was a man, who had doubts, which he wrestled with, as any man does, and overcame as God does. John's acknowledgment was important to Jesus, and this was the righteousness that was to be fulfilled, for if John had misgivings about Jesus beginning a public ministry, ... Jesus had to allow the opportunity for John to express any concerns he may have about such an endeavour on Jesus' part.

John had no misgivings about Jesus' ministry — he was overjoyed to see it coming! This must have been a great relief to Jesus, who had not acknowledged his own worthiness outside of his own mind. When he saw John's overwhelming Joy and encouragement of his decision, he must have felt wonderful, and this Joy was apparent to all present. John's emotion must have been greater than the joy of a father's when the lost son gets accepted to university and intends to follow in the father's career choice.

Both John and Joan have been working hard for a distant goal, that they may never see in their lifetime. They both know that whether Jesus, or the One, there is another who will take their work far further than they ever could. They long to see the completion of their work, by the saviour for whom they labour, every day. John is preaching a more thorough adherence to the law, and Joan is preaching a more thorough adherence to following Jesus, which she preaches leads to a One of marriage. Joan is not married, and John cannot die for the forgiveness of humankind's sins, yet they both long for their goals, whether the One of marriage or the salvation of humankind from their sins.

Both John and Joan know they need Jesus or the One more than Jesus or the One need them. This is why they protest. Nevertheless, both John and Joan are essential to the work. The One must be acknowledged, so that there is an outward and visible sign of inward and spiritual grace. That is it — there is no more! There is not any magic although there is likely a great deal of overwhelming emotion, for all present.

Finally, in today's marriages, the celebrant at the ceremony merely acknowledges the witness of the spouses that there is a sacred relationship, or One, that exists between them, the spouses. There may or may not be certain tests that the celebrant may attempt to use to verify the existence of a sacred relationship, but such a relationship is beyond any tests, so they are meaningless. But when there is a sacred relationship, or One, the celebrant needs to be acknowledged by the couple, and this is not such a radical idea. Many couples today, who have drifted away or outright chosen to not participate in any organized religion, have voted with their feet that the church or other religion has failed to serve their spiritual lives. They fail to acknowledge the validity of the celebrant and the organized religion, and therefore do not bring their relationship to be acknowledged by an organization that they themselves do not acknowledge. This is akin to Joan saying "I need to be acknowledged by you, and do you come to me ?" Couples procreate, so if there is to be a continued organized religious presence, it is very important to that organization that families participate. Don't get it mixed up the other way around! The fact that couples may be a greater resource than anything else demands religions' attention. Keep in mind that a religious marriage does not in any way incline the relationship to last. And a casual relationship without determined forgiveness will fail to last. This is more important than any ceremony.

Monday, June 6th, 2011

Verse 15

¹⁵Jesus replied, "Let it be so now; it is proper for us to do this to fulfill all righteousness." Then John consented.

Verse 15

¹⁵One replied: "Let it be so now, it is proper for us to do this to fulfill all righteousness." Then Joan consented.

Verse 15 Discussion

Now — why is it good enough for now ? How does one break out of a closed system and bring about an infinite system. There is no way out of a closed system, and that is why it is a closed system. Consider a building — if it is constantly in use every day how does one expand such a building ? Our cities have not been abandoned to become new — they have become new and modern while people have inhabited them. Modern economics demands growth but where does this come from in a closed system. First of all, many economies annex neighboring economies, but this practice has limits. The exploration of space may have begun but this world will be all we have for many more generations. Our world, Earth, is finite, as ecologists keep reminding us.

The universe may be infinite, but we are limited in our ability to access anything beyond this planet.

So we are all in a closed system, and the system somehow has to be changed to a new system for there to be growth. There was the Stone Age, the Bronze Age and the Iron Age. There was the colonial age and the industrial revolution. Each of these periods found opportunities to expand from within, which was followed by an outward expansion that was equipped with the technologies that were found within the original closed system. Jesus, the man, found new opportunities in the Hebrew religion and had to adjust and expand the awareness of the Hebrew religion to draw attention to these new opportunities. This was his ministry to the Hebrews. He was not to minister to any other people, although "even the dogs eat the crumbs that fall from the master's table". Jesus took advantage of the opportunity that John had built and began there, with a more intense look at the Hebrew law and where such a thorough understanding could lead. Joan is doing the same thing with christianity — taking a more intense look at where a society of people who have taken on the character of christ could lead, and proclaiming that marriage is the obvious direction in which to head. Both are beginning with what they have and wherever they find themselves — NOW !

Jesus was within the law, and could easily accept the baptism of repentance that John was offering, especially if Jesus was committing himself to a new extremely thorough following of the law. This is why he says "Let it be so for now" - this is where he was beginning. It was proper for him to do so to fulfill all righteousness, before he continued on into even more intense righteousness. The One of the couple, will take the world farther than the single person of Joan ever could, but before they become more intensely involved in their relationship, Joan's acknowledgment becomes a milestone and a cornerstone on the road of their One accomplishments. They need Joan to acknowledge that this is the One and this is what it is doing. Sure there will be other relationships worthy of the title One, but all these relationships are One.

It is very often forgotten that we are to dwell in peace with God with us. Few people believe this is possible in light of all the suffering they have witnessed in their lives alone. They have abandoned even the idea of an infinite purpose such as God, let alone a loving infinite person. When a child learns to ride a bike it is miraculous that they find that they can continue on if they respect the limitations of balancing left and right. They are full of joy at the realization. This is the nature of the infinite One. It seems impossible in the present reality but nevertheless it comes into our reality almost by accident and calls us toward it from then on.

An infinite awareness of an infinite balance of whole and part will lead to infinite possibilities within a finite world. The door to growth and expansion lies within this One balance of marriage. Infinity will sit with us and be an everlasting opportunity. This infinity will be an always available recourse in the event of a tragedy. It will be found that good is infinite and bad is finite within this infinity. This can become our world NOW !

Friday, June 10th, 2011

Verse 16

¹⁶As soon as Jesus was baptized, he went up out of the water. At that moment heaven was opened, and he saw the Spirit of God descending like a dove and alighting on him.

Verse 16

¹⁶As soon as One was acknowledged, One went up, out of the church. At that moment, heaven was opened, and Joan saw the spirit of God descending like a dove and lighting on One.

Verse 16 Discussion

People use to tell me, in my early adulthood, that it doesn't matter what I do with my life, as long as I get committed. A university professor told me I could write about anything that I want, as long as I get engaged; but that's another story. What's done is done, so move on. Jesus has made his commitment, and begins to head out of the river, but then notices that things are different, as his commitment has made a difference.

Once one has wrestled with a decision, there comes a time to decide, and then move on. What's passed is past. The decision is made and the issue is no longer open for deliberation, discussion or debate. Others may try to maintain a state of deliberation in one's mind, but this only makes one's resolve stronger, and one closes them self off to anyone who wants to question the decision. For me this was the issue of whether I would complete grade thirteen, on the path to university. I had already made up my mind and had obtained an offer to become an electrician's apprentice, and I was already employed on that decision. But then my parents returned and at least my mother, if not both my parents, as well as an uncle in a lengthy soliloquy, made it clear to me that they wanted me to attend grade thirteen, even going so far as to tell me they know I want to attend grade thirteen, and I found their audacity amazing. Solely out of respect for my parents' wishes, I attended another year of secondary school, and promised myself this was the last thing I would do out of deference to my parents' wishes.

There is a freedom and joy that comes when one's mind is made up and the decision has been made and the die has been cast. When I am drawing the animation, it takes extreme concentration, and then I am exhausted, relieved and pleased that it is done, regardless of the shortcomings I am all too well aware of in the quality of my work. This joy may be what Jesus felt once he had committed himself to his ministry, by deciding to follow the law in such an intense fashion. The decision had been made and he no longer deliberated on where why and how, only considering what he would do next to follow his Father on the path He chose for Jesus. The relief of having the decision made would be enough to invite the spirit of God to alight on him, like a dove landing, and it would remain with him into his temptation trials in the desert in the fourth chapter of the Gospel of Matthew. It was the same spirit that drove him into the desert, and the same spirit that brought him back out.

It is not clear to me who the "he" refers to in the original Gospel text — is it Jesus who saw the spirit of God, or was it John who saw the spirit of God descend upon Jesus. Perhaps it descended on both of them! In the animation, it is Joan who sees the spirit of God descending like a dove and lighting on One, the couple. We are not made aware of how the couple felt as they left the church to continue on in their relationship. They appear to be driven by the spirit that is upon them.

Heaven was opened so that one, or even the One, can have a glimpse of what where we are heading would be like. The environment is heavenly. Joy reigns.

The spirit of God is portrayed in the animation. It is two tori linked and moving. This is a finite, limited image of infinite existence. God is infinite, and made manifest in our finite world. This animated image of the spirit of God is the least limited image I can find for my understanding of the universe or the nature of infinite reality.

The Hebrews did not create any images of God that were endorsed, so this discussion excludes things they created like a golden calf. Even the name of God was never said out loud, only written as "YHWH", which lacking vowels could not be said. The gentiles added an "a" and an "e" to make it "YAHWEH", and pronounceable. In other writings, a German "j" pronounced as a "y" made the spelling "JHWH" or "JAWEH", which has become "Jehovah", as in "Jehovah's Witnesses". Regardless, Yhwh translates to "I am". This is God's name - "I am".

Jesus taught that we should call God our "Father", which implies he is a personal parent apart, who has a vested interest in each of us personally. This is more familiar than "I am", which comes across as a little cold. Nevertheless, if one is, there must be other than one, that is separate from one. So "I am" implies there is a "You are", or "It is". Jesus also taught that we are children of God and that the peacemakers will be called sons of God. Jesus presented a God that is much more familiar, personal and intimately involved in each one of us. Each of us at some time has used the phrase "I am" in contexts such as "I am happy" or "I am hungry".

Christianity uses the symbol of the cross (+), which implies two aspects perpendicular to one another. Jehovah's Witnesses claim there is only the upright and dismiss the horizontal, and others claim the horizontal bar is at the top of the upright, so that the upright does not pass through the horizontal. There is a mythology represented in these symbols, whether intended or not. Another symbol is the Jewish star of David, made up of an equilateral triangle pointing down into another equilateral triangle pointing up, creating a six pointed star. The mythology of this symbol could be that God is reaching down to us as we reach up to God. It appears to represent a dichotomy.

In this animated symbol of infinite existence, there are two tori oriented perpendicular to each other, and linked. Each surface of each torus is moving laterally and longitudinally, each at the same rate as the other, each completing one revolution both laterally and longitudinally in the same time period. This means that at the inside of each torus, where each touches the inside of the other torus, the motion is continuous and in synch, even though the tori are perpendicular to each other. However, where the outside of a torus touches the inside of the other torus, the outside the torus is moving at least twice the speed of the inside of the other torus! This is an inconsistency in the model. This would be a boundary between the two tori, but where the insides of each torus touch there would not be any boundary. This boundary gradually progresses from where the insides of the two tori touch and are in synch, where there is not a boundary between them, to where the outside of one torus touches the inside of the other torus, where the boundary is most distinct, due to the greatest discrepancy between the speeds of the two surfaces of the tori.

Friday, June 17th, to Sunday, June 19th, 2011

Verse 17

¹⁷And a voice from heaven said, "This is my Son, whom I love; with him I am well pleased."

Verse 17

¹⁷And a voice was heard: "This is my One, with them I am well pleased."

Verse 17 Discussion

Stepping back from the discussion of macro physics, and the nature of existence, the voice from heaven says that Jesus is his son, whom he loves, and with whom he is well pleased. In the animation text, there is not a statement of love. This may have originally been an oversight, but the die has been cast, and what was said is what was said. To make sense out of it, going back to the beginning of this discussion, everything has an inclination to either whole or part, female or male, and this inclination can be seen as love. So the love of an aspect is for it's inclination. Males love to be male, and females love to be female. The greatest joy, however, is when the two parts of the dichotomy are united. So this joy is beyond love, as love can exist in one part without the other whole reciprocating, yet when the whole reciprocates there is joy, and vice versa, and this Joy is the One.

Love is what animates existence, and this is the movement of the two tori, as animated. To illustrate this movement in the surfaces of the tori, I have illustrated an arrow on each torus pointing in the direction of the movement of each surface. As a further complication, the arrow on the male torus is a positive image, with anything other than the arrow being transparent. In the female or horizontal torus, the arrow is transparent and the remainder of the surface opaque. These two arrows have a positive resultant vector, but point in perpendicular directions — at right angles to one another. There are twelve divisions both laterally and longitudinally on each torus. The arrows are determined by drawing a grid on the arrow image and mapping the image onto each torus to create 24 images, which when viewed in order, animate the tori.

The result is a very complex animated image. Originally, in the computer animated image of the tori in **HESUS JOY CHRIST / Matthew's One Too!**, the tori simply rotated longitudinally, did not touch, and had a random pattern on their surfaces. Then in **HESUS JOY CHRIST / Matthew's Two**, the surface of each torus had a spiral on it, like a candy cane, with the male having blue stripes and the female having red stripes. If the animated image represented merely the idea of the One, the image was in black and white, but if the One was present, the image was in colour. Furthermore, if the idea was newly acquired, and juvenile, the tori were static and not moving, without any pattern on the surfaces. This appears in the section entitled **The Escape to Civilization**.

Even I, with the greatest familiarity with this animated image, still have a difficult time seeing the arrows moving on the tori. I completed the animation in faith, having confidence in the final output because I was able to be consistent in the mapping of the arrows onto the tori. Nevertheless, if this simple construction is the basis for such a complex animated image, it is easy to imagine how there could be so much confusion, discouragement and conflict in the world if this extremely complicated image is the nature of existence.

Yet this image appears to be consistent with my experience. In Physics, they are trying to unite quantum physics, or micro physics, with macro physics, or Einstein's Theory of Relativity, to determine the nature of the universe and physical existence. The last time I checked, the universe, of multiple dimensions, appeared to be saddle shaped, or at least that is what I remember from the book **A Brief History of Time** by Stephen Hawking. The shape of the surfaces of the tori, where the insides touch, is just such a saddle shape, and is homogenous and consistent, without any singularities or boundaries.

From another approach, Pope John Paul the second, wrote his book, **Theology of the Body** where all the aspects of relationships amongst people, including sex, are discussed in the light of God's revelation. It has been stated many times that this one writing, is a time bomb sitting in the church, that will blow popular thinking both within the church and within society, right out of the water! Suffice it to say that this book, written by the Pope, as Pope in all his official authority, claims that the sexual revolution of the nineteen sixties did not go far enough in opening up peoples ideas of relationships and sexuality. There is a lot of potential between the sexes and in our relationships.

Furthermore, when looking at this animated model of existence, it seems to suggest that there are places in time and existence where everything is homogenous and moving together, yet in other parts of existence there is conflict and discord. There is also an exterior area in which to expand, but expansion is not so simple in this model. This is because, although male or female may expand freely in the open area outside of the longitudinal circumferences, expansion beyond the longitudinal circumferences into the inner circumference of the other, across the boundary, will create conflict. This seems to suggest that under certain circumstances the male must lead, but also equally strongly suggests that the female must lead in other circumstances that occur just as often. And the corollary would seem to be true as well — that there are circumstances where the male must limit himself, and there are equally occurring similar circumstances where the female must limit themselves.

Sunday, June 19th, 2011

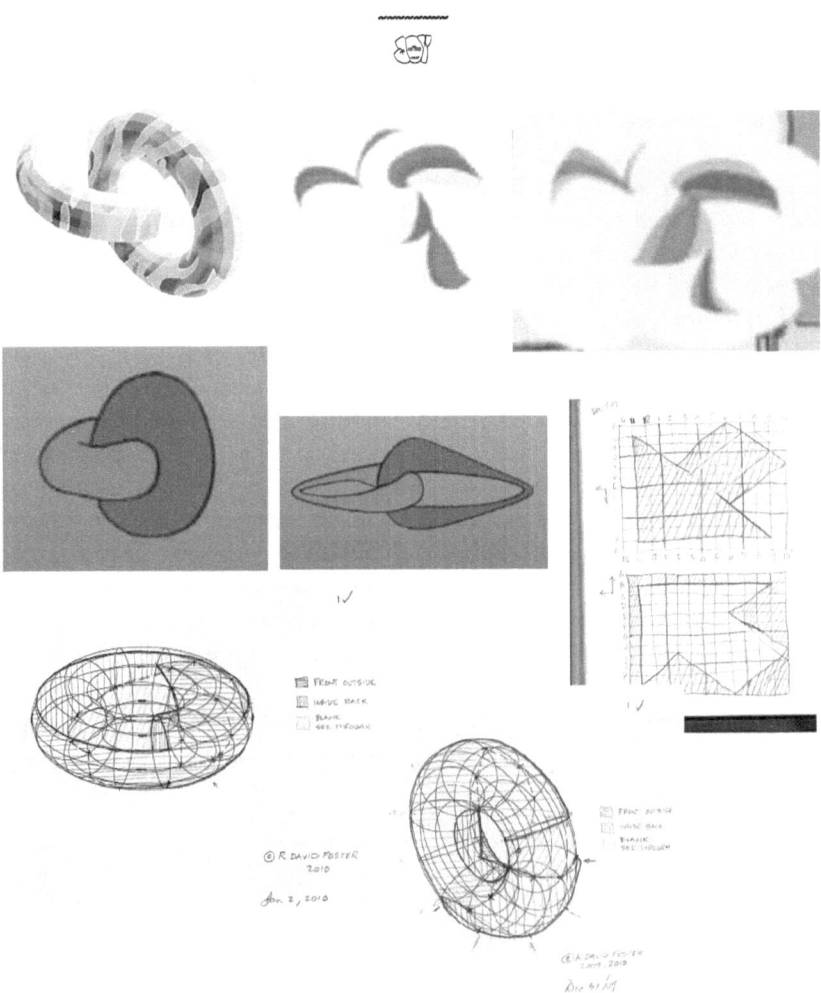

Closing Notes

OVERVIEW

  Well here we go ! We were a third of the way through discussing the seventeen verses of **HESUS JOY CHRIST / Matthew's Three Fold** , when I took a break to consider the wordage that was then pushing seven thousand words !

  A body of knowledge has it's limits, and one limit has nothing to do with how many pages are written about such a body of knowledge . When one (or a group) creates a body of knowledge they are making many decisions, or rather, assumptions that are not stated outright . These assumptions are made early on in the creation of a body of knowledge but seriously limit the effectiveness of that body of knowledge . So as an example of how creating a body of knowledge can become ridiculous, usually around the point at which academia takes over, I have chosen to write about everything I know about how to pick up a stick .

  I was fortunate to make the acquaintance of a man in his fifties who left the aerospace industry to go to school for landscaping . That alone is ridiculous enough, but the point is that this gentleman was accomplished in academia and technological industry, who when he decided he wanted to work outdoors it was only natural that he would go to school to learn an outdoor trade . He studied for three years at Humber College and graduated from the landscaping technician program . Sadly, he only lasted five months as a landscaper, in spite of working for a very reputable, good and established company, and was able to get into good enough shape in spite of his many years of age, but could not tolerate the bystanders looking at him with the expression of 'look at that nice old man picking weeds' ! His academic and thorough understanding was not appreciated by the casual observer, so was it worth anything at all ? Likewise, this thorough understanding of how to pick up a stick is ridiculous and not worth anything at all to the casual observer . And the discussion of **HESUS JOY CHRIST / Matthew's Three Fold** is not worth anything to the casual observer — unless an awareness is cultivated by considering the discussion, but a thorough consideration of the animation would have the same effect of cultivating an awareness, not to mention considering life would cultivate a thorough awareness .

  The moral of the story, here, is   PAY ATTENTION ! ! !

Tuesday, April 12th, 2011

HOW TO PICK UP A STICK!

Here is how to pick up a stick.

First determine the size of the stick. Is it a twig, a limb, or a full branch? If it is a twig, how many of them are there? If there are many, then get a rake and a tarp. If there are not enough to warrant a tarp than get a garbage bag or a bucket.

Drop the garbage bag or bucket in the general middle of the twigs, and begin a loop path, starting and finishing at the bucket and extending only far enough to allow you to fill your hands with twigs. If you make the loop path too big you will waste time walking back to the bucket when your hands are full. If you make the loop path too small you will be dumping too few sticks in the bucket for each loop and that wastes time loading too small a load of twigs in the bucket. This becomes a concern when the bucket begins to get full and the twigs must be stuffed into it and can no longer just be dropped into it. If you are using a garbage bag, however, this is always a concern as the twigs must be placed into the bag lengthwise as otherwise the bag cannot hold as much and is too quickly filled.

Actually picking up the twig must be done standing with legs extended but not locked. Lean down like you are touching your toes and bob down to pick up the twig, and as you bob up transfer it to your off hand until it is full, and by that time you should be more than halfway along your loop path. Finish the remaining path holding the sticks in the good hand that picks them up, so that you arrive at the bucket with two full hands. Do not crawl around on your hands and knees because you need your hands to hold as many twigs as possible. It likely isn't good for your knees, crawling in the damp ground. As well, bending your knees to crouch down to pick up the twigs will be too much bending for your knees. Bobbing will get you well stretched out.

In the case of many twigs, a rake can be used to gather the twigs into piles and onto the tarp, to be dragged or carried to the truck. The first sweep of the rake will orient the twigs perpendicular to the sweep of the rake, and then the pile can be rolled like a snowball as it gathers more twigs. Maintain the coherency of the pile if the twigs are to be tied into bundles, as such a fagot can be rolled onto the twine to allow the twine to be wrapped around the fagot and tied. Do not attempt to rake a twig that is parallel to the path of the rake. This will break the rake. It may still be necessary to gather the remaining twigs by hand. Larger sticks may need to be picked up by hand, following the above mentioned method, as they cannot be gathered by a rake. DO NOT BREAK THE RAKE!

Usually, a large area of twigs will occur in the spring as summer or spring maintenance is beginning, but may also occur when pruning. Pruning will produce limbs and perhaps branches. Branches may also need to be picked up at the beginning of spring maintenance or after a storm.

When picking up a limb or a stick that is larger, pick it up by the stump end as that will give you the most leverage over a tapered limb if you pick it up by it's heaviest end. Otherwise the limb will be unwieldy and if you can get it into your armload, you may not be able to toss it in the truck. Gather all that you can hold under one arm and make sure you are on your way back to the truck by the time you have a full load in your arms. Again, bob down and up to pick up the sticks, keeping in mind your armload. There is no way you could crawl or even crouch with an armload of sticks.

Branches are larger sticks that branch into more than one stick. They may be very large. If they are very large, do not cut them up, but instead drag them by the stump end, so that no further branches are broken off, and heave them by the stump end, into the truck. The best place to cut them, to pack them into the truck efficiently, is right in the truck. If one was to cut them up before they are in the truck, that is only more sticks to pick up and more sticks to throw in the truck and more sticks to pack into the truck to get a large load and reduce the number of trips with the truck. Once a few branches are aligned with the stump end at the head of the truck, tread on the branches carefully and with loppers, cut the branches at the crotches where the smaller branches head out from the main branch. It is the crotch that sets the limbs at angles to one another and prevents efficient loading in the truck bed. By cutting the branches at the crotches the limbs are able to fall into alignment with one another. I have seen a load of branches come out of the truck body and maintain the rectangular shape of the truck body as it sits on it's own after being dumped.

Finally, for a good laugh, try to wield a branch by the small end — it will wobble around and you may not even be able to get the stump off the ground! The use of a wood chipper greatly improves the packing and removal of large branches, but there will still be twigs to be gathered, according to the appropriate method.

1000 words

Tuesday, April 12th, 2011

HESUS JOY CHRIST / Matthew's Foretold DISCUSSION -

From Tuesday, April 24th, 2012,
to Tuesday, October 30th, 2012
as posted to the blog
of R. David Foster
entitled Vid'93 Bein' To Wordie . . .
@ www.vid93.blogspot.ca

© R. David Foster 2009, 2011, 2012

OVERVIEW
from the opening of the discussion of
HESUS JOY CHRIST / Matthew's Three Fold

Well here we go! Try to keep up because there are many angles to this text and it's discussion will cover all the angles I can find in both texts and the relationship between the two texts, which carries a fourth level of meaning. That is — the meaning of each text individually (2 meanings), the meaning when both texts are viewed together (3rd meaning) and the meaning of the relationship (3rd meaning) in the context in which we share — real life (the 4th meaning)!

Stepping back a bit, let's acknowledge a few things. We are talking about religion — specifically christianity, which I believe is essentially forgiveness to the ultimate degree. All religions have their strengths, in fact all are valid and relevant. Forgiveness is either a spoken or unspoken element in many religions. I believe forgiveness is essential, and that is why I am christian.

Many religions have elements of Whole and Part. Ying-Yang for example. Other terms are Agency and Communion, Reductionistic and Holistic, one and many, or male and female. All that exists has both a holistic aspect and a partial aspect. Everything that exists is part of a context, and wholly made of parts. To bring something into existence one must address both the whole and the part, both the context and the specific, aspects.

Furthermore, everything that exists has an inclination to either whole or part. The approach to anything assesses the balance of whole and part in that thing. An imbalance is always apparent, and the inclination of any approach is to correct the thing to obtain balance. If it appears too partial it must be corrected. If it appears too wholistic it must be corrected. The fallacy is that anything that exists is not in balance. In other words, if you may approach it then it does exist and if it exists it must already be in balance. Forgiveness allows the balance to exist without correction, and accepts that all things are in balance. This is somewhat a Buddhist opinion or faith. The important thing is to SEE the balance and not be moved to correction by any APPARENT imbalance. Otherwise the urge to correct leads to confrontation and a need to make things unbalanced and favouring whole or part over the other. A key thing about christianity is that it will forgive any apparent imbalance to the extreme of self destruction, but the self destruction is only apparent and not real! This last idea is explored in the animation entitled **HESUS JOY CHRIST / Matthew's Two Four** which is a chapter about ends.

If whole and part are termed female and male, then this forgiveness that exists between the sexes will allow marriage, which is capable of creation, if not joy and contentment. The whole of **HESUS JOY CHRIST** points to marriage as the further salvation of humankind, which is based on the essential character of Jesus that is essential for any successful marriage of any whole and part or female and male.

All people are called to different vocations, whether single celibacy, marriage, or other. Marriage is essential to society as a union of whole and part that creates new meaning and life. Marriage is a resource that produces new understanding and creates far more than just babies. This in no way diminishes christianity, because without ultimate forgiveness and sacrifice no marriage will survive. It will end when a partial or whole attitude fails to forgive a whole or partial attitude. Once one has taken up the challenge of Christ and begun to follow him, some sort of witness of the union of whole and part is where one must head, fully armed with forgiveness.

Moving on, evil is real, and forgiveness is how to deal with it. This third chapter of the Gospel of Matthew is about Jesus' baptism by his cousin, John the Baptist. John the Baptist was not preaching forgiveness, nor rebirth through death from forgiveness, but repentance which is turning from doing evil and trying again. Obedience to the Law, as turning from evil, will make balance apparent and allow the balance to be acknowledged and seen. But no one has ever been able to obey the fullest intent of the Law without the benefit of infinite grace. In other words, no one has ever been able to keep the Law when circumstances were against them. Jesus was able to obey the Law but it lead to his very public death. Many others have died obeying the Law in much less honoured deaths. Death — what is it really ? Death will be discussed elsewhere — perhaps in a further discussion of **_Matthew's Two Four_** .

Finally, one may choose to keep the issue of the existence of God out of this discussion. For my part, God is an infinite goal, infinitely present as an infinite goal, colouring our perception of existence. Whether God is a person, male or female, is beyond this immediate discussion, but worth discussing in some other writing. Suffice it to say, for now, that whatever has been created exists within infinity and it is all, entirely, good.

Ash Wednesday, March 9th, 2011

OVERVIEW

This is written after the discussion of **Matthew's Two Four**, the discussion of **Matthew's One Too !**, the discussion of **Matthew's Three Fold** and the discussion of **Matthew's Two** were written. Matthew, Chapter Four, is the story of Jesus' temptation by the devil in the desert, immediately after his baptism by John in the Jordan river, in Chapter Three. After he came out of the desert, Jesus began to preach, calling the first disciples, and healing the sick. **Matthew's Foretold** is a similar story of the life of the infant One, its effect on the community, and its ultimate dissolution and life continuing on after. **Matthew's Foretold** is not necessarily in chronological order as Chapter Four of the Gospel of Matthew is, but it is in the same order as the Gospel of Matthew, Chapter Four !

The One is the marriage relationship, or balance of male and female or part and whole. This discussion will be about the establishment of the infant One in the form of a marriage relationship. This One needs to be protected and nurtured to come to fullness and maturity, but once established, it is challenged.

The infant One is the understanding of the necessity of a balance of whole and part, and the faith of marriage, which must be nurtured and cultivated. It appears in relationships, especially romantic relationships, and must be taken care of and nurtured to reach maturity. This care can be interfered with and obstructed, as it frequently is, by other interests in the life of the spouses. Matthew's Foretold is the story of the trials endured by the One relationship, including the influence of the relationship on the community and the ultimate dissolution of the actual relationship, and the continuation of the influence of the One.

Wednesday, April 18th, 2012

OPENING NOTES

Wednesday, May 12, 2010
HESUS JOY CHRIST - Matthew Chapter Four
The animation of **HESUS JOY CHRIST - *Matthew's Foretold*** is complete. To double your viewing pleasure when the animation is posted, here, next Wednesday, I have provided the original bible text in this post below. All going well today, this animation will screen next Wednesday, May 19th, 2010 at the **Revue Cinema**'s open screening called **Drop Your Shorts**.
Be in the know - and get all the in-jokes.
David Foster

www.vid93.blogspot.ca

The Gospel of Matthew --- Chapter Four
New International Version

The Temptation of Jesus
4 1 Then Jesus was led by the Spirit into the desert . . . ...

Tuesday, May 18, 2010
HESUS JOY CHRIST - *Matthew's Foretold* -- text
. . . . below is the text of the animation, that is written very closely, in parallel, to the Gospel of Matthew Chapter Four. I will post the animation here after Wednesday evening, May 19th, when it screens at the **Revue Cinema**'s open screening called **Drop Your Shorts**.

Happy 19th everybody; including Gwen . . . .

Matthew's Foretold
© R David Foster December 26, 2009 --- January 10, 2010

/ The Temptation of the One /
/ 1 Then One was led by the Spirit into abundance . . . ...

Thursday, May 20, 2010
HESUS JOY CHRIST - *Matthew's Foretold* animation
. . . . below is the animation of **HESUS JOY CHRIST - *Matthew's Foretold***. It is embedded from the Youtube upload and can be found on www.youtube.com, with the rest of

the animation, by searching "RDavidFoster" (one word) in the Youtube search engine, as well as this posting on my blog . .
Vid93 bein' To wordie . . .
. . which includes previous postings of the original bible text and the text of the animation .

The Gospel of Matthew — Chapter Four

*Jesus Is Tested in the Wilderness**

¹Then Jesus was led by the Spirit into the **wilderness**** to be tempted^a by the devil. ²After fasting forty days and forty nights, he was hungry. ³The tempter came to him and said, "If you are the Son of God, tell these stones to become bread."

⁴Jesus answered, "It is written: 'Man shall not live on bread alone, but on every word that comes from the mouth of God.'^b"

⁵Then the devil took him to the holy city and had him stand on the highest point of the temple. ⁶"If you are the Son of God," he said, "throw yourself down. For it is written:

"'He will command his angels concerning you,
and they will lift you up in their hands,
so that you will not strike your foot against a stone.'^c"

⁷Jesus answered him, "It is also written: 'Do not put the Lord your God to the test.'^d"

⁸Again, the devil took him to a very high mountain and showed him all the kingdoms of the world and their splendor. ⁹"All this I will give you," he said, "if you will bow down and worship me."

¹⁰Jesus said to him, "Away from me, Satan! For it is written: 'Worship the Lord your God, and serve him only.'^e"

¹¹Then the devil left him, and angels came and attended him.

---

*	1	1973, 1978, 1984 NIV copy that HJC was written from is **The Temptation of Jesus**
**	1	1973, 1978, 1984 NIV copy that HJC was written from is **desert**
a	1	The Greek for tempted can also mean tested.
b	4	Deuteronomy 8:3
c	6	Psalm 91:11,12
d	7	Deuteronomy 6:16
e	10	Deuteronomy 6:13

Jesus Begins to Preach

¹²When Jesus heard that John had been put in prison, he withdrew to Galilee. ¹³Leaving Nazareth, he went and lived in Capernaum, which was by the lake in the area of Zebulun and Naphtali — ¹⁴to fulfill what was said through the prophet Isaiah:

¹⁵"Land of Zebulun and land of Naphtali,
the Way of the Sea, beyond the Jordan,
Galilee of the Gentiles—
¹⁶the people living in darkness
have seen a great light;
on those living in the land of the shadow of death
a light has dawned."*f*

¹⁷From that time on Jesus began to preach, "Repent, for the kingdom of heaven **has come***** near."

*Jesus Calls His First Disciples*****

¹⁸As Jesus was walking beside the Sea of Galilee, he saw two brothers, Simon called Peter and his brother Andrew. They were casting a net into the lake, for they were fishermen. ¹⁹"Come, follow me," Jesus said, "and I will **send you out to fish for people*******." ²⁰At once they left their nets and followed him.

²¹Going on from there, he saw two other brothers, James son of Zebedee and his brother John. They were in a boat with their father Zebedee, preparing their nets. Jesus called them, ²²and immediately they left the boat and their father and followed him.

---

f   **16** Isaiah 9:1,2

***   **17** 1973, 1978, 1984 NIV copy that HJC was written from is *is*

****   **18** 1973, 1978, 1984 NIV copy that HJC was written from is *The Calling of the First Disciples*

*****   **19** 1973, 1978, 1984 NIV copy that HJC was written from is *make you fishers of men*

Jesus Heals the Sick

²³Jesus went throughout Galilee, teaching in their synagogues, **proclaiming******** the good news of the kingdom, and healing every disease and sickness among the people. ²⁴News about him spread all over Syria, and people brought to him all who were ill with various diseases, those suffering severe pain, the demon-possessed, those having seizures, and the paralyzed; and he healed them. ²⁵Large crowds from Galilee, the Decapolis,⁹ Jerusalem, Judea and the region across the Jordan followed him.

******   **23**   1973, 1978, 1984 NIV copy that HJC was written from is **preaching**

g   **25**   That is, *the Ten Cities*

This **LEFT** Column is always the Original Gospel Text of the Fourth Chapter of the Gospel of Matthew, *New International Version.*

This **RIGHT** Column is always the text of the animation –

**HESUS JOY CHRIST /
Matthew's Foretold,**
written by R. David Foster.

Slashes (/) in the text of the animation indicate a scene change in the animation.

Verse 1

Jesus Is Tested in the Wilderness*

¹Then Jesus was led by the Spirit into the **wilderness**** to be tempted*ᵃ* by the devil.

* **1** 1973, 1978, 1984 NIV copy that HJC was written from is ***The Temptation of Jesus***
** **1** 1973, 1978, 1984 NIV copy that HJC was written from is ***desert***
ᵃ **1** The Greek for tempted can also mean tested.

Verse 1

The Temptation of the One

¹Then One was led by the Spirit into abundance to be tempted by the devil.

Verse 1 Discussion

'It is easier for a camel to pass through the eye of a needle than for a rich man to enter the kingdom of heaven.'
'Blessed are the poor in spirit, for theirs is the kingdom of heaven.'

So is it all that better to be rich, whether in wealth or spirit, living in abundance, rather than poor in wealth and spirit? Surely abundance can be a far greater environment of temptation than a deserted experience.
Having sought solitude to clear my head, and simple living to maintain a clear head, I understand Jesus going out into the desert as his wanting to clear his head and set his priorities. I have heard that the stones into bread is the temptation of an economic solution, but I cannot remember the correlation of the other two temptations to another two solutions.

Yet, if wealth is a hindrance to setting oneself right with the infinite, then, relatively speaking, North America, and all of western society, being wealthy, is on the wrong track. The success of the economic solution has left us bereft of spiritual leaders, and we import priests from the third world.

So I would suppose that Jesus wanted to put himself in a better position to face temptation, and so went off by himself into the desert to sort himself out without distractions.

But the achievement of the spouses, in attaining the sacrament of marriage, for their sacred One relationship balancing whole and part, female and male, has brought them prosperity, and the accompanying temptations. One temptation is complacency, that nothing is urgent and nothing too important. Another temptation is satisfaction, that the world has come to completion, and will therefore remain this way forever. A further temptation is that there is nothing to need to strive for, as all is accomplished. And don't forget the distractions of wealth with the many demands on one's attention, such as correspondence, accumulation, social events and more. Where is there any inclination to draw closer to one another, in meaningful discussion of how to take on further challenges as a team, or in discussion of each one's spiritual life and affinities, the life of the spirit before the infinite. And never mind learning about each other so that each may grow into the life of the other, the male growing in the world of the female, and the female fathoming the world of the male.

With all these distractions, no wonder Jesus sought out solitude in order to gain the high ground against temptation.

With all the possibility of renewable resources, why would Canada want to finish off the oil age, after the coal age, rather than develop the technology that reduces oil to a polymer source for plastics that technology can be made of and recycled as a renewable resource. This is but one example of the kind of challenges that are being overlooked because we are too distracted by the demands of our wealth. Really . . . steaming the oil out of the sand !! What were they thinking? I don't even steam my clothes to get the wrinkles out !!

Furthermore, who was it that said 'Movies were not made to be seen on a f£#%# %king telephone !!'. A smart phone is for a dumb arse who cannot organize themselves without a four inch screen. Napoleon conquered Europe without even a land line, let alone a walkie-talkie !! In considering my options for renewing my plan, I realized that all that these 'phones' can do is voice, voice messaging, email and internet. What is so important on the internet that one would squint to see it on the bus, not being allowed to use their 'phone' while driving, before they get home to view the internet on the desktop. If one is so busy that they cannot restrict their new boob tube use to certain times of the day than good luck with organizing anything else, including their eternal life. We are surely now living in a 'neon Rome'. We are agok at the shimmering darkness that titillates us and keeps us from real life. Honestly, when was the last time you dug a hole, or even more so, mowed a lawn, and better yet, walked for a half hour? When I had a car I was desperate for bicycle time. Having a car does not save transportation time, it only uses up more time in transportation going more places.

Even when I was dealing with blackberry people, and doing Autocad drafting near the airport in December, 2009, most people could not get over the technology far enough to count how many lanes of traffic Hurontario Street had just south of Burnhamthorpe. Sure, they had begun to take advantage of the customization possibilities of Autocad, but they had not thoroughly thought through their production process so no matter how versatile Autolisp may be, they were shooting themselves in the foot by not understanding their job to begin with!! Measuring along a curve! "£#%^%&^& !! Get real!! We are all staring at the pretty lights at the end of the tunnel and not realizing it is a truck heading for us !!

But I digress. I have been led by the spirit into a rant. Jesus was led by the Spirit into the desert to be tempted. The One was led by the Spirit into abundance to be tempted. We will all be tempted. The Spirit is always leading us to new challenges to our faith. We must rise to meet the challenges, and speak the truth of our environment as honest witnesses of our corner of the world. For the One, the environment of married life was found to be full of challenges that were to be overcome, but complacency is the standard of the day, to society's detriment. Marriage requires a supreme commitment, founded in christian forgiveness following Christ, by not only the spouses but the entire community, and this is lacking. Anyone who counsels spouses against one another, for whatever reason, is speaking against the spirit of the One sacred relationship balancing whole and part, and undermining society's greatest asset. Unless something illegal is occurring, than marriage must be supported by supporting both spouses as well as their union. The cost on society of the dissolution of a marriage is too great to take lightly, yet this is the case today. Keeping children as children, putting the well being of either spouse over the other spouse's well being, or anything else that undermines the infinite resource of a marriage relationship, limits society in too many ways to number.

Sunday, April 22nd, 2012

Verse 2

²After fasting forty days and forty nights, he was hungry.

Verse 2

²After feasting forty years and forty nights One was full.

Verse 2 Discussion

Jesus had reached a milestone — he had fasted and was hungry and had come to a turning point or point of decision. He was ready to face life choices and make lasting decisions. This was to be a landmark in his life.

Likewise, the One has come to a landmark in its life. Something has to be decided, which is mainly to stay the course or to correct the course, but things will not remain the same either way. If One stays on the course it is on, it will continue with a greater resolve, but if it changes course, it will be with determination.

It does not matter whether one has fasted or feasted — there will still be a completion to either fasting or feasting. Obviously one could continue to fast, and let the completion be their death, and likewise one could continue to feast, and let the completion be their death. But more likely one will come to a point where they will decide to continue or to change course in a life decision that will be made with determination.

Stepping back a bit, this sacred One relationship, Christlike, exists among the spouses as they balance whole and part, female and male, as Christ did with and in his life and ministry. But where Christ was one person, the One exists in the relationship of two people. Just as Christ could act with his left or right, as a whole or as a part, the sacred One relationship acts as a male or a female, in unity with the other spouse, yet each has their own role to play. If one is tempted, the One, the relationship is tempted. If one overcomes temptation, the One overcomes temptation. If one is full, the One is full, and at a turning point. Yet if one succumbs to temptation, the One succumbs to temptation, and this takes the forgiveness of the other spouse if the sacred One relationship is to survive. Yet God the Father, who is all powerful, oversees the existence of the One whether in a relationship or an individual, and will use both and either to fulfill His will, and see it accomplished. It is like the parable of the talents, where the slave that buried his talent in the ground, not even banking it to earn interest, has it taken away from him and given to the slave who invested his talents and returned even more talents to his master. If a sacred One relationship does not fulfill God's will it will be taken away to be bestowed elsewhere. This is why the One was full — it had accomplished all that it could. Likewise, Jesus was as empty as he could be, and ready to lay the foundation of his ministry.

It is generally accepted that Jesus was about thirty years old when he began his public ministry. He had probably experienced the death of his father, Joseph, and had settled into the trade of being a carpenter. Yet all this had turned his attention to his heavenly Father, and compelled him to take up another task that would require all his efforts and consume his life. He had just encountered his cousin, John the Baptist, and been acknowledged by John through Baptism. Jesus had to personally consider his life and what he would do with the remainder of the life God would allow him. Being fully human, Jesus had human reasons, regardless of divine reasons, for doing whatever he would do. He sorted this out as a human, and acted accordingly, fully considering the infinite ramifications of his actions.

Just as Jesus was human, we are all human, and when life events run their course we are all faced with decisions of what we as individuals, with full autonomy over our decisions, exercising our totally free will, will do with the remainder of the life we are allowed. We each, as individuals take stock of our assets and debts, our abilities and weaknesses, and decide what we as individuals may attempt to accomplish, in a very realistic assessment. This does not mean that we must limit ourselves to earthly goals, as we generally have the attitude that we will live forever, however unrealistic that may be, and this attitude admits a belief in the eternal, even if we cannot justify such a belief. So we may strive for an infinite goal, knowing full well that we have finite assets, as well as finite debts, finite abilities and limited weaknesses. Yet in the hymn "Lord of Creation", number 498 in the Catholic Book of Worship, there is the second verse that goes something like, as I paraphrase it:

(All powerful Lord, I surrender my will,
joyfully obeying, fulfilling your tasks.
Enslavement is freedom, service is harmonious joy,
and in your keeping, my inadequacies are strengths.)

paraphrased from **Lord of Creation, Catholic Book of Worship III,** #498

So many people strive for goals that are beyond them, like the soldier in the trenches of World War I, who fully aware of the barrage of fire that will greet him and his compatriots, still willingly chooses to go over the top and run headlong into likely death, even if that choice is the lesser of two evils, with court martial, execution or prison the alternative to fighting.

But for us today, having the witness and testimony of Jesus, the Apostles, the church, and many others, where are we to direct our efforts? I proclaim that the sacred One relationship, balancing whole and part, as in a sincere marriage, and the maintenance of such a relationship, is christianity applied, and the greatest resource society and individuals can draw on. When tempted, one should always choose marriage, or at least the local balance of whole and part, still in the light of the infinite, if marriage is not at hand.

But as Aristotle's Golden Mean, presents the problem of always taking the middle road, begging the question if always, is that not an extreme, rather than the middle road ? Marriage may not be a balance of whole and part, and this is for the infinite, God, to decide. Nevertheless the lay of the land is that marriage will likely be the best balance of whole and part with the greatest possibility, just as forgiveness is the best choice, with the greatest possibility, yet there are always exceptions, which will require forgiveness.

So the sacred One relationship balancing whole and part, has feasted and come to a point of decision. It has been acknowledged by Joan, in **Matthew's Three Fold**, and achieved abundance, and is now considering where to head. It could choose to continue as things are, regardless of shortcomings, in the faith that the union will bear fruit, or break the faith, and continue on a new path. This will involve deliberation, discussion and consideration, as well as action to confirm the choices as they are made. This is where temptation comes in, and it requires thorough understanding to chart the course of this local One sacred relationship. The twists and turns are wrenching as these two infinities dance and weave to accommodate the other, and consider their self awareness as well as their position before the infinite, both as a unit and as individuals. What are you, as an individual, exercising your total free will, going to do ?

Good Shepherd Sunday, April 29th, 2011

Verse 3

³The tempter came to him and said, "If you are the Son of God, tell these stones to become bread."

Verse 3

³The tempter came through him and said / " If you are the One of God, take this coin to become beer ! "

Verse 3 Discussion

For me, the temptation to resolve mysteries with a belief in magic short changes the issue and defeats the purpose of the mystery. Dwelling and deliberating on an apparently unresolvable mystery reveals numerous truths that likely shed light on the mystery without resolving it. This leaves the door open to the unexpected and miraculous. But attributing the mystery to magic short changes this process and the mystery fails to bear fruit. The place holder or unknown of magic closes the door on further consideration and renders the mystery of the situation impotent.

Whether Jesus could or could not have magically turned the stones into bread is not the point. Jesus knew his situation and waited on God to provide, rather than grasp at a solution. This is Jesus' life, in communion with the infinite, that loves and provides for Jesus and all of us. To grasp at a resolution to any problem short changes the purpose God has for the situation one finds themselves in.

I have heard that the temptation to turn stones into bread is the epitome of the economic solution. To settle for an economic solution to existence is pretty much what economists and the Roman Empire had done. Everyone had their physical needs pretty much met, yet this did not allow for an infinite purpose for each and every person. It short changed God's purpose for people and persons. We exist ultimately in an infinite existence, and merely meeting our economic needs negates the majority of our infinite existence. So just as magic short changes the consideration of a situation, accepting a finite solution to infinite existence short changes our awareness of the infinite.

Where the tempter came **TO** Jesus, the tempter came **THROUGH** the male spouse of the sacred One relationship. Seeking completion or satisfaction from the other spouse, the man requests beer. Beer may satisfy up to a point, but complete satisfaction cannot be had by beer alone. Complete satisfaction comes from the communion of the spouses, with or without beer, and with or without bread. Jesus knew he longed for the balance of whole and part, communion with the infinite, and neither bread or beer alone would satisfy his longing.

Where Jesus was a balance of whole and part in one person, the sacred One relationship is a balance of whole and part among two persons. Jesus came at a time and place that was ripe for a new understanding of the infinite. Yet someone had to acknowledge, proclaim and begin life enlightened by this new understanding. This new relationship with the infinite would not come on its own, and neither would the infinite impose a new understanding. A person had to recognise, proclaim and live this new understanding in a world of people that did not know it. Likewise, couples must live their relationship in a world that does not know why, where or how they relate to each other. Jesus lived a relationship with the infinite, and spouses live a relationship with the other half of infinity, their spouse.

It has been said that pondering the mysteries presented in christianity will make one loose their mind, or become crazy, and this is true. It has been said that instead, the mysteries must be accepted in faith, rather than considered so much as to change one's understanding of their world, and again, this short changes the mysteries and makes them impotent. Instead, considering the mysteries so much that they change one, opens up a new world to those considering the mysteries, and this world is unavailable to anyone that short changes the mysteries, so the actions of one who does consider the mysteries, become incomprehensible to those who do not consider such mysteries.

This is marriage, this taking up of a life before the other half of infinity, to bear fruit that no one else is able to comprehend the source of the fruit. Likewise, one who considers the mysteries offered by the infinite, will act seemingly without cause, and the cause will be their understanding of the infinite, which is unavailable to others not considering the infinite. This understanding may not be communicated by words but can be identified by the audience that considers the infinite as well. This is the witness of the Holy Spirit, the acknowledgment of one's actions by others who are likewise considering the infinite. Anyone who considers the mysteries of the infinite and acts on their understanding has taken up their cross and is following the path that Jesus took. This is necessary for any relationship with the infinite, whether as a person or as a spouse. To expect that one will be rewarded in a timely manner by those who do not consider the infinite is unrealistic, but to expect that one will make progress toward the infinite is reasonable.

In a world of distinct parts working with other distinct parts, as a machine would, there is little tolerance for changing the parts as that would make the other parts and the machine not work. This is the ego, and it does not allow for renewal. Those who are content with the way things work will not tolerate variation, yet for those who seek more than there now is, change must come. Only in a world acknowledging the infinite, will everyone, infinity, be content. This is a world considering the mysteries and growing before the infinite.

When one has reached as far as they can go, they turn back with a new understanding and recreate the world as much as they can, then continue on to infinity, and again turn back to recreate again. This is the whole of the parts, and many can fathom it, yet many do not consider it. This is not unreasonable, yet others who are content, fail to see it. So if marriage is not proclaimed, many will not see the need to maintain it as the infinite resource that it is, an infinite union of an infinite whole or female, with an infinite part or male. Jesus was the height of this union of whole and part in one person, yet the union of whole and part in a marriage relationship has the capacity to yield far more than one person on their own could.

(Height of wisdom, I offer my mind, receiving truth that is beyond knowledge.
What cannot be seen or heard is taught by the Holy Spirit, and glows in scripture.)

paraphrased from **Lord of Creation, Catholic Book of Worship III, #498**

Sunday, May 6th, 2012

Verse 4

⁴Jesus answered, "It is written: 'Man shall not live on bread alone, but on every word that comes from the mouth of God.'ᵇ"

    ᵇ 4 Deuteronomy 8:3

Verse 4

⁴One humbled him, "Why do we need beer ?"

Verse 4 Discussion

Bread or convictions — the eternal dichotomy ! Is it better to accept injustice so as to sustain our physical needs or to strive for justice at the expense of our physical needs ? This is dependent on whether our physical needs are met by the fulfillment of justice, or if instead, the two are independent of each other. But then again, is it better to gain the world and loose one's eternal life, or to save one's eternal life and loose the world.

Jesus' reply implies that the word from the mouth of God sustains, rather than just bread sustaining one. God may send bread, but he sends other things as well, and the entirety of the word sustains, where bread alone is insufficient. So Mabel may get you a (Black) Label beer, but there is more to Mabel than beer. It is the entirety of the situation that sustains, and this situation always includes the infinite, whether your other half of the infinite, your spouse, or plain old infinity.

The temptation is to neglect the infinite, the whole of the situation one finds themselves in, and to just take what one decides they need, rather than let things play out and allow one's needs to be met by the infinite. Attending to one's spouse may actually produce a beer without having to ask for it. This is the point of this verse — that one is always tempted to neglect either the whole or the parts of a situation and act without reference to the whole or the parts of a situation and to just exercise free will and take what one believes they need. Furthermore, one may even fight to gain what they either feel they deserve, or believe they have a right to maintain. This is not forgiveness and this is not what Jesus did. This is what Judas did. Judas, to my mind, thought that Jesus would surely stand up for himself if he was confronted by the Jewish leaders, and he thought that Jesus just needed a push for him to take over. This is why Judas was a disciple, because he believed in Jesus' ministry, and this is why Judas proceeded with his betrayal even though he knew Jesus knew what he was doing. He likely took Jesus' acknowledgment of what he was to do as approval of his betrayal of Jesus.

There is not ever any overpowering force demanding obedience — we are all free to choose life or else. Jesus ministry was not to dominate but to lure and encourage people to encounter and love God and their neighbour, infinity, for the wonder that it is. So Jesus, in his life before infinity, would not grasp at what he believed he needed, but would trust infinity to love and provide for him and those that followed. It is like the world of Disney's animated film, *The Jungle Book*, in which Baloo the bear sings - " Look for the bare necessities, the simple bare necessities, forget about your worries and your strife. I mean the bare necessities, that's why a bear can rest at ease, with just the bare necessities of life." Jesus' bare necessity was his relationship with infinity, and the demands of that relationship. He could have abandoned it at any time, yet he freely chose to accept it and be content with it.

So the husband asks the wife to buy beer, if she really appreciates him, but her response dismisses his request with the question "Why do we need beer?" True, beer is not necessary, but it does make for a celebratory mood, and the husband may have felt like celebrating. But the wife was cleaning, and did not feel like celebrating. There is a disconnect. Even though the wife is cleaning right in front of him, the husband neglects the truth of the situation and wants to celebrate. To him, cleaning could wait, especially until after the celebration, when it would make more sense to clean. Alternatively, the husband could have helped with the cleaning, and then suggested they celebrate together. As well, the wife could have realized that the husband was free to celebrate at this time, and taken advantage of the situation to celebrate with him, rather than tend to their home, putting it above her spouse.

There is not any right or wrong action here, only a disconnect. The temptation is more of an initiative that is not taken up. Jesus was hungry enough to eat stones, yet he chose not to test God or himself by attempting magic. He chose, rather than against magic, to be content and appreciate the solitude and clear head his environment was providing him, and to take advantage of that, to prepare for when he would not have solitude and be heady with wine. Rather than reject magic, he chose life. The spouses, in ignorance, or perhaps just lack of infinite will, do not choose each other in this verse. There is space between the pillars of the temple, but if there becomes too much space, the temple of the sacred One relationship, balancing whole and part, will fall.

Mother's Day, Sunday, May 13th, 2012

Verse 5

⁵Then the devil took him to the holy city and had him stand on the highest point of the temple.

Verse 5

⁵Then the devil took One downtown and placed them on the Order of Can-of-Duh list.

Verse 5 Discussion

For Jesus to just walk up and climb to the highest point in the temple, it must have been considered a public place. Likewise, to just go downtown and put yourself on the list for the highest honour in the capital, it must be a public nomination.

There was only an administrative distinction between religion and the state in Judea, as the Roman's ruled the state that would otherwise have been ruled by a king subject to the priests. Nevertheless, the high priest in Jerusalem, the holy city, was a political figure, regardless of Roman rule. So whether religious or secular, achieving the highest honour is the topic of this verse.

Jesus may not have thrown himself down and put God to the test when tempted by the devil in these verses, but he did allow himself to be brought down and crucified, so success or failure, achievement or loss, is not the issue here. The issue is about doing things idly, to just try things out, rather than putting everything into achievement. And this is the issue in this verse of the animation. Why would one attempt to honour themselves, and put any effort into their being acknowledged at all? Is there not enough to do to keep one busy fulfilling their purpose, rather than pausing to receive honours?

Furthermore, is there any advantage to receiving an honour? One may argue that recognition furthers one's purpose, but does it really draw the kind of attention that bears fruit? Jesus frequently tried to keep his miracles quiet, telling the cured lepers to tell no one other than showing themselves to the priests to be acknowledged as having been cured. Jesus did not rebuke all attention to himself, but he did rebuke the kind of attention that does not bear fruit — the seeking of signs and miracles. He performed his miracles for their own sake, to help those in need, rather than to draw people to himself. His teaching was enough to draw people to himself in a way that would bear fruit, or be productive and redemptive.

Standing on the highest point in the temple, regardless of Leonardo DiCaprio standing at the bow of the Titanic and proclaiming himself "King of the World", is a dubious honour. Most honours are dubious because they only go to those who put every means at their disposal into achieving such honours. This readily involves bending the rules, if not outright cheating. This is the Canadian response to winners — we think of them as overzealous and prefer to content ourselves with those who are good enough. This can become a political issue in the workplace, if not even in politics. One who only does the job they were hired to do can easily find themselves alienating the other ninety per cent of the workforce who are busy dodging work if not down right relaxing until their shift is over. Even management may take offense at someone who gets the work done correctly and on time. So there are two ends to this sword — a group that is overzealous and a group that is under zealous — both will be a threat to an honest person. Finally, when I delivered the Etobicoke Gazette advertising newspaper, I received an award for having a high collection rate — the rate of people I collected payment from compared to the number of homes I delivered to. This was truly a dubious distinction because, naively, I only delivered to those who would pay, and I never realized I was suppose to deliver to everybody and collect as much as I could !!

And then there is the idea that the first will be last and the last will be first! How is one a winner in such an environment ?! Jesus may be the first among people, but he was definitely the last as he hung on the cross. His greater honour was his criminal conviction and summary execution, rather than his standing on the highest point of the temple.

And then there is the whole question of why Jesus did not take up a career as a priest, if he wanted to work with religious ideas and minister to people? The short answer is that he was teaching a new understanding that would not fit into the old way of doing things — new wine cannot be stored in old wine skins. His life's work was not anything that would achieve any present honour in his present society, but would achieve honour in a new society of his own creation.

This time the temptation comes through the female spouse, who drags the male spouse downtown to place them on the Order of Can-of-Duh list! She wants acknowledgment and is grasping at it, rather than letting it come in its own time, as a gift of infinity, or a gift from God. The male spouse is fuming, and does not recognize the honour he may receive, and rather considers it an embarrassment, as if his co-workers were chastising him for self grandeur.

Once again there is a disconnect, as being nominated can be an honour in itself, let alone being voted for toward being selected. When one is working away, a little honest recognition can make all the difference and bolster a weary heart, if not transfigure it. And the view from the top of the temple must have been magnificent! It could have gone a long way toward imagining the vastness of the people to whom Jesus was ministering.

Ascension Sunday, May 20th, 2012

Verse 6

⁶"If you are the Son of God," he said, "throw yourself down. For it is written:

> "'He will command his angels concerning you,
> and they will lift you up in their hands,
> so that you will not strike your foot against a stone.'ᶜ"

_c   6   Psalm 91:11,12

Verse 6

⁶ "If I am the One of God, " he said, " why do we need this honour ?   / For:

> " 'You will tread on the lion and the cobra;
> you will trample the great lion and the serpent . ' ⸸ "

⸸ 6 Psalm 91:13

Verse 6 Discussion

      Again, an idle test of whether Jesus is the Son of God is rejected by Jesus. Yet in the animation text the question is put forward by the male spouse that their may not be a need for any honours and the seeking of any honours. Furthermore, why would One seek honours from those who ultimately oppose a new world of the sacred One relationship ?

      In the animation text, the lion is the earthly kingdom, and the cobra or serpent is knowledge, specifically medical knowledge. This is how I have taken this quote. The quote itself immediately follows the verses quoted by Matthew in this Gospel. Once again, quoting, taking something out of context to make a point, is dubious, yet I play along.

      Certainly it could be said that Jesus led a charmed life. Just the fact that he was executed as a criminal yet a worldwide religion was founded on this executed criminal is argument enough. So Jesus did have the supernatural supporting him, whether by magic or otherwise, that allowed him to accomplish all that he did. This means that what the devil quoted, Psalm 91, verses eleven and twelve, did apply to Jesus and did mean that he had supernatural help. So why is it a temptation for Jesus to test this to justify that it is true ?

      It is a temptation because it is not productive and will not redeem. But furthermore, since I am asserting that Jesus is the superlative balance of whole and part, it is a temptation for Jesus to act without respect to the whole, overlooking the details or parts.

      In the animation text, seeking after honour from the crown, or even the educated, is likewise neglecting the whole of the situation and running roughshod over the details or parts. If the sacred One relationship would change everything about present day society, why seek to be honoured by present day society ? Who would regard anyone who achieves a high honour and then proceeds to dismantle the source of that honour, as credible ? It would lack integrity to do so, and this lack of integrity is what the male spouse is trying to avoid by taking issue with seeking the honour of being a member of the Order of Can of Duh. The female spouse sees it differently, as presented in verse seven of this animation.

So where Jesus is tempted to throw himself down, the sacred One relationship is tempted, through the female spouse, to lift themselves up, with an honour from society. But accepting an honour from the society they wish to rebuild, would be disastrous and tantamount to throwing themselves down. Again, the female spouse sees it differently, as presented in the seventh verse, the next after this verse, of this animation.

The trick is to find a way to rebuild society while still living in it. Everyone has heard the phrase "live in the world, but do not be of the world". This is the fancy footwork that Jesus did when Pilate asked him if he was a king. His answer, that his kingdom is not of this world, because if it was, his followers would take up arms, disarmed Pilate. But for a people who were looking for an Anointed One, who never expected God to send His Son, Jesus' answer that "you will see the Son of Man at the right hand of God", is damning. But then again, it is only the truth, and a people with an absolute God, rather than a living God, condemn their saviour.

For the female spouse, this rebuilding requires a few steps back amongst the steps forward. The male spouse can relate to this, because he had to subdue his family's influence on him in order to prepare himself for marriage. The family crest for Foster, I am told, has a stag, a male deer, in it somewhere. In the second image of this verse, the male spouse has bagged a stag, while treading on the lion and the serpent. Jesus too, had to distance himself from his family, saying that those who hear his word and heed it are his brothers and sisters and mother. One must prepare themselves to be married, in a sacred One relationship, by putting away childish things, and entering a new heaven and a new earth, renewed daily, in a grand adventure. So the male spouse knows all about a few steps back amongst the steps forward.

Again, there is a disconnect between the spouses. The only solution is to accept the other's wishes and deny oneself and carry their burden. Jesus must have many times wondered why people just did not get what was so second nature to himself. He must have seriously wondered if they would even get it if he were to rise from the dead. But the kingdom of heaven exists, and there is great Joy in those who live in it. Rather than fear death, or loss, or failure, in the knowledge of their loving infinity's everlasting forgiveness, they carry on for the ride, and marvel at the sights!

Pentecost, Sunday May 27th, 2012

Verse 7

⁷Jesus answered him, "It is also written: 'Do not put the Lord your God to the test.'ᵈ"

ᵈ 7 Deuteronomy 6:16

Verse 7

/ ⁷One answered him, "For 'whoever is not against us is for us'.ᵇ"
/ She continued,

(" 'Fear the LORD your God, serve him only, and take your oaths in his name.
/ Do not follow other gods, the gods of the peoples around you;
/ for the LORD your God, who is among you, is a jealous God
/ and **her** anger will burn against you, and **she** will destroy you from the face of the land.
/ Do not test the LORD your God as you did at Mass . . . ah ! ' ᶜ ")

+ 7 Mark 9:40 ;
+ 7 Deuteronomy 6:13-16

Verse 7 Discussion - part A

Finally, now we come to it — Jesus' answer to the devil's temptation to throw himself down! "Do not put the Lord your God to the test." What is the issue here? Is it whether to humble oneself, or is it about testing, testing God?

Jesus did allow himself to be humbled — thrown down and executed. The difference in this case would have been that jumping off the highest point on the temple would only be a test, rather than actually accomplishing something. This is the temptation — to test God's love, forgiveness, and forbearance.

The best example I have, of the stupidity of testing, is my grade ten Ancient and Medieval History class. We frequently had true and false tests with really stupid questions that put me off of history almost altogether! The best example of such stupid questions is this - "Socrates asked too many questions — True or False?" Think about that . . . . Socrates was executed for corrupting the youth by asking questions, so he did ask too many questions, but then again, his questioning is the foundation of western philosophy! This question is both true and false, and depends on the context to determine one answer over the other. Testing is dubious.

Furthermore, even in science, the whole idea of cause and effect can only be proven if one can control the entire environment, in every whole possible, every context, to determine whether one set of circumstances will precipitate a specific different set of circumstances. And then to apply it, one can only be certain of the outcome if the circumstances are identical to those determined in the testing environment. Having said that, if observation provides a whole or a part that illuminates a situation, then it informs, but again, unless one is aware of all of the whole and all of the parts, one cannot predict accurately. Just ask a weather forecaster! Testing can illuminate, but fails to prove anything.

In the novel <u>**Zen and the Art of Motorcycle Maintenance**</u>, the case is made that it can be proven that nothing exists. I do not disagree with this, but what is the point? If nothing exists, than what good is that argument? At that point I stopped reading that novel. It may be a fact that gravity exists, but for something to fall it must have been elevated by something other than gravity, so even gravity has limits. Anything elevating does not disprove gravity, and likewise gravity does not disprove elevation.

And the Scientific Method cannot be the way one lives their life, because everything fails sooner or later, as one observes, hypothesizes, tests, observes, hypothesizes, and on and on. Sooner or later one will loose their faith in everything, as everything fails eventually, and at this point one should realize that the Scientific Method itself has failed! And so goes testing with it. At this point, one begins to enter the realm of faith and spirituality, and if one avoids magic, religion begins to have meaning. This is why testing God is irrelevant and misleading at best.

But there is more to this quote than just the line in this chapter of Matthew. In the animation text I have quoted Deuteronomy chapter 6, verses thirteen to sixteen, rather than just verse sixteen, as in verse seven of the fourth chapter of Matthew. But first, lets look at the female spouse's response.

The female spouse's response to the male spouse's question "Why do we need this honour?", is to quote Jesus as recorded in the Gospel of Mark, chapter nine verse forty, where Jesus says "whoever is not against us is for us." Elsewhere Jesus professes that whoever does not gather with him scatters, but in this quote from the Gospel of Mark, Jesus is responding to the disciples scolding others for casting out demons in Jesus' name, and he tells them to allow others to practice what Jesus is putting forward.

To the female spouse, one could benefit from an honour even if one is to change the source of that honour. This is like President John F. Kennedy, who was elected by Americans, and then proceeded to try to change Americans. Then again, he was assassinated, so it may be a weak example.

Once again, there is a disconnect, as the female spouse sees things one way, and the male spouse sees things alternatively. Both ways are valid, but it remains to be seen what action will prevail. I urge that it is better to work together, considering what the other spouse will do, and acting accordingly. This is teamwork, and when the whole and the part work together amazing things can happen. Joy reigns, like a sports car on a winding mountain road!

Thursday, May 31st, 2012

Verse 7

⁷Jesus answered him, "It is also written: 'Do not put the Lord your God to the test.'ᵈ"

^d 7 Deuteronomy 6:16

Verse 7

/ ⁷One answered him, "For 'whoever is not against us is for us'. ᵇ "
/ She continued,

(" ' Fear the LORD your God, serve him only, and take your oaths in his name.
/ Do not follow other gods, the gods of the peoples around you;
/ for the LORD your God, who is among you, is a jealous God
/ and **her** anger will burn against you, and **she** will destroy you from the face of the land.
/ Do not test the LORD your God as you did at Mass . . . ah ! ' ᶜ ")

⁺ 7 Mark 9:40 ;
⁺ 7 Deuteronomy 6:13-16

Verse 7 Discussion - part B

The animation text has veered away from the gospel text, but returns to it in the end of the second quote of this verse. This is because the animation text is about a relationship between two people before the infinite — God. Jesus was in a two way relationship between himself and God. The married couple is in a three way relationship — female, male and God. This marriage relationship reflects the Trinity of Father, Son and Holy Spirit, and this is what I understand the late Pope John Paul II's **_Man and Woman He Created Them — A Theology of the Body_** to be proposing — that the marriage relationship is at the very least, much like the relationships within the Trinity. And once again, it has been proposed in a Roman Catholic course I recently completed, that the mystery of the Trinity can be approached by considering the Father as being, itself, the Son as knowledge of being, itself, and the Holy Spirit as the love of being, itself. And then for the doers out there, the Trinity could, I suppose, be considered as doing, the knowledge of doing, and the love of doing. Perhaps that leads to the two approaches to infinity, the wholistic or being approach, and the partial or doing approach. Dare I say one is female and the other is male?

For Jesus, there was not any other option — he chose to not test God. But in the animation text, there are two approaches to infinity or God. The only correct choice is to cooperate to approach infinity. Bickering about how to go about it is stupid. If one can only see one way then that is the way both of them should proceed, for the integrity of the relationship and the maintenance of an approach to infinity. But rather, the two should try to see it both ways, the wholistic way and the partial way, the female way and the male way, so that they may have more options in how to proceed. This learning of the other's way is the number one benefit of a marriage relationship, for if one has an infinite capacity for one of the two ways, and must learn the other of the two ways, than the marriage relationship is the most fertile place to learn the other way.

This brings us to the temptation side of it. If one is lacking in their understanding of the other way, they will propose a way that is not balanced, and may lead to the downfall of the endeavour to approach infinity. The male spouse wanted beer, and the female spouse wanted honour. Both temptations draw the spouses apart, as well as jeopardize the two as persons.

But once again, there is a disconnect. This disconnect can only be overcome by determined free will — the will to stay together.

This begins to venture toward idolatry if one is to put their spouse above all other worldly concerns, but I insist it is only worldly concerns, with infinity, or God, remaining above all, as being and doing itself.

(" 'Fear the Lord your God, serve Him only, and take your oaths in his name.
/ Do not follow other gods, the gods of the people around you;
/ for the Lord your God, who is among you, is a jealous god, ... ")

Fear is a strong word, but respect may be more what is meant. Like respecting fire, not only for what it can provide, but for what it may become if not dealt with responsibly. So God must be addressed responsibly, or else infinity will get out of hand.

And we all know how an untended spouse can get out of hand! So in your approach to infinity, include your spouse or else.

And then there are all the worldly things that not only draw us away from our approach to infinity, or God, but draw us away from our spouse as well. And it is right there in the quote, that God is among us, and is jealous, so will nip us in the bud if we neglect him . . . ... or her.

The animation is of the other gods of the female spouse, and then the other gods of the male spouse. A god can in this case be considered a goal or something good, and is finite and achievable, rather than infinite and eternal. Putting any of these lesser goals, or gods, above an ultimate goal or infinite God, is just stupid.

Sunday, June 10th, 2012

Verse 7

⁷Jesus answered him, "It is also written: 'Do not put the Lord your God to the test.'ᵈ"

ᵈ 7 Deuteronomy 6:16

Verse 7

/ ⁷One answered him, "For 'whoever is not against us is for us'. ᵇ "
/ She continued,

(" ' Fear the LORD your God, serve him only, and take your oaths in his name .
/ Do not follow other gods, the gods of the peoples around you;
/ for the LORD your God, who is among you, is a jealous God
/ and **her** anger will burn against you, and **she** will destroy you from the face of the land .
/ Do not test the LORD your God as you did at Mass . . . ah ! 'ᶜ ' ")

ᵇ 7 Mark 9:40 ;
ᶜ 7 Deuteronomy 6:13-16

Verse 7 Discussion - part C

I have often heard about people's rights, as in the Charter of Rights and Freedoms, but I have only seen the connection between rights and responsibilities made in a poster in the hallway of a Catholic high school in Caledon East . I agree that along with rights there are responsibilities, and with responsibilities, there are rights .

Women, for whatever reason, were not held responsible for men's behaviour, and correspondingly did not have any rights in men's endeavours . This has changed . Women were recognized as persons in the 1920's and have the right to vote since around the same time . That was almost a hundred years ago . If there are still problems with society, women are to some extent at least, as responsible as men for those problems .

Nevertheless, women have taken on responsibility for society, for the benefit of all . The church has long honoured women in a distinct way, and this is becoming less distinct . There are some who celebrate the differences and others, both men and women, who dismiss the differences as cultural or otherwise . The time has come for women to stop hiding behind Mary and Jesus and step up and take up their cross, as Jesus did, and accept their consequential death and rebirth . The time has come for men to nurture, forgive, and accept the consequences . Women must engage their spouse, rather than their children, and men must honestly and truthfully accept the consequences of their actions, all of their actions and all of the outcomes, and be responsible for the outcome of their actions.

The age old optics debate about whether the church is patriarchal or matriarchal has run its course. The church is both, but from a man's point of view it appears matriarchal, and from a woman's point of view it appears patriarchal. Both are right. In reality, the time has come to see the church, the Body of Christ, for what it is, a communion of female and male, whole and part. This elevates women to an equal footing with men, and adds the role of women to the men's role. We are all persons first, and expressed secondly by our gender. We must not limit our responsibilities to our gender — men must take full responsibility and nurture as well, and women must get along with one another and deal directly, not obtusely or covertly. Women must become Christ, as well as Mary, and men must become Mary, as well as Christ.

The debate whether God is male or female is absurd. He is both and neither. This is like the story of the women who was widowed seven times and the answer to the question of who would be her husband in the resurrection. The answer is that in the resurrection there is no need for marriage as we are all and each fulfilled. This also implies that our earthly life's limitations are expressed in our gender and that when we are fulfilled we do not express gender. We can be fulfilled in this life, if we can take on both genders, and marriage is the greatest opportunity to do so.

So why do I even use the third person gender at all? Well in French, there is gender for just about anything, from a stone to a stag, and the stone can change gender depending on the context, from what I understand. So if one is speaking wholistically about something, they may use a female gender, and if speaking partially about something, they may use a male gender. So it goes with God. If referring to him as a present substantial being, as a mother, than why not use a female pronoun? And if referring to him as a loving parent apart, why not use a male pronoun? This is the best reason I know of for learning French, so sorry Quebec!

So when I change the quote from Deuteronomy to use the female pronoun, I am actually being more specific as to how infinity will get you if you devote yourself to finite goals at the expense of infinite goals. The situation will fester and rot all around you until you can no longer stand it. It won't come as a bolt out of the blue, striking you down in front of astonished onlookers, although it may be overwhelmingly dramatic. The point is that disregarding the totality of your situation brings a total failure, and likewise, disregarding the details, will give meaning to the phrase "The devil is in the details!"

Furthermore, what is illustrated in all of this animation, is that the other gender is a genuine resource to draw from for the only thing that one lacks. Does this not sound somewhat like an ultimate source, or an ultimate power, or an ultimate being? It does. But what is happening is that a distinction is being made between all this wholistic partial stuff and the actual person of infinity, God. What has been mired in the opposition of wholism and partiality is revealing itself to be an ultimate power beyond most imagining. And this revelation is a mere tool to approach infinity, or God, so closely that he may dwell among us, in the Kingdom of Heaven, right here on earth, within one's lifetime.

Can you imagine waking up next to God? This is what I understand the **Theology of the Body** stuff to be about. Now I may be incorrect, but I am being sincere and truthful. The practical solution, devoid of superstition, magic and anything supernatural, is to have one eye on the whole and the other eye on the part, and take advantage of any awareness that may be offered to assist in dealing either with the whole or the part.

Hanging a painting over someone's certificate is akin to putting one's priorities over another's, and this leads to anger, frustration and retaliation. Better to respect another's gods and have one's gods be respected, than to run roughshod over another's priorities.

Massah must have been some place where the Hebrew's tested God. I have, in my whimsical way, illustrated the male spouse sleeping in the Mass celebration at church. To the best of my knowledge, this never happened, but it has been known to happen, and this would test anyone's patience, including God's, although the man in the foreground is merely amused, as the female spouse is fuming!

Sunday, June 17th, 2012

Verse 8

⁸Again, the devil took him to a very high mountain and showed him all the kingdoms of the world and their splendor.

Verse 8

⁸Again, the devil took One to a very high mountain and showed her all the kingdoms of the world and their splendour.

Verse 8 Discussion

The devil is wooing Jesus. He is showing him all the worldly things he could do by applying his comprehension, understanding, and appreciation.

Certainly Jesus had a lot of potential with his insight and understanding. It has been said, at least in the **Jesus Christ Superstar** play and movie, that if only Jesus had come in modern times he could have done so much more. The issue is whether to apply oneself to finite goals that can certainly be accomplished, or to apply oneself to infinite goals, where it is unknown what may be accomplished.

I saw Justin P.J. Trudeau speak last night at the CMHA annual general meeting. He referred to the conservative majority government making a law against drive by shootings, as a boutique issue, to pander to the older voters, who do vote, who do not want anything to change and want to feel safe. But if you think about it, isn't it already illegal to shoot anyone, so why do we need a law specifically for a drive by shooting? Surely such a law will pass but it accomplishes little and nothing really changes. Instead, Mr. Trudeau put forth the idea that both space and time have changed for society, with the global economy and the youth disillusionment with politics.

A question was asked about the student protests in Quebec, and Mr. Trudeau suggested that since the youth do not vote it was easy for the Quebec government to shut them down.

Mr. Trudeau's point, as I understand it, is that the linear thinking of past generations that saw the world as infinite and never-ending has to change, and only the youth, who are accustomed to change, are capable of adapting and conceiving new understandings capable of solving the issues we are faced with today. These issues are the collapse of the global economy and the inability of the current institutions to solve this problem.

Mr. Trudeau put forth very good ideas about how things have to change, but where the Conservatives lack broad vision, they have diligently attended to details, and it remains to be seen if Mr. Trudeau, with his broad vision, is capable of working out the details.

Jesus was a balance of whole and part, with both a broad vision as well as diligent attention to detail. This gave him incredible, if not sacred and holy, potential. Jesus chose to address the biggest challenges he could fathom. These challenges were bigger than kingdoms and charted beyond this world, if not existence itself.

In the animation text of this verse, the devil takes One to a very high mountain to show her all the kingdoms of this world and their splendour. The temptation of the sacred One relationship is coming through the male spouse, as he tries to woo the female spouse with all that could be accomplished by the sacred One relationship. This is a serious temptation to the sacred One relationship.

In the nineteen-fifties marriage was held up as an ideal, and many who were unable to attain it were persecuted. Those persecuted were gays, lesbians, bisexuals, transgendered (if there were any), cross dressers, and unmarried pregnant women. This was because many that were married failed to apply their sacred One relationship to addressing the problems immediately around them by focusing on infinite goals, of living with God in a heaven on earth, and instead applied their relationship to finite goals such as wealth, health, offspring and personal happiness, at the expense of infinite goals such as a perfect society where everyone prospers. This practice was handed down to the next generation who were not taught to be aware of the priority of marriage and in the following half century marriage has failed.

Marriage, the sacred One relationship, has a lot to do with accepting reality and taking the attitude that "this will do" and that what one already has is sufficient to accomplish the immediate task one is faced with as they apply themselves to more infinite goals such as a perfect society. If one is not capable of heterosexual marriage one may still seek out a balance of whole and part in many other ways and thus continue to progress toward infinite goals such as a perfect society.

The Law is not to condemn anyone. It is only a means to see infinite perfection. Don't judge, because the measure you use on others will be applied to yourself. Condemnation is condemned. In this sense I support the Pride movement because they seek a balance of whole and part with what is immediately available to them.

Marriage as an economic and biological union for the purpose of procreation and wealth is by no means necessarily a sacred One relationship! The argument that marriage is a natural union between a man and women so therefore can only be legal between a man and a woman is a cop out and not a legitimate argument. Don't get me wrong, I do not want to see same sex marriages consecrated in the Catholic Church, although I see no harm in having them blessed, to acknowledge the existence of a relationship balancing whole and part as witnessed and testified to by the spouses. The point is that there must be a sacred One relationship, balancing whole and part, where the spouses are willing to suffer many deaths yet still maintain their spiritual relationship balancing whole and part. This is absent in the majority of heterosexual marriages today!!!

As far as gender is fundamental, heterosexual marriage is fundamental to society as an infinite resource because it balances an infinite whole with an infinite part, and this is why the church must honour it above same sex marriages. The argument that it is natural for procreation is not valid. The assumption that heterosexual relationships balance whole and part, without further investigation, is not valid. In a world that does not balance whole and part in heterosexual marriages, and instead applies a heterosexual relationship to finite goals instead of infinite goals, and where homosexual relationships that do balance whole and part do apply themselves to infinite goals, homosexual relationships should be as respected as, if not more respected than, heterosexual relationships. Yet the cycle will come around again.

So Jesus is tempted to apply his personal balance of whole and part to finite goals, and the sacred One relationship is tempted through the male spouse to apply itself to finite goals.

Wednesday, June 27th, 2012

Verse 9

9"All this I will give you," he said, "if you will bow down and worship me."

Verse 9

9 "All this I will give you," he said, "if you will bow down and subdue me."

Verse 9 Discussion

Where the devil is tempting Jesus, the person, the temptation in the animation, has come through the male spouse to tempt the sacred One relationship. The male spouse is grasping at straws, offering finite accomplishments to the infinity bound sacred One relationship.

Many people focus on eradicating evil, rather than promoting good. Eradicating evil, however, is a negative goal, as opposed to promoting good, which is a positive goal. Either way, one's world is structured around their goal, and setting up a goal system should have positive infinity as the primary goal, because focusing on negative infinity as the primary goal will at least leave one bereft if they ever achieve their infinite goal.

Furthermore, where are improvements to be found? I assert that in the set of everything that is wrong there are the elements that when correctly oriented toward positive infinity, form the achievements of tomorrow! Eradicating evil denies these elements and removes the opportunity for improvement by denying these elements that are essential to the solutions of tomorrow!

This is forgiveness — this allowing of negatively oriented elements so that they may have the opportunity to orient toward a positive infinity.

So in the Gospel text, the devil asks Jesus to worship him to achieve finite goals, and in the animation text, the male spouse asks the female spouse to subdue him to achieve finite goals, and eventually infinite goals. This, in the animation, is the offering to the female spouse, a negative goal of subduing the male spouse. Is this wrong?

No, the subduing of the male spouse by the female spouse is really only containing the male spouse within the limits of the female spouse's capability, and this is marriage, balancing infinite whole with infinite part, and limiting the part to the capability of the female spouse's whole, and parting the female spouse's infinite whole with the male spouses infinite part. Yes, I am using the buzz words of whole and part to represent the One and Many problem, female and male, as well as whole and part.

This is how evil will be swallowed up by good, and death will be swallowed up by life. Life is more fundamental than death, and good is more fundamental than evil.

Where the female spouse may subdue the male spouse, this will have elements of opposition to the male spouse. Satan is the opposer, and generally considered the prince of evil. But this prince of evil, the opposer, Satan, will be swallowed up in life, as the act of opposing will be oriented toward a positive infinity, including the growth of the spouses' awareness of the opposite side of infinity, the other spouse's infinity. As the female spouse limits the male spouse, the male spouse will grow in possibility and understanding of the female spouse, so as to be able to lead the female spouse in her growth and awareness of the male spouse's infinity, the partial capacity of the male spouse. This growth is symbiotic between the spouses, as they engage each other, with a partial growth, then a whole growth, then a partial growth, and on and on. . . . This is the growth of awareness for each spouse, and this awareness applies itself to all of existence, and has the capacity to accomplish what is even unimaginable today.

The female spouse has a choice, to either accept and forgive the limitations of the male spouse, or to instead turn to other finite goals, which I assert are far more finite than any sacred One marriage relationship. Nevertheless, real people are limited and can only take so much before it breaks them down. But this is what happened to Jesus — he was broken and destroyed for his love of people. This is death, and this is rebirth. If one may stay committed to their chosen approach to infinity, they will be destroyed yet arise again to a new approach to infinity.

So the real temptation is not to approve of the offer of finite goals — the real temptation is to give up on the sacred One relationship and assume other approaches to infinity would be more rewarding. It makes sense that the most promising approach to infinity, the sacred One relationship, would be the most challenging, full of death and disappointment, yet still promising real, adventurous and rewarding life.

The male spouse's offer, of being subdued by the female spouse, is the offer of life, for both spouses, but the illustration of the possible finite accomplishments of such a relationship is not a justification for subduing the male spouse. It is instead, finite solutions to infinite challenges — the infinite challenges and rewards of a sacred One relationship. This is both wrong and correct at the same time. This is why forgiveness, as a way of life, is so essential, and absolutely essential to the maintenance of a sacred One relationship, and the future of everything.

A final word about forgiveness — who benefits most from it? The person forgiven may feel they have received ultimate grace, and this is true. But the person who forgives has placed the burden of responsibility squarely on the person who has acted incorrectly and has been forgiven. If the person who acts incorrectly knows there will not be any opposition, they are in a position that demands that they seriously consider what will be accomplished by the incorrect act, and they would not be in such a position if they faced any opposition. Some times when you win you loose, and when you loose you win. Jesus lost and won everything.

Monday, July 2ⁿᵈ, 2012

Verse 10

¹⁰Jesus said to him, "Away from me, Satan! For it is written: 'Worship the Lord your God, and serve him only.'ᵉ"

ᵉ 10 Deuteronomy 6:13

Verse 10

¹⁰She said to him, "Away from me, Satan! Did I not just quote 'serve him only.'; "

⁓ 7, 10 Deuteronomy 6:13

Verse 10 Discussion

Jesus affirms that he will devote himself to infinite goals, or rather, THE infinite goal, which also affirms that there is only one infinite goal for everything. It follows that all the other finite and lesser goals will be met by the satisfaction of the one infinite goal.

The best example that I know of for why there is only one infinite goal is somewhat geometrical. The resultant vector, of a group of vectors, is the equivalent to the group of vectors together. It is like a path from A to B, from B to C and from C to D, being the same as the path from A to D. This is an oversimplification. The resultant vector could be explained by a force of 10 pounds pushing east, combined with a force of 20 pounds pushing west, combined with a force of 10 pounds pushing north; so that the resultant vector is the square root of 20 pounds west minus 10 pounds east, being 10 pounds west squared and added to 10 pounds north squared. The resultant vector is the square root of 200 pounds or 14.1421 pounds roughly, in the north west direction.

The idea is that the satisfaction of a multitude of goals can be achieved by understanding the primary goal of everything. This is why Bible thumpers are so adamant — they are trying to get everyone to their own individual and unique goal! This is why Bible thumpers are so intolerable — everyone thinks they are trying to tell us what our goal SHOULD be, rather than helping us achieve what we want. This is the disconnect — what they want for us is what we want for ourselves, but we cannot see eye to eye. Prayer, or rather pryer, where one prys at what they really want and how to get it, can illuminate or shed light on solutions, which demand certain things, requiring prying out solutions to those demands, and on and on.

So in the animation text, there is only one infinite goal for both spouses, but again there is a disconnect, where the female spouse feels she must serve him only, and the male spouse wants to remain engaged with the female spouse and sort out this one infinite goal amongst them.

There are many reasons to disengage oneself from a relationship — and all of them are futile. When we cut ourselves off from one another we fail to resolve the two or more world views, and this is to the detriment of all parties. The benefits of reaching solutions where all parties can see eye to eye are unfathomable. At the very least, reaching solutions where all parties can see eye to eye will reveal the primary infinite goal for all parties. This is the revelation of God. We were created to live forever with God amongst us, and this infinite goal has been abandoned in favour of finite goals. We have lost sight of our destiny. At the very least, most people hope for heaven after death, and although this is somewhat true, we were created to live beyond death, on earth with God amongst us. We may proclaim Jesus' death and profess his resurrection, but we do not practice what we preach. We are all children of God, offspring of the infinite, and are all on the path Jesus took, to our own resurrections, yet this is considered crazy talk. So be it. We will achieve what we expect and strive for, and nothing more.

There is always the line that one will give up the other for the other's sake, rather than for their own sake, but still, this is futile. Nevertheless, there is always the possibility of reconciliation, yet there are always limitations that cannot be overcome. Other commitments become dominant and original relationships become of secondary importance. This is reality, and this is the mess of choosing finite goals over infinite goals.

This is why it is so important to not fear any sort of death, but rather view death as the door to a new world, both heaven and earth renewed. The trick is to know what to hold on to and what to let go. Religion teaches us to hold on to God, and to let the chips fall where they may. I assert that one should hold on to God, and secondly, hold on to their primary relationship, letting the chips fall where they may, until the dust settles and both God and the primary relationship are renewed, as well as the world around one.

It is all about perceptions. When it looks darkest, the dawn is nearest. When we loose, we win. And the perceptions on the far side of failure are far more wonderful than any one on this side of death can imagine.

So when it looks like your relationship is over, stay alert, and stay together. Trust that the infinite purpose is at work in meeting both of your needs. And if the relationship does fail, an alternative will present itself to meet your needs, and satisfy them beyond your wildest expectations. I would never put a relationship above my relationship with God, but it is a very, very, very close second.

Finally, this death and rebirth is the experience about which **HESUS JOY CHRIST / Matthew's Two Four** is all about. This death and rebirth happens all the time, and will happen to many relationships, especially those where the spouses have the faith to hold on to each other. There is never any guarantee of what the other spouse will do, but one will know what they themselves intend to do, and may stay faithful to the end.

Sunday, July 8th, 2012

Verse 11

¹¹Then the devil left him, and angels came and attended him.

Verse 11

¹¹Then the devil left them, and they waited on angels.

Verse 11 Discussion

To tackle this verse, I propose an understanding of Evil. In the swirly animated conception of the sacred One relationship, the two rotating linked tori, there are local areas where the expansion of one torus will conflict with the other; and other local areas where the expansion of one torus will not affect the other in any way. As well, if the interior of a torus were to yield or give way to the expanding other torus, this would be considered something like Grace, and this yielding is directly proportional to the amount of Grace the other torus allows the first torus. Expansion of one torus into the other in a way that conflicts is Evil. The dominance of whole or part at the expense of the other is Evil. The communion of whole and part is good and brings great Joy!

In the last verse, verse ten, Satan, the opposer, would be swallowed up by good, as the limiting of one spouse by the other would maintain the communion. Here, in this verse, the devil leaves. Who is the devil? In the animation, the devil is the other spouse that twists and perverts what the first spouse tries to accomplish. This is the disconnect. This is the misunderstanding that is attributed to the devil, but once again, in a healthy sacred One relationship balancing whole and part, the devil will be swallowed up by good. The perversions of what one spouse tries to accomplish will shed light on that spouse's goals and illuminate the limitations of those goals to bring them to awareness so that they may be adjusted toward infinity.

Having tackled Evil, as well as Satan and the devil, let's go for broke and figure out what in the world an angel is! There is no advantage to appealing for blind faith, so let's stick to common knowledge. There is the expression of gratitude - "You're an angel!", that expresses appreciation beyond the value of the act or gift. When someone mildly acts in another's favour and the act is appreciated well beyond its nominal value, then the circumstances have created a supernatural event for the recipient. Infinity has blessed the recipient by the act of a person who thereby becomes a spiritual power for the recipient.

So as angels came and attended Jesus, the sacred One relationship spouses waited on angels. This could be taken either way. The spouses could be waiting on angels as servers serving the angels, or they could be waiting for angels to appear and be present to them. Either way, the spouses, now separated, need not neglect the infinite, and continue to seek God.

Many may make the case that to put one's spouse so high on the list of priorities, second only to God, is too close to idolatry. That's idolatry, not adultery! To them I answer that to put one's entire faith on a book, be it the Bible, or anything else, is idolatry. To put one's faith in symbols, or even a lack of symbols, is idolatry. To pray like the pagans, trying to be heard by their many words, is idolatry, and believing in some sort of magic words, praying the same words over and over again without any consideration, is idolatry. Even refuting an extreme idea citing common sense or reasonableness, is idolatry.

For every thing, there is a context, and denying either is idolizing the other. The Anointed Saviour is a balance of whole and part, uniting heaven and earth, good and evil, God and people, Infinity and the individual. Many believe that reductionistic thinking is God like, and many others believe that wholistic thinking is God like, and both are correct and incorrect, as God is beyond and both wholistic and reductionistic. To truly approach God, the infinite, one must get beyond both being wholistic and reductionistic to a reality of Joy and infinite possibility. Marriage is the fundamental way to do this, and it is as fundamental as gender.

Other's propose that a spouse cannot bear the weight of God put on them by the other spouse, and this is true. But Jesus died carrying the weight of God put on him by the people, and this is our calling, to take up our cross and follow Jesus to our own resurrection of the body. To try for anything less will achieve only that. If we fail we will be forgiven, and may find ourselves in a position to pick up the pieces and try again, with a greater experience and wisdom.

So let's take a stab for heaven. If the movie **The Matrix** has any sense, it is that the mind does not know the nature of its existence, yet it is apparent. So it could be argued that heaven exists in the mind, or that the mind exists in heaven. Thus the sacred One relationship continues on in the minds of the spouses, and they continue to seek it, even though they have lost an incidence of it. The ideal exists in heaven, the mind, and continues to influence the mind of all who have encountered it, whether they have encountered it in their mind or their experience. The sacred One relationship, or any other balance of whole and part, is the closest thing I have encountered to Joy and an appreciation of God, the Infinite Person.

Sunday, July 15th, 2012

Verse 12

Jesus Begins to Preach

¹²When Jesus heard that John had been put in prison, he withdrew to Galilee.

Verse 12

One Gets Preachy

¹²When One heard that Joan was ministering elsewhere, he became secular.

Verse 12 Discussion

I remember, when I was dating Lois, the daughter of a Baptist Minister, and attending Yorkminster Baptist Church with her, she claimed that it was God's will for her to break up with me. At that time I bought two books just because of their titles. One was **Decision Making and the Will of God**, and the other was **Evangelism As A Lifestyle**. I bought them at a protestant book store, and I was Anglican at the time. I thought that decision making and the will of God was too easily glossed over by most people, and when I dated another Baptist, I remember remarking to their Baptist Minister that circumstances could be created by the devil as much as they could be created by God, so there is more to discerning God's will than just appreciating signs in one's life. The other book title I found very amusing since even as an Anglican, I believed my lifestyle was my evangelism! My experience of Catholics, both before and after my conversion, was that they were constantly ministering and evangelizing by and through their own lifestyle. This was John the Baptists' ministry as well — his life, as well as his teaching, was his ministry and evangelism.

So just because John was in prison does not mean his ministry was at an end. Sure, he was unable to teach and preach, but he did send his disciples to ask if Jesus was the one, or should they wait for another. And he maintained his condemnation of Herod for taking his brother's wife. This precipitated John's beheading.

Sooner or later we all become unable to express ourselves and communicate, but this is not the end. Our witness prevails through our choices and attitudes. My mother was aggressive towards her nurses when she was given poor care in her last months, but she stopped pinching and punching toward the end, probably because she was unable to, but for me it seemed that her attitude had changed to one of accepting her circumstances. If she had only accepted her circumstances earlier, and taken up the attitude that she was going to make her nursing staff look good by being a exemplary patient, they might have been more attentive and provided better care. Who knows?

Martyrdom is not simply being killed for who you are, it is being faithful to the end, no matter what the end — death or any other end. The Iroquois killed many Frenchmen, as allies with the British, but not every Frenchman kept proclaiming Christ as they were tortured, so much that they cut out their tongue. My mother seemed to be faithful to proper nursing practice, being a Registered Nurse, and a Community Care Access Coordinator, who also taught Nursing, to the end.

My understanding is that Galilee was a secular community. This is where Jesus, as far as I know, began his ministry. Although he only ministered to the Jews, with a few exceptions, he ministered mostly to the Jews who had gone astray, the secular Jews. Although he did preach in the synagogues, or Jewish places of worship, he preached everywhere else as well. He preached in the synagogues as a lay person, being a carpenter, rather than as a Scribe, Pharisee or other ordained religious teacher and official. He was asked by what authority he ministers, but failed to give a direct answer. He answered with the question " Was John the Baptist's ministry from God or from man ? ", and the religious leaders who put the question to him would not answer for political reasons being that the people believed John's ministry was from God, yet the religious leaders denied John's ministry. So to answer either way, as an ordained religious leader, would tempt fate. Jesus was a regular person who chose to preach and minister to the outcast as well as the prominent and regular people, secular or religious.

So in the animation text, the preacher from **Matthew's Three Fold**, Joan, is apparently ministering elsewhere, and this has an effect on the sacred One relationship that was acknowledged by Joan. The sacred One relationship, now existing only in heaven or the mind of the spouses or spouse, drives them to a secular community, yet still participating in the religious ordinances as an approach to infinity.

For both Jesus, and the witnesses of the sacred One relationship, there is more than just maintaining the religious ordinances that needs to be done, and this " more " becomes a new and unique ministry. Jesus did not copy John's ministry, but built on it. Even John proclaimed that there is one who would come after him, who would be greater than him. John baptized with water, but Jesus would baptize with the Holy Spirit.

At the very least, in our baptisms, we are all called to be priests, prophets and kings, to minister, proclaim, and maintain our individual corners of existence, and this expression is unique to each and everyone of us baptized individuals. It is not solely the role of the professionals to profess the good news, the burden, although light and wonderful, is upon each one of us who was ever baptized.

Rather than create a world of conflict and opposition, this role of priest, prophet and king calls each of us to engage one another in witnessing our experiences and understandings so that we may grow amongst each other to an eternal newness of life, rather than an isolated bearing of stagnant eternal walking waking death. There is so much to learn from each other, that to not engage in, at the very least, a sincere and passionate discussion, is to pass up on the life we are offered and called to by the loving infinite person.

There is a wonderful christian music economy that puts the Gospel into new words and songs, which I greatly appreciate, even though I want three classic hymns to be associated with me

— 498 "Lord of Creation", 476 "Come and Journey", and 395 "Lord of the Dance". This proclamation of the ancient faith with new and intriguing words and music opens us up to a more filling understanding of how our faith may be applied in our new world and present day circumstances. The best t-shirt I have seen that is a part of this pop christian culture is a parody of the Home Depot logo and tagline "You can do it — We can help." Instead of "The Home Depot" this t-shirt says "The Holy Spirit", "You can do it — He will help." This pop christian culture, although generally failing when the rubber hits the road, may be the door to both the secular as well as the religious communities, to which Jesus directed his ministry.

Sunday, July 22nd, 2012

Verse 13

¹³Leaving Nazareth, he went and lived in Capernaum, which was by the lake in the area of Zebulun and Naphtali— . . ...

Verse 13

¹³Leaving the hill, he went and lived in a rooming house, down toward the lake, . ./ . . in the area of the mall, ...

Verse 13 Discussion

What does where one, or the One, lives have to do with anything? Really, it doesn't have that much to do with anything, other than that Jesus, as well as everyone else, has to move from time to time. Perhaps the reasons we move have some significance.

Really though, this verse is a good example of this whole **HESUS JOY CHRIST** writing. The point is not to elevate anyone's personal experience to the level of worship, but to illustrate how scripture relates to everyone personally, using this one example, and that is its value. Too many people have the attitude that church and scripture are some kind of moralizing fairy tale that everyone needs to grow out of as they mature into adulthood, but this is false. Sure, one must mature, but our understanding of scripture and church is capable of maturing with us, as it is alive and relevant to all of existence, not just childhood. This verse is a simple example of how Jesus had life events that everyone has, and his response to such events is relevant in that we all face similar life events, and may respond in a similar way.

Flight is really just rising above one's limitations and life events and riding them out to a positive resolution. This is what spiritual truths are about. Everyone who reaches will fall short, and dealing with these shortcomings successfully, carries one on to new life. Failure can devastate one spiritually, but it can also be an opportunity to move beyond what one was trapped in, to a new life with new and better challenges.

Flight can also be considered as "falling with style", as in the movie **Toy Story**, where the character Buzz Lightyear proclaims "to infinity and beyond". The joke is that there is nothing beyond infinity, or is there?

There is a school of thought that the universe may be finite without bound. This means that the universe is a determined size, but doesn't have any boundaries. The best example of this idea is the earth itself, as a sphere. A sphere has a two dimensional surface, of a finite size dependent on the diameter of the sphere, yet nevertheless a finite size. But even though the surface of the sphere is limited, there is not any boundary or end of the surface of the sphere. One can travel the globe and never come the the end of the earth. But if one travels the globe, they do not come back the same person.

The same with infinity. Each encounter with infinity sends one back a different person, to a different world, one that is new in every way, yet still the same world. In this way it could be said that one has passed through infinity to a new world!

Jesus had just spent a lot of time alone. He considered the infinite, and came back a new person. The One had spent a length of time amongst the two spouses, and then moved on to a new set of circumstances. The end of the sacred One relationship leads to a new life, different than the life before the sacred One relationship.

Death is real, yet one may progress through a death or failure, to a new world, if they are open to life, and do not choose to remain in death. The question is not how high God will lift you, but rather what elevation can one tolerate, endure or remain in an awareness of how high one is. It is fear that limits one's elevation, rather than faith, grace, or death. Death is real, but life remains so that one may die with so much style that they appear to have conquered death. This is more than just an appearance. It is real.

Jesus had just heard that his greatest advocate, John the Baptist, had been put in prison. Jesus went to Galilee, and left Nazareth, to go and live in Capernaum, by the lake, in the land of Zebulan and Naphtali. Consider this! Jesus was a real person, with an emotional response to the events of his life. We are all like that, and when things happen we respond emotionally. Jesus' response was to raise the bar, carry on, and shoot for higher stakes, upping the ante, and making his life, as well as John's, count for as much as possible.

But what if he failed? Who knew whether he had a chance? It doesn't matter, when one gets right down to it. Not trying ensures a 100% failure rate. A half hearted try may reduce the failure rate to 95%. But a full press reduces the rate of failure even more, and to not give 100% is to accept failure. Failure may be certain, but a good shot reduces that certainty. What else is there to do?

I do not know anything about Zebulan or Naphtali. I just assume it is some sort of locality around Galilee. I do know that the mall is a secular wonderland. So this emphasizes that Jesus was in a secular world. He related to that world in such a way that he found a following.

But the secular world may be considered a life of darkness, within which there is no one worthy. Jesus entered this type of region, and remained worthy. This is the hope of the spouse, to be able to honour the secular world with some sort of redemption, as Jesus remained worthy in an unworthy region.

This is what we are all called to do — to remain worthy in unworthy circumstances, to turn water into wine, to find life amongst death, to honour the dishonoured, to shine in the darkness.

Sunday, July 29th, 2012

There was not a Discussion of **HESUS JOY CHRIST** this week as I was away on the ***Cross of Victory Walking Pilgrimage*** to Martyr's Shrine in Midland, Ontario.

Martyr's Shrine was created to honour the seven North American Martyrs who were killed by the Iroquois in their attack on the Hurons (Ouendat) and the French Jesuit Mission of St. Marie (Among the Hurons), in the 1630's.

We left Saturday morning, August 4th, after Mass, and started walking from Terra Cotta to Midland, with a one day retreat and rest on Sunday, August 5th, at a Catholic high school in Caledon East. Then from Monday to Saturday we walked up to 25km a day, with Mass each morning, until we arrived at Martyr's Shrine on Saturday, August 11th, for Mass around 2 pm.

We met up with about 50 pilgrims from Brampton on Saturday night, then we were joined by about 50 pilgrims from Guelph, and 10 pilgrims from Hanover on Monday night. On the last Saturday, if not earlier, we met up with anywhere from 500 to 1000 Polish pilgrims from Toronto.

So to tide you over, here is a reference to the introduction to **_Man and Woman He Created Them — A Theology of the Body_**, by Pope John Paul II.

"**_Theology of the Body_**" was proclaimed by Pope John Paul II, in his general audience addresses in St. Peter's Square on Wednesdays from September 5th, 1979 to November 28th, 1984. There was a brief break in these addresses in May of 1981 until November of 1981 when the Pope was shot by an assassin.

As I find it difficult to find references for the idea of balancing whole and part, I was pleased to find this reference, which I have paraphrased below, in the Introduction to **_Man and Women He Created Them — A Theology of the Body_** by Michael Waldstein:

> (It may seem apparent that analysis and meditation are opposed to each other. In meditation one receives insight by pondering a whole, and in analysis, one actively resolves a whole into its parts.
> The two approaches, although opposite, complement each other.)

Page 17, paragraph two, Introduction by Michael Waldstein, **Man and Woman He Created Them – A Theology of the Body**, Pauline Books & Media, 50 Saint Paul's Avenue, Boston, MA 02130-3491. www.pauline.org   ISBN 0-8198-7421-3

Copyright © 1986, 2006, Librerea Editrice Vaticana, 00120 Città del Vaticano, for the original catechetical texts of John Paul II and the then Cardinal Karol Wojtyla. The texts may be found on the Vatican website: www.vatican.va

Introduction, index, and translator's notes accompanying text © 2006, Michael Waldstein

Edition copyright © 2006, 1997, Daughters of St. Paul

Verse 14

. .. ...¹⁴to fulfill what was said through the prophet Isaiah:

Verse 14

. . . . . .¹⁴to fulfill what was said through the prophet Isaiah:

Verse 14 Discussion

In chapter nine of the book of Isaiah, he prophesies about the birth of the Messiah. Chapter nine, verse six reads:

> **"For to us a child is born, to us a son is given, and the government will be on his shoulders. And he will be called Wonderful Counselor, Mighty God, Everlasting Father, Prince of Peace."**
>
> *New International Version*

So let's consider what it means to prophesie. If one knows all the parts, one can predict the outcome, depending on whether the whole is consistent and without change. Likewise, if one knows all of the wholes, one can predict the outcome, depending on whether the parts change or not. So when Jonah was commanded to prophesie to Ninevah, which he eventually did after chilling out in a fish, the parts, or the people, changed, and the destruction of Ninevah was averted. Jonah was aware of the wholes, and could foresee the future, but the parts, the people, changed and changed the future of Ninevah.

So when Isaiah prophesies about a light coming to the people in darkness, he understands the wholes and does not anticipate any parts changing. This prophesy is taken to be about Jesus — his birth and ministry, and this quote is used to support his ministry in Galilee.

But just as the book of Matthew quotes Isaiah 9, the second part of verse one, and verse two, I have quoted only verse one, up to where Matthew's quote begins. Actually, Matthew's quote juggles the words a fair bit.

So all this quoting of prophesies is generally used to show how there is order and awareness of that order. If Isaiah could know, or be aware, of the coming of the Messiah, there must be an order that is apparent to Isaiah. But just as we are all aware, today, of how spin doctors can massage the facts, details and parts to create an approvable whole, quoting and prophesying can be done pretty much by anyone with anything to predict anything. The world is suppose to end on December 21st, this year, 2012, because the Mayan calendar runs out. Jehovah's Witnesses have been predicting the end and the Second Coming since the late 1800's until today. And don't forget the Y2K business at the last turn of the century, whether it was January 1st, 2000, or January 1st, 2001. I remember actually getting a notice from my bank that they were ready for the turn of the century and that I need not fear for my bank account.

So once again, we come back to a balance of whole and part. To predict anything, one must know all the parts and all the wholes. And how does one go about knowing all this? By paying attention! If either the part or the whole changes unexpectedly, the forecast becomes incorrect. But this has a flip side. If one is faced with insurmountable odds, one may change the whole or the part to overcome such odds. This is what David did with the giant Goliath. There was a part that Goliath did not expect. This part was that David could drive a small stone with his sling, with such force and accuracy that it killed Goliath by striking him square in the forehead. It must have been a formidable forehead, but nevertheless, David's shot was sufficient.

These two ways of understanding and awareness fully complement each other, so that when the parts are exhausted, the wholes may prove fruitful, and vice versa. This is so common that it is almost always overlooked. It is as simple as walking. The left foot can only stride so far, but the right foot is there to stride as well, and set up the left foot for another stride, which sets the right foot up to continue, and on and on again! The potential is limitless!

Consider Calculus. The limit of a sum is the sum of the limits. This limit of the series approaching the slope of a curve, is the slope of a curve at a single point, with rise and run both at zero! This is using both the whole and the part to achieve what was considered impossible — the slope of a curve, normally calculated by rise divided by run, when the rise and run are infinitesimal — zero! This is the possibility of balancing whole and part — infinity.

The idea that one can prophesie is nothing when compared to the possibility offered by a full awareness of whole and part. I prophesie that a full awareness of whole and part, female and male, would allow one an infinite awareness, even of the infinite person, God, and so much so that such an awareness would be as if the infinite person were right here with us, on earth. There is so much possibility it can hardly be imagined.

A homily was given by a newly ordained deacon last Friday at Our Lady of Lourdes in Elmvale, Ontario, to the pilgrims walking to Martyr's Shrine. The idea that intrigued me from this homily was that an unborn baby has absolutely no idea what the world beyond birth is like. How could they possibly imagine jet aircraft, bunnies, chocolate, swimming, or anything else, including meeting their mother from the outside. All they know is that they are being forced out of everything they have ever known, and it must seem like the end of everything. This can be likened to death. It seems the end of everything, but who can imagine what is beyond death.

The trick is to become aware of the infinite life before one leaves their body, so that they may choose life when the time comes. I have witnessed the loss of everything and all meaning, or at least at the time it seemed so, only to find myself in much more wonderful circumstances beyond that apparent death. And this balance of whole and part has the potential to bring us more than any unborn baby can imagine beyond their birth to new life.

Tuesday, August 14th, 2012

Verse 15

¹⁵"Land of Zebulun and land of Naphtali,
the Way of the Sea, beyond the Jordan,
Galilee of the Gentiles—
    ᶠ 16 Isaiah 9:1

Verse 15

¹⁵ "Nevertheless, there will be no more gloom for those who were in distress." . . . . . . ᵈ

+ 15 Isaiah 9:1

Verse 15 Discussion

" . . . ... Galilee of the Gentiles - - - " A gentile was anyone who was not a member of the Jewish faith. They were considered pagan, or at the very least, were secular. Almost all christians are gentiles to this day. Some Jews are christian, but almost all christians are gentiles. This is where Jesus began his ministry, in a Jewish district, full of gentiles. Jesus' ministry was to the Jews, but "crumbs" fell from the master's table to be taken up by the "dogs". Paul's ministry was almost entirely to the gentiles. He travelled from Judea to Greece and Rome, evangelising as he went. Peter held down the fort in Judea, while Paul reaped a large harvest of believers from far and wide. To the best of my knowledge, Philip went to India, and James went to Spain. Jesus preached to the Jew's, but his apostles spread the word to the world.

There was an issue that is presented in the book of Acts, where Peter has a dream where he is commanded to consume unclean animals, and refuses, only to be told to not call anything that God has declared clean, unclean. This is taken that God wants to accept gentiles into the Way, the christian faith.

Nevertheless, Jesus' ministry was directed toward the Jew's, albeit the secular and sinners. I take the reason for this to be that Jesus needed to direct the Jewish faith, which at the time was a beacon for the world. Being new, making all things new, Jesus' ministry was different, and this difference was seen as incorrect because it was different. Jesus' ministry was new wine only containable in new wine skins.

Likewise, the sacred One relationship, balancing whole and part, which may be consistent with Pope John Paul II's **Theology of the Body**, is appreciated by, and directed towards "pop" christians, who may accept a deeper faith, rather than be content with customs. It has been said that **Theology of the Body** is a time bomb in the Catholic Church, that will echo down through the ages when it eventually goes off. Likewise, Jesus was foretold by the prophets, as **Theology of the Body** is based on the ancient faith, yet rejected by the clergy of the day.

So in the first part of the first verse of Isaiah nine, there will be no more gloom for those who were in distress, whether the people of Galilee, or those in the presence of the sacred One relationship, as the people of Galilee were in the presence of the Messiah. But where the people of Galilee witness the beginning of Jesus' ministry, in **Matthew's Foretold**, the two women witness the end of the presence of the sacred One relationship. Nevertheless there will be no more gloom, since the ministry is fulfilled and everyone is safe. The trials and temptations are at an end, and victory, the victory of the sacred One relationship, is complete. The sacred One relationship has been made known, and will be present to all involved, to the end of their days. The sacred One relationship will shine upon all those who were in darkness, as the people of Galilee " . . . have seen a great light."

So the ministry is toward those who practice the faith, but accepts those who do not practice, yet calling them back to practice, finding those who do practice obstinate and not open to this ministry.

But where the protestant reformation was change from the outside, here we have change from the top, the Pope himself, declaring a challenging teaching for both Catholic and Protestant alike. The Catholic Church is not only under attack for the abuse of boys by priests, but for its stand on abortion, birth control, and heterosexual marriage.

Just as the protestant reformation attacked abuses in the Catholic Church, the Catholic Church is now under attack for its lack of understanding of marriage, which the Pope himself has resolved in **Theology of the Body**, and this is a greater challenge. All the accusations being directed at the Catholic Church, including but not limited to, the abuse of boys by priests, its stand on abortion, birth control, and heterosexual marriage, are answered in **Theology of the Body**, yet even the Pope's own church fails to comprehend his teaching. The church has its work cut out for it, not only in the New Evangelization, evangelising Catholics themselves to be able to speak about their faith, but evangelising the world to understand marriage, when many Catholics themselves do not comprehend its sacred nature. Catholics must be able to communicate their faith, and not only their faith, but **Theology of the Body** as well, to answer the accusations made against the Catholic Church.

But Catholic evangelization has been by example, so that is why **Theology of the Body**, more so than **HESUS JOY CHRIST**, must be comprehended and practiced, to shine as a light in the darkness, among the gentiles.

I put the question of why the Ontario Catholic schools do not refuse public funding, in order to maintain Catholic values in their schools, to a discussion group of Catholics. A deacon who was informed about recent legislation responded that even if the Catholic schools rejected public funding to retain their values, effectively becoming private schools, they would still be subject to provincial law and bound to teach birth control and homosexuality. This is similar to how government law in both Ontario and the United States is compelling Catholic hospitals to provide birth control and abortions. As well, a teacher expressed to me at the end of the discussion, that the province owns the assets of the Catholic schools, so there would be considerable hardship incured if public funding was rejected.

This rejection by the ordained clergy, this rejection by government authority, and the necessity of the message, all lead to a death and resurrection. Jesus said and did his bit, and then died for it only to live and conquer the empire as well as the ordained clergy. This is what we are called to do. Our sacred One relationship has been rejected and has ended, but lives on to conquer our awareness. And if the Catholic schools rejected public funding, government legislation and popular opinion, to maintain **Theology of the Body**, to the point of imprisonment, not to mention the vast number of students not attending schools, there would be an end for certain, but more certainly there would be a new beginning in Christ.

Sunday, August 19th, 2012

Verse 16

... ¹⁶the people living in
 darkness
have seen a great light;
on those living in the
 land of the
 shadow of
 death
a light has dawned."ᶠ

ᶠ 16   Isaiah 9:1,2

Verse 16

¹⁶" . . . In the past she
 humbled the land of
 Zebulun and the land
 of Naphtali,
but in the future he will
 honour."ᵈ

✝ 16 Isaiah 9:1

Verse 16 Discussion

I have taken another liberty in referring to God with a feminine pronoun. This could be taken as Wisdom, referred to in the feminine, if not God, referred to in the feminine. Nevertheless, the gift of self discussed in **Theology of the Body** is implied to be a gift to God as the church, the Body of Christ, is given to God, and the analogy that this gift is like a marriage, where God gives themself freely to each of us, as we give ourself freely to God, as discussed by St. John of the Cross. Can the analogy be taken as far as marriage, where the spouse is God incarnate to the other spouse? I'll continue reading **Theology of the Body** and let you know how it turns out.

So whether it is Wisdom or the female spouse, she humbles the land where the sacred One relationship resides, but in the future he will honour it. The trials continue for the sacred One relationship, as Christ is continually assaulted, yet both will triumph.

In **Eusebius' Church History**, the trials prevailed upon the christians for three hundred years, until Constantine condoned christianity in the early three hundreds. Even then, he had to subdue his brother in law for persecuting the christians when his brother in law ruled the eastern empire. Constantine pressured the church to agree amongst itself by forcing the Council of Nicea, which produced the Nicene Creed. This made it clear who was the church and who wasn't the church, so that benefits could be bestowed by the emperor onto the church. These benefits included the return of church assets, including buildings, to the church, as well as monetary gifts from the state to the church, and the exemption of the church and its clergy from taxes. But the majority of **Eusebius' Church History**, the majority of the three hundred years after Christ, is a litany of persecution.

Why would one dare to be a christian and suffer such abuse? It is because the christian has encountered something that he or she will not deny, even under duress, to put it mildly, that consisted of severe torture, mutilation and other suffering worse than death. Many did deny under persecution, but enough did not deny, and were faithful to the end, however slowly it may have come, to inspire the remainder, the meek, to carry on in the faith. I too, would rather die and be done with this false life, than deny the faith I have found. And this faith includes the divine role of marriage. Yet I remain, so I proclaim, as best I can, that the applied christian faith points to marriage and beyond. If there is any honour, let it be for Christ, and christianity applied — marriage.

Today's readings begin with Joshua 24, verses 1-2, 15-17, 18, where Joshua declares he and his family will serve the Lord, and the people proclaim they will serve the Lord as well. The second reading is the notorious bit from Ephesians, chapter four verse 32 to chapter five verse 2, and chapter five verses 21-32. Paul calls the faithful to imitate God and live in love, and then goes on to call wives to be subject to their husbands as the church is subject to Christ, and calls husbands to love their wives as Christ loved the church, giving up his life for her, and also calls husbands to love their wives as they love their own body. Paul goes on to say that a husband and wife will become one flesh, and that this is a great mystery, that he applies to Christ and the church.

So much of the christian culture is illustrated with the analogy of marriage that it is but a small step to see marriage as the focus of christian culture. This step is not uncommon. If all of created life can be seen as a relationship, than perhaps the relationship is more fundamental than all of created life, and more real than all of created life, existing before, after and beyond created life.

This type of step, if not a leap, can be found in a resolution of evolution versus creation. If religion deals with existence before infinity, as Genesis One, verse 1, which states that "In the beginning when God created the heavens and the earth, the earth was a formless void and darkness covered the face of the deep, while a wind from God swept over the face of the waters.", then the awareness of evolution is a gift from God, bringing awareness into creation and remaining fundamental to all awareness, including awareness of evolution. If one is unaware, God brings awareness to them. It is God's creation that awareness is practiced by God's creation, including awareness of evolution. This encounter with existence begins and ends with God.

It is all very simple, if not extremely profound, and so simple that words fail to adequately express it. It must be encountered and experienced first hand before another can point to it and communication of it can begin. This "it" is an infinite awareness of infinity leading to an awareness of the infinite person. It may be anthropomorphizing existence, but then again, why not? Why are we the way we are, and not any other way? It is so simple it is almost impossible to communicate.

This may or may not honour, but it is sincere and honest. The argument may be made that the **HESUS JOY CHRIST** animation is not true, and this would be true, in a literal sense, but once again, the truth that is there is what is being communicated, and if anything is false, discard it and continue to search for what is true, and one will find the truth that is there to be found.

Sunday, August 26th, 2012

Verse 17

¹⁷From that time on Jesus began to preach, "Repent, for the kingdom of heaven **has come***** near."

*** **17** 1973, 1978, 1984 NIV copy that HJC was written from is **is**

Verse 17

¹⁷From that time on One got preachy: "Rebirth, or the kingdom of heaven is ne'er."

Verse 17 Discussion

So begins the preaching. On the one hand, Jesus preaches "Repent, for the kingdom of heaven is near." and the sacred One relationship, balancing whole and part as Jesus himself embodied a balance of whole and part, preaches to all who encounter it - "Rebirth, or the kingdom of heaven is ne'er."

On the one hand, the kingdom of heaven is near, and can be attained by repenting, which is to stop, correct oneself, and continue on within the law. This is successful if one is close to the kingdom of heaven already. On the other hand, the kingdom of heaven is never, contracted to the form of "ne'er", unless there is rebirth. Both repentance and rebirth are common in christian culture, but they are not the same thing.

Webster's New World Dictionary defines "Repent" to mean both to feel sorry for a sin, and to feel such regret that one changes one's mind. "Rebirth", on the other hand, is defined as a new or second birth; a reawakening or revival. The essential difference is that repentance deals with a part of one's life and rebirth encompasses the whole of one's life.

If one exists in a closed system, than nothing new can enter that system. The only glimpse of a larger more thorough system that one can encounter is in the mistakes or errors made in that existing closed system. If the existing closed system were complete and accurate, then mistakes or errors would not occur. Repenting maintains the existing closed system, and attempts to correct errors or mistakes, regardless of why or how they occur. Rebirth is the self destruction of a closed system due to its own failure to account for mistakes and errors, revealing a more complete and accurate system, whether closed or not.

A very good example of rebirth is the two views of the solar system. When knowledge of the planets began, they were observed to be in motion with respect to the earth. But as the knowledge of the planets increased, it became obvious that it was easier to understand the motion of the planets if the sun was considered the centre, rather than the earth. This allowed the motion of the planets to be understood as orbiting the sun, rather than far more complex motion with respect to the earth. The totality, or whole, of the motion of the planets changed, from being understood with respect to the earth, to being understood with respect to the sun. The facts remained the same, but the understanding changed entirely.

If one's system is working well, then correct the errors and maintain the system. But if one's understanding is failing in an onslaught of errors, than scrap it and look toward a better system that more accurately accounts for existence. For some, the kingdom of heaven can be achieved by repenting, but for others, and societies, there are times when rebirth is the overwhelmingly essential solution. We are in such a time.

All the ordinances can be understood by a balance of whole and part, and gender can be understood as well. Marriage is the solution, but to see this solution, one, and society, must experience a reawakening and reorient themselves around marriage, and the overwhelming Joy of such a rebirth, rather than around law, ordinances, values, comfort, condemnation, dismissal and apathy.

Jesus did call for repentance as John the Baptist did, but Jesus also called for rebirth. I cannot find the exact quote, but I believe it goes something like this. If a seed remains, it is just a seed, but if it is sown, it dies and becomes a large plant, bearing fruit. The plant is more magnificent than the seed. The purpose of the seed is the plant, and the purpose of the plant is the seed. Rebirth is the death of the seed and the creation of the plant bearing fruit.

Rebirth is necessary for the comprehension of the sacred role of marriage. One must die to other authorities, relinquishing their demands, to become obedient to God and their spouse, rather than law, parents, career, or other earthly demands. Christ is the way, the truth and the life, and is there to be found in, around, and pointing to marriage, the sacred balance of whole and part.

If repentance has led us this far, and death and rebirth are necessary to move forward, than rebirth is necessary to move forward. Jesus has come and now is the time to move on, in the path of Jesus, to the new world that we have encountered. This world is navigated by balancing whole and part, and is more vast than anything yet imagined.

This new world is like electromagnetics. It is within our existing understanding, but draws our understanding beyond the obvious, to a new understanding that can account for more than the old understanding could, as well as account for everything the old understanding offered.

This new world is not like Mars. It is not beyond our physical experience, out there somewhere. This new world is within us, around us, among us, and at hand.

Sunday, September 2nd, 2012

The image for this verse is of the animation of Verse Two of _Matthew's Three Fold_, on the computer screen of the former spouse, as he creates the **HESUS JOY CHRIST** animation.

Monday, September 3rd, 2012

Verse 18

Jesus Calls His First Disciples****

¹⁸As Jesus was walking beside the Sea of Galilee, he saw two brothers, Simon called Peter and his brother Andrew. They were casting a net into the lake, for they were fishermen.

**** **18** 1973, 1978, 1984 NIV copy that HJC was written from is **The Calling of the First Disciples**

Verse 1B

The Calling of Discipline

¹ᴮAs One was seeking employment, . . ./ . . two siblings saw One, Simone called Stress Rocks and her brother in arms, Andrew. / They were playing a line for they were grifters.

Verse 1B Discussion

Everyone knows what a fisherman is, but a grifter is less commonly known. This is because it is slang, from the 1930's in the Great Depression in America, for a small time con artist. These people, grifters, would make a living by confusing and outwitting someone out of their money or assets. I know this term, grifter, from a movie that came out in the 1970's called **The Sting**, which was about a small time grifter, played by Robert Redford, getting back at a big time gangster, with the help of a big time con artist, played by Paul Newman. The movie's soundtrack featured big ragtime hits from the 1920's, such as **"The Entertainer"** by Scott Joplin.

So as Jesus begins to apply himself, the spouse of the sacred One relationship seeks to apply himself by seeking employment, armed with his resume. Jesus came across men employed legitimately as fishermen, yet the one encounters employed landscapers who are also applying themselves as grifters.

Where Jesus comes across two brothers - Simon, who would be called "Cephas", which means "Rock" and is translated with the Greek word for rock - "Petros", and his brother Andrew; the One comes across two siblings — an amply endowed woman, Simone, nicknamed "Stress Rocks", and her brother, Andrew. Peter and Andrew are working as fishermen, but Stress Rocks and Andrew, are pausing from their work as landscapers to conduct some grifting business. They are playing a line, which means to con someone, as well as meaning fishing with a line, while Peter and Andrew are fishing with a net.

The Sea of Galilee, would be in Galilee, which is a secular area of Judea. Likewise, the One seeks secular employment, but Jesus is seeking to apply himself spiritually.

So that's a fair bit of wordplay. There, as always, are four meanings in this animation. There is the meaning of the original Gospel text, the literal meaning of the animation text, the meaning that presents itself when the two texts are compared, and finally, the meaning of the whole exercise to each of us in today's world.

All that happens in the Gospel text is that Jesus sees two fishermen, Simon and Andrew, casting their nets. We are told that Simon was called Peter, but we are not told why. The meaning I take from this is that when one attempts to apply themselves, opportunities will present themselves. As well, Jesus is content with what is readily at hand, which happens to be two working individuals, actually working, and in charge of their own work. We do not know what Jesus knew of these brothers, if anything. But we know that Jesus goes on to commission these two brothers right away.

The animation text is similar, in that the One is on the lookout, as Jesus was, albeit more actively seeking than Jesus who just walked along the shore. The siblings, Simone and Andrew, see the One, as they are doubling up by being on the clock as landscapers as well as conducting a bit of grifting business. They are employed by someone else, the business owner, to which the One would like to apply for work.

Where Jesus saw Simon and Andrew, Simone and Andrew see the One. This forwards and backwards, inside and out, is typical of the sacred One. Balancing whole and part can be unstable, but once one is experienced, this inversion and reversion becomes easy to manage, and allows for a high level of mental agility and diligence. Simone and Andrew are employed by someone else, not presently working at landscaping, but on the clock, and conning someone. They are stealing from their employer by not working while being punched in, as well as stealing from the object of their con.

So it may seem a simple thing for Jesus to see two fishermen, but it carries a lot of meaning. These two, Simon and Andrew, have many strong attributes when compared with Simone and Andrew. Jesus could have done far worse, even though Simon and Andrew are likely illiterate and uneducated, as well as knowing full well that they are sinners. Jesus sees the positive in people and builds on that, because that is what exists. A person's shortcomings do not exist. Only what they are capable of actually exists.

Nevertheless, as the animation plays out, there is the common practice of the attitude that "this will do", that reality is adequate, which acknowledges not that God will provide, but that God is, has, and is always providing abundantly. This is the calling of discipline.

Monday, September 10th, 2012

Verse 19

¹⁹"Come, follow me," Jesus said, "and I will **send you out to fish for people*******."

***** **19** 1973, 1978, 1984 NIV copy that HJC was written from is **make you fishers of men**

Verse 19

¹⁹ "Can we lead you," they said, "we can get you lots of friends."

Verse 19 Discussion

The people of God, the Church, the Body of Christ, is often compared to a flock of sheep, being led throughout their lives by a shepherd, who is what God or Jesus is like, always aware of His flock. But then where do the leaders come from, and are they still following as they lead? I would assert that leading and following are not that different, and really are practised simultaneously.

Consider the European explorers of North America. Sure, they led the way into the wilderness, but they followed first nations guides, who worked for them. So the guides were told where the explorers wanted to go, and the guides told the explorers how to get there. So the leaders followed, and the followers lead.

"There are three that bear witness, the spirit, the water and the blood, and the three into the one thing are." That is a literal translation from the Greek that I remember, of a verse, First John 5:7, that is often used as a proof of the Trinity, the three in one Godhead of Father, Son and Holy Spirit. Don't ask me how each of the three corresponds. There is a constant relationship between Being, Knowledge of Being, and Love of Being, or instead, Doing, Knowledge of Doing, and Love of Doing. Who is to say which is the leader?

Likewise, using landscaping as an example, the crew members follow the crew leader, each for their own reasons, and each at different tasks, yet the crew leader follows the manager as he leads the crew around the different sites, and the manager follows the owner, as well as the property managers, who are directed by the home owners. Yet the home owners are told what they can and cannot have by the owner, and this symbiotic relationship will or will not exist. Each person is both following and leading. The Apostles, when Jesus left them a prepared place, lead others as they followed Jesus to martyrdom. The flock is both following and leading. The Church endeavours to lead the world to God, the infinite person, as the Church follows Christ.

So in this verse, where Jesus says "Follow me" to Simon and Andrew, in the animation text, Simone and Andrew ask to lead the spouse of the sacred One relationship. Jesus commands Simon and Andrew, but Simone and Andrew request of the One. Is there a difference?

If, as in the last verse, God, the infinite person, is always providing, then the One accepts this offer of following Simone and Andrew as an opportunity from God. This is just as the opportunity presented by Simon and Andrew is taken up by Jesus.

So who cares who is leading and who is following? Sure, there is the illusion that the crew leader has more control and self determination, but try to believe that with a crew full of people like Andrew, who are constantly questioning the leader and opposing every direction that leader gives. And we have already mentioned how the crew leader is not that far up the ladder, since he answers to not only the manager, but the owner, the property manager and the home owners as well. This is why I would not be a crew leader, even though I had a crew in my truck and mostly drove them around to sites with the manager's truck and crew, as well as to sites this crew worked alone. The manager was not interested in working so much as in being the leader so as to have more self determination. Good luck.

As well, often one is chosen to represent the crew to others. This is leading with someone. Although Jesus called Simon Peter to follow him, Jesus eventually led with Peter.

Finally, we are all called as individuals by our Baptism, to be priest, prophet and king. We are to minister to others, proclaim to others as witnesses of our experience and faith, and to administer and manage our corner of the world, based on our experience and understanding. A nation of kings!! This is not so bizarre, as this is what free enterprise is suppose to accomplish. Nevertheless, free enterprise fails to function once the concept of an employee is allowed. But one may remain a priest, prophet and king, regardless of the roles imposed by the secular world, as the infinite person is constantly providing opportunities to fulfil those three duties, regardless of how the world views one's role.

Tuesday, September 18th, 2012

Verse 20

²⁰At once they left their nets and followed him.

Verse 20

²⁰At once they left their line and led with them.

Verse 20 Discussion

Without hesitation, surprisingly, the opportunity is taken up, and many question how the decision could be made so quickly, and without looking back. The assumption is that something was so obviously apparent that there wasn't a question whether one should or shouldn't take up the opportunity. These are people who know where they stand and are capable of making a decision on the spot, fully aware of the circumstances surrounding the opportunity, and confident enough in their understanding to boldly act on their decision.

This is the nature of the One, when anyone follows a balance of whole and part, holistic and reductionistic, female and male. They are living in the moment with a vast comprehension of their situation and their purpose. It is like a fighter pilot, who not only takes their life in their hands, like a motorcyclist, but further as a pilot, without their feet on any physical foundation, other than air; and commits themselves constantly and repeatedly to the consequences of their many choices and decisions. There is all the thrill of the movie **Top Gun**, and all the Joy. This is real life, rather than a waking death.

It is not reckless risk taking, but it does not shirk away from risk. The awareness of the whole enables calculated risks, and the awareness of the part manages the details from moment to moment.

Many people talk of giving one's life to Jesus. Jesus the man is no longer with us so what are they talking about? Jesus may be physically present in the Eucharist, but that may not be an obvious presence and using the same buzz words over and over again will not make the message any clearer. Neither will using the buzz words of whole and part and balancing them, make the message clearer, just perhaps be a different approach. Every generation must make the message their own in their own words.

But balancing whole and part, as Christ is, leads to a wonderful life of adventure, communion, peace and Joy. One may not know where it will lead or how it will end, if ever, but there is certainty as well as surprising Joy.

In this verse, compared to verse eighteen, Simon and Andrew seem reckless and irresponsible to leave their nets and business, and Simone and Andrew seem to be taking a step toward responsibility by leaving the line they were stringing and taking up the use of the sacred One, as referred to by "them". If the sacred One spouse is virtuous, then taking up the use of him, rather than conning others out of something, is a move toward responsibility.

And sending out a virtuous person to do one's work may seem like an advantage to the person who sends them out, but a virtuous person may come across less than virtuous circumstances and proceed to resolve those circumstances to a virtuous end. So there is a certain amount of honesty in a dishonest person who makes use of an honest person, for whatever end.

Likewise, it becomes irrelevant whether Jesus knew the character of Simon and Andrew, and only relevant whether they are willing to do the will of Jesus, because the work he will send them out to do will forge them into virtuous characters. And the work that the sacred One spouse does will bring the purposes of whoever leads with him to light, and begin to resolve those purposes to a virtuous end.

Once again, the duties of priest, prophet and king are placed upon every baptized person, and rest with them regardless of that person's role in society, work or before infinity. Balancing the whole and part of existence is a task constantly before any one who may become aware of existence — that is everyone.

So let's discuss an idea that has been on my mind lately — intelligent disobedience. It is a phrase that is common in service dog training. The idea may be expressed by an example. If a blind person commands a service dog to lead them across a street, but the dog sees cars coming, the dog will disobey the command to cross the street. That is intelligent disobedience.

Perhaps all disobedience is intelligent. Certainly the person who disobeys sees some intelligence in their actions. The problem only arises when the person who disobeys has a lesser awareness of the whole and part of the situation than the one who commands them. Often the one who commands has a lesser awareness of the whole and part than the one who is to obey.

When I was working for Etobicoke Electric, Mike told me to go to a site and hang the lights now that the plasterers had finished the ceiling. I arrived and the electrical boxes for the lights were in the wrong spot, and had old wires in them. I realized that we had only left cable hanging down and did not remove the old electrical boxes, so the plasterers just pushed the wires up and plastered around the old boxes. I could not make this clear to Mike on the phone, and he said "Are there boxes? Then hang the damn lights!!" A week or so later, I was unloading when I heard Mike yelling from the area that I hung the lights and had a laugh to myself because I knew he had screwed up the work because the person, Mike, who commanded, had a lesser awareness than myself, who obeyed. I should have intelligently disobeyed.

Sunday, September 23rd, 2012

Verse 21

²¹Going on from there, he saw two other brothers, James son of Zebedee and his brother John. They were in a boat with their father Zebedee, preparing their nets. Jesus called them, ...

Verse 21

²¹Going on from there, two others saw them, Mandy of Paul and her brother John. / They were in the same boat as their father, repairing their bets. / They called One, ...

Verse 21 Discussion

A bit of wordplay, where ". . . in a boat with their father . . ." becomes ". . . in the same boat as their father, . . .", is the core of this verse. Hopefully everyone knows the expression: to be "in the same boat", which means to share the circumstances with others "in the same boat".

First though, many people may recognize value in one, or the sacred One relationship, and begin to participate in that balance of whole and part. Such people can come from anywhere, whether relatives, in-laws, co-workers, acquaintances or even strangers. Likewise, many people, no matter how close or involved, may overlook one's efforts to balance whole and part, including overlooking one's accomplishments at balancing whole and part. One may never assume that there will or will not be appreciation of one's efforts.

These two in-laws, siblings of the female spouse, took notice of the sacred One relationship, and sought to include that relationship in their lives, so that it became an example of a balance of whole and part to them. They were busy at maintaining their financial security, taking calculated risks to advance responsibly and independently. Yet they took notice of the sacred One relationship, and ventured into communion with the spouses, to understand further what had sparked their interest.

This is very common. Even the two landscapers, Simone and Andrew, took notice, even if they did not fully appreciate the balance of whole and part that they had witnessed. This is like sowing seed — some sow and others harvest. The seed may have been sown with Simone and Andrew, but the harvest was for someone else to take on. With Mandy and John, there is a greater appreciation, but the busyness of their lives may have crowded out the maturing of their understanding of the benefits of balancing whole and part in the form of a relationship. Perhaps they will recognize it again elsewhere, and invest themselves further into appreciating it.

As life goes on, one may never anticipate where others who appreciate one's efforts at balancing whole and part may come from. I have been very surprised by who does appreciate my efforts, and who completely overlooks or dismisses my efforts.

And once again, where James and John are called by Jesus, Mandy and John call the spouses of the sacred One. It, again, does not matter who is following and who is leading, as even by following one may express their balance of whole and part, that those leading will consider considerably, so much so that they will in reality be following those they lead.

This is the nature of balancing whole and part — it can seem volatile, unwieldy and destabilizing, but this is the great potential of this ever present guide — agility, diligence, facility, velocity and power. Consider a formula one race car — just the slightest motion on the steering wheel translates into a considerable steering correction. These cars are finely tuned and designed to be so responsive that they are uncontrollable by a novice. Yet this lack of control is the very thing that allows one to have so much control that they easily outperform other more manageable vehicles.

This is the reason the Roman Empire fell, and this is the reason marriage is so volatile. The many gods of the Roman Empire were easily understood and allowed a certain amount of control. But when Christ came along and amalgamated the many gods into the one God, the understanding of goals and logical behaviour directed toward those goals became more complex as well as simpler — one god is simpler than many gods, but resolving many purposes to one purpose is a more complex undertaking. So if one is to place marriage, the balance of whole and part, as the top practical priority, then lesser priorities will be overrided at times to defer to the priority of marriage. This will confuse others who cannot justify placing marriage at the pinnacle of purposes. And actually pursuing marriage, a balance of whole and part, will mean that lesser purposes will be disregarded from time to time, when they do not serve the higher purpose of marriage, and this will be considered everything from a simple mistake to a capital crime.

Marriage is so volatile, as any balance of whole and part is, because it is so powerful, and must be understood and managed. The novice will crash and burn many times before he accomplishes much, as society has crashed and burned many times, especially in the dark ages of medieval Europe, since the beginning of Christianity.

Flight is a very good example of the power and volatility of balancing whole and part. A modern jet is extremely powerful and capable of great feats, but the last century began with many deaths and defeats in the efforts to achieve reliable flight. Indeed, many people thought it was sheer folly to even attempt flight, yet nevertheless, those who struggled were eventually successful, although it is still a highly complex skill and technology to attain and maintain. Today, as discovered September 11th, 2001, flight is taken for granted. Likewise, the social accomplishments of generic christianity are taken for granted, and one day the achievements of balancing whole and part, as well as the understanding of the necessity, primacy and power of this goal, will be taken for granted.

Tuesday, October 2nd, 2012

Verse 22

… … .²²and immediately they left the boat and their father and followed him.

Verse 22

… … . ²²and immediately they left the boat of their father and kept track of One.

Verse 22 Discussion

For James and John to leave their business and father to follow Jesus is a big decision, demanding a spur of the moment commitment. But for Mandy and John to pay attention to the witness of the sacred One relationship requires much less of a commitment. It only requires a bit of attention, and they need not leave anything in their life, other than manage their attention so as to be aware of the sacred One relationship. They may not pay so much attention to their finances and business, as their father has, and spend a little more time paying attention to the balance of whole and part in the witness of the sacred One relationship.

This may seem irresponsible to not pay full attention to the demands of self sufficiency, but in reality, this is what their father has done so as to raise a family and maintain a marriage to their mother. Likewise, following the sacred One relationship is not so radical at all!

I am reading the Qu'ran, and up to only Surah 3 — Al-'Imran, or The Family of 'Imran, page 29 of 429 pages, and the third chapter of 114 chapters. For those interested, the translation I have is by Abdullah Yusuf Ali. To me it comes across as a litany of rules, each numbered, and they all seem unconnected. My understanding is that all of these rules, when understood as a whole, will create a profound understanding of existence, or at least that is my hope. It seems written to be a concrete, knowable and practical guide to the infinite, and the infinite person, God.

Christianity, on the other hand, is full of parables that seem to confuse many people, although they are readily ripe with meaning for me. As well, Christianity has many mysteries, of which one is the Trinity, which are to be believed without a full understanding, seemingly demanding blind faith. I have found, however, that blind faith is a dead end, the same dead end as the belief in magic, and I instead ponder the mysteries presented, in faith, and receive insight from day to day as I ponder these mysteries.

So where Islam demands accepting the litany of rules, and considering them all as one, Christianity demands accepting quite a few mysteries, and considering them as one, to benefit from a thorough understanding of each of these guides to the infinite, and the infinite person, God. Where Christianity presents lofty ideas, full of complex relationships, Islam provides concrete rules, that are to be taken as a whole, both leading to a comprehension of the infinite, although each approach is unique.

So one must consider all the seemingly disconnected elements of their existence, and develop a single, as each person is a single entity — one, comprehension that approaches infinity, both within one's own practice of faith, as well as amongst the secular world they find themselves in, if not the approaches to infinity presented by other faith practices, and manage a comprehension of their own. My experience and comprehension points to a concrete guide, that of balancing whole and part, and in pursuit of this balance, marriage stands out as a fundamental foundation for this way of life, balancing whole and part. In such a practice, one may encounter revelations that are overwhelmingly obvious, once encountered. Mandy and John may come to an awareness of the importance of marriage, balancing whole and part, both by the witness of the sacred One relationship, and the witness of their father, as well as mother. It makes sense that Mandy and John's parents would value marriage, yet Mandy and John, as single people, have to come to value marriage in their own awareness, and when and if this happens, it will seem overwhelmingly obvious, once they are aware of such value.

Zebedee may have been quite pleased to see his sons take up the opportunity Jesus presented to them, and Zebedee may have been comforted that his sons were able to do what he never had the opportunity to do, and could not now take up the opportunity due to commitments and physical inability. There may be hardships for Zebedee, who has lost the efforts of his sons, but he may endure these hardships willingly and joyfully, knowing that the tasks his sons have taken up are worth his efforts at enduring his own hardships. John the Baptist knew he must decrease as Jesus and his ministry increased.

This is the attitude that parents need to take toward their adult children. They must make do without their offspring so that their offspring can mature and grow into what they may become and succeed as persons. This is what Jesus did with his disciples. He left to prepare a place for them. This is often taken as if Jesus would do such things as build a house where they would all live together. This understanding is mistaken. Jesus did not leave to go to another place to prepare a place for his disciples — Jesus' departure alone prepared a place by leaving a hole for the disciples to fill. Jesus promised to be with them, but only in spirit, and not physically, so that they would take up the work Jesus did for themselves, and grow into the likeness of Jesus and take on his role for themselves. This is why parents must allow their adult children to leave, and live apart from them, so that they will grow into full adults, and perhaps nurture others of their own.

If the word "man" means "human" or "person", and includes both genders, then it should also mean that a person will leave their father and mother and cling to their spouse, so that the two will become one flesh. And whatever God has joined, let no person separate.

Thanksgiving Weekend, Sunday, October 7th, 2012

Verse 23

Jesus Heals the Sick

²³Jesus went throughout Galilee, teaching in their synagogues, **proclaiming********* the good news of the kingdom, and healing every disease and sickness among the people.

******* **23** 1973, 1978, 1984 NIV copy that HJC was written from is **preaching**

Verse 23

One Feels the Sick

²³One went thoroughly secular, learning in their malls, . . / . . preachy about the good news of the kingdom, . . / . . and bearing every disease and sickness among the people.

Verse 23 Discussion

Once again, Galilee is a secular area, and this is where Jesus taught in the established religious institutions, as a lay person, preaching about a new thing called the Kingdom of Heaven. He also healed "every" disease and sickness among the people.

Jesus was a carpenter, a tradesman, and not any kind of ordained religious leader. He did however, proclaim a new religious ideal called, among other things, the Kingdom of Heaven. It is understood that this new religious ideal was based in the established faith and religion of the region, and Jesus called people of this established religious faith to follow him, whether they were in good religious standing, or not. This included sinners, but did not include gentiles. Jesus was open to gentiles appreciating his lead, but he directed his efforts toward the Jews.

Jesus' healing "every" disease and sickness is an interesting statement. It is not generally understood that Jesus healed every instance of every disease, leaving an entirely healthy population in his wake. Rather, he healed those that came to him, and frequently gave credit to his patient's faith, saying things like "your faith has healed you".

It could be understood that Jesus healed specific instances of pretty much every known disease, from leprosy to demon possession, which is often taken to mean mental illness. This is how I understand the statement that Jesus healed "every" disease and sickness.

Likewise, one spouse of the sacred One relationship gets by in the secular world, professing both in churches and elsewhere, as a lay person, about a new idea called the sacred One relationship, or marriage, balancing whole and part. He also "bore" every disease and sickness among the people.

Getting by in the secular world means that one has to understand the collective mind of people who do not play any religious game. They worship, yes, but they do not even know what they worship, and do not have any awareness that they are worshiping. There are many reasons that they give for excluding religious behaviours and trappings from their lives and they do not have any understanding of the fundamentals so they are unable to relate to christianity, or any other faith. Theirs can be considered a faith of the one with the most toys at the end wins — or any variation of anything like that. Nevertheless, where they are successful, however limited, this spouse watches and learns, and incorporates their understanding into his. The mall is a common place of secular worship, with rituals and communion.

This spouse, may or may not be considered to have a trade, but gets by in the secular world, as opposed to being a religious devotee, not being provided for as such. This spouse proclaims a new religious ideal called, among other things, the sacred One relationship, balancing whole and part, female and male, holism and reductionism, and communion and agency. It is understood that this new religious ideal is based in the established faith and religion of the region, and this spouse called people of this established religious faith to follow him, whether they were in good religious standing, or not. This included sinners, but did not include anyone other than those of a christian culture. This is open to members of other faiths appreciating this lead, but it is directed toward christians, whether in good standing or not. This is because christianity is fundamental to any approach balancing whole and part, because christianity proclaims forgiveness as fundamental, rather than forgiveness as a special favour. The path of marriage requires the method of Christ, based on constant fundamental ever present unfailing forgiveness.

This bearing "every" disease and sickness is an interesting statement. It is not generally understood that anyone ever bears every instance of every disease, leaving an entirely burdened population in their wake. Rather, they bear those that come to them, and frequently give credit to their faith, believing things like their faith has healed them.

It could be understood that this spouse bore specific instances of pretty much every category of every known disease, from chicken pox to demon possession, which is often taken to mean mental illness. This is how I understand the statement that they bore "every" disease and sickness.

Sunday, October 14th, 2012

Verse 24

²⁴News about him spread all over Syria, and people brought to him all who were ill with various diseases, those suffering severe pain, the demon-possessed, those having seizures, and the paralyzed; and he healed them.

Verse 24

²⁴News about One was unheard of throughout the community and they encountered all who were / . ill with various diseases, those suffering severe pain, / . the demon-possessed, / . . those having seizures, / . . and the paralyzed, / . . and they healed One.

Verse 24 Discussion

This was news. This news spread quickly and far. The news about Jesus was that he was healing the people who were ill with various diseases, and so much so, people would bring the ill to him to be healed.

Likewise, the news of the sacred One relationship spread throughout the community. It was unheard of for two members of this community to unite in marriage, so the news of the sacred One relationship spread quickly and fast.

This is common. The news of a marriage will break through the silence of unmaintained family relations, and will draw the family and compatriots together to celebrate.

Everyone wants to meet the other spouse who has grown united to their relative or friend. Everyone in this community hopes to be blessed by this union so that they too may one day participate in just such a union.

The sacred One relationship, in the likeness of Christ, has the capacity to heal. But where Jesus Christ healed the sick, the sick heal the shortcomings of the sacred One relationship. This relationship sees the weaknesses and sufferings of others in the community and treasures this relationship more and more. The union of whole and part, female and male, in this sacred One relationship is Joy for all who encounter it.

This Gospel passage tells of the Event that Jesus' healing was. This Event, as we consider it two-thousand years later, is very hard to verify, and this leaves us with only the consideration that whatever was happening, it did make news all over Syria. This is important and this is the purpose of this passage of scripture — that Jesus' healing was an event. Even if it were only a spiritual healing, rather than a miraculous physical healing, it remains a remarkable event, as witnessed by the fact that the news spread all over Syria. There was something going on for certain, even if it was a hoax, for it must have been a very impressive hoax. It must have been such an impressive hoax that one must consider that there must have been something to it, even as hoaxes go! The fact that Jesus was an Event on the basis of his healings, is the importance of this verse of the Gospel of Matthew, Chapter Four.

Likewise, the news of the sacred One relationship is an event in the community. News of this spread fast and far, and had an impact. This drew spectators from the community and from afar, and the illnesses these spectators bore, as they came to encounter the sacred One relationship, healed the sacred One relationship so that the spouses forgave each other their shortcomings for the sake of the sacred One relationship. This kept the sacred One relationship aware of its strengths and benevolence. This healed One.

Jesus was also impacted by the needs of the people that both came to him and were brought to him. It is often expressed in the Gospels that Jesus felt this or that emotion toward someone who either came or was brought before him. This would have driven home, to Jesus, the importance of Jesus' ministry, and that it was not just some academic intellectual exercise he was re-committing himself to, each time he encountered suffering and need. Jesus knew and was constantly reminded that his mission was practical and capable of resolving the roots of sin, suffering, physical suffering, oppression and even death.

Likewise, the spouses of the sacred One relationship, impacted by the needs of the people that they encounter, are keenly aware of the problems of today and re-commit themselves to their attempts to resolve what they believe to be the roots of sin and suffering, proclaiming the solution offered by a balance of whole and part, founded in marriage, in whatever way grace presents to them.

So the diseases . . . . The severe pain is the solitary life, united with no-one, lacking full communion with all of life, and shut out from marriage, the fundamental balance of whole and part, and more importantly, the fundamental basis of Joy !

The demon possession is the enslavement to ideology. This does not allow for grace to act and redeem. As Christ was broken and bled for the sake of us all, we too are to be broken and bled for the sake of our community, and this includes most importantly, and above all, our ideologies and understanding of our existence. For a new comprehension, the incorrect must be acknowledged and incorporated into our understanding and this requires the destruction of ideology to be born again as a new ideology, to face its own shortcomings and be reborn again and again to a new ideology.

The seizures are suffered by those who are oppressed by others for whatever reason, be it legitimate or otherwise, and have not experienced grace and forgiveness from their oppressors, as Jesus would forgive their oppressors. This makes it impossible for the siezed person to act, and they can only act incorrectly in the eyes of their oppressors.

The way out of this is to die to the oppression, and surface elsewhere where the possibility of blossoming may present itself.

The paralyzed are the walking waking dead, who have accounted for all they experience, and have excluded mystery, miracles and wonder from their lives. Because they believe they have created themselves to be eternal, they have closed themselves off from grace and forgiveness, believing they are quite fine without it. They are dead long before they physically die, and may, by the grace of God, realize it before they physically die, if even only on their death bed. They are the flipside, often seized themselves, of seizured people, and frequently the oppressors.

Sunday, October 21st, 2012

Verse 25

²⁵Large crowds from Galilee, the Decapolis,ᵍ Jerusalem, Judea and the region across the Jordan followed him.

ᵍ 25 That is, *the Ten Cities*

Verse 25

²⁵Large crowds of secularism, / . municipalities, / . churches, / . hospitals, / . and the far side led with them.

Verse 25 Discussion

Sure — it is curious, perhaps, to know where the people who were fans of Jesus came from, but what difference does it make to us today? He was executed anyways, and probably most of his fans weren't fans any more after such a disappointment.

We have already touched on how Galilee was a secular area, so this verse tells us that secular people were fans of Jesus. Reading this scripture today tells us that secular people saw value in Jesus' ministry, and that there could be secular value in the Gospel for us today. So how many religious people today are towing the line only as far as the secular value and not investing in the existential value of scripture and faith? How many secular people acknowledge that the secular values they hold have roots in religion?

Balancing whole and part, female and male, has the advantage of both whole and part, but comes under attack for being wholistic, by those who only have faith in "part", and also comes under attack for being partial, by those who only have faith in "wholes". This is christianity, balancing whole and part, female and male, each forgiving the other. When one acknowledges value, essentially they are acknowledging an integration and balance of whole and part. Many people acknowledge only either the whole or the part, and will support only either of those two aspects, overlooking the balance of whole and part that accomplishes. This is prevalent both within and without organized religion. This is rampant both within and without of organized religion. Sunday school teachers impress the importance of the whole, even at the expense of the part. Preachers insist the importance of the part, at the expense of the whole. Almost all of society promotes and dismisses in ignorance of any balance of whole and part, yet balancing whole and part is the only thing that works, so often in an individual's understanding they are unaware that what they are promoting is a specific instance of a balance of whole and part.

So the sacred One relationship presents value, by balancing whole and part, to society, and is put to work promoting either whole or part, depending on the inclination of those in control. Society, and every part of society, leads with individuals that they have faith in. Since the sacred One relationship has a great deal of value, the spouses are often called upon to lead on behalf of those in control. This practice is prevalent.

Jesus, as an original balance of whole and part, was able to shock and awe with his ability and ideas. Today, the opportunity to balance whole and part is present to everyone, and so the capabilities of such a balance are taken for granted. Rather than lead, the sacred One relationship is at work in the trenches, on the ground floor, getting their hands dirty and pulling themselves up by their boot straps! Rather than taking the lead, like an executive or an officer, the sacred One relationship has the respect of its peers for what it can accomplish first hand.

So where large crowds followed Jesus, there is an abundance of people looking to make use of the spouses of the sacred One relationship.

The secular world hires, trains, educates, empowers, delegates to, and holds the spouses of the sacred One relationship, or anyone balancing whole and part, responsible.

Urban planners, on behalf of municipalities, create suburbs for those who balance whole and part in the forms of consumption and work.

Churches are valued for the regular attendance they can muster from those balancing whole and part.

Hospitals are almost religious institutions themselves and promote the healing and cures they accomplish, disregarding the people who die there.

Even the far side of society can employ the accomplishments and capabilities of those balancing whole and part. The spouses of the sacred One relationship, as well as any one else who balances whole and part, are who everyone is looking for, seeking to hire, seeking to heal, seeking to attend, and seeking to live.

The municipalities are the same as a region of ten cities. The churches are the same as the sacred city Jerusalem. The hospitals are the same as the benevolent region supporting the churches and Jerusalem. The region beyond the Jordan is the far reaches of society, extending as far as, and including, those on the far side of society.

I'm sure Mike is still singing "*My Sharona*" on karaoke without me, and enjoying not having a crew under the maintenance manager!

Sunday, October 28th, 2012

Closing Notes

OVERVIEW

Well here we go ! We were a third of the way through discussing the seventeen verses of **HESUS JOY CHRIST / Matthew's Three Fold**, when I took a break to consider the wordage that was then pushing seven thousand words !

A body of knowledge has it's limits, and one limit has nothing to do with how many pages are written about such a body of knowledge. When one (or a group) creates a body of knowledge they are making many decisions, or rather, assumptions that are not stated outright. These assumptions are made early on in the creation of a body of knowledge but seriously limit the effectiveness of that body of knowledge. So as an example of how creating a body of knowledge can become ridiculous, usually around the point at which academia takes over, I have chosen to write about everything I know about how to pick up a stick.

I was fortunate to make the acquaintance of a man in his fifties who left the aerospace industry to go to school for landscaping. That alone is ridiculous enough, but the point is that this gentleman was accomplished in academia and technological industry, who when he decided he wanted to work outdoors it was only natural that he would go to school to learn an outdoor trade. He studied for three years at Humber College and graduated from the landscaping technician program. Sadly, he only lasted five months as a landscaper, in spite of working for a very reputable, good and established company, and was able to get into good enough shape in spite of his many years of age, but could not tolerate the bystanders looking at him with the expression of 'look at that nice old man picking weeds' ! His academic and thorough understanding was not appreciated by the casual observer, so was it worth anything at all ? Likewise, this thorough understanding of how to pick up a stick is ridiculous and not worth anything at all to the casual observer. And the discussion of **HESUS JOY CHRIST / Matthew's Three Fold** is not worth anything to the casual observer — unless an awareness is cultivated by considering the discussion, but a thorough consideration of the animation would have the same effect of cultivating an awareness, not to mention considering life would cultivate a thorough awareness.

The moral of the story, here, is PAY ATTENTION ! ! !

Tuesday, April 12th, 2011

HOW TO PICK UP A STICK!

Here is how to pick up a stick.

First determine the size of the stick. Is it a twig, a limb, or a full branch? If it is a twig, how many of them are there? If there are many, then get a rake and a tarp. If there are not enough to warrant a tarp than get a garbage bag or a bucket.

Drop the garbage bag or bucket in the general middle of the twigs, and begin a loop path, starting and finishing at the bucket and extending only far enough to allow you to fill your hands with twigs. If you make the loop path too big you will waste time walking back to the bucket when your hands are full. If you make the loop path too small you will be dumping too few sticks in the bucket for each loop and that wastes time loading too small a load of twigs in the bucket. This becomes a concern when the bucket begins to get full and the twigs must be stuffed into it and can no longer just be dropped into it. If you are using a garbage bag, however, this is always a concern as the twigs must be placed into the bag lengthwise as otherwise the bag cannot hold as much and is too quickly filled.

Actually picking up the twig must be done standing with legs extended but not locked. Lean down like you are touching your toes and bob down to pick up the twig, and as you bob up transfer it to your off hand until it is full, and by that time you should be more than halfway along your loop path. Finish the remaining path holding the sticks in the good hand that picks them up, so that you arrive at the bucket with two full hands. Do not crawl around on your hands and knees because you need your hands to hold as many twigs as possible. It likely isn't good for your knees, crawling in the damp ground. As well, bending your knees to crouch down to pick up the twigs will be too much bending for your knees. Bobbing will get you well stretched out.

In the case of many twigs, a rake can be used to gather the twigs into piles and onto the tarp, to be dragged or carried to the truck. The first sweep of the rake will orient the twigs perpendicular to the sweep of the rake, and then the pile can be rolled like a snowball as it gathers more twigs. Maintain the coherency of the pile if the twigs are to be tied into bundles, as such a fagot can be rolled onto the twine to allow the twine to be wrapped around the fagot and tied. Do not attempt to rake a twig that is parallel to the path of the rake. This will break the rake. It may still be necessary to gather the remaining twigs by hand. Larger sticks may need to be picked up by hand, following the above mentioned method, as they cannot be gathered by a rake. DO NOT BREAK THE RAKE!

Usually, a large area of twigs will occur in the spring as summer or spring maintenance is beginning, but may also occur when pruning. Pruning will produce limbs and perhaps branches. Branches may also need to be picked up at the beginning of spring maintenance or after a storm.

When picking up a limb or a stick that is larger, pick it up by the stump end as that will give you the most leverage over a tapered limb if you pick it up by it's heaviest end. Otherwise the limb will be unwieldy and if you can get it into your armload, you may not be able to toss it in the truck. Gather all that you can hold under one arm and make sure you are on your way back to the truck by the time you have a full load in your arms. Again, bob down and up to pick up the sticks, keeping in mind your armload. There is no way you could crawl or even crouch with an armload of sticks.

Branches are larger sticks that branch into more than one stick. They may be very large. If they are very large, do not cut them up, but instead drag them by the stump end, so that no further branches are broken off, and heave them by the stump end, into the truck. The best place to cut them, to pack them into the truck efficiently, is right in the truck. If one was to cut them up before they are in the truck, that is only more sticks to pick up and more sticks to throw in the truck and more sticks to pack into the truck to get a large load and reduce the number of trips with the truck. Once a few branches are aligned with the stump end at the head of the truck, tread on the branches carefully and with loppers, cut the branches at the crotches where the smaller branches head out from the main branch. It is the crotch that sets the limbs at angles to one another and prevents efficient loading in the truck bed. By cutting the branches at the crotches the limbs are able to fall into alignment with one another. I have seen a load of branches come out of the truck body and maintain the rectangular shape of the truck body as it sits on it's own after being dumped.

Finally, for a good laugh, try to wield a branch by the small end — it will wobble around and you may not even be able to get the stump off the ground! The use of a wood chipper greatly improves the packing and removal of large branches, but there will still be twigs to be gathered, according to the appropriate method.

1000 words

Tuesday, April 12th, 2011

Appendices

EPILOGUE

This ends the writing of the discussion of the **HESUS JOY CHRIST** animation to date. So where are we left?

As outlined in the Overviews, reality can live in our awareness in two ways that are the same but different. One way is to be aware of the wholes, and the other way is to be aware of the parts. Women have a naturally infinite capacity to comprehend the wholes, to the extent of their gender. People are persons, beyond their gender. Men have a naturally infinite capacity to comprehend the parts, to the extent of their gender. People are persons, beyond their gender.

Our infinite capacity and purpose is beyond gender — both wholistic and partial, and our infinite capacity and purpose for both individuals and all of us is an image of God. God is beyond and within the wholes and the parts.

Christ is the balance of whole and part, and portrays the remarkable potential of the balance of whole and part.

To condemn anything that exists as being too wholistic or too partial, by denying forgiveness, is not toward the infinite purpose or Person. Christ and God do not condemn. Evil exists, and is the expression of either wholism or partialism **at the expense of the other**. The way to deal with Evil is to forgive.

Many people feel that the infinite purpose is to analyze, to reduce everything to its parts. Many people feel that the infinite purpose is to compound everything into wholes. Both are necessary but neither is the infinite purpose. The Infinite Purpose is a balance of wholistic and partial awareness, and has unimaginable potential, that is lacking in popular society, yet it is the basis of all success, and has always been the basis of all successes.

Both within religion, whether spirituality, Buddhism, Hinduism, Judaism, Islam or Christianity; and outside of religion; many condemn the other aspect and will give their lives for their own aspect. This limits our awareness. The secular world has found success in the balance of whole and part that is all too frequently condemned by members of religions. Some of the truth of the infinite purpose is carried by each religion, yet another religion will condemn one religion as easily as the secular world will condemn a religion.

If there is any positive effect of this project, **HESUS JOY CHRIST**, I hope it will be to **both commend** the balance of whole and part *in the secular world*; **and** to **discern**, in **religion**, the **difference between** the affinities of wholism and partialism, **and** the infinite purpose or infinite person, commonly known as God, or "I am who I am", which is both and beyond, both wholism and partialism, being present in the **balance** of wholism and partialism, female and male, left and right.

In **HESUS JOY CHRIST / Matthew's Five's Nine** the personification of the balance of whole and part will speak plainly as Jesus spoke in the Sermon on the Mount portrayed in the Gospel of Matthew, Chapter Five.

Your patient consideration is greatly appreciated. Your appreciation will not go unnoticed, as there is little apparent appreciation for this concept. Just "google" "wholistic", "reductionism" or "agency" and see if you can find any promotion of balancing the two. Yet the balance of whole and part is an ever present, endless and eternal source of JOY !

Sunday, October 20th, and Saturday, October 26th, 2013

I'll find you in JOY !   I'll find JOY in you !

. . . now that you know how it turns out, you can check out how it all started, and may I suggest the first three sentences of the Preface on page 19 !

HESUS JOY CHRIST theme lyrics

HESUS JOY CHRIST!
What are you doing?
Can you not hear that?
That's the Lord wooing!
He has come!
He has come!

HESUS JOY CHRIST!
Hallelujah, praise the Lord,
The Word is tabled
And the Spirit's poured!
Hear Him come!
Hear Him come!

HESUS JOY CHRIST!
John baptized to repent—
Submersed to consider
The life you've spent.
Here He came!
Here He came!

HESUS JOY CHRIST!
We died with you
To all the evil
To ever oppose you.
Here we go!
Here we go!

HESUS JOY CHRIST!
In faith we go —
To be cheeky with evil,
Death's freedom we know!
Here we come!
Here we come!

HESUS JOY CHRIST!
Arise you dead!
God's love is given!
In grace we're wed.
Here He is!
Here He is!

HESUS JOY CHRIST!
Alive in You!
We praise one and other—
'Til we see You!
Here we are!
Here we are!

JESUS LORD CHRIST!
We praise and adore!
Our Father and Spirit
Forever more!
Here we are!
Here we are!

JESUS LORD CHRIST!
You've been so patient!
Let all praise raise
The love that's latent
Here we are!
Here we are!

HESUS JOY CHRIST theme August 20th, 2009, 11:30pm – 12:07 am

Bibliography

Here is a list of the literature works that have influenced the understanding presented in **HESUS JOY CHRIST**. This Bibliography includes fiction as well as non-fiction.
In this list each entry is accompanied by a brief comment as to how the book relates to this work, as well as further information that may assist the reader who may wish to order their own copy.

The majority of these listed are books I have read. Those listings marked with **Recommended Reading** are recommended reading, mainly because I have not yet completed reading them.

Nowadays, the internet is the best way to follow up on these leads.

ASIN: Amazon.com's identification number

Effort has been made to find the original publication that I read. This cannot be done for every publication in this bibliography, so I have done my best to cite the closest available publication.

ISBN numbers have been sourced from www.amazon.com and verified at www.isbnsearch.org .

Major Works

Holy Bible
Chinese/English *New International Version*

ISBN-13: 9781563208010
ISBN-10: 1563208016
Author: International Bible Society
Binding: Hardcover
Publisher: International Bible Society
Published: December 2005

Having been raised in the church, from Protestant to Catholic, I have known almost all the major Bible stories my entire life.

Man and Woman He Created Them: A Theology Of The Body

ISBN-13: 9780819874214
ISBN-10: 0819874213
Author: John Paul II
Binding: Paperback
Publisher: Pauline Books & Media
Published: October 2006
List Price: $29.95

I am currently reading this, and all indications point to this work being a major influence in my life for some time to come. If I am correct my animation and discussion may serve to flesh out this profound proclamation of the late Pope John Paul II.

This material is commonly referred to as __Theology of the Body__.

Childhood Reading 1974 – 1982

The Boy's King Arthur: *Sir Thomas Malory's History of King Arthur and His Knights of the Round Table*

ISBN-13: 9780684191119
ISBN-10: 0684191113
Author: Thomas Malory
Binding: Hardcover
Publisher: Atheneum
Published: September 1989
List Price: $28.00

This encouraged virtue above all, with the promise of adventure, and the old English writing made both the King James Bible and Shakespeare easy to comprehend in later life.

Two Little Savages *(Dover Children's Classics)*

ISBN-13: 9780486209852
ISBN-10: 0486209857
Author: Ernest Thompson Seton
Binding: Paperback
Publisher: Dover Publications
Published: November 2011
List Price: $12.95

Encouraging me to read for the sole sake of reading, my parents gave me this book about two boys pretending to be Indians, playing in the woods.

Early Reading 1983 - 1986

The Search
ISBN-13: 9780425081976
ISBN-10: 0425081974
Author: Tom Brown
Binding: Mass Market Paperback
Publisher: Berkley Trade
Published: January 1985
List Price: $6.95

This is a contemporary book of an adult playing Indian in the woods, with real North American Natives, and practicing "survival" skills and tracking skills.

The Prophet
ISBN-13: 9781851689453
ISBN-10: 1851689451
Author: Kahlil Gibran
Edition: Annotated
Binding: Paperback
Publisher: Oneworld Publications
Published: January 2013
List Price: $12.95

The profound poetry of Islam and Christianity by a resident of the Middle East.

Western Theology

ISBN-13: 9780915321001
ISBN-10: 0915321009
Author: Wes Seelinger
Binding: Paperback
Publisher: Spring Arbor Distributors
Published: August 1985
List Price: $6.95

ISBN-13: 9780913618066
ISBN-10: 0913618063
Author: Wes Seeliger
Edition: First Edition
Binding: Hardcover
Publisher: Forum House
Published: December 1973

This was given to my family in 1982 by an Episcopalian Priest, and became the basis for my Youth Sunday Sermon in 1982. It basically makes the case that partial, agency, is better than wholistic communion, comparing two views of the church — a Settler Town, wholistic; and a Wagon Train, agentic or partial.

The Men of the Last Frontier *(Voyageur Classics)*

ISBN-13: 9781554888047
ISBN-10: 1554888042
Author: Grey Owl
Edition: Reprint
Binding: Paperback
Publisher: Dundurn
Published: February 2011
List Price: $26.99

As I lost interest in society in my mid teen years I turned my attention toward spending my life beyond society and educated myself in preparation for doing so.

Never Cry Wolf : Amazing True Story of Life Among Arctic Wolves

ISBN-13: 9780316881791
ISBN-10: 0316881791
Author: Farley Mowat
Edition: Reprint
Binding: Paperback
Publisher: Back Bay Books
Published: September 2001
List Price: $12.99

I read this book almost entirely in one sitting, only interrupted by a high school teacher's attention or a meal. This was the first fiction work that I ever appreciated at all, except it wasn't really fiction!

Emanuel Swedenborg

I greatly appreciated the scope of this mystical author's writing, but I was otherwise unimpressed with his conclusions. At university we discussed Emanuel Swedenborg's overwhelming influence on Wilhelm Wundt, a founder of psychology.

Religion and Life

I could not find a citation for this book, but it is very similar to the other two books cited here.

Life in Animals and Plants

ISBN-13: 9780854480821
ISBN-10: 085448082X
Author: Emanuel Swedenborg
Edition: 1ST
Binding: Paperback
Publisher: The Swedenborg Society
Published: December 1981

God, Providence, Creation

ISBN-13: 9780854480869
ISBN-10: 0854480862
Author: E. Swedenborg
Edition: New Ed
Binding: Paperback
Publisher: The Swedenborg Society
Published: December 1976

Pre-University Reading 1987 – 1988

Kipling: Poems *(Everyman's Library Pocket Poets)*

ISBN-13: 9780307267115
ISBN-10: 0307267113
Author: Rudyard Kipling
Binding: Hardcover
Publisher: Everyman's Library
Published: October 2007
List Price: $13.50

The poem If better be in this collection !!

This poem really puts life as a whole into perspective.

The Best of Robert Service

ISBN-13: 9780070898073
ISBN-10: 0070898073
Author: Robert Service
Binding: Paperback
Publisher: McGraw-Hill Ryerson
Published: December 2001

*This collection includes the poem, **The Men Who Don't Fit In**, that had a profound affect on my attitude toward committing to something rather than dismissing most everything as inconsistent.*

Confessions (Penguin Classics)

ISBN-13: 9780143105701
ISBN-10: 0143105701
Author: Augustine
Binding: Paperback
Publisher: Penguin Classics
Published: December 2008
List Price: $16.00

A sinner's sincere approach to God, and consequently sainthood, which merely means the church is officially of the opinion that this person, the saint, has definitely made it into heaven, so I suppose one could use him as a reference.

Escape from Freedom

ISBN-13: 9780805031492
ISBN-10: 0805031499
Author: Erich Fromm
Edition: Owl Book ed
Binding: Paperback
Publisher: Holt Paperbacks
Published: September 1994
List Price: $17.00

This book identifies that everyone commits to some form of enslavement in order to mitigate the vastness of freedom.

Obedience to Authority: An Experimental View
(Perennial Classics)

ISBN-13: 9780061765216
ISBN-10: 006176521X
Author: Stanley Milgram
Edition: Reprint
Binding: Paperback
Publisher: Harper Perennial Modern Classics
Published: June 2009
List Price: $14.99

This documents an experiment where subjects freely killed others in obedience to authority.

The Last Days of Socrates *(Penguin Classics)*

ISBN-13: 9780140455496
ISBN-10: 0140455493
Author: Plato
Binding: Paperback
Publisher: Penguin Classics
Published: January 2011
List Price: $14.00

This illustrates how critical thought is irrelevant to conclusions but integral to comprehension. Socrates practiced a method of questioning, Plato wrote examples of this method, and Aristotle compiled these mere examples into a closed system, that ran its course and quickly became irrelevant and an abuse of Socrates' efforts. Some assert Socrates was a precursor of Christ.

The Duality of Human Existence: Isolation and Communion in Western Man

ISBN-13: 9780807029695
ISBN-10: 0807029696
Author: David Bakan
Edition: First Edition
Binding: Paperback
Publisher: Beacon Press
Published: December 1966

This book makes the case that communion is better than agency. It was the first encounter I had with the terms communion and agency, which represent wholistic, female, and partial, male, respectively.

The Denial of Death

ISBN-13: 9780684832401
ISBN-10: 0684832402
Author: Ernest Becker
Edition: 1
Binding: Paperback
Publisher: Free Press
Published: May 1997
List Price: $15.99

This book makes the case that insanity is the inability to cope with the inevitable death.

A Brief History of Time: From the Big Bang to Black Holes

ISBN-13: 9780553053401
ISBN-10: 055305340X
Author: Stephen W. Hawking
Binding: Hardcover
Publisher: Bantam
Published: March 1988
List Price: $27.95

This book is the product of a very active imagination applied to concrete investigations. It presents ideas that are consistent with <u>The Geometry of Meaning</u>.

During University Reading 1988 – 1989

The Geometry of Meaning

ISBN-13: 9780440049913
ISBN-10: 0440049911
Author: Arthur M Young
Edition: y First printing
Binding: Hardcover
Publisher: Delacorte Press/S. Lawrence
Published: December 1976

*This book was the basis for an essay in a Social Science course on Evolution that I took in University. It illuminates the management of non-linear thought, by creating a set of frameworks including a two, a three, a four, and a twelve dimensional framework for dealing with multiple aspects at once. As well as **A Brief History of Time**, this book greatly influenced my animated image of the **Spirit of One**.*

Jonathan Livingston Seagull

ISBN-13: 9780743278904
ISBN-10: 0743278909
Author: Richard Bach
Edition: 1
Binding: Paperback
Publisher: Scribner
Published: February 2006
List Price: $12.99

I first encountered this work through the soundtrack of the movie when I was less than ten years old. I accidentally stole this small paperback from the library, and read it straight through. The book is far better than the movie, which is a live action film of a seagull thinking about god and perfection, although the soundtrack is worthwhile on its own.

The Reflexive Universe:
Evolution of Consciousness

ISBN-13: 9781892160119
ISBN-10: 1892160110
Author: Arthur M. Young
Edition: Revised
Binding: Paperback
Publisher: Anodos Foundation
Published: September 1999
List Price: $18.95

- Recommended Reading -

http://www.nfb.ca/film/cree_hunters
Cree Hunters of Mistassini

Directed by	Boyce Richardson
	Tony Ianzelo
Produced by	Colin Low
Written by	Boyce Richardson
Narrated by	Boyce Richardson
Cinematography	Tony Ianzelo
Editing by	Ginny Stikeman
Studio	National Film Board of Canada
Release date(s)	1974
Running time	57 min 53 s
Country	Canada
Language	English
Budget	$95,602[1]

This tells the story of life on the land, which is abhorrent to some but loved by others. Would you like fresh meat in a clean new house, or would you prefer processed feed in an dusted dirty old house?

Post University Reading 1989 – 1998

The World According to Garp

The Novel

ISBN-13: 9780345366764
ISBN-10: 034536676X
Author: John Irving
Edition: 0020-Anniversary
Binding: Mass Market Paperback
Publisher: Ballantine Books
Published: November 1990
List Price: $7.99

Reality is more bizarre than most people can imagine.

The Film

Actors: Robin Williams, Mary Beth Hurt, Glenn Close, John Lithgow, Hume Cronyn
Directors: George Roy Hill
Format: Anamorphic, Closed-captioned, Color, Dolby, HiFi Sound, Subtitled, Widescreen, NTSC
Language: English (Unknown), French (Unknown)

Subtitles: English, Spanish, French, Portuguese
Region: Region 1 (U.S. and Canada only.)
Aspect Ratio: 1.85:1
Number of discs: 1
Rated: R (Restricted)
Studio: Warner Home Video
DVD Release Date: April 3, 2001
Run Time: 136 minutes **Average**
Customer Review: 3.9 out of 5 stars
ASIN: B000056WRE

The Power of Myth

The Book of the Interviews

ISBN-13: 9780385418867
ISBN-10: 0385418868
Author: Joseph Campbell
Binding: Paperback
Publisher: Anchor
Published: June 1991
List Price: $16.00

This PBS television series where Bill Moyers interviews Joseph Campbell is very intriguing and led me to purchase the book of the interview series. Joseph Campbell has found common ground amongst the multitude of myths, religions and faiths in the world in not only our time but ancient times as well. There is truth out there for those who pursue their bliss.

The Film of the Interviews

Actors: Joseph Campbell, George Lucas, Bill Moyers
Producers: Alvin H. Perlmutter, Joan Konner
Format: Color, NTSC
Language: English
Region: Region 1 (U.S. and Canada only.)
Aspect Ratio: 1.33:1
Number of discs: 2
Rated: NR (Not Rated)
Studio: Athena
DVD Release Date: September 21, 2010
Run Time: 360 minutes
Average Customer Review: 4.3 out of 5 stars
ASIN: B003SXHZEA

My Side of the Mountain

The Book
(Puffin Modern Classics)

ISBN-13: 9780142401118
ISBN-10: 0142401110
Author: Jean Craighead George
Binding: Paperback
Publisher: Puffin Books
Published: April 2004
List Price: $6.99

I could have easily become the protagonist who escapes the city to live in the woods.

The Movie

Actors: Teddy Eccles, Theodore Bikel
Directors: James B. Clark
Format: Widescreen, Color, NTSC
Language: English
Region: Region 1 (U.S. and Canada only.)

Aspect Ratio: 1.85:1
Number of discs: 1
Rated: G (General Audience)
Studio: Paramount
Run Time: 100 minutes
Average Customer Review: 3.6 out of 5 stars
ASIN: B004IE0YJQ

The Man Who Planted Trees

The Book

ISBN-13: 9781933392813
ISBN-10: 1933392819
Author: Jean Giono
Edition: 20th Anniversary Edition
Binding: Paperback
Publisher: Chelsea Green Publishing
Published: October 2007
List Price: $10.00

Recommended Reading -

The Book of the Film

ISBN-13: 9780773757332
ISBN-10: 0773757333
Author: J Giono
Edition: First Edition
Binding: Paperback
Publisher: Fitzhenry and Whiteside
Published: December 1995
List Price: $9.95

Recommended Reading -

The Video of the Film

Directors: Frederic Back
Number of tapes: 1
Studio: SRC Video
Run Time: 30 minutes
Average Customer Review: 4.5 out of 5 stars
ASIN: B006G1MYAQ

This story impressed upon me what one person may accomplish through sustained solitary effort, regardless of others' efforts for or against. The animation confirmed the possibilities of which animation is capable.

I would refresh myself while studying animation by watching this film in the school library, but originally I watched the 16mm film in the Metro Toronto Reference Library, as I would go there to browse.

The DVD of the Film

Directors: Frederic Back
Format: Animated, Closed-captioned, Color, Digital Sound, NTSC
Language: English
Region: Region 1 (U.S. and Canada only.)
Number of discs: 1
Rated: Unrated
Studio: CBC Radio-Canada
DVD Release Date: November 1, 2004
Run Time: 60 minutes
Average Customer Review: 4.5 out of 5 stars
ASIN: B0006HDBU8

_____

Great Mambo Chicken And The Transhuman Condition: Science Slightly Over The Edge

ISBN-13: 9780201567519
ISBN-10: 0201567512
Author: Ed Regis
Binding: Paperback
Publisher: Basic Books
Published: September 1991
List Price: $17.50

This illustrates how unbridled investigation and construction can lead anywhere, including nowhere.

The Emperor's New Mind: Concerning Computers, Minds, and the Laws of Physics (Popular Science)

ISBN-13: 9780192861986
ISBN-10: 0192861980
Authors: Roger Penrose; Martin Gardner
Edition: 1St Edition
Binding: Paperback
Publisher: Oxford University Press, USA
Published: December 2002
List Price: $19.95

More intriguing math and physics.

The Power of One

The Novel

ISBN-13: 9780316158251
ISBN-10: 0316158259
Author: Bryce Courtenay
Edition: First Thus
Binding: Paperback
Publisher: Little Brown & Co.
Published: September 1995
List Price: $25.00

The power of the many when they come together as one. The power of the parts when they come together as a whole.

The Film

Actors: Nomadlozi Kubheka, Agatha Hurle, Nigel Ivy, Tracy Brooks Swope, Brendan Deary
Directors: John G. Avildsen
Format: Closed-captioned, Color, Dolby, Letterboxed, Widescreen, NTSC
Language: English (Dolby Digital 2.0 Surround)
Region: Region 1 (U.S. and Canada only.)
Aspect Ratio: 1.85:1
Number of discs: 1
Rated: PG-13 (Parental Guidance Suggested)
Studio: Warner Home Video
DVD Release Date: June 22, 1999
Run Time: 127 minutes
Average Customer Review: 4.0 out of 5 stars
ASIN: 0790740850

A Prayer for Owen Meany

ISBN-13: 9780062204226
ISBN-10: 006220422X
Author: John Irving
Edition: Reprint
Binding: Mass Market Paperback
Publisher: Harper
Published: April 2012
List Price: $7.99

Not for the merely pious.

The 158-Pound Marriage

ISBN-13: 9780345367433
ISBN-10: 034536743X
Author: John Irving
Edition: Reprint
Binding: Paperback
Publisher: Ballantine Books
Published: December 1990

The staying power of a marriage.

The Outport People

ISBN-13: 9781552636473
ISBN-10: 155263647X
Author: Claire Mowat
Binding: Paperback
Publisher: Key Porter Books
Published: February 2005
List Price: $19.95

Life in the vast communion of an isolated outport community.

The Real Messiah? A Jewish Response to Missionaries

ISBN-13: 9781879016118
ISBN-10: 1879016117
Authors: Aryeh Kaplan; Berel Wein; Pinchas Stolper
Binding: Paperback
Publisher: Mesorah Pubns Ltd
Published: December 1976
List Price: $8.99

The case is made — now what?

The Hitchhiker's Guide to the Galaxy

Actors: Bill Bailey, Anna Chancellor, Warwick Davis, Mos Def, Zooey Deschanel
Directors: Garth Jennings
Format: Widescreen, NTSC, DTS Surround Sound
Language: English (Dolby Digital 5.1), English (DTS 5.1), French (Unknown), Spanish (Unknown)
Subtitles: Spanish, French
Region: Region 1 (U.S. and Canada only.)
Aspect Ratio: 2.35:1
Number of discs: 1
Rated: PG (Parental Guidance Suggested)
Studio: Buena Vista Home Entertainment / Touchstone
DVD Release Date: September 13, 2005
Run Time: 109 minutes
Average Customer Review: 3.5 out of 5 stars
ASIN: B000A283AW

In such chaos, does the balance of whole and part prevail ?

Recent Reading 1999 – 2013

The Snow Walker

Actors: Barry Pepper, Annabella Piugattuk, James Cromwell, Kiersten Warren, Jon Gries
Directors: Charles Martin Smith
Writers: Charles Martin Smith, Farley Mowat
Producers: Barry Pepper, Christina Toy, Ellen Dinerman Little, John Houston, Michael Ohoven
Format: Closed-captioned, Color, Dolby, Subtitled, NTSC
Language: English (Dolby Digital 5.1)
Subtitles: Spanish
Region: Region 1 (U.S. and Canada only.)
Aspect Ratio: 1.78:1
Number of discs: 1
Rated: PG (Parental Guidance Suggested)
Studio: First Look Pictures
DVD Release Date: May 31, 2005
Run Time: 90 minutes
Average Customer Review: 4.6 out of 5 stars
ASIN: B0007UDC80

Male, agency, finds the value of female, communion, and is saved by the union of the two.

What Dreams May Come

Actors: Robin Williams, Cuba Gooding Jr., Annabella Sciorra, Max von Sydow, Jessica Brooks Grant
Directors: Vincent Ward
Writers: Ron Bass
Producers: Stephen Simon, Barnet Bain
Format: Closed-captioned, Color, Dolby, NTSC, Special Edition, Widescreen
Language: English (Dolby Digital 2.0 Stereo), English (Dolby Digital 5.1)
Subtitles: Spanish, French
Region: Region 1 (U.S. and Canada only.)
Aspect Ratio: 2.35:1
Number of discs: 1
Rated: PG-13 (Parental Guidance Suggested)
Studio: Polygram Filmed Entertainment
DVD Release Date: March 4, 2003
Run Time: 114 minutes
Average Customer Review: 4.1 out of 5 stars
ASIN: B00007GZR5

This proposes a supernatural power to intensely sincere marriage in a supernatural environment.

Praying Our Experiences

ISBN-13: 9780884896494
ISBN-10: 0884896498
Author: Joseph F. Schmidt
Edition: 20th
Binding: Paperback
Publisher: Saint Mary's Press
Published: March 2000
List Price: $5.95

This acknowledges the severe amount of thought I've put into considering my experiences.

Acedia & Me:
A Marriage, Monks, and a Writer's Life

ISBN-13: 9781594489969
ISBN-10: 1594489963
Author: Kathleen Norris
Edition: First Edition
Binding: Hardcover
Publisher: Riverhead Hardcover
Published: September 2008
List Price: $25.95

This book takes the reader on a journey through the mind of a life plagued by melancholy. It is an example of non-analytical consideration.

The Shack

ISBN-13: 9781609414115
ISBN-10: 160941411X
Author: Wm. Paul Young
Edition: Reissue
Binding: Mass Market Paperback
Publisher: Windblown Media
Published: June 2011
List Price: $8.00

This book is the fledgling venture of a protestant into wholistic thought.

The Pagan Christ: Is Blind Faith Killing Christianity?

ISBN-13: 9780802777416
ISBN-10: 0802777414
Author: Tom Harpur
Binding: Paperback
Publisher: Walker & Company
Published: May 2006
List Price: $14.95

Recommended Reading -
Academia at play. Is this for real, or just an academic exercise?

Catholicism

Actors: Fr. Robert Barron
Directors: Matt Leonard
Format: Box set, Color, Dolby, NTSC, Surround Sound, Widescreen
Language: English, Spanish
Subtitles: English, Spanish
Region: All Regions
Aspect Ratio: 1.33:1
Number of discs: 5
Rated: NR (Not Rated)
Studio: Word on Fire
DVD Release Date: August 25, 2011
Run Time: 500 minutes
Average Customer Review: 4.8 out of 5 stars
ASIN: B005J6U77Q

The full power of communion in unity with agency is apparent in the apostolic tradition of the Roman Catholic Church.

http://www.catholicismseries.com/
http://www.wordonfire.org/

Eusebius: The Church History

ISBN-13: 9780825433078
ISBN-10: 082543307X
Author: Eusebius
Binding: Paperback
Publisher: Kregel Academic & Professional
Published: May 2007
List Price: $15.99

The full power of the Gospel in action redeeming, and amongst, an ignorant, ancient society.

The Collected Works of St. John of the Cross

ISBN-13: 9780935216141
ISBN-10: 0935216146
Author: Saint John of the Cross
Edition: Revised
Binding: Paperback
Publisher: ICS Publications
Published: January 1991
List Price: $22.95

Recommended Reading -
From what I've read and heard, mostly from the Catholicism course, anything by this author, St. John of the Cross, is worth reading. This work is referred to heavily in __Theology of the Body__ .

Story of a Soul: The Autobiography of St. Therese of Lisieux, Third Edition

ISBN-13: 9780935216585
ISBN-10: 0935216588
Author: Therese de Lisieux
Edition: 3rd
Binding: Paperback
Publisher: I C S Publications
Published: January 1996
List Price: $13.95

Recommended Reading -
From what I've read and heard, mostly from the Catholicism course, anything by this author, St. Therese of Lisieux, is worth reading. This work is referred to heavily in __Theology of the Body__ .

Theology of the Body for Beginners

ISBN-13: 9781934217856
ISBN-10: 1934217859
Author: Christopher West
Edition: Revised
Binding: Paperback
Publisher: Ascension Press
Published: September 2009
List Price: $12.99

This is just one publication that Christopher West wrote that tries to make **Theology of the Body** *accessible to a lay audience. The problem is that although simple, the priority of marriage is more or less unprovable, and demands the participants truly follow the path of Christ, with all the challenges and tragedies as well as the immense joy and achievements. Simplification may not make the priority of marriage any clearer, and may in fact, just confuse the audience. The priority of marriage is truly a gift of the Holy Spirit. This work is based on* **Theology of the Body** *.*

Hermeneutics: Principles and Processes of Biblical Interpretation

ISBN-13: 9780801020674
ISBN-10: 0801020670
Author: Henry A. Virkler
Edition: First Edition
Binding: Paperback
Publisher: Baker Academic
Published: February 1996
List Price: $19.99

Reductionism in the form of reducing scripture by using a consistent system, so that it may only mean certain things in certain circumstances unnecessarily limits the divine in the words. Integration of scripture with lived experience has been far more effective for me, rather than consulting any "authority" as to how I should understand scripture. I do however greatly appreciate sources of additional information and comprehensions of scripture, even when I do not agree or appreciate such information and comprehensions, as they force me to integrate my comprehension further. The greatest wealth of additional information and comprehension I have found to date, is in the Roman Catholic Church.

Links

Here are sites where all the animation and other artwork may be viewed.

It is my sincere hope that few people will come across my work by any way other than my animation.

If this publication is your first encounter with my work, I apologize and plead that you view my animation and other work on the following sites.

www.sites.google.com/site/hesusjoychrist

https://www.sites.google.com/site/hesusjoychrist/home/hesus-joy-christ

www.sites.google.com/site/vid932008

http://ca.linkedin.com/in/vid932008

www.vid93.blogspot.ca

www.wawacolour.blogspot.ca

http://www.behance.net/vid932008

About the Author

Richard DAVID FOSTER was born, in the late 1960's, and raised in The Borough of Etobicoke, in Metropolitan Toronto, Ontario, Canada.

Educated in the public school system, he excelled without recognition, drawing comics in grade six, to be tested and admitted to the advancement program. By grade nine, thoroughly disillusioned with academics, he made an effort in grade ten in College Station, Texas, but lost faith in grade eleven in Toronto. He excelled in a college level structural drafting program at Texas A&M University Extension Service at the end of grade ten, but was unable to find employment in drafting until 1988.

By grade twelve he was determined to find an alternative to the academic stream and pursued work as an electrician's helper. But to honour his parents wishes, he returned to the academic stream but then refused to pursue academics beyond high school. After a brief period of employment with the Hudson's Bay Company — Northern Stores, in Povungnituk, Quebec, in the arctic, he returned to Toronto. Returning to work, he took extended periods to pursue a life in the bush, paddling his kayak along Lake Ontario and the Trent-Severn waterway. After a trip to Moosonee, Ontario, he decided not to begin an Electrician's Apprenticeship, and began to pursue marriage. This led him to attend York University, but he was so thoroughly disillusioned he abandoned academics once again.

After a brief visit to Newfoundland, he returned to Toronto and began employment in Autocad drafting, which again ended in disillusion. Pursuing marriage led him again into school for art, where he excelled, but left the animation program that was intended to get grads hired through a government subsidy.

Working in a kitchen found David getting married, and this became a basis for Landscaping drafting work, which became landscaping construction labour and then landscaping maintenance labour. Completing **HYPOTHERMIA / My Kayak Prayer** saw the end of his marriage and the beginning of his writing and animation.

INDEX

Be sure to browse this Index as there is an interesting vast range of agents touched upon in the whole of this publication!

A Brief History of Time 268, 365
Abraham 41, 76, 78, 89, 103p., 106p., 109, 111, 141p., 175, 229, 251
Abram 41, 104, 111
abundance 30, 92, 117, 132, 140, 145, 147, 277, 282, 284, 287, 344
academia 160, 221, 232, 270, 347
acedia . . . . 28, 132p.
Acedia 132
acknowledged 24, 88, 90, 101, 149, 165, 173, 227, 241, 255, 259pp., 265, 275, 286p., 292, 313, 342
agency 171, 187, 215, 339, 359, 364, 375, 377
Agency 100, 164, 226, 274
analysis 28, 35, 50, 155
angel 79p., 84, 86, 148, 156, 196p., 210p., 310
angels . . . . 62, 67, 92p., 239, 279, 294, 310p.
Anglican 31, 52, 128, 312
animation . . . . 19pp., 24p., 27, 29pp., 35p., 42, 50, 59p., 68, 70pp., 77p., 80, 100, 102, 105, 109, 113, 127pp., 140p., 147, 150, 155pp., 164, 167, 170, 173, 178pp., 185, 187p., 190p., 197pp., 201, 203, 206, 208pp., 212pp., 221, 226, 228, 231, 235, 237p., 241, 245, 247, 249, 253pp., 258, 260, 265pp., 270, 274, 277p., 282, 292, 294p., 297pp., 302, 304, 306, 309p., 313, 325, 327pp., 331, 347, 357, 383p.
Animation 19, 23, 130, 254
ANIMATION 73, 97
anthropomorphizing 325
Aristotle 63p., 287, 363
Baker, Jim 232
balance of whole and part 43, 100, 110, 133, 136, 143, 151, 159, 164, 166, 171, 176, 178, 181p., 185p., 188, 191pp., 201, 203pp., 207, 211pp., 220, 226, 248pp., 253p., 256, 260, 264, 274, 276, 286pp., 294, 304p., 311, 320p., 326p., 332, 334pp., 342, 344

balancing whole and part . . . . 19, 33, 198, 201, 204, 212, 217p., 220, 250, 283p., 286p., 291, 305, 310, 318, 320p., 325, 327, 332, 334pp., 339, 344pp.
Balancing whole and part 329, 344
baptism . . . . 101, 165, 227, 255, 259p., 264, 275p.
Baptism 90, 230, 259p., 286, 331
Baptist Church 31, 128, 312
baptize 26, 31, 56, 89, 151, 229, 255p., 259p., 313, 333, 354
baptized 26, 31, 56, 88, 90, 151, 229p., 241, 255p., 259pp., 265, 313, 333, 354
Bernardo, Paul 244
birth 21p., 29, 54pp., 76, 79p., 102, 104, 109, 112, 142, 144, 150p., 153, 157p., 173p., 179pp., 187, 202, 209, 217, 235, 319pp., 326
Birth 79, 119, 144, 159
bisexual 304
blind faith 252, 310, 337
Body of Christ 302, 323, 330
Buddhist 100, 164, 226, 274
Calculus 320
Catechism of the Catholic Church 28
catholic 29, 240
Catholic 19, 21, 28p., 31, 145, 171p., 215, 233, 286, 299, 301, 305, 317, 322p., 357
Catholicism . . . . 28p., 377p.
Cephas 328
christ 19, 23pp., 30, 33, 36, 58p., 78pp., 83, 100pp., 109p., 112, 115, 133p., 137p., 140, 145p., 149p., 152, 154, 157p., 164p., 171p., 177p., 186, 190, 195, 212, 214p., 217, 220, 226p., 233, 237, 240p., 252, 254, 256, 262, 264, 274p., 284, 286, 288, 301p., 313p., 321p., 324, 326, 336, 339, 383
Christ . . . . 31, 36, 42p., 52, 55, 59p., 62pp., 68, 70, 82, 101p., 109p., 136, 143pp., 147, 149pp., 159, 165p., 170pp., 174pp., 190pp., 198p., 207p., 216p., 219, 227, 231, 233, 238, 246, 254, 256, 258pp., 266, 275, 284p., 302p., 312, 323p., 327, 330, 332, 335, 337, 339, 341p.

CHRIST 20p., 24pp., 39, 42, 45, 50, 70pp.,
75, 81, 87, 91, 99pp., 105, 109, 151, 159p., 163p., 167, 170, 205,
207, 220p., 225p., 228, 231, 235, 241, 245, 253, 260, 268, 270,
273p., 277, 282, 310, 314, 317, 322, 325, 327, 347, 354, 356
christian 30, 100, 110, 133, 138, 145, 157, 164,
190, 195, 226, 254, 274, 284, 313p., 321, 324, 326, 339
Christian 31, 36, 145, 151, 261
christianity 19, 100pp., 150, 152, 154, 164p., 195,
215, 217, 226p., 237, 240p., 252, 254, 264, 274p., 286, 288,
324, 336, 339, 344
Christianity 52, 153p., 190, 192, 207, 246, 254,
266, 335, 337
christly 233
Christopher West 152
church 30p., 42p., 50, 52, 63, 82, 86, 88, 90,
110, 116, 128, 136, 154, 170pp., 177, 181, 184, 198, 209, 211pp.,
220, 233, 239pp., 247p., 252, 254p., 259p., 263, 265p., 268,
286, 301pp., 305, 314, 322pp., 357
Church 19, 21, 28p., 31, 128, 154, 171p., 210,
232, 252, 254p., 258, 305, 312, 322, 324, 330
CHURCH 27
Church of Latter Day Saints 232
closed system 220p., 243, 263p., 326, 363
communion 82p., 145, 170pp., 181, 185, 187, 191,
199, 204, 215, 288, 302, 310, 332, 334, 339
Communion 100, 164, 170p., 226, 274
communion and agency 171, 187, 215, 339, 364
conceive 79, 153, 170, 186
confess 256
Confess 243
confessing . . . . 243p.
confession 243
Confession 241
consummate 22, 80, 158
crazy 288, 309
Crazy 147
critical thought 30
Critical thought 30, 220, 249
Critical Thought 30
cross dresser 304

Dark Night of the Soul 28
David 25, 30p., 50, 56p., 63, 76pp., 82, 84, 88, 92, 99, 103, 109p., 112, 114p., 123, 141p., 146, 148, 156, 163, 167, 170, 178pp., 203p., 225, 231, 266, 273, 277, 282, 320, 384
DAVID 384
David Foster 76, 82, 88, 92, 99, 109p., 163, 167, 170, 179, 225, 231, 273, 277, 282
death 55p., 60, 63p., 69, 71p., 89, 101, 115, 127, 133, 138, 140, 143p., 149pp., 154, 157, 165, 173p., 179, 191, 193pp., 199, 201p., 206, 209pp., 213, 217p., 227, 232, 234pp., 248, 252p., 255pp., 261, 275, 285p., 295, 301, 307, 309p., 312p., 315p., 320p., 323p., 327, 332
Decision Making and the Will of God 312
desert . . . . 132p., 221, 231p., 236, 240, 265, 276p., 282pp.
devil 32, 92p., 276, 279, 282, 292, 294, 296, 302pp., 306, 310, 312
deviles 32
DiCaprio, Leonardo 292
die 55, 64, 70, 122, 127, 134, 154, 181, 190, 193, 195, 199, 236, 252p., 256p., 259, 262, 265, 267, 315, 324, 327
disciple 35, 50, 155, 290
doored 72
Drop Your Shorts 20, 105, 157, 167, 228, 277
ego 35p., 155, 289
Ego 35, 155
Einstein 268
Einstein, Albert 249
emmanuel 154
Emmanuel 22, 79p., 153p., 158, 261
Episcopalian 31
Etobicoke Electric 333
Eucharist 152, 170p., 173, 332
Eusebius 210, 324
Eusebius' Church History 324
Evangelism As A Lifestyle 312
evil 26, 101, 124, 127, 165, 196, 198p., 201, 215, 227, 244p., 256, 275, 306p., 311, 354
Evil 261, 310

fagot 161, 222, 271, 348
female 19, 22, 31, 33, 100pp., 109p., 113p., 130, 135p., 147, 149pp., 164pp., 171, 174p., 187p., 192p., 195, 197p., 211pp., 220, 226p., 267pp., 274pp., 283, 285, 289, 293, 295, 297pp., 302pp., 306p., 309, 320, 324, 332, 334, 339, 341, 344, 364, 375
Female 100, 164, 226, 274
finite 143, 191, 193, 196, 234, 240, 242, 245pp., 263p., 266, 286, 288, 300, 302pp., 315
fishermen . . . . .95, 280, 328p.
forgive 100p., 140, 145, 150, 152, 157, 164p., 185, 198p., 201, 210p., 213, 215, 220, 226p., 236p., 239, 241, 243pp., 253, 256pp., 261pp., 274p., 284p., 287, 290, 295p., 301, 306p., 311, 339
Forgive 100, 164, 226, 258, 261, 274
forgiveness . . . . .100p., 140, 145, 150, 152, 157, 164p., 198p., 201, 210p., 213, 215, 220, 226p., 239, 241, 243p., 253, 256, 258p., 261pp., 274p., 284p., 287, 290, 295p., 306p., 339, 342p.
Forgiveness 33, 100, 164, 226, 258, 261, 274
Foster, David 3p., 25, 30p., 50, 56p., 63, 76, 82, 88, 92, 99, 109p., 163, 167, 170, 179, 225, 231, 273, 277, 282
free DVD 245
Galilee 86, 90, 94pp., 169, 216, 230, 259p., 280p., 312p., 315p., 319, 321p., 328, 338, 343
gay 43, 304
genealogy 76, 102p., 106, 109, 115, 137, 142, 159
Genealogy 76, 103p., 106, 109, 142
Gentiles 321
god 93, 146, 156, 178, 217, 299p., 335, 365
God 6, 22, 25p., 28pp., 32p., 35p., 52pp., 58, 60pp., 64, 79p., 89p., 92p., 101, 108, 110p., 115, 127, 134, 140, 142p., 146, 150pp., 158p., 165, 170, 172, 174p., 178p., 181p., 184pp., 189, 192, 195pp., 209pp., 215, 217pp., 227, 229p., 232pp., 236, 238pp., 244pp., 251pp., 255pp., 261p., 264pp., 268, 275, 279, 285pp., 290pp., 308p., 311pp., 315, 319pp., 323pp., 327, 329pp., 335pp., 343, 354
Golden mean . . . . .49, 62p.
Golden Mean 64, 287
Greek 114, 133, 178p., 182, 190, 201, 207, 212, 220, 238, 251, 254, 264, 266, 303, 328, 330

grifter 95, 328
grifting . . . . 328p.
Hawking, Stephen 268
heaven . . . . 29, 33, 62, 65pp., 72, 88, 90, 94, 110, 151pp., 181, 189, 195, 205, 209pp., 217p., 229p., 233pp., 238, 241p., 261, 265, 267, 280, 282, 295, 304, 309, 311, 313, 325p.
Heaven 33, 61, 175, 217, 261, 266, 303, 338
Hebrew 114, 133, 179, 190, 201, 207, 212, 220, 238, 251, 254, 264, 266, 303
Hermeneutics 379
Herod 82pp., 86, 168pp., 173pp., 178, 183pp., 193, 196, 199p., 202p., 206, 210pp., 216, 312
heterosexual 239, 243p., 305, 322
holistic 274, 332
Holistic 100, 164, 226, 274
holy spirit . . . . 89, 112, 255p.
Holy Spirit 29, 79, 89, 102, 107, 144, 148p., 152, 172, 175, 178, 181p., 192, 194p., 197, 212, 219, 229, 255p., 260, 289, 299, 313p., 330
homosexual 117, 244, 305, 322
husband . . . 78p., 114p., 135pp., 144, 146, 176, 239, 291, 302, 324
I am 6, 20p., 32, 43, 51pp., 59, 76, 89p., 92, 100, 102, 109pp., 116p., 123, 133, 140, 147, 153, 157, 164, 180, 191, 201, 215, 226, 229p., 232p., 237, 243, 251, 255, 261, 265pp., 274, 294p., 302p., 306, 336, 357
I AM 42
identifying what the members of the congregation are brandishing 245
idol 143, 217p., 299, 311
Immanuel . . . . 79, 153p., 158p.
infinite . . . . 28p., 33, 101, 110, 117, 127, 133, 135, 142p., 146pp., 153p., 165, 174, 184pp., 188, 190, 193p., 196p., 199, 203p., 211, 213, 215pp., 220, 227, 234p., 237, 239pp., 252, 254, 256, 258pp., 263p., 266, 275, 283p., 286pp., 298pp., 302pp., 311, 313, 315, 320, 325, 330p., 336p.
Infinite 234, 311
infinite person . . . . 33, 142, 215, 264, 313, 320, 325, 330p., 336p.
Infinite Person 311
infinite purpose 110, 127, 142, 153, 186, 211, 234, 240, 252, 264, 288, 309

infinity . . . . .28p., 33, 101, 110, 117, 127, 133, 135, 143, 146pp., 153p., 165, 174, 184pp., 188, 190, 193p., 196p., 199, 203p., 211, 213, 215pp., 220, 227, 231, 234p., 237, 239pp., 252, 254pp., 258pp., 263p., 266, 275, 283p., 286pp., 293, 295, 298pp., 302pp., 313, 315, 320, 324p., 330p., 333, 336p.
Infinity 264, 311
intellectualisation 233
intelligent disobedience 333
Islam 237, 252, 337
Jehovah's Witnesses 19, 31, 128, 150, 232, 266, 319
Jerusalem 6, 82, 88, 96, 133, 168, 170p., 173pp., 212, 229, 236, 239p., 254, 281, 292, 343, 346
Jesus . . . . .21p., 33, 35p., 50pp., 60, 65pp., 71, 76, 78pp., 82, 90, 92, 94pp., 101pp., 106pp., 115, 134, 137p., 140, 142pp., 147, 150pp., 158p., 164p., 168, 170, 172, 174p., 177pp., 184pp., 190, 192p., 195pp., 201pp., 205, 207pp., 212pp., 219p., 227, 230pp., 244, 246pp., 255p., 259pp., 264pp., 275p., 279pp., 288pp., 301, 303pp., 311pp., 319, 321pp., 325pp.
JESUS 26, 354
Jesus Christ Superstar 303
Joan . . . . .88, 90, 94, 231p., 235pp., 240p., 247pp., 253, 255, 258pp., 287, 312p.
John 19, 24pp., 28p., 56, 71, 88, 90, 94p., 101, 128, 136, 145, 152, 165, 192, 194, 215, 227, 229pp., 236pp., 240p., 247pp., 253pp., 257pp., 266, 268, 275p., 280, 286, 297, 299, 312p., 315p., 318, 321, 323, 326, 330, 334pp., 354, 357
Joplin, Scott 328
Jordan 88, 90, 94, 96, 229p., 240p., 259p., 276, 280p., 321, 343, 346
Joseph 35p., 78pp., 84, 86, 102p., 109, 115, 137, 142, 144pp., 155p., 158, 177pp., 185, 196pp., 212, 214, 216, 286
Joshua 114, 150, 324
Joy 53, 55, 82p., 100, 140, 143, 154, 164, 171pp., 175, 177, 183, 185, 187pp., 191p., 195, 215, 226, 232, 238p., 254, 257, 262, 264p., 267, 274
Joy . . . . .65, 145, 204, 209, 211, 234, 258, 262, 266p., 295, 298, 310p., 326, 332, 341p.

JOY 19pp., 24pp., 39, 42, 45, 50, 54, 62, 70pp., 75, 81, 87, 91, 99pp., 105, 109, 151, 159p., 163p., 167, 170, 199, 205, 207, 220p., 225p., 228, 231, 235, 241, 245, 253, 260, 268, 270, 273p., 277, 282, 310, 314, 317, 322, 325, 327, 347, 354
kayak 59, 76, 118p., 154, 201p., 384
Kayak 3p., 19pp., 32, 39, 41p., 105, 384
king 6, 36, 82p., 115, 156, 168, 170, 172pp., 179, 187, 193, 247, 283, 292, 295, 313, 331, 333
King 6, 21, 52, 76, 82, 103, 106, 109, 114, 142, 166, 168, 170, 173pp., 178pp., 190, 199, 292
kingdom of heaven . . . . .88, 94, 154, 189, 205, 218, 229, 233pp., 238, 241, 280, 282, 295, 325p.
Kingdom of Heaven 217, 261, 303, 338
koan 35p., 50, 64, 155, 158
Koan 35
law . . . . .55, 79, 82, 114, 137, 146, 154, 158, 177, 210p., 233p., 239, 241pp., 249, 260, 262, 264p., 304, 322pp., 326p.
Law 79, 101, 134, 153, 165, 227, 233p., 237, 275, 305
lesbian 43, 304
Liaison of Independent Film of Toronto 19
liar 185
lie 147, 185p., 261
LIFT 19
Lord 26, 68, 79p., 82, 84, 86, 88, 93, 107p., 115, 148p., 152p., 156, 169p., 175, 179pp., 196, 200, 205p., 209p., 215, 229, 236, 279, 286, 296, 298p., 301, 308, 314, 324, 354
LORD 26, 150, 296, 298, 301, 354
Lord of Creation, Catholic Book of Worship III, #498 286
lust 244
macropolis . . . . .82, 84, 178, 182, 203p.
Macropolis 179
Magi . . . 82pp., 166, 168pp., 181, 183, 187, 189, 192pp., 203, 205
magic 216, 260, 262, 287p., 291, 294, 297, 303, 311, 337
male 19, 22, 31, 33, 100pp., 109p., 135p., 147, 150p., 164pp., 171, 174p., 188, 192p., 195, 197p., 211pp., 220, 226p., 267pp., 274pp., 283, 285, 288p., 293pp., 297pp., 302pp., 309, 320, 332, 339, 341, 344, 364
Male 100, 164, 226, 274, 299, 375

Man and Woman He Created Them — A Theology of the Body . . . 299, 318
Man and Woman He Created Them : A Theology of the Body 27, 215
marriage 100pp., 108, 110, 113, 124, 127p., 131, 133pp., 138, 144pp., 149pp., 157p., 164pp., 175pp., 188, 190, 193pp., 207, 215pp., 226p., 233, 237pp., 241, 244, 246pp., 252pp., 274pp., 283p., 286pp., 295, 299, 302, 304pp., 322pp., 326p., 335pp., 339
Marriage 22, 79p., 101, 123, 132, 134, 141, 143p., 146, 148, 150pp., 157p., 164p., 227, 239, 249, 253, 259, 261, 275, 284, 287, 304p., 311, 326, 335
Marriage and the Eucharist 152
Mary . . . . 33, 36, 78pp., 83, 102, 109p., 112, 115, 134, 137, 144pp., 148p., 156, 158, 171p., 177p., 186, 214, 256, 262, 301p.
matrigeneosophy 24, 102, 109p., 114, 127, 141
Matrigeneosophy 76, 109, 159
Messiah 35, 54, 58, 76, 78p., 82, 109, 137, 141, 144, 147, 155, 172, 176, 179, 201, 207, 238, 319, 322
Mormons 31
mysteries 216, 287pp., 337
mystery 287, 299, 324, 343
Nazarene 86, 169, 219
ne'er . . . . 88, 94, 233, 235, 325p.
Ne'er 235
New Evangelization 322
Newman, Paul 328
Nicene Creed 324
oppose 26, 32, 137, 177, 185, 219, 241, 245, 294, 354
opposer 185, 199, 201, 219, 245, 307, 310
ordained 89, 246p., 251p., 313, 320, 323, 338
ordination 89, 251
otherene 86, 219
part . . . . 19, 29, 33, 35, 42p., 52, 62, 100pp., 109p., 113, 124, 133, 136, 143, 147, 150pp., 155, 157, 159, 164pp., 171, 174, 176, 178, 181p., 185pp., 191pp., 195, 197p., 201, 203pp., 207, 209, 211pp., 226p., 232, 240, 245, 248pp., 253p., 256, 260pp., 264, 267, 274pp., 283pp., 291, 294, 296pp., 301pp., 310p., 314, 318pp., 325p., 329, 332pp., 339, 341p., 344pp.
Part 100, 164, 226, 274
PART 42

partial 100p., 143, 164p., 171, 181, 214p., 220, 226p., 245, 256, 274p., 299, 302, 307, 344
partially 123, 181, 249p., 302
person . . . . 28, 33, 36, 42, 53, 55, 59, 64, 68, 101, 117, 132, 140pp., 149, 151, 156, 165, 171, 173, 177p., 183, 185, 187p., 192, 198, 202pp., 211p., 215p., 218, 227, 231, 235, 242pp., 246p., 249p., 256, 260p., 264, 275, 285, 288p., 293, 302, 306p., 311, 313, 315, 320, 325, 329pp., 336pp.
Person 311
person's 130, 192, 250, 255, 257, 329, 333
Petros 328
Pharisee 35, 155, 313
Pharisees 89, 229, 246
physics, macro . . . . 267p.
physics, micro 268
Plato's Philebus 214
Pope John Paul 19, 24p., 136, 145, 152, 192, 215, 268, 299, 318, 321, 357
Povungnituk 76, 118p., 147p., 186, 384
preach 94, 276, 280, 309, 312p., 325
Preach 94, 280, 312
preachy 94, 96, 325, 338
Preachy 94, 312
Presbyterian 31
proclaim 88, 138, 157, 236pp., 248, 251, 260, 286, 288, 309, 313, 324, 331, 338
proclaiming 25, 96, 234, 237, 264, 281, 292, 312, 338, 342
profess 150pp., 193, 209, 243p., 246, 309, 313
Profess 243
professing 243pp., 256, 339
profession 29, 50, 243
prophesie . . . . 319p.
prophet 57, 79, 82, 84, 88, 94, 153, 178, 182p., 200, 205p., 208, 236, 252, 313, 319, 331, 333
prophets 56, 58, 86, 154, 169, 207, 219, 313, 322
Prophets 56, 79, 153, 237
psalm 137 133
Psalm 137 6

purpose . . . . 28p., 33, 101, 110, 117, 127, 133, 135, 142p., 146pp., 153p., 165, 174, 184pp., 188, 190, 193p., 196p., 199, 203p., 211, 213, 215pp., 220, 227, 234p., 237, 239pp., 252, 254, 256, 258pp., 263p., 266, 275, 283p., 286pp., 298pp., 302pp., 311, 313, 315, 320, 325, 330p., 336p.
Qu'ran 336
quantum physics 268
ragtime 328
rebirth . . . . 29, 33, 70, 89, 101, 136, 140, 149, 151p., 165, 181, 190, 194p., 199, 201p., 209p., 213, 217, 227, 234p., 248p., 252pp., 261, 275, 301p., 307, 309pp., 323, 326p.
Rebirth . . . . 33, 88, 94, 233pp., 248, 325pp.
Redford, Robert 328
reductionistic 28, 171, 215, 311, 332
Reductionistic 100, 164, 226, 274
Relativity, Theory of 268
repent 26, 56, 140, 194p., 260, 354
Repent . . . . 88, 94, 229, 233, 280, 325p.
repentance . . . . 56, 89, 101, 165, 194p., 210, 227, 229, 234p., 248p., 255, 259p., 264, 275, 326p.
Repentance 56, 194p., 233p., 248
resode . . . . 83, 193p.
resurrection 29, 140, 149, 151p., 181, 190, 199, 209, 217, 302, 309, 311, 323
Resurrection 33
Revue Cinema 20, 105, 157, 167, 228, 277
righteous 79, 145p., 239
Roman Catholic 19, 21, 29, 31, 377
Roman Empire 52, 170, 185, 220, 288, 335
sacred One relationship . . . . 201, 203pp., 208pp., 220, 283, 285pp., 291, 294p., 304pp., 310p., 313, 315, 321pp., 328, 331, 334, 336p., 339pp., 344pp.
saddle shape 268
Sadducee . . . . 246p.
Sadducees . . . . 89, 229, 246p.
Salvation Army, The 233
Satan . . 32, 93, 172, 181, 185, 199, 201, 219, 245, 279, 307p., 310
saviour 239, 262, 295
Saviour 68, 152, 236p., 311

secular 19, 30, 94, 96, 137, 215, 220, 247, 292, 312pp., 316, 321, 328, 331, 337pp., 343, 345
September 11th, 2001 335
serve 61, 93, 127, 134, 159, 175, 179, 192, 233, 245, 249p., 256, 263, 279, 296, 298p., 301, 308p., 324, 335, 357
Sheen, Charlie 231, 244
sin 33, 79, 88, 140, 150p., 211p., 234, 236, 241p., 244, 255, 262
Socrates 63p., 296, 363
son of God 54
Son of God 52, 64, 92, 279, 287, 294
spirit of God . . . . 90, 265p.
Spirit of God 90, 230, 265
Spirit of One 365
spouse . . . . 28, 32, 116, 129p., 134pp., 143, 152, 154, 157, 176p., 188, 192, 197, 199, 201p., 204p., 216, 239, 248, 253, 256, 258, 261, 284p., 288pp., 293pp., 297pp., 303pp., 309pp., 313, 316, 323p., 327p., 331pp., 338pp.
St. John of the Cross 28, 323
St. Therese of Lisieux . . . . .28p.
star 59, 82p., 168, 172p., 183, 187, 189, 266
Star 189
subdue 93, 295, 306p., 324
Sword in the Stone, The 240
The China Syndrome 69
The Entertainer 328
The Geometry of Meaning 207
The Great Gatsby 63
The Hitchhiker's Guide to the Galaxy 204
The Jungle Book 291
The Man Who Planted Trees 219
The Matrix 311
The Pagan Christ 231, 377
The Real Messiah ? A Jewish Response to Missionaries 172
The Sting 328
theology 29
Theology of the Body . . . . 19, 24, 27pp., 136, 145, 152, 171p., 192, 215p., 268, 299, 303, 318, 321pp.
Top Gun 332

tori . . . . 150, 266pp.
torus 151, 266pp., 310
Toy Story 315
transgendered 304
Trudeau, Justin P.J. 304
Two and a Half Men 244
ugknown 63, 256
union 19, 21p., 29, 31, 42p., 77, 79p., 82p., 101, 118, 127, 132, 145, 150pp., 157p., 164p., 170pp., 178, 181, 185, 187p., 191pp., 195, 199, 204, 207, 211, 215, 219, 226p., 275, 284, 287pp., 302, 305, 310, 332, 334, 339, 341
UNION 42
union of whole and part 19, 42p., 101, 151p., 157, 164p., 176, 178, 188, 192p., 227, 275, 289, 341
UNION OF WHOLE AND PART 42
united . . . . 77, 132, 151, 173, 219p., 267, 341p.
United 31, 154, 171, 252, 323
United Church 31, 154, 252
virgin 79, 102, 153, 158, 178
West, Christopher 136, 152
whole . . . . 19, 33, 42p., 53, 59, 71, 100pp., 109p., 113, 117, 124, 127, 133, 136, 143p., 146p., 150pp., 157pp., 164pp., 171, 174, 176, 178, 181p., 185pp., 191pp., 195, 197p., 201, 203pp., 207, 211pp., 226p., 231p., 248pp., 253p., 256, 258, 260p., 264, 267, 274pp., 283pp., 293p., 297p., 302pp., 310p., 314, 318pp., 325pp., 329, 332pp., 339, 341p., 344pp.
Whole 100, 164, 226, 274
WHOLE 42
wholistic 28, 100, 143, 151, 164, 171, 181, 214p., 220, 226, 245, 274, 299, 302, 311, 344
wholistically 181p., 249p., 302
wife 41, 54, 77, 79p., 110, 112, 114p., 135p., 144p., 148, 156p., 176, 179, 210, 236, 239, 291, 312, 324
wilderness 59, 88, 92, 147, 215, 229, 231p., 236, 260, 279, 282, 330
Wilderness 92, 279, 282
wise men 166, 170, 173
Wise Men 24, 170p., 173, 181, 187, 189, 192p., 196
witnessing 77, 127, 232, 251, 313

worship 21, 30, 32, 82p., 93, 110, 150, 158, 168, 172p., 184p., 191p., 203, 212, 214p., 217p., 239, 279, 306, 313p., 339
Worship 93, 192, 279, 286, 308
www.youtube.com 237, 277
Ying-Yang 100, 164, 226, 274
Zen and the Art of Motorcycle Maintenance 249, 297

www.ingramcontent.com/pod-product-compliance
Lightning Source LLC
Chambersburg PA
CBHW031959220426
43664CB00005B/76